SPAIN AND THE ABOLITION OF
SLAVERY IN CUBA, 1817–1886

LATIN AMERICAN MONOGRAPHS, NO. 9
INSTITUTE OF LATIN AMERICAN STUDIES
THE UNIVERSITY OF TEXAS

Spain and the Abolition of Slavery in Cuba, 1817-1886

ARTHUR F. CORWIN

PUBLISHED FOR THE INSTITUTE OF LATIN AMERICAN STUDIES
BY THE UNIVERSITY OF TEXAS PRESS • AUSTIN

Copyright © 1967 by Arthur F. Corwin
First paperback printing 2014

All rights reserved
Printed in the United States of America

Requests for permission to reproduce material from this work
should be sent to:
 Permissions
 University of Texas Press
 P.O. Box 7819
 Austin, TX 78713-7819
 http://utpress.utexas.edu/index.php/rp-form

Library of Congress Catalog Number 67-64700

ISBN 978-1-4773-0133-3, paperback
ISBN 978-1-4773-0134-0, library e-book
ISBN 978-1-4773-0135-7, individual e-book

RESPECTFULLY DEDICATED TO

Dr. and Mrs. J. Fred Rippy

PROLOGUE

At last, at the end of the thirteenth century the struggle ended, and so great was the number of Slavs condemned to slavery and scattered by the Germans that the name came to mean a man reduced to that condition . . . in this way originated the word "eclavus," which is *esclavo* in Spanish; *esclave* in French; *schiavo* in Italian; *slave* in English; and *sklavu* in Polish.

José Antonio Saco[1]

It is generally accepted that slavery or serfdom was gradually disappearing from Europe during the late Middle Ages, even though Christian and infidel continued to enslave one another. Whether this be true or not, a new and more terrible form of human servitude arose as a consequence of the expansion of European powers overseas. In this sense, the Dark Continent was as much a discovery as America. The Portuguese, whose descendants today bear marked Negroid characteristics, found a new source of wealth—new to the Portuguese at least —as they pushed the frontiers of maritime exploration farther south along the unknown coast of Africa. Around the middle of the fifteenth century, it is said, the intrepid Lusitanians, as the Romans once called them, shipped the first boatload of Senegalese blacks to Lisbon.

Not that the Portuguese had the dubious honor of founding the African slave trade, for that trade had been known to African and Arab peoples long before the founding of Rome. If we are to believe the reports of twentieth-century international commissions, this trade inland over the ancient caravan routes still provides servants and concubines for tribal potentates.[2] The Atlantic slave trade, which

---

[1]José Antonio Saco, *La historia de la esclavitud desde los tiempos más remotos hasta nuestros días*, II, 262.

[2]See, for example, Sean O'Callaghan, *The Slave Trade Today* (including extracts from Parliamentary Debate, July 14, 1960).

flourished for four centuries and made possible the great plantation economy in the New World, however, was founded by the Portuguese, even though more powerful nations soon shouldered little Portugal aside in their eagerness to lay hands on one of the most lucrative articles ever known to the annals of barter and trade.

Because of the economic value of the slave trade and because systems of domestic and patriarchal slavery can be found to exist almost naturally in all periods of written history, including the present, it seems something of a miracle that a consolidated movement eventually arose to destroy this Atlantic commerce, and, more so, that it eventually succeeded. The society of the Western World can take pride in this fact as surely as it can feel shame at what preceded it, even though exponents of historical determinism might find neither the heroic nor the diabolic in the story of the rise and fall of Negro slavery in America.

Through an exchange fellowship made possible by the University of Chicago and the Instituto de Cultura Hispánica (August, 1954, to August, 1955) I was able to examine in the libraries and archives of Madrid one aspect of this story, namely Spain's problem of abolishing African slavery in the Spanish Antilles. Later, through a two-year association with the University of Puerto Rico and several extended visits to the Latin American Library of The University of Texas I was able to amplify the sources of information on this subject.

One could not hope, however, to consult all the unpublished and published materials that bear upon the subject. Undoubtedly, the archives and libraries of Spain, Havana, London, and Washington contain much that could further illuminate Spain's problem of abolishing slavery in Cuba and Puerto Rico, not to mention the Brazilian abolition problem, which presents striking similarities. But we hope that this study will be considered a step forward in giving more attention to the abolition problem in Latin American history and diplomacy.

We have limited this study chronologically to the period of 1817–1886, that is, from the origin of the abolitionist problem in Spain's promise to apply the first slave-trade treaty with Great Britain until Spain finally took effective legislative and executive steps to end slavery in Cuba. In the nature of things attention was drawn to the relation between the abolitionist problem and Spanish colonial policy and foreign diplomacy. At the same time it was found necessary to portray the character of the abolitionist movement, the slavist arguments, and the acts of abolition, as well as to offer interpretations of motives and

Prologue xiii

considerations, real and alleged, that served to justify or obstruct abolitionism. But no claim is made that this study is, per se, a history of slavery in Cuba, or of the slave trade, or of slave-trade diplomacy. As the title suggests, this study has limited its focus to Spain's abolitionist problem in Cuba.

It is, of course, well known that the struggle to abolish Negro slavery in the New World has attracted in varying degrees the attention of many historians and sociologists in such countries as the United States, Brazil, and even Jamaica. Yet in the Spanish Antilles and in Spain the subject has thus far received relatively less attention.

No Spaniard has yet undertaken a serious study of the abolition of slavery in Cuba.[3] As for the Cubans, they have produced several interesting studies on slavery, but none treat the problem of abolition directly. The works of the Cuban Fernando Ortiz Fernández, for example, *Hampa afro-cubana*,[4] deal with the legal, sociological, cultural, and anthropological aspects of Cuban slavery. Raúl Cepero Bonilla's *Azúcar y abolición*[5] is the closest approach to a study of abolition, but it is largely confined to a Marxist study of the relation between economic factors and the attitude of the planter toward the abolitionist question.

The earlier, general works of Hubert S. Aimes, *A History of Slavery in Cuba, 1511 to 1868*, and José Antonio Saco, *La historia de la esclavitud de la raza africana en el Nuevo Mundo*,[6] first published in 1879, are more concerned with the history of the slave trade and do not cover the abolitionist problem in its most crucial period. Recently, Philip S. Foner has given the abolition problem an important place in his *A History of Cuba and Its Relations with the United States*. Mr. Foner, who had access to our study when it was still in the form of a doctoral dissertation, has already incorporated a good part of the re-

[3]Nor of slavery in Spain itself for that matter. See the brief explanatory study by Antonio Domínguez Ortiz on the forgotten subject of slavery in modern Spain, "La esclavitud en Castilla durante la edad moderna," *Estudios de Historia Social de España*, II, 370–428.

[4]Fernando Ortiz Fernández, *Hampa afro-cubana: Los negros esclavos. Estudio sociólogo y de derecho público*.

[5]Raúl Cepero Bonilla, *Azúcar y abolición. Apuntes para una historia crítica de abolicionismo*. Frequent reference will also be made to another Cuban writer, Ramiro Guerra y Sánchez, whose several works on nineteenth-century Cuban history provide a most helpful framework for a study of abolition.

[6]José Antonio Saco, *La historia de la esclavitud de la raza africana en el Nuevo Mundo y en especial en los países Américo-Hispanos*, edited by Fernando Ortiz.

search into his own narrative.[7] Generally speaking, however, modern works of reference on the Spanish abolitionist question in Cuba are scarce. One is forced to reconstruct the foundation of such a study from a mass of unorganized material, much of which is of a polemic nature.

As to documentary sources, a genius for centralized bureaucracy had made possible a thorough documentation of Spanish government in America. It is so in the case of Cuba. The Archivo del Ministerio de Ultramar (colonial or overseas archive), which forms part of the National Archives in Madrid, contains the record of Spanish government in Cuba for the period 1830–1898. In the Sección de Política are found the instructions and correspondence passing between the metropolis and the captains general.

On some questions the government of Cuba was nearly autonomous in the sphere of foreign relations. Spanish diplomats in Washington—incidentally, supported by the Cuban treasury—often communicated directly with Cuba first and then with Spain, owing largely to what were considered the immediate perils surrounding the island. The Archivo de Ultramar therefore contains much of this interesting correspondence.

The strict regime of censorship in Cuba meant that many prohibited newspapers and pamphlets fell into the tentacles of the censor. These, duly remitted to Madrid, became another valuable resource of the Archivo.

Unfortunately, it is difficult to work in these colonial archives, at least, for the present. Shortly after the disaster of 1898 they were absorbed by the archives of the National Library of Madrid. Some three thousand bundles were moved to the basement of the Library, where they lay neglected and in disorder until 1954 when they were moved to a new location, El Centro de Investigaciones Científicas, Madrid. Although they are now readily accessible to scholars, they are not adequately indexed.

At some future date the Archivo de Ultramar will be moved to Seville to become a part of the Archives of the Indies. It was not found necessary to study in Seville because the great bulk of nineteenth-century colonial documentation is still to be found in Madrid.

El Archivo del Ministerio de Asuntos Exteriores (Archive of the

---

[7] The dissertation, "Spain and the Problem of Slavery in Cuba, 1817–1873," was originally presented to the University of Chicago in 1958.

Prologue   xv

Ministry of Foreign Affairs) conserves the records of Spain's foreign and colonial policy during the nineteenth century, and serves to complement the Archivo de Ultramar. Here special permission must be secured to examine documents dated within the last hundred years. The works of the Spanish historian and archivist Gerónimo Becker on nineteenth-century Spanish diplomacy are a useful introduction to the contents of this archive.

The archives of the Biblioteca Nacional (National Library) contain important primary sources. The Sección de Estado, for example, contains documents on Anglo-Spanish slave-trade diplomacy for the period 1817–1865.

The National Library of Madrid has also the greatest collection of published material on the Cuban problem, including a rich store of contemporary newspapers, pamphlets, and books, for which the *Catálogo de Ultramar*, published in 1900, serves as a partial guide. Originally, the greater part of this collection was housed, along with the colonial archives, in a special edifice (La Biblioteca y Archivo de Ultramar) dedicated in 1896 to the purpose of arousing more interest in Spain's overseas possessions, namely, Cuba, Puerto Rico, and the Philippines. Two years later all was superfluous. As in the case of the colonial archives, the library was abandoned, and the contents of its shelves became a part of the National Library and Archives, including the great collection of Cuban material of Don Justo Zaragoza.

Other important collections of published documents used in this study which deserve special mention are various volumes from the Great Britain Foreign Office, *British and Foreign State Papers*. Much of British slave-trade correspondence has been printed in this series. Also useful were certain volumes of the series edited by William R. Manning, *Diplomatic Correspondence of the United States: Inter-American Affairs 1831–1860*, especially Volume VII, *Great Britain*, and Volume XI, *Spain*.

It is difficult to assess the depth of sentiment on African slavery in Cuba. Since discussion of the slave question was forbidden in the colonies, few Cubans dared to discuss the abolitionist question in print before 1865. Even following the Liberal revolution in Spain (1868) and the establishment of the Republic, colonial officials continued to discourage public discussion of *la cuestión social*. The residents of Cuba, however, did address to the government petitions and projects concerning the pros and cons of abolition, or speak obliquely on "the social question" in Havana newspapers, or publish a pamphlet surreptitiously. It is mostly from such sources that one attempts to reconstruct public opinion in Cuba on the abolition question.

A most informative study in this regard is Roland T. Ely, *Cuando reinaba su majestad el azúcar. Estudio histórico-sociológico de una tragedia latinoamericana: el monocultivo en Cuba, origen y evolución del proceso.* At a time before the State Department's embargo on North American visitors to Castro's Cuba, Ely was able to consult such important archives as the *Real Consulado de Agricultura, Industria y Comercio y La Junta de Fomento* and the *Memorias de la Sociedad Económica de Amigos del País.*

In Spain also, where the press was relatively more free, it is difficult to ascertain public opinion on the abolitionist problem. Spanish colonials lamented that the Spanish public paid little attention to the colonies. A perusal of Spanish newspapers, proceedings of sessions of the Cortes, and biographies of prominent political figures of the time largely sustain the complaint. We will later suggest some causes of this indifference to colonial problems. For now, it remains to be said that much of what was written or said about the colonial problem in Madrid was said by colonials who had gone there for that purpose, or by a handful of Spanish officials who had served in the insular administrations.

As to the abolitionist question and the relation of Spanish policy thereto, the many pamphlets of the abolitionist Rafael María de Labra are primary. Labra was such a monumental figure in the Spanish abolitionist question that a study of this problem cannot exclude his writings and influence.

NOTE: The following abbreviations will be used in the footnotes:

A.H.N.	:	Archivo Histórico Nacional, that is, the National Archives, of which the Archivo de Ultramar forms a part.
A.M.A.E.	:	Archivo del Ministerio de Asuntos Exteriores.
BFSP	:	*British and Foreign State Papers.*
Leg.	:	Legajo — a box or bundle of documents.
HAHR	:	*The Hispanic American Historical Review.*

Spanish words and phrases frequently used in this study will be italicized upon first appearance, thereafter not. A listing of these words and phrases appears in the Glossary.

CONTENTS

Prologue xi
1. How African Slaves Were First Brought to the Antilles . 3
2. The Planting of a Diplomatic Problem, 1815–1820 . . 17
3. A Chapter in Slave-Trade Diplomacy, 1820–1825 . . 35
4. A United Front in Cuba, 1825–1840 47
5. Britain Grows More Aggressive, 1840–1848 69
6. The Status Quo Reaffirmed in the Face of New International Threats, 1848–1851 93
7. A More Serious Effort To Suppress the Slave Traffic, 1851–1860 107
8. Signs of Change, 1855–1865 129
9. Abolitionism Invades Spain, 1863–1866 153
10. Two Hesitant Steps Forward, 1865–1866 173
11. Great Expectations: The Reform Commission of 1866–1867 189
12. The Glorious Revolution: A New Horizon, 1868–1870 . 215
13. The Moret Law: An Entering Wedge, 1870 239
14. Behind the Scenes: Failure To Enforce the Law, 1870–1872 255
15. Application of the Moret Law and Abolition in Puerto Rico, 1872–1873 273
16. Epilogue: Last Days of Spanish Slavery, 1873–1886 . . 293

Bibliography 315

Glossary 331

Index 335

ILLUSTRATIONS

Frontispiece. A Map of the West Indies

Following page 140:

1. Julio L. de Vizcarrondo y Coronado
2. Harriet Brewster de Vizcarrondo
3. Henry John Temple, Third Viscount Palmerston
4. José Antonio Saco
5. Domingo Dulce y Garay
6. Juan de la Pezuela, Marqués y Conde de Cheste
7. Francisco Serrano y Domínguez, Duque de la Torre
8. José Gutiérrez de la Concha, Marqués de la Habana
9. Antonio Cánovas del Castillo
10. Juan Prim y Pratts
11. Abolitionist Literature
12. Rafael María de Labra y Cadrama
13. Segismundo Moret y Prendergast
14. Emilio Castelar

SPAIN AND THE ABOLITION OF
SLAVERY IN CUBA, 1817–1886

1. How African Slaves Were First Brought to the Antilles

> The impossibility of finding Indians . . . to do the work of breaking and cultivating the land demanded that this work . . . be delivered to more robust arms.
>
> Apology of Fernando VII,
> December 19, 1817[1]

The New World lay before the conquerors in all its primeval splendor, exciting vivid awe and wild imagination—but in reality it was not the fabled Indies of the East, where commercial exploitation had been known for centuries and where a dense population of laboring hands stood ready to supply the demands of overseas markets. If those who directed the course of European expansion westward were to realize immediate commercial rewards, obviously a source of labor had to be found, organized, and set to work to fulfill these expectations.

From the very beginning Spaniards employed forced labor to develop their vast territories in the American hemisphere. The native inhabitants were immediately seized for that purpose. Did not the great admiral Columbus set an example by enslaving Indians who did not accept the Christian faith? And once that road was opened, how difficult it would be to close! In spite of the peculiar servile institutions developed by the Spaniards for the utilization of Indian labor, the Indians themselves constituted poor slave material. In the Antilles the Indian population melted away rapidly, but the conquerors lost no time in replacing red slavery with black slavery. From the earliest

---

[1] From the Preamble of the treaty of September 24, 1817, with Great Britain, José María Zamora y Coronado, *Biblioteca de legislación ultramarina*, III, 126–127.

times, therefore, slavery, and only slavery, in the words of Fernando Ortiz, was the basis of the socioeconomic structure of Cuba.[2]

One of the earliest known references to imported Africans in the Antilles was in 1511 when King Fernando, acceding to the advice of the Casa de Contratación of Seville, gave permission to introduce fifty black slaves into Santo Domingo for work in the mines. A short time afterward, Alvaro de Castro, dean of the Church of the Concepción of that island, was authorized by the crown to import two hundred slaves and to employ them on his lands.[3] In this manner black slavery began in Spanish America.[4]

Sometimes Bartolomé de las Casas, the great Spanish missionary, has been blamed for counseling the crown to introduce African slaves in order to save the Indians from extermination, since the latter could not endure the regimen of work imposed upon them by the conquerors. It is true that for this reason the crown issued licenses permitting the introduction of Africans in the Indies.[5] But this recommendation was not made until 1517 or later, when Las Casas was a member of a commission sent to govern the Indies. Already the system of introducing Negroes by royal license had begun, and already, in 1510, the Order of Predicators, the first religious order in the Indies, had urged the necessity of relieving the Indians through African labor. In fact, it seems to have been generally felt that the work of one Negro was worth that of four Indian slaves.[6] Even so, Las Casas could complain that the introduction of Negroes did not result in the liberation of Indian slaves,[7] and the fact was that Indian slavery lasted until the end of the seventeenth century.[8]

Black slavery appeared to be an institution accepted naturally by the Spaniards. Even before the Portuguese expansion into Africa

[2]Fernando Ortiz in the Prologue of José Antonio Saco's *La historia de la esclavitud de la raza africana en el Nuevo Mundo y en especial en los países Américo-Hispanos*, I, viii.

[3]*Ibid.*, I, 104.

[4]Ramón de la Sagra, in his *Historia física, política y natural de Cuba*, says that as early as 1505 seventeen slaves were listed among passengers going to the Indies; cited by Zamora, *Legislación ultramarina*, III, 110.

[5]Bartolomé de las Casas, *Historia de las Indias*, III, 274.

[6]Saco, *Historia de la esclavitud de la raza africana*, I, 106.

[7]Las Casas, *Historia*, III, 275.

[8]José Antonio Saco, *La historia de la esclavitud de los Indios en el Nuevo Mundo*, I, 227.

there were Negro slaves in Spain.[9] After the reconquest of Seville by Fernando III in 1248 many of the Negro slaves of the vanquished Moors continued as slaves with the Spanish conquerors, as did likewise their descendents until the epoch of the Catholic Kings. The introduction of slaves into Spain by the Portuguese added to this class of Negroes, some of whom accompanied the conquerors to America, apparently in the very ships of Columbus. As early as 1501 the crown, wanting to protect Indian neophytes from possible contamination, forbade the immigration from Spain of slaves, Jews, Moors, and New Christians.[10] The law of May 11, 1526, again prohibited the exportation of Spanish-speaking slaves (*ladinos*) to America.[11]

A flourishing contraband trade in slaves developed in Spanish America at an early date. A decree of June 28, 1527, prohibited the importation into Spanish America of all slaves without royal license and ordered that slaves fraudulently introduced should be confiscated from their owners and placed at the disposition of the government. This decree was repeated in 1530 and several times thereafter, but without much effect.[12]

Although in the beginning the system of exporting slaves to the Indies was by royal license, the tendency toward the *asiento*, or contract, system soon was evident. Sometime before the year 1527 the crown sold to the governor of Breda, a Fleming, a license to introduce four thousand slaves into Spanish dominions in America. The Fleming, in turn, sold the concession to Genoese merchants for 25,000 ducats. How revealing that Las Casas could complain to the king that the concession should have been given to the Spaniards since "they are poor."[13]

The Spanish crown did not fully exploit the slave trade in the beginning. Royal licenses were given only sporadically as special concessions to the king's subjects in the Indies, for the crown since the days of Isabel I regarded the enslavement of Africans as a necessary evil which should not escape from royal control. But the crown could

---

[9]Antonio Domínguez Ortiz, "La esclavitud en Castilla durante la edad moderna," *Estudios de Historia Social de España*, II, 370–428.
[10]Rolando Mellafe, *La esclavitud en Hispanoamérica*, pp. 17–18.
[11]"Informe de la Comisión nombrada por la Sección de Comercio sobre la abolición del tráfico y esclavitud de los negros y próxima pérdida de la Isla de Cuba," Junio del año de 1851, A.H.N., Ultramar, Leg. 3548–3549.
[12]*Ibid.*
[13]Las Casas, *Historia*, III, 283.

not resist the demands for slave labor in the colonies, and as the demand grew, the crown saw the possibility of a new source of revenue. In 1513 a charge of two ducats was imposed on each slave imported in the Indies, and the price rose thereafter.[14]

After the union with Portugal in 1580 the asiento system was fully established whereby the permission to import slaves into royal dominions was placed exclusively in the hands of Portuguese contractors for a certain number of years. The need to conciliate the Portuguese after a forced marriage, to reduce the amount of contraband trade, and to meet complaints of disorder, inequity, and high prices brought about the turn to the asiento system. One should also add increasing financial difficulties. By 1590 the Spanish treasury was exhausted. The pious Philip II, in outfitting the Invincible Armada, had exhausted his credit with the Genoese bankers, but he had still to assume the burden of all Christendom. The asiento system promised larger and steadier revenues.

The first asiento contract was made with the Portuguese Pedro Gómez Reynel on January 30, 1595. The contractor, in alliance with the governor of Portuguese Angola, agreed to ship annually for nine years 4,250 slaves to the Indies, paying the crown the yearly sum of ten thousand ducats.[15] In like manner eighteen additional asientos were granted between the years 1615 and 1713.[16] During this period the Dutch often supplied the Portuguese contractors.

Asiento contractors often suffered serious financial losses. Contraband trade, the Seville monopoly, and various intermediaries claimed a share of the profits. Cries of fraud and corruption were heard from all concerned, including the monopoly ports of Spanish America. Briefly, from 1651 to 1662, the Seville merchants were given the privilege of supplying Spanish America with African *piezas* (African slaves). After 1676 the Casa de Contratación held temporary control. But the Spanish monopolists were unable to supply colonial demands, and, as always, the asiento was returned to those contractors who had connections with foreign factors. Several foreign countries, following the Dutch example, organized powerful trading companies in order to

---

[14]Mellafe, *Esclavitud*, pp. 30–31.
[15]Zamora, *Legislación ultramarina*, III, 111; Saco, *Historia de la esclavitud de la raza africana*, II, 91–93.
[16]Jacobo de la Pezuela y Lobo, *Diccionario geográfico, estadístico, histórico de la isla de Cuba*, II, 280–283.

compete effectively in the slave trade.[17] All coveted the Spanish asiento because it was much more than a slave-supply contract. It was a screen to hide contraband goods, ". . . and that is why the Dutch, Portuguese, French and English contended for the privilege."[18]

The Spanish government, which would later allege that Spain was not responsible for the African slave trade to America, made every effort to encourage Spanish participation in the trade, but to little effect. The asiento of 1696 was granted to the Portuguese Guinea Company, and that of 1701 to the Royal French Guinea Company as a result of the Bourbon family pact. But England, having by now outstripped all competitors in maritime power and joint-stock companies, was not content with this arrangement, and in 1713 the asiento passed to the English South Sea Company, a transfer which the Spanish Bourbon king was forced to accept by the terms of the Peace of Utrecht. And so this mercantilist plum passed from the Portuguese to the French, and from the French to the English, who rushed madly to buy stock in the favored company.

By means of the asiento of 1713 English merchants obtained a monopoly of the slave trade to the Spanish Indies for thirty years, agreeing to import 4,800 slaves annually via the English Royal African Company and to pay the Spanish crown 33.5 pesos in silver for each one.[19] They were also allowed to send annually to the Spanish colonies one ship laden with merchandise. It is well known, however, that the English, like other foreign contractors, grossly exceeded their legal quota of merchandise and slaves. Spanish attempts to stop smuggling led to the War of Jenkin's Ear with Britain, and this in turn to the abolition of the asiento in 1740.[20]

To fill the place formerly occupied by English merchants, the Spanish Bourbons created a privileged Royal Company of Havana in 1740 for the introduction of all articles, including slaves. This privileged company was an attempt to duplicate the successful trading companies of the Dutch and English, but when it failed in 1760 the crown was obliged to return to the policy of awarding asientos to private

---

[17]Mellafe, *Esclavitud*, pp. 34–42.
[18]Georges Scelle, "The Slave Trade in the Spanish Colonies," *American Journal of International Law*, IV, No. 3 (July, 1910), 618.
[19]Saco, *Historia de la esclavitud de la raza africana*, II, 182–184.
[20]Hubert S. Aimes, *A History of Slavery in Cuba, 1511–1868*, p. 22; Vera L. Brown, "The South Sea Company and Contraband Trade," *American Historical Review*, XXXI, No. 4 (July, 1926), 662–678.

contractors, some of whom were Spaniards. Asientos were thus conceded in 1765, 1773, 1780, and 1783. The last was with Baker and Dawson of the Liverpool slave emporium, who introduced 5,306 slaves under this contract.[21]

The hope that Spain could still monopolize the slave trade to America died hard. In 1778 Spain acquired the islands of Annobón and Fernando Po on the west coast of Africa. Here were potential slave supply bases. When Spanish capitalists, formerly involved with the moribund Caracas Company, organized the Philippines Company in 1785 they were given an exclusive asiento with the intent of exploiting the newly acquired islands. As a supplier of African slaves the Company was a fiasco.[22]

Finally, the asiento system came to an end by a decree of the enlightened Charles IV, dated February 28, 1789, but even more significantly the slave trade was now opened, with some restrictions, to Spaniards and foreigners alike. Decrees of 1791 and 1792 amplified this liberty.[23] At the same time the crown reduced taxes for Spaniards investing in the trade.[24]

From 1789 until the independence outbreaks of 1810 the slave trade to Spanish America increased notably. It has been estimated that during the entire colonial period more than one million Africans were shipped under legal guise, more or less, and perhaps an equal number as contraband.[25]

Perhaps a final observation on Spain's attempt to control the slave trade to colonial Spanish America is in order here. Although a weak commercial power, said Georges Scelle, Spain could maintain her colonies under the yoke of her exclusive monopoly system and defend her vast underdeveloped empire from more powerful nations because contraband trade and the asiento served as safety valves. The colonies were supplied with European goods and slaves at lower prices, the foreign merchants gained access to the Spanish empire without hav-

---

[21]Pezuela, *Diccionario*, II, 283.

[22]James F. King, "Evolution of the Free Slave Trade Principle in Spanish Colonial Administration," *HAHR*, XXII, No. 1 (February, 1942), 34–56.

[23]Pezuela, *Diccionario*, II, 283.

[24]For example, a royal order of 1793 exempted Spaniards outfitting slave voyages from export taxes on goods employed in the trade. Also, a Spaniard purchasing a foreign-built slave ship was exempted from the registry tax. James F. King, "Free Slave Trade Principle," p. 54.

[25]Mellafe, *Esclavitud*, 58–59.

How African Slaves Were First Brought to the Antilles

ing to conquer it (other than supply depots in the Caribbean), and Spain could maintain the illusion of imperial control.[26]

Attention must now be drawn to Cuba in particular. It is said that the first large-scale introduction of Negro slaves to Cuba occurred in the year 1524, when permission was granted to import three hundred Africans to work the Jagua gold mines.[27] Later, in 1550, "because of the laziness of the Cubans," who resisted all kinds of work, an exclusive privilege was given by the crown to import African slaves in order to cultivate tobacco and sugar cane.[28]

The Pearl of the Antilles was not then so precious a pearl, for Cuba's economic development was slow and relatively unimportant in the first three centuries after its discovery. Here only a few details will be given for purposes of contrast with the prosperous nineteenth century, for it is easy to agree with Pezuela who wrote:

> The small importance of commerce to the island of Cuba during the two and a half centuries that followed its occupation by the Spaniards would not merit our sketching a picture of this long epoch of poverty; however, we might attempt to explain the principal elements of its early life, so that the reader may better comprehend the metamorphosis that has taken place in all aspects of the modern period.[29]

Once the island had been explored and subdued, 1511-1515, and the fact determined that it was relatively poor in precious metals, Cuba, with its deadly tropical climate, ceased to have much attraction for restless Spanish adventurers. During the first century of Spanish dominion the island fulfilled the mission of a base of operations for the conquest and settlement of the American continent. Its population, like that of the city of Havana, was largely transient. Early settlers, such as Cortés, Pedro de Alvarado, Cristóbal de Olid, Juan de Grijalva, and Bartolomé de las Casas, deserted Cuba for exciting adventures elsewhere. By the year 1602 Cuba's population was only twenty thousand, of which number thirteen thousand lived in and around Havana, the port city. The seventeenth century saw, besides

---

[26]Scelle, "The Slave Trade in the Spanish Colonies," p. 661.

[27]*Cuadro estadístico de la Siempre Fiel Isla de Cuba, correspondiente al año de 1846, formado bajo la dirección y protección del Exemo. Sr. Gobernador y Capitán General Don Leopoldo O'Donnell, por una Comisión de Oficiales y Empleados particulares* (Published Manuscript).

[28]"Informe de la Comisión nombrada por la Sección de Comercio," A.H.N., Ultramar, Leg. 3548-3549.

[29]Pezuela, *Diccionario*, II, 26.

a turbulent era of pirate raids, the slow development of sugar cane and tobacco, but livestock continued to be the most important occupation. The population barely reached thirty thousand by 1655, but refugees from the English conquest of Jamaica soon expanded it.[30]

Not until the Bourbons began to rule in Spain was a new commercial impulse given to Spanish America. The establishment by the English Royal African Company of factories in Havana and Santiago de Cuba (1716) stimulated the trade cycle and the consequent importation of slaves. As previously mentioned, the English asiento monopoly was broken in 1740. The Royal Company of Havana was then formed for the purpose of providing Cuba with foodstuffs and manufactures in exchange for tobacco and sugar. In twenty-two years of operation this company introduced 4,986 slaves.[31]

In 1762, the year that the English took Havana, there were an estimated seventy sugar plantations, which produced hardly as much as one of the great plantations a century later. Nevertheless, this represented real economic progress. By this year an estimated 60,000 slaves had been introduced into Cuba.[32]

The brief occupation of the British forces gave the inhabitants a taste for free commerce—Havana was opened to the British colonial trade, and merchandise and slaves were sold at reduced prices. It is said that British merchants sold 10,000 slaves to the Cubans during the occupation.[33]

By the middle of the eighteenth century agricultural activities included stock raising, and the growing of sugar cane and tobacco. Of much less importance were indigo, cotton, coffee, and beeswax, the last exported to Mexican churches. Still, the modest scale of these activities did not as yet demand many slaves.

Stock raising served local consumption and provided hides for export, hides being Cuba's most important product for some two centuries. Communal *haciendas* arose with several family members or settlers having through custom a recognized claim in the original royal grant.[34] During the first three centuries the continual process of

[30]"Informe de la Comisión nombrada por la Sección de Comercio," A.H.N., Ultramar, Leg. 3548–3549.
[31]Pezuela, *Diccionario*, II, 57.
[32]*Ibid.*, II, 56.
[33]*Ibid.*
[34]Ramiro Guerra y Sánchez, *Azúcar y población en las Antillas*, pp. 62–63.

How African Slaves Were First Brought to the Antilles

subdividing land helped lay a broad basis for the Creole agricultural prosperity that was to come.

Sugar was especially favored by royal concessions and subsidies. For example, a decree of April 14, 1531, authorized loans from crown revenues for two years to proprietors for the purchase of slaves to be used in sugar mills. A decree of October 23, 1598, exempted sugar mills from attachment for debt. "To give an account of the successive royal concessions to the sugar planters," said Fernando Ortiz, "would be to travel the main highway of Cuba's history as a colony."[35]

In spite of these feudal privileges the sugar industry developed slowly. Among the factors that retarded growth were trade restrictions prohibiting free entry of sugar in the metropolitan and foreign markets.[36] At best, Spain could offer a very limited market owing to the poverty of its people and to the fact that sugar was produced in Spain also. According to Humboldt no sugar exports were mentioned for Cuba until after 1553.[37] As late as 1763 the annual export of sugar was reported as only thirteen thousand boxes.[38]

Tobacco was introduced in the seventeenth century. The European demand for this leaf, the favorable soil and climate of Cuba, and the relatively small financial and technical investment it required led to a steady though not phenomenal growth of tobacco, so that by the end of the eighteenth century its value equaled that of cattle and sugar in the domestic and foreign markets. The British occupation of Havana in 1762 and the occupation of Spain by foreign armies during the Napoleonic wars led to a popularization of Havana tobacco.[39]

Tobacco cultivation, however, was hindered by many restrictions, including the monopoly enjoyed by the Spanish government. It was confined largely to the poorer classes, who sold their product to the established factory. Tobacco, like sugar, was also destined for better days.

Coffee was introduced into Cuba by immigrants fleeing Santo Domingo in the last decade of the eighteenth century. By 1800, accord-

[35]Fernando Ortiz Fernández, *Cuban Counterpoint: Tobacco and Sugar*, pp. 280–281.
[36]*Ibid.*, p. 66.
[37]Alexander von Humboldt, *The Island of Cuba*, p. 251.
[38]*Ibid.*, p. 252.
[39]For an interesting discussion of the history and place of tobacco in the economy of Cuba, see Ortiz, *Cuban Counterpoint*, pp. 55–60, 67–70.

ing to Humboldt, there were sixty coffee plantations in the district of Havana.⁴⁰

The commercial decrees of Charles III gave the first consistent stimuli to the agricultural and commercial development of Spanish America, especially the Antilles. That of August, 1764, broke the commercial monopoly of Seville and Cadiz and opened other Spanish ports to the American trade, notably Barcelona. That of May 3, 1774, permitted the free entry into Spain of sugar, hides, beeswax, coffee, and tortoise shells. That of October 12, 1778, amplified this liberty still more and reduced the tariff on numerous imports from Spanish colonies. That of August 24, 1784, established a monthly packet line from Spain and made Havana the center of the Spanish American commercial system.⁴¹

Shortly, positive results were obtained from this policy of stimulation. The trade with Cuba required about six ships in 1765 and two hundred in 1778.⁴²

In the early 1790's important commercial organizations were founded or approved by royal decree in Havana. La Sociedad Económica (Economic Society), Junta de Fomento (Council for Economic Development), and Real Consulado de Agricultura, Industria y Comercio (Royal Consulate of Agriculture, Industry, and Commerce) are examples.⁴³

These various concessions and organizations contributed greatly to the growing commercial spirit in Cuba. The need for slaves began to rise precipitously in the last quarter of the eighteenth century. Yet, compared with that of Haiti, for example, Cuban agricultural and commercial development was more potential than real. The census of 1792 listed 399 large stock ranches, 478 sugar plantations, and 7,814 smaller properties devoted to tobacco growing, truck farming, and stock raising on a minor scale.

The population had now risen to 172,620, and included 96,440 whites, 31,847 free Negroes, and 44,333 slaves. Since the island contained about 44,000 square miles of land, there was about one slave to the square mile—a very low concentration of slaves compared with

⁴⁰Humboldt, *Island of Cuba*, p. 284.
⁴¹Aimes, *History of Slavery*, p. 39; Saco, *Historia de la esclavitud de la raza africana*, III, 2–4.
⁴²Aimes, *History of Slavery*, p. 35.
⁴³For the enlightened spirit of these organizations, see Robert J. Shafer, *The Economic Societies in the Spanish World, 1763–1821*.

How African Slaves Were First Brought to the Antilles

Haiti with its 452,000 slaves (and 38,000 whites) in an area of 11,000 square miles, or Barbados with its 62,115 slaves in an area of only 166 square miles.[44]

The proprietors had long wanted the free introduction of slaves. Now that a free market for sugar and coffee existed in Spain, with a widening one in the United States, the problem was one of productive forces. The agroindustrial cycle of cutting, hauling, grinding, clarification, filtration, evaporation, and crystallization required many hands at the right time, all simultaneously coordinated. Fernando Ortiz discusses this requirement of the sugar industry and contrasts it with other industries, namely tobacco.[45]

As noted in another context, the slave trade was thrown open to the ships of all nations on February 28, 1789, for a period of two years. The ports of Havana, San Juan, Puerto Cabello, and Santo Domingo were designated to receive slave cargoes.

Cuban slave interests were largely responsible for the new law. They readily foresaw that William Wilberforce's proposals in the British Parliament of 1787 were a real threat to the British slave trade, still the most important source of supply for Spanish America. With shrewd prevision, therefore, the Cuban proprietors wanted the slave trade thrown open to the world.[46] Since it is said that twenty thousand slaves were admitted during the two years of free trade, it is safe to assume that the beneficiaries of this short-term policy would sue for renewal.

A number of influential men promoted the plantation economy of Cuba. One was Luis de las Casas, captain general, 1790–1796; another was Alejandro Ramírez, intendant of the Treasury. But more than any other man, Francisco de Arango y Parreño, Cuban born (1765–1830), sometimes called the "Colbert of Cuba," was representative of the foundations of the new slave prosperity. Delegate of the economic interests of the island, Arango was in Madrid with the object of renewing the concession of 1789 for at least six more years.[47] When the news arrived in November, 1791, of the great slave rebellion in Haiti,

[44]Guerra, *Azúcar y población*, p. 71.
[45]Ortiz, *Cuban Counterpoint*, pp. 33–35.
[46]Saco, *Historia de la esclavitud de la raza africana*, III, 3–4.
[47]Francisco de Arango y Parreño, "Representación manifestando las ventajas de una absoluta libertad en la introducción de Negros y solicitando que se amplíe a ocho la prórroga concedida por dos años, 10 de mayo de 1791," *Obras de Don Francisco de Arango y Parreño*, I, 97–102.

Arango saw this not as a threatening example to Cuba, where slaves were still relatively few, but as Cuba's golden opportunity at French Haiti's expense.

The opportunity was obvious to the Cuban producers and to many Spaniards. Arango, speaking for these economic interests, convinced the king's ministers that the high price of cane sugar after the Haitian disaster could make Cuba rich like Mexico or Peru. In a memorandum to the crown, *Discurso sobre la agricultura de la isla de Cuba y los medios de fomentarla,* published in 1792, Arango projected the economic future of Cuba, analyzed the defects of the Spanish colonial system, and suggested reforms that were later conceded by a series of royal decrees. In the name of the aspiring economic interests of the island, Arango asked for a larger measure of free commerce, especially free commerce in slaves so that Cuban sugar and tobacco could compete favorably with produce of the French and British West Indies.

The series of wars and events connected with the French Revolution inclined the Spanish Crown toward Arango's free-trade ideas, especially since the Spanish merchant fleet in time of maritime wars could in no way serve the interests of the colonies. The decree of November 24, 1791, not only renewed the free commerce in slaves for six years and indefinitely thereafter but also lowered taxes on other importations into Cuba.[48]

Arango, who served forty years in the public administration of Cuba, lived to see the day when he regretted, perhaps like Las Casas, advocating the importation of more Negro slaves. Instead of becoming a uniformly prosperous land of small holders, as he had planned, the island became a disparately prosperous land of great estates and merchant fortunes, where the Africans frightfully outnumbered the whites.

But Arango and the Cuban agriculturists were at the moment less concerned with the dangers of an excessive slave population than with prosperity. Previous indications had been that the slaves tended to be absorbed easily into the island's free population. From 1774 to 1791 the proportion of slaves was actually diminishing in relation to the growing free population. In 1791 only one in every four inhabitants was a slave.[49] It was therefore generally felt in Cuba that, com-

[48]*Ibid.,* III, 18–20.
[49]Ramiro Guerra y Sánchez, *Manual de la historia de Cuba (económica, social y política),* p. 188.

pared with the saturated islands of Haiti and Barbados, Cuba could maintain many more slaves without danger.

In 1804 the Council of the Indies, remembering Haiti, cautioned against the unlimited introduction of slaves. But the royal decree of April 22, 1804, granted a twelve-year extension of the slave trade to Spaniards, and a six-year extension to foreigners, at the same time stipulating that the *ingenios* (sugar mills) should be provided with slave women so that by the procreation of Creole slaves the slave trade would naturally diminish.[50] The proportion of female slaves in Cuba was always very low, usually estimated at one third the number of males. Neither this provision of the decree of 1804 nor other efforts to increase the percentage of females had any appreciable effect. A certain resistance existed in Cuba against having female slaves on the plantations, since they were considered a source of distraction; nor were slave marriages generally thought desirable. This meant that Cuba must continue to depend heavily upon the slave trade as a source of labor supply.

The rate at which the slave trade increased under the stimulating afore-mentioned factors may be appreciated from Humboldt's calculations.

Imported through Havana, according to the customhouse returns:[51]

Year	Number	Year	Number
1790	2,534	1806	4,395
1791	8,498	1807	2,565
1792	8,528	1808	1,607
1793	3,777	1809	1,162
1794	4,164	1810	6,672
1795	5,832	1811	6,349
1796	5,711	1812	6,081
1797	4,552	1813	4,770
1798	2,001	1814	4,321
1799	4,919	1815	9,111
1800	4,145	1816	17,737
1801	1,659	1817	25,841
1802	13,832	1818	19,902
1803	9,671	1819	17,194
1804	8,923	1820	4,122
1805	4,999		
		Total in 31 years	225,574

[50] Aimes, *History of Slavery*, p. 61.
[51] Humboldt, *Island of Cuba*, p. 218.

These figures by themselves may not be so impressive, but when compared with previous periods their significance is obvious:[52]

>From 1521 to 1763 60,000
From 1764 to 1790 33,409
In Havana alone:
From 1791 to 1805 91,211
From 1806 to 1820 131,829
316,449

Increase by the illicit trade and by the importations in the eastern part of the island (approximations):

From 1791 to 1820 56,000
Total 372,449

[52]*Ibid.*, p. 219.

2. The Planting of a Diplomatic Problem, 1815-1820

> And considering that just and enlightened men of all centuries have thought that the commerce known by the name of the African slave trade is contrary to the principles of humanity, and universal morality: . . .
>
> Declaration of the Congress of Vienna[1]

A stroke of abolition in Haiti had given Cuba a golden opportunity. But was there not a danger that the same hand might strike in the Spanish islands as well? As the nineteenth century approached, there was every indication that the Cuban planter must fight against the impending doom of black servitude, for while Cuba (and Brazil) were beginning an unprecedented era of slave prosperity, a movement for the abolition of the slave trade appeared almost simultaneously in several different countries. Of the currents that gave rise to the movement, two above all were decisive: rational humanitarianism and the evangelical religious conscience of Protestantism.

The American Revolution and then the French Revolution signified the triumph of the rights of man and opened the modern age of democratic idealism. In adopting a new constitution in 1789 the Americans

[1] Declaration of the Congress of Vienna condemning the traffic of slaves, February 8, 1815, signed by the representatives of the powers: Castlereagh, Stewart, Wellington, Nesselrode, Löwenhielm, Gómez Labrador, Palmella, Saldanha, Lobo, Humboldt, Metternich, and Talleyrand, found in José María Zamora y Coronado, *Biblioteca de legislación ultramarina*, III, 134; or José Antonio Saco, *La historia de la esclavitud de la raza africana en el Nuevo Mundo y en especial en los países Américo-Hispanos*, III, 122–124.

seriously debated the question of civil rights and the slave. Some constitution makers recognized that servitude was obviously inconsistent with a free and democratic society, but a compromise had to be made with slave interests. The American constitution therefore did not go beyond providing for the cessation of the slave traffic within twenty years.

In France, before the Revolution, an abolitionist society had been formed (La Société des Amis des Noirs), headed by such aristocratic apostles of enlightenment and faith in mankind as Condorcet and Lafayette. As an effect of the society, the revolutionary French Assembly was disposed to decree the abolition of slavery in Haiti, as it did in 1793. When Napoleon in 1802 attempted to restore slavery to that rebellious island his decree remained without effect, and the spirit of Toussaint L'Ouverture remained to mock the white planter everywhere in the Caribbean.

In England the business community had celebrated the slave asiento of 1713 as a national victory, but, as the eighteenth century progressed, an emergent humanitarian spirit questioned the necessity of human slavery. Such rationalists as John Locke, philosopher; Samuel Johnson, man of letters; Adam Smith, economist; William Robertson, historian; Tom Paine, world citizen; and Jeremy Bentham, utilitarian, all raised their voice against Negro slavery. But it was first the gentle Quakers, and then the Methodists (John Wesley, for one, had been converted to the Quaker view of human bondage), who began an active movement to arouse the English conscience against the African slave trade.[2]

A new stimulus was felt when Granville Sharp, a reformist Anglican, obtained in 1772 a court decision declaring free all slaves held in England. In 1787 various outspoken reformers founded the Society for the Abolition of the Slave Trade, which expanded the abolitionist mission of an earlier Quaker committee. The emblem of the Society was a chained Negro on bended knee with the inscription "Am I not a man and a brother?" Realizing that a demand for the complete abolition of slavery in the colonies would be self-defeating, the Society devoted itself first to the abolition of the slave trade, and, second, to the amelioration of the slave's condition in the colonies.[3] Under the leadership of William Wilberforce the abolitionists attempted to in-

[2]Frank J. Klingberg, *The Anti-Slavery Movement in England*, Chap. II: "Public Opinion and Slavery."
[3]Earl L. Griggs, *Thomas Clarkson: The Friend of Slaves*, pp. 54–55.

duce Parliament to abolish the English share of the slave commerce.

Planter interests in Parliament, as well as English reaction to the excesses of the French Revolution, frustrated the abolitionist cause for nearly two decades. Bills proposing the abolition of the English slave trade were repeatedly blocked by conservative majorities. Finally, in 1807 Parliament abolished the slave trade. The following year the Americans did the same, and Sweden in 1813.

Although England was not the first to abolish the slave trade—Denmark, for example, did so in 1792—it is to the honor of England that she led the nineteenth century in advancing the cause of enslaved peoples. Having ended the British slave trade the English abolitionists, now organized as the "African Institution," set out to block the African slave trade everywhere. The approaching Congress of Vienna was a superb opportunity. English abolitionists besieged kings and statesmen with pamphlets and personal visits. Wilberforce, for example, wrote Talleyrand soliciting his support,[4] while Thomas Clarkson educated the Emperor Alexander and the Duke of Wellington as to the ugly facts of the African trade. Clarkson, whom the poet Coleridge called "the moral Steam-Engine," addressed the august potentates with these words:

> When it is considered that the destiny of the world will probably be fixed at the Congress about to be held in Vienna . . . It is to be presumed that you are totally ignorant of what takes place on the continent of Africa . . . Not to put an end to crime, when you have the power, is to make yourselves accomplices to it . . . divine providence has restored you to your former comforts and to your hereditary dominions . . . let the Era of your own deliverance be known in the history of the world as that of the deliverance of others also![5]

Castlereagh, who at one point complained that misunderstood abolitionist pressure was doing more harm than good, noted that European statesmen could not understand the deep feeling in England against the slave trade, and that they imagined, since Britain had foolishly deprived her planters of cheap labor, that British policy at Vienna had only the purpose of depriving other nations of this economic advantage.[6] Of course, the British abolition law of 1807 did

---

[4]Letter to His Excellency Monsieur le Prince de Talleyrand, October, 1814, cited by Saco. *Historia de la esclavitud de la raza africana*, III, 114–115.
[5]Griggs, *Thomas Clarkson*, p. 116.
[6]Klingberg, *Anti-Slavery Movement*, p. 152.

add British planters to the abolitionist ranks. Wilberforce himself noted the fact when he said: "Every consideration impelled us to stop a traffic like this. If it were not put an end to, any hope for our colonies selling their produce beyond our possessions would be at an end."[7]

On the other hand, while reform movements sprouted on both sides of the English Channel, Spain appeared to lie in mystic hibernation, even though, to be sure, there was a stir in the second half of the eighteenth century, as Masonry and the French Enlightenment invaded Spain via *el pacto Borbónico*. But in her egocentric culture Spain resisted the dynamics of the Enlightenment and the Reformation. If the ruling classes mimicked French manners and philosophy, the masses, steeped in tradition, resented reforms, as "foreign-inspired." If this was characteristic of the eighteenth century, it would be more so of the nineteenth and twentieth. There arose as the counterpart of the reformer the reactionary, who could easily denounce reform as alien to Spain. Thus was opened a schism in the Spanish soul that has not yet been healed. Whither Spain? Back to the glorious days of the Catholic Kings, or forward after the lead of other nations?

Surely Spain of the Golden Age suffered no such dilemma. In the sixteenth century Spanish doctors and jurists were reputed the equals of any in Europe and, if anything, their thoughts on war and peace and human dignity were in advance of their European contemporaries. Spanish language and letters were *a la moda* in Europe.[8] One reflects, however, on the fact that the Spanish Abolitionist Society will not be founded until 1864, and then by a Puerto Rican of Protestant tendencies. Apologists for the Spanish Inquisition and the Counter Reformation have pointed out the benefits of conformity and pure blood—how it preserved Spanish culture intact, how it saved Spain from the scourge of the seventeenth-century religious wars.[9]

[7]Eric Williams (ed.), *The British West Indies at Westminster, Part I: 1789–1823*, p. 64.

[8]For a succinct analysis of Spanish culture in the sixteenth century, its content, and its international influence, see Salvador de Madariaga, *Spain*, pp. 30–42.

[9]Some of the more noted apologies for the black legend of Spanish intolerance are Marcelino Menéndez y Pelayo, *Historia de los Heterodoxos españoles;* Julián Juderías, *La leyenda negra;* and Jaime Balmes, *El Protestantismo comparado con el Catolicismo en sus relaciones con la civilización europea* (see *Obras Completas del Dr. D. Jaime Balmes,* editada por el P. Ignacio Casanova, S. J.). Balmes, theologian, philosopher, and political writer, exercised great influence in nineteenth-century Spain. While Protestant sects were demanding the abolition of

The Planting of a Diplomatic Problem, 1815–1820

On the other hand, critics ask whether it destroyed the humanism of Vitoria, the zeal of Las Casas, the science of Salamanca? Or whether it declared a scholastic status quo leaving Aristotle triumphant over the Christian conscience? Or whether it merely put off the scourge of ideological strife until modern times?

La decadencia española is now a theme made popular by the generation of '98, but even before this date there were those who pointed their finger to the Holy Office for its evil effects upon Spanish character. For what they are worth we cite the words of Cánovas:

> The idea of servitude, so opposed to Christianity, was thus fortified among us, and with it, as sister and companion, the justification of tyranny gained entry into all spirits ... From philosophy the nation far from receiving doctrines of progress and sentiments of humanity, gathered nothing more than the resignation of the stoics ... and a greater sum of intolerance.[10]

What seems certain is that when abolitionism arose in Europe, Spain could not respond. She had not an abolitionist conscience, and subsequent events could only serve to abort its birth.

The Napoleonic invasions undermined ancient institutions and divided the people into two mutually frustrating forces: the conservatives would defend traditional Spain, while the liberals would modernize Spain through reforms. As the nineteenth century opened, questions arose infinitely more important to Spanish factionalism than abolition and reforms in distant Cuba, Puerto Rico, and the Philippines. The Diary of the Spanish Cortes and the newspapers rarely would refer to the slave problem but they would revel in the burning questions of papal concordats, anticlerical reforms, Carlist wars, new constitutions, and party rivalry.

If we say that what abolitionism there was would be identified more with Spanish liberalism and its ephemeral triumphs, then we must immediately add that, unfortunately, the liberals formed an op-

---

black slavery, Balmes was proving that Protestantism had done nothing to form the true spirit and conscience of Christian civilization.

[10]Antonio Cánovas del Castillo, *Historia de la decadencia en España desde el advenimiento de Felipe III al trono hasta la muerte de Carlos II*. It is customary to blame Spain's misfortune on intolerance, but since Cánovas was a conservative, a great statesman, and a historian, his observations are, perhaps, more trustworthy than the polemic type. For a more modern but essentially coincident viewpoint see Claudio Sánchez Albornoz, *España: Un enigma histórico*.

portunistic minority. In order to triumph they had identified themselves with militarism with all the ideological perversion that the word implies. The liberals were fully capable of reactionary conduct, above all in the case of the Antilles. The reforming Cortes of 1810 and 1822 and the slave question coincided with the beginning of the colonial revolts in Spain's American colonies. Spanish liberals and conservatives alike blamed the loss of continental America on reforms conceded at that time. Men swore not to repeat the same mistake in regard to Cuba, now pathetically called "the Everfaithful Isle." It was no accident that Cuba was governed in the nineteenth century as in the time of the *adelantados* (frontier governors). Merely declaring oneself a radical, a progressive, or a liberal could not overcome the heritage of centuries.

Other reasons were involved, also. To Spain, progressively stripped of her empire, the revenues from the Cuban sugar trade were to become the life's blood of her public treasury, always in penurious circumstances, while the preservation of slavery was to serve at the same time to keep the powerful merchant and slaveholding class loyal to Spain in an era when incendiary ideas of independence and republicanism were taking root among the Cuban *criollos*. The conservation of Cuba, the conservation of Cuban revenues, and the conservation of slavery would become inextricably woven into Spanish foreign policy. These last considerations, being of "high policy," help to explain why the Spanish government would ignore or repress any abolitionist argument for many years and would look indulgently on slave-trade treaty violations.

In view of the afore-mentioned considerations, should it surprise anyone that the abolitionist question was seldom raised by a Spaniard? When the first important abolitionist threat arose in the revolutionary Cortes of Cádiz during the Napoleonic wars,[11] it was significantly a colonial deputy from New Spain, Miguel Guridi y Alcócer, who presented the first formal abolitionist project in Spain on March 26, 1811.[12] His eight propositions provided for the immediate abolition of the slave trade, the freedom of all children born to slave moth-

---

[11]It is said that in 1802 Isidro Antillón read before an academy of Spanish law a dissertation against the commerce and enslavement of Negroes. Luis Díaz Soler, *La Historia de la esclavitud negra en Puerto Rico*, p. 119.

[12]Another American deputy, Ramón Power, Puerto Rican, had instructions from the City Council (Cabildo) of San Juan to support the gradual abolition of slavery, *ibid.*, p. 120.

ers, wages for slaves, the right of the slave to purchase his freedom, and better treatment for those remaining in slavery.[13] The Cortes agreed that the commission on the new constitution should study the project.

On April 2, 1811, the noted liberal politician Don Agustín Argüelles presented a more limited project asking only for the immediate abolition of the slave trade. Argüelles also proposed that "His Britannic Majesty" should be immediately informed so that the two powers could work in harmony toward the same philanthropic end.[14] Argüelles was supported by several other members. No doubt, as Saco suggested, the fact that it was the revolutionary Cortes of Cádiz made some deputies wish to appear liberal.[15]

The story behind the Argüelles proposal, according to Saco, is as follows: The British ambassador intended to hand a note to the Spanish government requesting that the slave commerce be abolished in Spanish dominions. Argüelles dissuaded the British minister, promising to propose the same in the Cortes so that it would seem to have a national and spontaneous character free of foreign pressure.[16] "Spain ought to be in line with Great Britain," said Argüelles in the Cortes of 1811,[17] and added that he himself had the sweet satisfaction of witnessing the triumph of light and reason when the British abolition bill passed the House of Lords in 1807.[18]

The two proposals mentioned, and the discussions concerning them in the Cortes, caused great alarm in the Antilles. The Marqués de Someruelos, captain general of Cuba, in a communication that was read to the Cortes in secret session on July 7, 1811, stated that such

---

[13]The preamble to these propositions revealed the prevailing philosophy of a revolutionary era. Slavery was declared as contrary to natural law and to the liberal maxims of the present government, and about to be abolished in any case by the civil laws of cultured nations. Saco, *Historia de la esclavitud de la raza africana*, III, 83–85; or given in Rafael María de Labra, *América y la constitución española de 1812*, pp. 127–129.

[14]Saco, *Historia de la esclavitud de la raza africana*, III, 86.

[15]*Ibid.*, III, 87.

[16]Saco claimed that Argüelles personally explained this strategy to him, *Ibid.*, III, 85–86.

[17]Quotation from *Recueil des diverses pieces*, p. 8, as cited by Hubert S. Aimes, *A History of Slavery in Cuba, 1511 to 1868*, p. 64.

[18]Francisco de Arango y Parreño, "Discusión sobre el comercio de esclavos, habida en las Cortes," el 2 de abril de 1811, *Obras de Don Francisco de Arango y Parreño*, II, 229.

proposals were causing great commotion in Cuba and that there was great fear the catastrophe of Santo Domingo (Haiti) would be repeated. He requested the government to treat the matter with great reserve "in order not to lose this important island."[19] How often in the years to come would the captains general repeat those words!

The Ayuntamiento of Havana together with the Consulado and the Sociedad Económica addressed a memorandum to the Cortes complaining loudly against a public debate on the abolition question. The memorandum blamed the introduction of Negroes on the misplaced piety of Las Casas. "The Negroes have come and are here to our misfortune; not by our fault, but that of those who first initiated and encouraged this commerce in the name of law and religion." In essence, the memorandum argued that the fortunes of Spanish Cuba inevitably depended on slavery and that even the slave trade should be allowed to continue for a time.[20]

Francisco Arango, the spokesman for the slave interests in the Cortes of Cádiz, made a brilliant defense against the abolitionist propositions, especially that of Argüelles. Arango condemned the slave trade as unjust, of course, but he opposed as equally unjust a sudden resolution of the problem, arguing that the Cortes of Cádiz was not empowered to make such a decision until a constitution for the Spanish monarchy had been adopted; that such an immediate step could not be justly taken without hearing the colonial interests concerned; that the British and the Americans had given a twenty-year notice before abolishing the slave trade and that the decision of the Cortes should be just as gradual; that the haciendas of Cuba lacked a sufficient number of slaves and especially a sufficient number of female slaves for reproduction purposes; that before the Cortes considered such a measure others of greater importance, such as administrative reforms in the island and the promotion of white immigration, demanded attention.[21] These arguments of Arango were to be advanced again on other occasions, not only by him but also by other defenders of a moratorium on the abolition of the traffic.

[19]"Oficio del Marqués de Someruelos, La Habana 27 de Mayo de 1811," Saco, *Historia de la esclavitud de la raza africana*, III, 90.
[20]Quotation from *Recueil des diverses pieces*, pp. 55–56, cited by Aimes, *History of Slavery*, pp. 67–69.
[21]Arango y Parreño, "Representación de la Comisión de la Habana a las Cortes," el 20 de julio de 1811, *Obras*, II, 145–187; or Saco, *Historia de la esclavitud de la raza africana*, III, 90–112.

A more dangerous abolition motion arose spontaneously in the session of November 23, 1813. In a debate on a motion to remove the *alcabala* (excise tax) on the sale of slaves, the deputy Antillón suddenly proposed the abolition of slavery. But Arango managed to quell this motion, too, by confining it to the oblivion of a secret session.[22]

The arguments of Arango and the powerful remonstrances of the colonial interests finally led the Cortes of Cádiz to discard these proposals. No doubt, many men in that liberal assembly sincerely believed that revolutionary perils surrounding Cuba made immediate abolition impossible. The time did not seem propitious, but then it never would. And so passed a rare opportunity to make abolitionism appear national and spontaneous, and not foreign.

Foreign pressure, a factor henceforth ever present, now came openly into play. Britain attempted after the Napoleonic wars to induce her allies, especially the French, Portuguese, and Spanish kings, to promise to abolish the slave trade in their respective dominions. In the first Treaty of Paris (May 30, 1814) France agreed to join with Britain in the suppression of the slave traffic, and both powers brought pressure to bear on the newly restored Spanish monarchy. But Fernando VII and his ministers, like the Cortes, were impressed by the arguments of the Cuban slave interests.[23]

Hence in the Treaty of Madrid (July 5, 1814) His Catholic Majesty did no more than express a conformity of feeling with His Britannic Majesty respecting the injustice and inhumanity of the slave trade, and promised only to prohibit Spanish subjects from supplying other possessions with slaves and to consider the means for abolishing the trade.[24]

At the Congress of Vienna, Britain attempted to secure a joint declaration from the allied powers abolishing the slave trade immediately, and it was a significant fact that Spain and Portugal opposed. Since Spain was still faced with a chain of revolutions in Spanish America, she was doubly concerned with conserving the loyalty and prosperity of Cuba and Puerto Rico; for those reasons the Spanish representative, Pedro Gómez Labrador, opposed Castlereagh's maneuver to discuss the matter among the eight powers instead of among the colonial powers of Britain, France, Spain, and Portugal. Natural-

[22]Labra, *América y la constitución*, p. 130.
[23]Aimes, *History of Slavery*, p. 71.
[24]Jacobo de la Pezuela y Lobo, *Diccionario geográfico, estadístico, histórico de la isla de Cuba*, II, 286.

ly, the noncolonial countries—Russia, Austria, Prussia, and Sweden—would have little difficulty in accepting a resolution abolishing the slave trade.

The resolution affirmed in part that just and enlightened men of all centuries had considered the African slave trade as contrary to the principles of humanity and universal morality, and therefore said representatives had resolved to put an end by all means possible to a calamity that had desolated Africa, disgraced Europe, and afflicted humanity. But—and this reflected the concern of Spain and Portugal—although this objective was very honorable, no action would be taken without just consideration for the interests of the various sovereigns concerned.[25] Each nation would be left to determine when it would be convenient to abolish the African slave trade.

This was the delaying principle for which the Spanish and the Portuguese representatives fought. Gómez Labrador explained that if the Spanish colonies had been in the same condition as the English, His Catholic Majesty would not have hesitated one moment in abolishing the slave trade. But the English proprietors had been warned since 1788 concerning the abolition of the trade and therefore had been given twenty years of grace to fill their colonies with slaves.[26] Jamaica, which had 200,000 slaves in 1787, had 400,000 by 1807, the date when Britain abolished the traffic. On the other hand, Spanish colonial proprietors had "found it impossible to acquire slaves in the last 20 years," especially since Spain's involvement in the war had prevented sending ships destined for this object. The proprietors had hardly been able to offset the mortality rate among their slaves.[27] There were ten blacks to one white in Jamaica, but in Cuba the ratio was about one to one. It was simply too soon to abolish the Spanish slave economy.[28]

[25]Declaration of the Congress of Vienna condemning the traffic in slaves, February 8, 1815, previously mentioned; full text given by Zamora, *Legislación ultramarina*, II, 114.

[26]In Parliament the abolitionist Zachary Macaulay admitted the truth of foreign criticism of Britain's hypocritical delay in formulating the abolition law of 1807. The horrors of the slave trade were as well known in 1792 as in 1807, he said, but British slave interests wished first to saturate the colonies with slaves in the hope of keeping sugar trade to themselves. The sugar market was soon glutted; only then was abolition possible. Williams (ed.), *British West Indies at Westminster*, p. 126.

[27]Saco, *Historia de la esclavitud de la raza africana*, III, 119.

[28]Pezuela, writing from 1863 to 1866, condemned the treaty as immature:

The Planting of a Diplomatic Problem, 1815–1820

Certain aberrations were present in the figures given by the Spanish plenipotentiary, according to Saco. The number of slaves in Jamaica in 1807 was 317,351 and not 400,000, and, according to the official registers, 104,000 Negroes entered the port of Havana during the said twenty years (1795–1814).[29] In fact, if contraband were taken into account the total figure would be 130,000. Obviously the absence of Spanish ships dedicated to the slave commerce was a negligible consideration. How else can one explain that in 1795 there were 84,590 slaves in Cuba and in 1814 a total of 212,000?

In spite of the reservations made in the declaration of Vienna, February 8, 1815, Britain had won her point: the abolition of the slave trade was admitted in principle. Immediately, Castlereagh asked the signatory powers to implement the declaration through treaties. Approached on this matter, the Spanish plenipotentiary answered negatively. The Spanish monarch, after consulting colonial interests, especially Cuba and Puerto Rico, had decided on the impossibility of immediate abolition, nor would Spain fix a definite date (eight years), as she had previously thought possible.[30] But Castlereagh placed Spain under great pressure by enlisting the cooperation of the other powers, with the exception of Portugal, in further negotiations on the subject.

The twelve-year license for slave trafficking conceded by the crown to Spaniards in 1804 was due to expire on April 22, 1816, creating a difficult problem for the crown in the midst of negotiations with Great Britain. The Council of the Indies' majority report, based on the broad principles of humanity, recommended to the king on February 15, 1816, that the slave trade be immediately abolished. Also represented, however, was a powerful dissident minority in which the irrepressible Arango, now a member of the Council, figured. The minority voiced the same protests as in 1811. Why this hurry to abolish slavery? There had always been slaves in the world and there always

---

"When they celebrated this treaty, so premature, so impolitic, so prejudicial, so inopportune, there were only 199,145 slaves in Cuba alongside 114,058 free blacks and 239,830 whites." *Diccionario*, II, 285.

[29]Saco, *Historia de la esclavitud de la raza africana*, III, 120.

[30]Spain could only promise that the Spanish ships would not engage in the slave traffic with other foreign colonies, nor loan her flag to cover expeditions contrary to the laws of the other countries—promises that Spain had already made in the Anglo-Spanish treaty of July 5, 1814. *Ibid.*, III, 125.

would be. Now, suddenly, Britain pronounced the strange doctrine that Negro slavery was contrary to human rights.[31]

Nor did the opposition fail to suggest that Britain had in her West Indian colonies motives of self-interest for wishing the ruin of the prosperity of Cuba, an allegation that was readily believed throughout Cuba. Thus the spokesmen for the slave interests developed, in addition to their "too soon" argument, a "patriotic argument" to foil British demands or, better, to impute whatever action the Spanish government might take in this regard to humiliating British pressure.

Even the dissenters, however, realized that they could not demand too much under the circumstances. They were willing to see the traffic abolished north of the equator immediately, and south of the equator on April 22, 1821. Along with this proposal were demands that Britain pay full indemnity for all losses incurred in the abolition of the traffic, and that the Spanish government adopt measures for promoting free immigrant labor.[32]

Meanwhile, Fernando VII and his ministers fought a delaying action in Madrid that never received its due appreciation from the Spanish slave interests. But in the end, Spanish officials gave in before the prestige and diplomacy of their British ally, and thus was born the controversial treaty of September 23, 1817.[33]

By this treaty the Spanish king prohibited Spanish subjects from engaging in the slave trade on the coasts of Africa "north of the equator." The captains and masters of ships captured in contravention of the law were to be subjected to ten-years imprisonment in the Philippine Islands, and their slave cargoes declared free. This part of the agreement was put in force by the decree of December 19, 1817. Beginning May 20, 1820, Spanish subjects were forbidden to engage in the slave trade on the coast of Africa "South of the Equator, under the same penalties." Foreign ships introducing slaves in the Spanish dominions were subject to the same laws.[34] It was also provided that the British government would pay an indemnity of 400,000 pounds (10,-

---

[31]"Voto particular del Sr. Don Francisco de Arango y de otros Consejeros de Indias en el asunto de la abolición del tráfico de negros," Madrid, 15 de febrero de 1816, *ibid.*, III, 307–319.

[32]Aimes, *History of Slavery*, p. 76.

[33]According to Pezuela, the king and his ministers resisted with constancy to the end before the threats of British diplomacy. *Diccionario*, II, 286.

[34]Real Cedula del 19 de diciembre de 1817 y del 20 de mayo de 1820, A.H.N., Ultramar, Leg. 4815 (1880–1882).

000,000 pesetas) to the Spaniards for losses suffered in "legitimate trade" as a result of these treaties, to be paid in London on February 22, 1818.[35] The warships of both nations were authorized to register the merchant ships from either nation whenever there was a well-founded suspicion of illicit cargo. If contraband cargo was found aboard, the ships and their crews were to be detained and taken before the tribunals established for the purpose. These mixed courts were composed of an equal number of judges named by both nations. One was to be established on the coast of Africa (Sierra Leone) and another in the Spanish colonies (Havana). There was to be no appeal beyond these courts.[36] The royal decree of December 19, 1817, ordered the treaty to be published in all the leading cities throughout Spain and the empire.

The decree of 1817 putting into effect the agreement with the British government was prefaced by some interesting remarks. The spirit of humanity that had devoted its efforts to restoring the edifice destroyed by the usurper (Napoleon), said Fernando VII, as if Thomas Clarkson were peeking over his shoulder, had also given rise to a general wish among the sovereigns of Europe to see the slave traffic abolished. Fernando apologized at some length for the decision of his august predecessors to permit the slave trade. Slavery had been a positive benefit for the Africans but, circumstances having changed, it was no longer necessary to transport them to the new world for their own salvation, since an enlightened nation, England, had taken upon itself "the glorious enterprise of civilizing them on their own soil."[37]

Perhaps more indicative of Fernando's calculated philanthropy was the fact that before signing the treaty, José Pizarro, the negotiating minister, sent secret instructions to Cuba and Puerto Rico urging that Spanish slave expeditions reserve at least one third of the cargo for female slaves so that "by propagating the species, the abolition of the slave trade may be less noticeable in the future."[38]

[35]The indemnity sum given to Spain aroused considerable debate in parliament. Sir R. Heron, for one, feared the money might be employed to subjugate Spain's revolted colonies. Williams (ed.), *British West Indies at Westminster*, p. 68.

[36]Real Cédula del 19 de diciembre de 1817, A.H.N., Ultramar, Leg. 4815 (1880–1882).

[37]*Ibid.*, Also in Zamora, *Legislación ultramarina*, III, 126–127.

[38]Jacobo de la Pezuela y Lobo, *Historia de la isla de Cuba*, IV, 49–50. Cited by Duvon C. Corbitt, "Immigration in Cuba," *HAHR*, XXII, No. 2 (May, 1942), 289.

The Anglo-Spanish treaty of 1817 was not unique. It was, after all, but a link in a chain of treaties designed to eradicate the African slave trade in the Western World. The spread of revolutionary ideas to Hispanic America made easier the problem of abolishing black slavery there. Early independence leaders, such as San Martín, Bolívar, and Hidalgo, had declared the abolition of slavery, and congressional ratification had followed. Argentina formally abolished slavery in 1816; Gran Colombia and Chile in 1821; Peru, Guatemala, and Uruguay in 1828; and Mexico in 1829. England herself did not abolish slavery in her colonial possessions until 1833.

The glory of being the first to abolish slavery, however, was a relative thing. The Spanish American republics did not possess a flourishing plantation economy such as the English had in Jamaica, the Spanish in Cuba, and the Portuguese in Brazil. A declaration abolishing slavery or the slave trade was for most of these governments mere paper work; it involved little effort at enforcement. Even so, Argentina did not fully abolish Negro slavery until the 1840's, and Peru waited until 1854. But such countries were really more concerned with peonage labor.

Where the plantation economy consumed thousands of Africans annually, there the British faced the problem of enforcing compliance with abolition agreements. In an attempt to close the great Brazilian slave market Britain pressed treaties on Portugal (January 22, 1815, and July 28, 1817). Like the Spanish treaty, these agreements empowered British cruisers to visit and search suspected vessels flying the Portuguese flag, and to adjudicate captured slavers through mixed commissions. Portugal received 300,000 pounds compensation for retiring after 1820 from four centuries of slave trading north of the equator. But, unlike Spain, little Portugal did not specifically commit herself to abolish the trade south of the lines, and insisted on an additional article reserving the right to terminate her treaty obligations fifteen years after the so-called universal closing of the Portuguese slave trade.[39] The British would have cause to regret such reservations, for not only would the Portuguese flag reappear on slave ships, necessitating unilateral seizures of suspected ships under the Portuguese flag, but independent Brazil would follow the Portuguese example.

[39]Viscount Palmerston to Lord Howden, Foreign Office, June 4, 1847, *BFSP* (1847–1848), XXXVI, 601–602.

The Planting of a Diplomatic Problem, 1815–1820

As early as 1810 Portuguese Brazil, in the name of the prince regent in exile, signed a commercial agreement with Great Britain, making at the same time a pious declaration against the slave trade and a promise to prohibit Portuguese participation beyond Portuguese Africa. But quasi-independent Brazil, where Portuguese capitalists continued to invest in the African traffic, never felt bound by this declaration nor by Portugal's treaties with Britain. At the Congress of Verona in 1822 Canning announced that the African traffic was greater than ever before, even north of the equator, where supposedly the Portuguese had agreed to abolish the slave trade. He then made proposals against the use of the Portuguese and Brazilian flags by foreigners, and against the importation of Brazilian products. He asked that each nation declare the slave trade piracy. France opposed and Canning's proposals were ignored.[40]

Later, facing the usual British threat to withhold diplomatic recognition, the independent monarchy of Brazil—which also needed the support of the slaveholding class, as Spanish sovereignty would need it in Cuba—agreed to halfhearted cooperation in the "complete closing" of the Brazilian slave trade. But by Brazilian interpretation the treaty of 1826, which repeated the Anglo-Portuguese treaty of 1817, was limited to a fifteen-year period (1830–1845).[41]

How the British forced Brazil, a more important slave mart than Cuba, to cooperate further is of course another story.[42] We wish only to point out here that British slave-trade diplomacy encountered in Spanish Cuba and Brazil a similar series of trials and tribulation, and that the Cuban and Brazilian slave markets were to a great extent responsible for the whole chain of British treaties against the slave trade.

At first Britain did not attempt to bind all maritime nations to cooperate in abolishing the African slave trade, only those where this trade had previously been important. The standard British procedure was to withhold diplomatic recognition or ratification of a treaty of commerce, amity, and peace, or to refuse to facilitate a loan in the London money market until the lesser power agreed to cooperate with British

---

[40]Klingberg, *Anti-Slavery Movement*, pp. 167–168.
[41]Palmerston to Howden, June 4, 1847, *BFSP* (1847–1848), XXXVI, 601–602.
[42]See, for example, Lawrence F. Hill, "The Abolition of the African Slave Trade to Brazil," *HAHR*, XI, No. 2 (May, 1931), 169–197; and Percy A. Martin, "Slavery and Abolition in Brazil," *HAHR*, XIII, No. 2 (May, 1933), 151–196.

cruisers in closing the traffic. In 1825 the Argentine Confederation signed such a treaty. Gran Colombia and Mexico did so in 1826. The slave trade was considered virtually at an end in such countries, but later, as the slavers moved with agility from one flag to another, mainly to supply the Cuban and Brazilian markets, Britain closed the gaps methodically through a new series of world-embracing treaties which expressly conceded British cruisers the right of search and arrest. To mention only some of these: France in 1833; Bolivia, Tuscany, and Asiatic cities in 1837; the Kingdom of Naples in 1838; Haiti, Venezuela, and Chile in 1839; more stringent treaties with Argentina and Uruguay in the same year; Texas in 1840; Ecuador in 1841; Mexico again in 1842; and the Dominican Republic in 1850.[43] The United States, which (like Peru) steadfastly refused the British the right of search, did agree by the Webster-Ashburton Treaty of 1842 to join in maintaining a patrol squadron on the coast of Africa.

In regard to closing the Cuban slave market, it appears that neither contracting power foresaw the extent of future difficulties. True, Spain had agreed to abolish the slave trade by 1820, but Cuba immediately received compensations that served only to incite demands for cheap labor. In 1816 the Creole Arango was named counselor of the Indies, from which position he could even better promote the Cuban plantation economy. In 1817 the royal tobacco monopoly was abolished, thus giving a stimulus to small, independent producers. The decree of October 21, 1817, promoted white Catholic immigration to Cuba, including non-Spanish for the first time;[44] that of February 10, 1818, opened Cuban ports to foreign vessels and allowed Cuba to trade directly with foreign nations, so long as the mother country received the customs revenues; and that of 1819 granted full title rights

---

[43]"Informe de la Comisión nombrada por la Sección de Comercio sobre la abolición del tráfico y esclavitud de los negros y próximo pérdida de la Isla de Cuba, Junio del año de 1851," A.H.N., Ultramar, Leg. 3548–3549. Not all agreements were immediately ratified; for example, Ecuador did not ratify the agreement of 1841 until 1847. Again, Austria, Prussia, and Russia never ratified the agreement of 1841. For further details see James F. King, "The Latin-American Republics and the Suppression of the Slave Trade," *HAHR*, XXIV, No. 3 (August, 1944), 387–411.

[44]Foreigners were divided into three classes: transients, domiciled foreigners, and citizens by naturalization. To enjoy civil rights one had to declare his intention of permanent residence, embrace the Catholic religion, and foreswear allegiance to his native country. Willis F. Johnson, *The History of Cuba*, III, 19–20.

The Planting of a Diplomatic Problem, 1815–1820

to property which formerly had been tenuously held by royal grace.⁴⁵

As an effect of these decrees land and slaves in Cuba were more in demand than ever before, and this in spite of the fact that the crown had for three centuries an almost fixed policy (at a time before Spain fully realized that slavery was the key to holding Cuba) to promote a white labor force in Cuba. Even before the Anglo-Spanish treaty of 1817, Arango and the various economic corporations were pushing hard for free white labor, calculating that the slave trade would soon end, and that the presence of a large number of whites would permit more slave labor to be used without fear of a Negro rebellion. In 1815 the Intendant Ramírez and Captain General José Cienfuegos founded the Junta de Población Blanca for promoting white population. The immigration decree of 1817, with its special land privileges for new settlers, was one of the concessions given the Junta. From February 7, 1818, until the slave trade should close in 1820, a tax of six pesos was imposed on each male slave imported. This revenue was to be used by the Junta for bringing free white labor to Cuba. At the same time, female slaves were exempted from the tax so as to encourage the domestic breeding of slaves.⁴⁶

The white immigrants came, but not the kind that added to a white labor force or contributed to support Spain's abolitionist commitment. As always, few Spanish immigrants could be induced to labor like serfs in the tropics, and, lacking capital and planter experience, few settled on the underdeveloped lands in the interior of Cuba. On the other hand, refugees from Santo Domingo, Louisiana, and Florida took advantage of reforms such as the immigration and land act of 1817. Then during the wars of independence in South America and Mexico, 1810–1826, an estimated twenty thousand Spanish exiles were admitted to Cuba. Many of the refugees were wealthy with commercial and planter experience, and Cuban sugar, coffee, and tobacco production owed much to them. But they were also additions to the slaveholding forces and, as a consequence, they served not to diminish but to increase the demand for slaves.

Furthermore, being exiles from New World republics many of them were reactionaries, and bitterly disposed toward equalitarian doctrine. They were an important element in the foundation of a fanatically pro-Spanish party dedicated to conserving whatever remained of

⁴⁵Philip S. Foner, *A History of Cuba and Its Relations with the United States*, I, 95.
⁴⁶Corbitt, "Immigration in Cuba," 283–288.

the old privileged order in the Spanish empire, and their new-found prosperity. Such elements could easily join with Spanish officials in making it a patriotic duty to resist British abolitionism and to silence any abolitionist-minded Creoles.

Thus opened an era of slave-trade diplomacy characterized by British efforts to force a contracting power into full compliance with formal agreements. The task that the English government took upon its shoulders at the behest of her abolitionists was truly gigantic.

3. A Chapter in Slave-Trade Diplomacy
1820-1825

> One could compose volumes on the claims addressed by the English government to the Court of Madrid at different times, in order to demand the fulfillment of the treaty.
>
> Valiente, 1869[1]

There was, of course, a rush to fill Cuba with slaves before the application of the treaty of 1817. Between 1817 and 1820, through Havana alone, 67,059 Africans entered *la gran Antilla*.[2] Meanwhile the treaty had been applied north of the equator after May 30, 1820. Since five months were allowed for completion of all voyages, the deadline established was October 30, 1820. But even after this date slavers continued to arrive in Havana with impunity. From October 31, 1820, to September, 1821, twenty-six slavers had entered Havana with 6,415 slaves. Of these, eighteen still used the Spanish flag, five the French, two the Portuguese, and one the American.[3]

Cuban officials, apparently in agreement that five months were too short a period for completing voyages started before May 20, 1820, did nothing. At the same time, a Cuban delegation was in Madrid urging the Spanish government to agree to an extension of five months, since the original period was not sufficient time for a ship to make cargo.[4]

[1] Porfirio Valiente, *Réformes dan les isles de Cuba et Porto-Rico*, p. 8.
[2] Alexander von Humboldt, *The Island of Cuba*, p. 218.
[3] Report of R. F. Jameson, British commissioner in Havana, in Hubert S. Aimes, *A History of Slavery in Cuba, 1511 to 1868*, p. 97.
[4] *Ibid.*, p. 96. José Antonio Saco, *La historia de la esclavitud de la raza africana en el Nuevo Mundo y en especial en los países Américo-Hispanos*, III, 140–143.

In the meantime a military revolt in Madrid (April, 1820) forced Fernando VII to restore the liberal constitution of 1812, and to accede to the election of a new Cortes. This turn of events probably gave added strength to British protests against extending the traffic.[5] In any case, on December 10, 1820, the British commissioners in Havana were informed that orders to carry out the treaty had been received. The newly assembled liberal Cortes appointed a commission, March 26, 1821, to propose measures to stop violations of the treaty, and to decree that the treaty of 1817 be included in the new criminal code.[6] On paper these were promising beginnings.

But the events of 1820–1823, though promising in an abolitionist sense, only served, in the end, to fortify the old pattern. Fernando VII, being frightened, agreed to the restoration of the constitution of 1812. The Cortes of 1820 again included deputies from the colonies. The corporations of Cuba (la Diputación Provincial, el Ayuntamiento Constitucional, y el Consulado de la Habana) gave the three elected deputies explicit instructions on the slave-trade question. They were to try to revoke the treaty of 1817 or at least secure a delay of six years in its application.

Again following arguments similar to those presented by Arango in the Cortes of 1811 the instructions of the Provincial Deputation said: "This does not concern the permanence of the slave trade. The signs of the time resist it." A delay of six years at least was needed in order to provide the haciendas with the needed slaves, ". . . and especially African women for the conservation of the species and the plantations, as has happened in the English islands which were given ten years of grace for this purpose."[7]

The following words indicate why, in the first place, the commercial class in Cuba was so opposed to abolition, and why, in the second place, it would prove so difficult to extirpate the slave trade:

Of all the provinces of the Spanish empire, the most involved and prejudiced in this business is the island of Cuba. No other one had undertaken

---

[5]Aimes, quoting from *British and Foreign State Papers*, Vol. IX, and *Parliamentary Papers*, 1822, is a valuable source for this early period of negotiations, *History of Slavery*, p. 96.

[6]*Ibid.*, p. 97. Also, Saco, *Historia de la esclavitud de la raza africana*, III, 143–144. The commission decided on new measures to stop the slave trade, since it was decided that the treaty of 1817 had not provided sufficiently for the enforcement of same.

[7]Saco, *Historia de la esclavitud de la raza africana*, III, 141–142.

the African slave trade directly with its own ships and capital. Therefore the damages caused by the sudden cessation . . . are incalculable. The quantity received for compensation is most inadequate . . . And if no delay is obtained . . . an enormous weight of debts and obligations will weigh upon the subjects of the nation.[8]

Apparently the liberal commitment of the Cortes outweighed the foregoing instructions, because none of the Cuban deputies in the session of 1821–1822 dared to ask for the revocation of the treaty. Such a move would have hardly been consistent with the liberal principles for which that Cortes stood. On the contrary, voices such as that of the Count of Toreno were raised in favor of punishing infractions of the treaty, and this proposal was approved by the Cortes.[9]

Three new deputies were elected in Cuba to serve the Cortes of 1822–1823. They were given the same afore-mentioned instructions, but, as has happened more than once in Cuban history, the elected deputies proved to be surprisingly liberal and patriotic. Father Félix Varela y Morales, Cuban deputy, philosophy teacher, and one of the founders of Creole patriotism, more than ignored the instructions by proposing the gradual abolition of slavery in Hispanic America.

Varela's prologue throws some light on the suppressed feelings of a liberal minority concerned about the future of *la Patria Criolla*. He argued that until slavery was abolished the Antilles would always be in grave danger of slave insurrections, especially since the Haitians and the revolutionaries of continental Hispanic America had designs for liberating the island. It would be foolish to imagine that the slaves would remain tranquil and content while the whites rejoiced in their new-found liberties, including the constitution of 1812 revived in 1822. "The barbarian is the best soldier when he finds someone to lead him," said Varela; Santo Domingo had proved that there would be no lack of leaders. Varela dared to say that "the general wish of the people of Cuba is that there were no slaves, they only want to find some other way to supply their necessities." Abolition, astutely controlled, would provide the answer.[10]

On presenting these arguments, Varela could not refrain from attacking the so-called philanthropy of the British. England, the first to sacrifice humanity to avarice, now flaunted a philanthropy which was

[8] *Ibid.*, III, 141.   [9] *Ibid.*, III, 144.
[10] "Memoria que demuestra la necesidad de extinguir la esclavitud de los negros en la Isla de Cuba, atendiendo a los intereses de sus propietarios," por el presbítero don Félix Varela, diputado a Cortes, *Ibid.*, III, 1–17.

as much a child of her own self-interests as were her past cruelties: "Englishmen, on your lips the word philanthropy loses its value; excuse the expression, you are bad apostles of humanity." Repeating the common objection of Arango and others, Varela innocently asked why Britain did not put the same pressure on Brazil, and other slavist countries.[11]

Varela's project provided for the liberty of all slaves who had served fifteen years with the same master, the liberty of all those born after the publication of this decree, the establishment of a lottery whereby the slave selected would be enabled to purchase his freedom, and the foundation of philanthropic juntas charged with gathering funds, protecting slaves, and directing abolition.[12]

Although this project did not receive much public notice the news reached Cuba, where Varela's action was roundly condemned and cursed: "The deputy from Cuba that would ask for abolition of slavery ought to have his tongue torn out."[13] It seems that the Cortes of 1822, if it had not been preoccupied with other important political matters, would have been disposed to a more radical solution of the slave-trade question.

In the midst of the liberal interval in Spain, another Cuban deputy, the ecclesiastic Juan Bernardo O'Gaban, published his *Observations on the Condition of African Slaves* in 1821. In company with prominent slave proprietors, O'Gaban reiterated the demand that the Cortes protect the slave trade against the British. O'Gaban said that he was not a defender of slavery; yet, "work was ordained of God" and "the Africans were the laziest people known." His pamphlet contained all the sophisms—the slave trade was a means whereby the Africans were made more civilized; hence, wise legislators, "if humanitarianism were truly understood," not only would compel the Negroes to work but also would protect their transition to America.[14]

---

[11]*Ibid.*, III, 7. In fact, Britain was exercising similar pressure on Portuguese Brazil. See Lawrence F. Hill, "The Abolition of the African Slave Trade to Brazil," *HAHR*, XI, No. 2 (May, 1931), 169–197.

[12]"Proyecto de decreto sobre la abolición de la esclavitud en la Isla de Cuba y sobre los medios de evitar los daños que pueden ocasionarse a la población blanca y a la agricultura." Saco, *Historia de la esclavitud de la raza africana*, III, 18–31.

[13]Saco claims he personally heard this remark made about Varela. *Ibid.*, III, 146.

[14]Juan Bernardo O'Gaban, *Observaciones sobre la suerte de los negros de Af-*

In a way, this was a reflection of earlier protests, for example, that of the *Consulado* of Havana, October 21, 1818, whereby illustrious Cuban landholders, such as Juan O'Farrill, Andres de Juaregui, and Fernando de la Maza Arredondo, asked for a protected slave trade.[15]

The slave interests regarded the treaty with Britain as a national humiliation, and a most untimely threat to the island's dynamic economy. But they soon could feel at ease, for a change of events put a sudden end to hopes of ephemeral liberalism. In April, 1823, the King of France sent to the Peninsula "100,000 sons of St. Louis" in order to wipe out the revolutionary infection there. Spanish masses who had fought to the death against the illegitimacy of the Napoleonic invasion, threw flowers in the path of a legitimate invasion. There was no better proof of the deep conservative nature of Spain. The beloved despot Fernando VII, feeling his strength again, dissolved the upstart Cortes and dispersed the liberals to the four winds. All propositions leading to a more radical solution of the slave question were abandoned.

Meanwhile political conditions in Spain and the limited nature of the treaty of 1817 frustrated any efforts to intercept slave ships, even though the Cuban officials might try. In the first three years after 1820 no captures were made, although the French ship *Mario* was detained briefly in September, 1822.[16]

The Spanish government had perhaps two ships patrolling the coast, the British government not many more. These were not sufficient to blockade over two thousand miles of indented coastline. Nor was it easy to stop slavers from hiding among the fifteen hundred ships that now entered Havana annually. It was difficult to distinguish a slave ship from any other and a bothersome task to examine scrupulously each one. Furthermore, shipment of slaves between the Spanish colonies was still permitted and protected by law. One hesitated to question all ships indiscriminately.[17]

In the interim, mixed commissions, or Admiralty Courts, had been established both at Sierra Leone and at Havana. As provided by the treaty, each of the two contracting governments named their own

---

rica, considerados en su propia patria y reclamación contra el tratado celebrado con los ingleses, p. 7.

[15]"Representación del Consulado, La Habana, octubre de 1818," *ibid.*, pp. 23–24.

[16]Aimes, *History of Slavery*, p. 102.

[17]*Ibid.*, p. 98.

representatives to the mixed commission, or tribunal. The commissary judge and the commissioner of arbitration were officials authorized to hear and determine all cases involving the seizure of slave ships according to treaty stipulations. At Havana, Alejandro Ramírez, the intendent, was named commissary judge for Spain, and Francisco Arango, commissioner of arbitration. J. T. Kilbee and R. F. Jameson represented Great Britain.[18]

From the standpoint of Anglo-Spanish relations, Article Seven was the most important provision of the treaty of 1817. This gave rise to the famous question of the *emancipados*, a class of Negroes coming from captured slave ships. According to Article Seven, when the mixed court declared a slave ship fair prize it was subject to sale at public auction, the proceeds being divided between the two governments. But the slaves found aboard were to receive from the mixed commission a certificate of emancipation. These emancipados were then to be delivered to the government in whose territory the mixed commission had pronounced sentence.[19] For example, if the emancipados were captured off the coast of Cuba by either British or Spanish ships, they were to be delivered to the government of Cuba. Each government promised to guarantee the liberty of these Africans committed to their charge.

Spain pledged her national honor in accepting the following obligations: (1) to issue a certificate of emancipation to captured Africans; (2) to place these emancipados under the patronage of the government of Cuba; (3) to give employment to the emancipados as servants or free workers; and (4) to guarantee to the British government the liberty of this class of Negroes.[20] These were the provisions whereby Britain would justify her audacious intervention in the slave affairs of Cuba. Spain would rue the day she had signed such an agreement with Britain, and would try, but in vain, to free herself from the obligations of Article 7.

Since the emancipado question is in a certain sense the beginning of the abolition question in Spanish colonial slavery, the problem will henceforth be treated in some detail, for it may well serve as an introduction to the greater problems to come.

By 1824 the first slave cargoes were captured off the coast of Cuba

[18]*Ibid.*, p. 95.
[19]Reglamento de las Comisiones mixtas, A.H.N. Ultramar, Leg. 3548-3549. Index N. 2.
[20]*Ibid.*

and declared free by the mixed court of Havana. From this point on, the question of the emancipados became a major diplomatic problem, and remained so for the next fifty years. As soon as emancipados were placed under the patronage of the Cuban government, reports of gross abuses were circulated.

English consuls in Havana, presuming to enforce treaty obligations, charged that the captains general were selling the emancipados to the great slave owners. It was also charged that the slaveowners, instead of teaching the emancipados a trade or working them as free men as provided by law, treated these ignorant Africans exactly as slaves. Since, according to treaty regulations, the emancipados were to emerge after four years of tutelage as free men capable of sustaining themselves, their lot was all the more cruel. The patrons tended to squeeze out of them all the labor possible in this given time. According to Saco, the emancipado was more a slave than the slave himself.[21]

The alert English consuls and commissioners were clamoring for the intervention of the British government in behalf of the hapless people. Consul Kilbee in Havana suggested to the government of Canning that the emancipados should be protected by the naming of a general superintendent of emancipated Negroes, and that a fine of five hundred pesos should be imposed on those proprietors who substituted emancipados for dead or missing slaves. The Council of the Indies (April 14, 1825) could not accept such a forceful suggestion but contented itself with a few paternal exhortations to the children of the Indies: for example, the Council recommended that the emancipados be given to persons of good character, preferably to owners of plantations where there were fewer slaves. Emancipados could thus be more certain of learning a trade or profession, "so that later they could live on their own." The Council charged the planters to treat the emancipados well, and established a register wherein the names of the emancipado and the plantation were recorded.[22] The purpose

[21] At first the emancipados were placed with civil or religious corporations, with widows, and with proprietors who promised to care for them, but soon the placing of emancipados became a lucrative business (Ramiro Guerra y Sánchez, "Illustración: libertad de comercio" in *Historia de la nación Cubana*, Ramiro Guerra y Sánchez et al. [eds.], III, 81). As Lord Palmerston observed, the emancipado did not have a permanent owner who would care for him like a working animal, *First Report from the Select Committee on the Slave Trade Together with the Minutes of Evidence and Appendix*.

[22] Varias comunicaciones y consideraciones sobre el problema de los emanci-

of the register was to prevent the emancipado from being treated as a slave, and to provide for a checkup on his condition. But soon complaints were heard of false names and details being entered in the register.

The capture of *bozales* (slaves proceeding from Africa) by British ships off Cuba, and their subsequent status as emancipados, even though not many in number, produced the greatest alarm in Cuba. It was feared that the existence of this free class of Negroes would undermine the morale of the slave system, or that such Negroes, filled with "English ideas of liberty," might prove to be incendiary personalities.

When the British man-of-war *Lion* captured the Spanish slaver *El Relámpago* in Cuban waters (1825), 150 slaves were entitled to certificates of liberty under the law. Yet the Spanish judges of the mixed court voiced the popular feeling that if these Negroes were placed at liberty they would represent a dangerous example to the other slaves of the island.[23]

Some Spanish officials, in view of the agitated state of opinion, asked why the Cuban government could not return the emancipados to Africa. In a communication of May 1, 1825, the government of the island had explained that this was impossible for several reasons: first, the expenses involved; second, the difficulty of finding ships destined to Africa; third, the foolishness of returning the emancipados to "the darkness of paganism"; fourth, the certainty of exposing the same emancipados to recapture and resale into slavery.[24]

No mention was made of the most important reason obstructing the return of the emancipados to Africa. The government of Cuba, for a consideration of money and influence, was now delivering the emancipados to the slave owners for a period of seven years. Since this arrangement represented a source of revenue for the authorities and a source of labor for the proprietors, there was not the least demand in Cuba for the return of the emancipados to Africa.

The captains general of the island complained bitterly that the activities of the English consuls endangered the maintenance of public order and disturbed the slave class. They frequently suggested to the Madrid government that the conduct of the English consuls

---

pados, Consejo do Indias, 17 de noviembre de 1825. A.H.N. Ultramar, Leg. 3548–3549, N. 1.
[23]*Ibid.*
[24]*Ibid.*

was part of a plot to destroy slavery in the Spanish Antilles, and thereby Spanish dominion.

In turn, the continuance of illicit trade very early led the British commissioners to suggest to their government the connivance of Cuban officials. Frequent British protests led to the decree of January 2, 1826 (repeated August 2, 1830), ordering every ship captain to deliver his log book to the naval commandant of Havana for inspection. This was a useless provision since anything or nothing could be entered in the log book. Another clause of the decree, however, provided that any person could denounce slave disembarkations, including the slave himself, and if this was the case, the slave would be set free. Purchasers of illegally imported slaves were to be fined two hundred pesos for each slave acquired, and to suffer confiscation of the same. Also His Spanish Majesty implored the Archbishop of Cuba and the Bishop of Havana to announce in their diocese that the traffic was against the Christian conscience, as well as His Majesty's.[25]

The decree of early 1826, in its latter provisions, was a positive step in attempting to close the slave market, especially the part providing for the denouncement of slave disembarkations, and there seems to have been at least a temporary reduction in the slave trade after this order.[26]

The abolitionist efforts of the English officials in Havana were not the only influence feared by the slave interests of Cuba. Dangerous currents threatened from many directions and it was difficult to separate fact from rumor. Republican and abolitionist propaganda coming from the adjacent republics of Haiti, Santo Domingo, and the United States kept the Spanish government in a continual ferment of fear as already suggested. Weak, decrepit, divided at home, Spain could at best fight a delaying battle against the ideas and movements of the century. Rumors that South American Republics were plotting the independence of Cuba, rumors that abolitionist agents were plotting slave revolts, rumors that the *yanquis* were plotting to seize or buy Cuba, rumors that Cuban criollos were secretly plotting independence — in all this there was much tilting with windmills. Fears were, no doubt, exaggerated but no less genuine for that.

[25]Real Orden del 2 de Enero de 1826, José María Zamora y Coronado (ed.), *Biblioteca de legislación ultramarina*, III, 126–127.

[26]According to Aimes there was a definite fall off from 7,000 slaves in 1825 to 3,500 in 1826 and 1827, but by 1829 the figure had risen to 7,500 and to 9,000 in 1830, *History of Slavery*, Appendix II, "Slaves Imported into Cuba."

Ostensibly to prepare the island against attacks from all quarters, the captains general had been invested with near "omnipotent faculties" by the decree of 1825. This was, in fact, the island's only constitution, as Callahan has said.[27] The island was considered a besieged fortress *(plaza sitiada)* and was thus to be governed. The captain general could at his discretion lay aside precedents of local government. Although Governor Vives did not invoke the decree arbitrarily, his successors would. It would now be possible to reduce the influence of the insular corporations and local Creole interests; commerce, travel, social affairs, even the most innocent activities, could now be placed under the scrutiny of the military. A strict censorship would be exercised over all discussions in the press, public meetings would be outlawed, and mention of the "inciting words" *slavery* and *independence* would be forbidden, as would also any public reference to political reform.[28]

Henceforth the most careful scrutiny would limit the entry of all classes of foreigners, since they could be potentially dangerous agents. Among other prohibitions, the Council of the Indies, by decree of April, 1833, revived the act of February 25, 1796, forbidding the introduction of Negroes proceeding from neighboring islands and foreign nations, "... since they are educated with ideas opposed to moral health and offer a bad example to the many slaves of the Spanish colonies."[29]

According to the census of 1817 the population of the island was 630,980, a figure which represented a remarkable increase of 358,680 over the census of 1791. The population had more than doubled in less than thirty years! Even more impressive, there were now 224,268 slaves in Cuba. The combined black population, including the free blacks, outnumbered the whites for the first time:[30]

---

[27]The Royal Order of May 29, 1825, James Morton Callahan, *Cuba and International Relations: A Historical Study in American Diplomacy*, p. 15.

[28]Expressions unfavorable to the government were never allowed in print, except for a short period in 1812, and from 1820 to 1823, when the liberals briefly triumphed in Spain. Johnson describes at length the rigidity of the regime, including the tax burdens, censorship, and other inconveniences of an overcentralized government. Willis F. Johnson, *The History of Cuba*, III, Chap. I.

[29]Callahan, *Cuba and International Relations*, p. 16.

[30]The census of 1817 taken under the command of Captain General José Cienfuegos Jovellanos, as given in Ulpiano Vega Cobiellas, *Nuestra América y la evolución de Cuba*, pp. 74–75.

Whites	291,021	(45.96%)
Slaves	224,268	(54.04%)
Free Blacks	115,691	
	630,980	

There were now 625 sugar plantations, 779 coffee plantations, 1,601 tobacco plantations (*vegas*), and 2,127 cattle farms.[31]

In terms of sugar exportation, progress was astounding. According to Humboldt's estimates, based on official documents, only 13,000 boxes of sugar were exported annually around 1760. By 1780 the number had risen to 50,000. Following the destruction of the Haitian sugar industry, the widening of the American and British markets, and the commercial reforms of 1792, exports rose steadily, reaching a total of 103,629 boxes by 1794. During the Napoleonic period up to 1825 the annual average was over 200,000 boxes. Thereafter sugar exports climbed even more precipitously.[32] The British commissioner estimated in 1822 that about 155,000 slaves were on the sugar plantations, 54,000 on coffee farms, 36,000 on minor estates such as vegas, farms, and cattle ranches, and 20,000 employed in household service.[33]

A comparative view of Cuba and the other sugar islands in the West Indies in 1823 offers interesting contrasts:[34]

Slave Population and Export of Sugar in 1823

	Slaves	Export
Cuba	260,000	1,520,000 cwt.
Jamaica	342,382	1,417,488 cwt.
Barbadoes, Granada, and St. Vincent	128,000	794,567 cwt.
Trinidad	23,500	189,891 cwt.
All the English Antilles	626,800	3,005,366 cwt.
French Antilles	178,000	794,760 cwt.
Dutch, Danish, and Swedish Antilles	61,300	354,386 cwt.

Brazil with 1,960,000 slaves produced only 650,000 cwt. in 1816 and even less thereafter, due to domestic disturbances and an increasing shift to coffee planting. An over-all view of sugar exports in the Western hemisphere in 1825 showed that the Caribbean islands supplied 62 per cent, Brazil 27 per cent, and Guiana, with 206,000 slaves, 9 per

---

[31]Humboldt, *Island of Cuba*, p. 280.
[32]*Ibid.*, pp. 252–253.
[33]*Parliamentary Papers*, 1822, cited by Aimes, *History of Slavery*, p. 100.
[34]Thrasher's notes, Humboldt, *Island of Cuba*, p. 255. Not all slaves listed were engaged in sugar production, however.

cent. The British population of over 14,000,000 people consumed one third of the New World sugar exports of 460,000,000 kilograms.[35]

Obviously, given this picture of prosperity, the Cuban slave proprietor was not disposed to follow a revolutionary path to economic ruin, even if he sympathized with the revolutionary heritage of America. The Haitian massacre made the Cuban whites cautious about revolutionary ideologies. The conspiracy of the free Negro José Antonio Aponte, 1813, was a reminder.[36]

[35]*Ibid.*, p. 257. Again one must keep in mind, particularly in the case of Brazil, that not all slaves were employed in sugar production.
[36]Vega Cobiellas, *Nuestra América*, p. 70.

4. A United Front in Cuba, 1825-1840

> Spain has often made resolutions for reforms, but has always postponed the first step till tomorrow. The motto of Columbus was "Sail on!" but this has not been the motto of Spain in regard to politics and government. "Forward, march!" has been used only as an order to the troops of the standing army. Procrastination and delay have been the notes of Spanish diplomacy and politics. This misfortune has often been the result of political complications rather than of any determined opposition to reform.
>
> Callahan, 1899[1]

Before continuing the exasperating story of Anglo-Spanish diplomacy on the slave-trade question, it would be well to describe more fully the complex nature of the colonial situation. If Spanish policy seemed to be decidedly one of increasing resistance to abolitionist demands and of status quo on reform questions in general, the explanation lies not only in the Peninsula, whose political problems we have already touched upon, but also in Cuba, where a peculiar set of circumstances gave rise to an almost solid block of vested interests.

During the second quarter of the nineteenth century progress continued on the major agricultural fronts. Tobacco, now freed of government monopoly, enjoyed great prosperity. In the period 1825 to 1830, 128,644 quintales (1 quintal = 1 cwt.) of leaf tobacco and 245,097 millions of cigars were exported. By the period 1845 to 1850

---

[1]James Morton Callahan, *Cuba and International Relations: A Historical Study in American Diplomacy*, p. 136.

these figures had risen to 364,183 and 896,000, respectively. Tobacco was now second only to sugar in the employment of slave labor.[2]

The annual sugar export, which had reached an average of 200,000 boxes by 1825, was still pushing upward, so that ten years later the annual average was 500,000. By 1850 this figure had trebled to 1,500,000.[3]

Coffee production, which had always been more sporadic in nature, competed seriously with sugar for slave labor. For the first quarter of the nineteenth century prices were good, from thirteen to seventeen pesos a quintal, and coffee exports rose steadily. As a result, by 1825 an estimated 28,000 slaves were engaged in coffee cultivation, compared with 66,000 slaves working on sugar plantations.[4] After 1835, however, the coffee industry, centered mainly in the eastern province, began to decline, largely due to Brazilian competition. The annual average export of 499,000 quintals in 1825 declined to 192,061 quintales in 1850.

Sugar was obviously king of Cuba, but as the nineteenth century progressed the picture of a sugar bonanza developed uneven spots, suggesting that not all the planters were as happy as one might think.[5] As often happens in a plantation economy that inclines toward monoproduction, the fortunes of the planters were subject to violent fluctuations in accord with the often capricious demands of the international market ever sensitive to such disturbing events as embargoes between warring countries. The English blockade of Napoleonic Europe, for example, led to the rapid spread of a German discovery for extracting sugar from beet crystals. To encourage this industry European governments were soon erecting tariff walls against Cuban and Brazilian cane sugar.

The major markets of Cuba were soon limited to England and the United States and even these were insecure. Until 1833 England still retained in the Caribbean her own sugar islands operated by slave labor, while in the United States production of sugar cane in the South was ever on the increase. Only by more-efficient methods could

---

[2]Thrasher's notes, Alexander von Humboldt, *The Island of Cuba*, p. 289. Allowance must be made for contraband tobacco not included in these calculations.
[3]*Ibid.*, Thrasher's notes, pp. 252–253.
[4]*Ibid.*, Thrasher's notes, p. 282.
[5]See Roland T. Ely, *Cuando reinaba su majestad el azúcar. Estudio histórico-sociológico de una tragedia latinoamericana: El monocultivo en Cuba, origen y evolución del proceso.*

the planters of Cuba compete effectively in an unsteady market. Mechanization of the sugar industry would begin early in the nineteenth century. Steam engines were introduced in the refining mills as early as 1820, and railroad construction from the port of Havana to the interior sugar fields began in the early 1830's.[6]

This forced mechanization, which required greater capital and more efficiency, gradually resulted in expansion of production, and as the size of the mill and the size of the cultivated area grew, concomitantly a new political and economic pattern began to unfold. A solid link took form between the commercial interests, mostly Spaniards of Catalan origin, and the agricultural interests, mostly criollos, not on political questions but on the slave question. In order to extend sugar production (and to lesser extent coffee) by the importation of machinery, the cultivation of more land, and the increase in the laboring force, the *hacendados* (sugar planters), in their competition with one another and with other sugar-producing countries, were forced to borrow heavily from Spanish merchants. The nature of sugar production was such that a further capital investment was always required, and this produced, said Humboldt, "a state of absolute dependence"[7] of the proprietors on the merchant. Loans were made in anticipation of sugar or coffee crops, and loan rates were as high as 12 to 16 per cent or higher.

The vicious circle of harvest loans to negligent planters was undoubtedly encouraged by the feudal *privilegio de ingenios*, special protective legislation first given by the crown in the sixteenth century to encourage the sugar industry. A creditor could not confiscate the property of a planter but only that part of the harvest which remained after the planter had met the expenses of cultivation. After many complaints by merchant creditors, a royal order of April 12, 1852, determined that all new plantations would be subject to common law, and that after January 1, 1865, all plantations would be so subject.[8] The result, meanwhile, was interdependence, which would force the two interests to a common front on slave policy. Abolition would be considered a threat both to the increasing capital investment of the hacendados and to the collection of the merchant's loan.[9]

[6]Ramiro Guerra y Sánchez, *Azúcar y población en las Antillas*, pp. 78–80.
[7]Humboldt, *Island of Cuba*, p. 281.
[8]For more details, see Ely, *Cuando reinaba su majestad el azúcar*, pp. 320–341.
[9]Hubert S. Aimes, *A History of Slavery in Cuba, 1511 to 1868*, p. 91.

This pattern, however, would not be uniform throughout the island. The western end of Cuba (Provincia de Occidente) differed greatly from the eastern end (Provincia de Oriente). In the former, Havana was the radiating center of merchant capitalism and in this province the hacendados developed the larger and more-efficient sugar mills. The Oriente province would tend to fall behind due to outmoded methods; small planters there would struggle to keep abreast of the rising costs of sugar production, and dissatisfaction would grow among them. Thus began between the two classes of planters a gradual rift of interests, which would have important consequences in the future.

For the moment the deciding voice lay in Havana. Here would be found the Casino Español, social and directive center of the Spanish merchants, and here would meet the Junta de Hacendados, which spoke for Cuba's agricultural interests. This union of interests would have consequences fundamental to understanding Spanish slave policy.

Neither the captain general nor the government of Madrid could afford to ignore these interests, seated as they were in the major corporations of the island. Wealthy, they could afford to leave Havana to spend sojourns in Spain.[10] Ambitious, some were able to secure titles of nobility by money or other means. Needless to say, some representative figures of Cuba's "true interests" were always on hand in Madrid, ready to fight for the status quo to the exclusion of other interests. As opposed to the less articulate Creole masses, the slave interests spoke for the island, its loyalty, its patriotism, its fears, its political ideology, and its interests. Slavery would make possible the "Spanish party" that vaingloried in the titles "the Ever-Faithful Isle" and "unconditionally Spanish."

The price that Spain was expected to pay for such fervent loyalty was, of course, the unconditional protection of the vested interests, who would have extraordinary influence over colonial policy, partly because the confused political situation in Spain utterly debilitated metropolitan administrations in the face of their demands.

Some of the hacendados, it is true, were not properly of the Spanish

---

[10]Wealthy Cuban proprietors, like the British planters in Jamaica, were often absentee landlords, according to David Turnbull, *Travels in the West: Cuba, with Notices of Puerto Rico and the Slave Trade*, p. 47.

party, nor were they associated with the slave traders. They would have wanted to be of liberal spirit, for they were sympathetic with Bolivar's achievements and with the republican destiny of the Americas. Since they were nearly all criollos, born and bred on the island, they could not be "unconditionally Spanish." They would have demanded from Spain equal political rights with the *peninsulares*. But any question involving the civil liberties of the white man in Cuba led logically to the dangerous question of civil liberties and the possible rebellion of the black man. Political reforms, therefore, were to be suppressed as dangerous innovations, and the Creole planters for the most part would be forced to abide by their *mariage de convenance* with the arrogant peninsulars.

This would constitute the terrible dilemma of nineteenth-century Cuban liberalism. One might predicate political liberties for the whites, but where could the line be drawn? The Creoles, whether within the hacendado group or outside of it, hardly dared to be liberals, above all on the slave question, where one would be immediately branded a Negrophile, an Anglophile, or a demagogue threatening the peace and economy of the island. As Saco would write: to be called a Negrophile was worse than to be called a traitor.[11]

Another result of the increasing investment in the slave economy, and the fear that some firebrand might spread rebellious ideas among the increasing concentration of Negroes on the new model plantations was that slavery would become more institutionalized than formerly, more sharply defined socially, economically, and legally. The position of the slave, though perhaps more fortunate than that of his fellows in eighteenth-century Haiti or Jamaica, nevertheless tended to worsen in the measure that Cuba came to depend more on slave economy, the same process that one had seen earlier in Haiti.

According to the laws of *coartación*, a slave could buy his freedom on the installment plan, providing he made an initial payment of 25 to 50 pesos to his master. If he were valued at $600 he could then continue to pay off the balance in small payments, recovering a percentage of his freedom with each step. The master was obliged by law to accept these payments, and the slave could appeal to the magistrate

---

[11]In a letter to Domingo Delmonte, 1843, quoted by Fernando Ortiz in prologue of José Antonio Saco, *Contra la anexión*, I, xv.

if he were overvalued. Humboldt could say in 1825: "In no part of the world where slavery exists, is manumission so frequent as in the island of Cuba." Spanish legislation placed no obstacles in the way as English, French, and American legislation did.[12]

David Turnbull, who had served on the mixed court of Havana, claimed that the number of *coartados*, that is, slaves purchasing their freedom, was insignificant.[13] The fact was, however, that a large class of free blacks (controlled by vagrancy laws) existed in Cuba, as in Brazil. Humboldt said that "the position of the free Negro in Cuba is much better than it is elsewhere, even among those nations which have for ages flattered themselves as being most advanced in civilization."[14]

It is true that before the new prosperity an enlightened and humane slave code had been decreed by the Spanish monarch Carlos IV (May 31, 1789). This code was based largely on precedents extracted from the laws of the Indies and contained provisions which were humane in their religious and material concern for the slave. Masters were obliged to instruct their slaves in the Catholic religion, to compel them to hear mass, and to sustain the cost of a priest for the purpose. They were to feed and clothe the slave according to customary standards enforced by the syndic who served as protector of slaves. Masters who abused their slaves, punished them excessively, or failed to fulfill the requirements of the law were subject to fines, criminal prosecution (as if the injured slave were a free man), and the expropriation of the slave. The slave was then to be sold to another master, or on previous complaint to the syndic he was permitted to choose another master. Provision was also made for their diversions, and this included all Sundays and religious feasts. There were in all 270 working days a year.

On the other hand, all the requirements for enforced servitude were present in the code. Slaves were obliged to obey and respect their masters, and to discharge duties in accordance with their ability. Excepting those slaves older than sixty years or younger than seventeen, they could be obliged to work from dawn to sundown. The recalcitrant slave could be subjected to stocks and irons and the whip

---

[12] Humboldt, *Island of Cuba*, p. 212. The privilege extended to the slave of purchasing his liberty was first decreed in 1708. Rafael María de Labra, *América y la constitución de 1812*, p. 125.

[13] Turnbull, *Travels in the West*, p. 148.

[14] Humboldt, *Island of Cuba*, p. 213.

(not more than 25 lashes). In times of harvest the slaves could be obliged to work longer.[15]

But to what extent these provisions were enforced is the question. There exists the often-cited old Spanish saying to characterize the colonial's indifference to metropolitan laws: *se obedecen pero no se cumplen* (the laws are obeyed but not fulfilled). Arango, for one, reported that the humanitarian provisions of the slave code were not enforced, especially in the rural areas.[16]

Turnbull, although speaking from an abolitionist criterion (1840), claimed that Cuban slavery was deceptively cruel, that domestic slaves were treated well and this is what the visitor saw in Havana, but that field hands left to the mercies of mayordomos were wretchedly treated, which he could affirm "as a result of personal inquiry and minute observation."[17]

Although the phenomenal prosperity of Cuba was not evenly distributed, or consistent, the increasing demand for slave labor was almost uniformly great. The demand was not merely for field hands, *los nuevos ricos* demanded domestic servants in greater numbers. Unlike Puerto Rico, where the mixture of races blurred caste lines and where slavery was far less profitable, Cuba's flourishing slave economy was accompanied by a growing fear of slave rebellions and caste distinctions. As we shall see, the slave code of 1842 would be more strict than that of 1789.[18]

During this period the Cuban slave trade thrived in the face of British abolition efforts, for much the same reasons as in Brazil. "The Treaty of 1817 was always a dead letter," according to the Cuban historian Ramiro Guerra. During the period 1821-1831 an estimated three hundred slave expeditions landed 60,000 slaves in Cuba. Mahy, Kindelán, and Vives, captains general during this period, were said to

[15]*Ibid.*, pp. 53-56. Or José María Zamora y Coronado (ed.), *Biblioteca de legislación ultramarina*, III, 130-135.

[16]"Informe sobre los negros fugitivos" (1796), in Francisco Arango y Parreño, *Obras de Don Francisco de Arango y Parreño*, Vol. I.

[17]"As I frequently had been told that the slave owners of Havana were the most indulgent in the world, I was not a little surprised to find, as the result of personal inquiry and minute observation, that in this last particular I had been most miserably deceived . . . in no quarter, unless perhaps the Brazils [where Turnbull had not been] . . . is the state of slavery so desperately wretched." Turnbull, *Travels in the West*, p. 47.

[18]Both codes are found in José Ferrer de Couto, *Los negros en sus diversos estados y condiciones; tales como son, como se supone que son y como deben ser.*

have given unlimited tolerance to the trade.[19] Pezuela claimed that English ships captured scarcely 4 per cent of these expeditions.[20]

Documents presented to the Engish Parliament give a comparative view of the number of slaves imported during the years 1788–1830:[21]

Year	Spanish Colonies (Mainly Cuba)	Portuguese Colonies (Mainly Brazil)	Other Countries
1788–1798	25,000	18,000	44,000
1798–1805	15,000	20,000	38,000
1805–1810	15,000	25,000	33,000
1810–1815	30,000	30,000	20,000
1815–1817	32,000	31,000	17,000
1817–1819	34,000	34,000	12,000
1819–1825	39,000	37,000	1,000
1825–1830	40,000	50,000	4,000

After 1830 British cruisers made greater exertions; yet it is estimated that some 200,000 more slaves entered Cuba illicitly between the years 1830 and 1850, an average of 10,000 per annum.

As suggested previously, it was one thing to sign agreements promising the abolition of the slave trade, but another to enforce them. The government of Fernando VII had been too impotent, too penniless, and too harassed by political instability to provide for adequate enforcement of treaty obligations. But something of calculation was in Spanish ineptitude.

Cuba, it was often said, had replaced Mexico, with her gold and silver pieces, as the pearl in the Spanish diadem. A decadent Spanish government, already in debt to Britain, hungered for tax revenues.[22]

---

[19]Ramiro Guerra y Sánchez, "Ilustración" in *Historia de la nación Cubana*, Ramiro Guerra y Sánchez et al. (eds.), III, 80.

[20]Jacobo de la Pezuela y Lobo, *Diccionario geográfico, estadístico, histórico de la isla de Cuba*, II, 285–287.

[21]Francisco de Armas y Céspedes, *De la esclavitud en Cuba*, pp. 120–122.

[22]The Creole planter Cristóbal Madan listed the following taxes as imposed by the oppressive Spanish regime: duties on sugar exports and imported consumer items, taxes on property and business transactions, ecclesiastical contributions, and miscellaneous. Madan estimated that a plantation of three hundred slaves producing four thousand boxes of sugar annually would pay twelve thousand pesos in taxes per annum, a sum which would represent 23 per cent of total expenses (*Llamamiento de la isla de Cuba a la nación española*, cited by Ely, *Cuando reinaba su majestad el azúcar*, pp. 449–450).

"The result of all this," said John Glanville Taylor, "is, first, certainly an im-

Why kill the only hen that laid a golden egg? In Cuba, government complicity in the slave trade was common knowledge. Governors filled their pockets and counseled Madrid that slavery must be protected if Cuba was to remain dependent on Spain. The testimony of Domingo Delmonte, Cuban liberal, to Robert Madden, judge of the mixed court of Havana, characterized this policy:[23]

> Did the government have enough power to suppress the traffic?
> More than enough.
> Did the government want to suppress it?
> No.
> Did the Captain-General have instructions from his government to suppress it?
> Yes, *public ones*, when the Madrid cabinet was instigated by that of London.

As Valiente put it, the Spanish government pretended to give satisfaction to British demands by issuing orders to the insular authorities urging them to enforce the laws against the traffic, "... but, in reality, all these excitations had as their unique objective the safeguarding of an appearance of legality."[24] The Spanish king could sign an abolition treaty, but that act did not make it a national decision, for, as we have seen, even the king and his ministers resisted the act. Spain lacked abolitionist sentiment, as previously said, and the problem was to create one. As Saco had observed, it was possible for Britain to enforce laws against the slave trade because there was a press and a public opinion in England (and we might add a navy), as well as a parliament and a government that had been occupied with the problem for twenty years.[25]

In the meantime, with the arrival of General Miguel Tacón on the island in 1834 the policy of toleration toward the criollos exercised by his predecessors, Vives and Ricafort, came to an abrupt end. The new policy assumed that the Creole interests were fundamentally opposed to the interests of the metropolis. The Creole agricultural interests

---

mense revenue to Spain, but secondly, a system of smuggling elsewhere unknown." *The United States and Cuba: Eight Years of Change and Travel*, p. 303.

[23]"Interrogatorio de Mr. R. R. Madden, Absuelto, el 17 de septiembre de 1829," por Domingo Delmonte. In Saco, *La historia de la esclavitud de la raza africana en el Nuevo Mundo y en especial en los países Américo-Hispanos*, IV, 330–340.

[24]Porfirio Valiente, *Réformes dan les isles de Cuba et Porto-Rico*, p. 8.

[25]Saco, *Historia de la esclavitud de la raza africana*, III, 136.

wanted, as exemplified by Arango, a policy of free trade which would favor agricultural exportation and lower the prices of imports. They had obtained a number of concessions, especially toward a freer trade with Spain, but they were not satisfied because now the bulk of the Cuban trade lay not with Spain but with the United States and to a lesser degree with Britain. Since 1790 the center of commercial gravity had been shifting toward the United States. By 1833 the bulk of the export trade and an increasing percentage of the import trade, namely flour, was with the United States.[26]

The peninsulars, representing commerce and bureaucracy, wanted protective tariffs and monopolies against foreign economic powers. The metropolis, unable to supply Cuba's wants and needing tariff revenues, could not but sustain the claims of Spanish merchants and bureaucrats.

Spain had other reasons for favoring the peninsulars as against the Creoles. The Creoles, influenced by the ideology of the revolutionary period, naturally envisioned the possibilities of eventual autonomy or independence, and closely linked to this vision was the rapid development of a cultural milieu distinctly Cuban. The phenomenal economic development of the island in the first decades of the nineteenth century also developed Creole cultural and educational facilities. The previously mentioned economic societies and corporations, the presence of foreign merchants and investors, the University of Havana where Varela taught—products of the reform spirit of the late eighteenth and early nineteenth century—were focal points for the diffusion of all kinds of knowledge, including political economy, philosophy, and chemistry. Since these organizations were largely dominated by the Creoles—almost all the agricultural interests were of the Creole class with, so to speak, roots in the soil of Cuba—they became the schools of a nascent nationalism. The young outstanding liberals of this period—Saco, Delmonte, Luz Caballero, Escobedo, and others—were products of this new enlightenment.[27]

The peninsulars, however, were not disposed to admit the educated Creole on equal political terms and this widened the caste differences between them. Tacón, suspicious of the Creoles and fearing their progress, chose the Spanish side of the argument, and surround-

[26]*Historia de la nación Cubana*, Guerra (ed.), III, 230–231.
[27]The division between peninsulares and criollos and the inter-relation of cultural, racial, social, and political factors is explained by Ramiro Guerra y Sánchez, *Manual de la historia de Cuba (económica, social y política)*, pp. 296–324.

ed himself with "patriotic" counselors only. The Creole voice, such as Arango's, that hitherto had played so important a part in Spain's colonial policy in Cuba, was now to suffer diminishing influence.

Yet another point of friction was growing between the peninsulares and the Creoles. Among the young liberal generation, which owed so much to Varela, was a growing realization that the slave trade served only as a Spanish tool for holding the Creoles in a form of political and economic servitude. The young Creoles began to blame Spanish merchants and officials, in connivance with slave traders, for selling Cuba's birthright and compromising her future. But it was as yet a Creole birthright and a Creole future, with little place for the Negro.[28] For, although the liberals might be willing to close the traffic, they were not ready to abolish the existing institutions of slavery in Cuba.

The most significant facet of this division between the peninsulars and the Creoles, and the siding of the government with the former, was that reformism became almost exclusively associated with discontented Creoles. Since the patriotism of the Creoles was now highly suspect it meant that all reform suggestions were unpatriotic or tainted with treason and disaffection. On the other hand, the Spanish party conveniently confounded their patriotism with resistance to British abolitionist pressure and political reforms.

The few Creoles, such as Saco, Varela, Delmonte, or Arango (in his last years an abolitionist), who might have been capable of cultivating an abolitionist sentiment were ignored, silenced, or exiled. Arango's *comunicaciones* to the government from 1828 to 1832 urging the extinction of the slave traffic and better treatment for slaves as one solution to the labor problem, were filed away and never known outside official circles.[29]

Saco's article, "Análisis de una obra sobre Brasil," which appeared

[28] As Cepero has said, the Cuban hacendados never included the colored race in their political projects, even though some of the ideologists of this class foresaw in the future the emancipation of the slaves and the problem of a free colored class. Raúl Cepero Bonilla, *Azúcar y abolición: Apuntes para una historia crítica de abolicionismo*, pp. 9–10.

[29] "Informes de Don Francisco de Arango y Parreño a Su Majestad el Rey sobre la condición de los esclavos en la Isla de Cuba y la urgente necesidad de la supresión de la trata, 1828 y 1832," cited by Saco, *Historia de la esclavitud de la raza africana*, III, 150.

Also, "Representación al Rey sobre la extinción del tráfico de negros y medios de mejorar la suerte de los esclavos coloniales" (La Habana, 28 de mayo de 1832), Arango, *Obras*, II, 529–536.

in the *Revista Bimestre Cubana,* aroused a great discussion on the slave-trade problem. It was characteristic of the sophisticated Saco that he did not treat the problem from the humanitarian point of view "because this is not respected when interests speak," but suggested the political and international dangers to Cuba of protecting the slave trade, and the advantages to be derived from increasing the white population through immigration.[30]

Saco was speaking for emergent Cuban nationalism when he said that the problems of vagrancy, political ineptitude, and low cultural level that had plunged Haiti and Santo Domingo into a miserable national existence must not cloud Cuba's future.[31] Saco was the first to discuss the problem publicly. The shrill cry of the slavists caused an even wider circulation of Saco's pamphlet, and revealed that there was in Havana a feeling larger than expected, although timid, against the continuation of the slave trade. The most enlightened element of the island, those who could see beyond the narrow confines of the present, and the Creole youths, who had their eyes fixed on the national future of the island," sincerely applauded the enlightened thought" of Saco.[32]

The pamphlet was condemned by the Cuban government, and shortly afterward Saco was expelled from the island of Tacón (July 17, 1834), who wanted to crush incipient Creole liberalism among the young of Havana.[33]

From Tacón onward until the 1860's the captains general with few exceptions sided with the Spanish party against the Creoles, whose most humble reform suggestions would be interpreted as the entering wedge to independence. Reform sentiment, political and abolitionist, was now to be ruthlessly extirpated. Tacón is symbolic of the best and the worst of the military despotism to which Cuba was subjected. He

---

[30] Among other things, Saco commented upon slavery in Brazil, the clandestine slave traffic in Cuba, with statistical proofs, and the inconvenience for the Cuban society of the continuance of the trade. "Análisis de una obra sobre Brasil entitulada: Notices of Brazil in 1828 and 1829, by Reverend R. Walsh, author of a journey from Constantinople, etc.," *Revista Bimestre Cubana,* Año II (June, 1832). Given fully in Saco, *Colección de papeles científicos, históricos, políticos y de otros ramos sobre la isla de Cuba,* II, 28–84.

[31] Saco's interesting article on vagrancy, "Memoria sobre la vagrancia en la Isla de Cuba," 1831, may also be found in *Colección de papeles,* Vol. I.

[32] J. S. Jorrin, *Biografías de Cubanos distinguidos: José A. Saco.* Cited by Fernando Ortiz in prologue of Saco's *Contra la anexión,* I, xliv.

[33] Guerra, *Manual de la historia,* p. 319.

was the first to exploit fully the omnipotent powers conceded in 1825.[34] The emergency of that year passed, but the island was still surrounded by republican enemies, and in 1833 the British raised a new threat by abolishing slavery in Jamaica. Not only this but the British anchored the *Romney* in full view of Havana harbor and collected whatever emancipados they could. Spain, torn by internal dissention, was too weak to protest effectively this act, ". . . offensive to Spanish honor and a dangerous stimulus to Cuban slaves." But at least Tacón was fully armed to deal with any seditious attempts to penetrate the island.[35]

As far as his administration was concerned, Tacón, like all efficient despots, was preoccupied with two things: public order and public works. These were the only criteria of a good colonial administration, and in this regard Tacón's administration was beneficial.[36] But so far as the slave trade was concerned, Tacón, who had once fought in vain against the independence movements in South America, did nothing to hinder a business which enriched the colonial officials of Cuba, advanced the agricultural interests of the island, and, more important, contributed to holding Cuba dependent on the metropolis. Some Cubans maintained that Tacón was personally honest and gained nothing from the slave trade. Others accused him of profiteering. It was a public and notorious fact, said Domingo Delmonte, that Tacón took his half ounce of gold for every slave landed on the island illicitly, and in 1835 alone there were an estimated 19,000 of these.[37]

British commissioners in Cuba stated that "never since the establishment of the Mixed Commission has the slave trade of Havana reached such a disgraceful pitch." In 1834 a reported sixty-two ships left Cuba for African shores, thirty-three landed their cargoes safely, only twelve had been captured. In 1835 at least eighty ships sailed for Africa, ". . . the greatest number yet known . . . Tacón builds public

---

[34]Along with unlimited powers there was at the disposal of the captain general a military commission with authority to judge all political offenses that ordinarily belonged to the civil tribunals. Guerra, "Ilustración" in *Historia de la nación Cubana*, III, 67.

[35]Jacobo de la Pezuela y Lobo, *Ensayo histórico de la isla de Cuba*, p. 606.

[36]See Callahan, *Cuba and International Relations*, p. 172, or Turnbull, *Travels in the West*, p. 57.

[37]Domingo Delmonte, "La Isla de Cuba tal cual está" (1836). Found in Saco, *Historia de la esclavitud de la raza africana*, IV, 269–297. Delmonte, along with Saco, was one of the Creole reform leaders of the 1830's. He favored the closing of the slave trade for the same cultural and national reasons.

works with the payoffs ... giving a legal aspect to the commerce." The commissioners explained that the recent abolition in Jamaica, and the consequent fear that the traffic would soon end, "is without doubt one of the principal causes of the increase."[38] Also, one should note that another cause was the Asiatic cholera that swept through the Western World in 1833–1834, and took some thirty thousand lives in Cuba, many of them slaves.[39]

As to the emancipados, Vives had given them as "apprentices" to poor widows, underpaid officers, government employees, and other "deserving people," but Tacón began to charge a fee for "speculative reasons," such money being applied to public works and the celebrated Teatro Tacón, "which alone would have sufficed to perpetuate his name."[40] Understandably, English officials and abolitionists charged that under Tacón the condition of the emancipados worsened.[41]

In England at this time the crusade to abolish the slave trade and protect the emancipados found a mighty champion in the person of John Henry Temple, the third Viscount Palmerston, who became foreign secretary in 1830. For the next thirty years Palmerston's personality was destined to dominate British foreign policy. But, for the moment, Palmerston addressed himself to the fact that slavers were evading British searchships—practically the only ones that prosecuted the trade—by sailing under nontreaty flags. This was the more intolerable after Britain abolished slavery in the British West Indies, for now British planters demanded abolition everywhere.

As already indicated, Britain commanded a new series of treaties designed to snatch every protective flag from the slavers, or, in Palmerston's words, to enlist in a league against the slave trade every state in Christendom which has a flag that sails on the ocean.[42] British abolition policy wanted two things of Spain: a greater measure of authority to search suspected ships, and a law from the Spanish

[38]British Commissioners (W. S. Macleay and E W. H. Schenley) to Viscount Palmerston, The Havana, January 1, 1836. *BFSP* (1835–1836), XXIV, 80–83.

[39]José García de Arboleya, *Manual de la isla de Cuba: Compendio de su historia, geografía, estadística y administración*, p. 52.

[40]Pezuela, *Ensayo histórico*, p. 604.

[41]Emancipados were also treated contemptuously by other slaves, who called them "English slaves." Turnbull, *Travels in the West*, p. 162.

[42]James F. King, "The Latin-American Republics and the Suppression of the Slave Trade," *HAHR*, XXIV, No. 3 (August, 1944), 387.

A United Front in Cuba, 1825–1840

Cortes putting teeth into the treaty of 1817.

The new government of Spain was admittedly more liberal and receptive to British demands, especially since British diplomatic power had assured the victory of Isabel II in the dispute then raging over the succession to the Spanish throne. The result was the treaty of June 20, 1835, ratified on August 24, 1835,[43] which again declared (Articles 1 and 2) the Spanish slave traffic abolished in all parts of the world, and promised that as soon as the treaty was ratified Spain would adopt within two months the most efficacious measures against participation of her subjects in the slave trade. Article Three again threatened severe punishment for shipowners, captains and crew members involved.

Articles Four and Five established the mutual right of search by warships especially authorized for the purpose, but only upon just suspicions could a ship be subjected to registration and examination. Article Six provided for indemnization for losses incurred by respective subjects due to arbitrary detention.

Articles Seven and Eight reconfirmed the powers and organization of the mixed commissions established by the treaty of 1817. Article Nine provided for satisfaction in case any official deviated from treaty instructions.

Articles Ten, Eleven, and Twelve declared that a ship could be seized as a fair prize (*buena presa*) if any of the paraphernalia used in the slave trade were found aboard, for example, rice, cornmeal, kitchen utensils, or water barrels in quantities more than necessary for the needs of the crew, or if hatchway and deck structures were suspiciously arranged.

The final articles provided for the disposition of prizes and cargoes, and for instructions to naval commanders of both nations.[44] Again, as in the earlier treaty, Negroes found on board were to belong to the government making the capture, and to be immediately set at liberty. Information as to their condition was to be furnished from time to time.

[43]Pezuela, *Diccionario*, II, 294.
[44]*Ibid*. Or Zamora (ed.), *Biblioteca de legislación ultramarina*, III, 115–118. In the "Regulations of the Mixed Tribunals" that accompanied this treaty, the much disputed Article Seven of the treaty of 1817 was altered. Now bozales were no longer put ashore on the territory where the nearest mixed tribunal was established—which so alarmed Cuba—but instead were to belong to the cruiser that made the capture, and treated according to established regulations.

The new treaty was hardly a major advance over that of 1817. True, the right to search suspected ships and to detain them on prima facie evidence was a promising innovation; formerly, suspected ships could be detained only if slaves were found aboard. Yet, as Turnbull pointed out, ship carpenters could make and dispose of prima facie evidence such as water barrels and deck arrangements with relative ease.[45]

More significant than the treaty of 1835 was the fact that after this date British cruisers began to concentrate less on Cuban waters and more on African waters at notorious points of embarkation. It was too easy to land slaves on the unguarded coasts of the great Antille. The Spanish colonial authorities were still unwilling, either for reasons of impotency or complicity, to sharpen their vigilance, and once slaves were disembarked there was no legal way to pursue the matter further. The Spanish government consistently refused to alarm proprietors by enforcing a system of search. As a result of the British decision to concentrate on darkest Africa, fewer slave vessels were captured on the coast of Cuba after 1835. The mixed commission in Havana handled few cases thereafter.[46]

The treaty of 1835 changed the character of the slave trade without essentially reducing it. Ships were no longer openly fitted out in Cuban ports. The arrival and departure of such ships no longer appeared in the papers, nor did the names of slave captains appear in the registers of the slave exchange in Havana.[47] At first Havana insurance offices refused to insure ships bound for African coasts, for ships could now be detained on prima facie evidence. All this forced new tactics. The slavers changed from the Spanish to the Portuguese and American flags. In 1835 seventy-eight out of eighty slave ships sailed under the Spanish flag, but in 1838, forty-four out of fifty ships carried the Portuguese flag. American-built ships became more frequent—in 1837 there were eleven, in 1838 nineteen. Since the British could not search American ships the American flag was used in African waters,

[45]Turnbull, *Travels in the West*, pp. 383–384.
[46]Two slavers were condemned in 1836, one in 1848, and one in 1870. (Aimes, *History of Slavery*, p. 132). The fact that fewer ships henceforth fell into the hands of the cruisers did not mean, however, that the source of emancipados had ceased. Some slaves were confiscated upon landing, and these were added to the emancipado class.
[47]From *BFSP*, Vols. XXX and XXV, given by Aimes, *History of Slavery*, p. 128.

A United Front in Cuba, 1825–1840

and since the Americans could not search Portuguese ships the Portuguese flag was useful in American waters.[48] Apparently slavers were little concerned about Spanish waters, since the Spanish navy made no captures, except the *María de la Gloria* in 1824.[49]

The United States consul at Havana, Nicholas P. Trist, was accused by the British of complicity in the Spanish slave trade because he authenticated registration papers of American ships secretly sold to Spanish slave interests and cleared the ships for slave voyages under the American flag.[50] British cruisers, in spite of protests, seized some of these "American ships." Such incidents would eventually lead to the agreement of 1842, whereby the American government agreed to station a force of eighty-eight guns on the African coast—little more than a token force—in order to search ships flying the American flag.

According to Aimes, it was not difficult to mix the slave trade with the great volume of legitimate traffic. An American vessel arriving in Havana with legal cargo of codfish, staves, or salt was then actually or nominally transferred to the slavers with the proper papers. She would then sail for Africa, picking up the proper equipment in some small isle like the Danish St. Thomas, and protecting herself by the proper set of flags.[51]

The British at first hoped that Spain would at once give force to the agreement of 1835, an expectation really without precedent. The British were doomed to disappointment even though the Progressive Party in Spain would make a further declaration against slavery. During the first year of Isabel's reign the Progressives had considerable influence at the Court. Reflecting this new spirit, the royal decree of March 29, 1836, abolished whatever remained of slavery on the Spanish Peninsula.[52] Some of the Progressives wanted the matter to be voted by the Cortes of the nation. To this end, they prepared a formal project of abolition presented to that assembly on March 5, 1837. But

---

[48] Aimes, *History of Slavery*, p. 130. Turnbull, *Travels in the West*, pp. 158–159, 350–384.

[49] Aimes, *History of Slavery*, p. 131.

[50] For more details, see Warren S. Howard, *American Slavers and the Federal Law, 1837–1862*, especially Chap. 2, "Pirates and the Government."

[51] *Ibid.*, p. 129.

[52] Antonio Domínguez Ortiz in his exploratory study agrees with Saco that slavery had gradually disappeared in Spain before the nineteenth century, "La

the project was never discussed, even though it referred only to the Peninsula and not to the colonies, because many feared that such a discussion would serve to alarm the proprietors of Cuba and Puerto Rico, who had already protested against the project. Even liberal sentiment in Spain could defend the economic benefits of the slave trade.[53] As to the meaning of the decree abolishing whatever remained of slavery in Spain, it was an empty gesture, having no bearing on blockading the slave traffic in Cuba.

Even more unfortunate for abolitionist hopes, the latest treaty coincided with the first Carlist War, 1833–1844. It was the old story of one unfortunate situation after another disrupting the good intentions of transient ministries. It is true that the royal order of November 2, 1838, advised the colonial authorities to pursue slave-trade infractions with a strong and zealous hand, ". . . subjecting perpetrators to competent tribunals and exemplary punishment."[54] But José Antonio Saco has well qualified such orders as "more formula than conviction."[55] Nor, apparently, could the papal bull of Gregory XVI (December 3, 1839) published in the *Gaceta de Madrid*, January 1, 1840, condemning the slave traffic have any appreciable effect.[56]

Furthermore, the exclusion of Cuba and Puerto Rico from the liberal Cortes of 1834–1837 and the adoption of an article in the constitution declaring that the colonies would be ruled henceforth by "special laws," had a further deleterious effect in that it served to justify this iron-handed rule of the military government in the Antilles and to exclude Creole liberal and abolitionist sentiment from the Cortes.

The great liberal of 1810–1812, Agustín Argüelles, masterminded the exclusion of the Antilles from the Cortes of 1836–1837 on the reactionary grounds that the admission of American deputies in 1810 and 1822 had led to the loss of the greater part of Spanish America. Naturally, denying the oppressed Creoles of Cuba a voice in the Cortes

---

esclavitud en Castilla durante la edad moderna," *Estudios de Historia Social de España*, II, 370–428.

[53]No less a person that Canga Argüelles, an outstanding Spanish liberal, expressed this view in his *Diccionario de Hacienda*, Vol. II, cited by Saco, *Historia de la esclavitud de la raza africana*, III, 156.

[54]Real Orden del 2 de Noviembre de 1838. Zamora (ed.), *Biblioteca de legislación ultramarina*, III, 127–128.

[55]Saco, *Historia de la esclavitud de la raza africana*, III, 149.

[56]*Ibid.*, III, 65.

intensified their bitter feelings. Saco, who had been among those liberal deputies elected to represent Cuba in Madrid, in spite of Tacón, suffered the humiliation of being denied admission to the Cortes. The frustrated Saco thereupon led his fellow delegates in the preparation of a famous protest: *Protesta de los diputados electos por la Isla de Cuba a las Cortes generales de la nación.*[57] At the same time, Saco published a powerful essay "Parallel between the Island of Cuba and Some English Colonies" in which he compared the administration of Cuba so unfavorably with that of Canada, and pulverized the legend abroad in Spain, and propagated by the Spanish party, that Cuba was the most happily governed of colonies.[58] The Creoles of the island were greatly influenced by the pen of Saco, who was now their acknowledged spiritual leader in exile. Many of them chose to read this as an argument in favor of annexation to the British system, or the American one. Since the Creoles felt that they were not strong enough to achieve and maintain the independence of the island, this thought of annexation began to gain ground rapidly, especially since their exclusion from the Cortes dashed reform hopes, and because, "They have no national privilege except that of undergoing taxation."[59]

There was no doubt that the existence of slavery in the Antilles contributed to "justify" the exclusion. Since Cuba was surrounded by "special circumstances," namely slavery, she must be ruled by "special laws," which, in effect, turned out to be the law of 1825, conceding unlimited emergency powers to the governor. The powers could be conveniently used to expell all abolitionist agents, Creole or foreign.[60]

Rumors were rife in the period 1836–1839 that the disaffected

---

[57]Published in Madrid, February 21, 1837, signed by Saco, Francisco de Armas, and Juan Montalvo. Given by Valiente, *Reformes dan les isles*, or in *Información: Reformas de Cuba y Puerto Rico*, Vol. I.

[58]José Antonio Saco, "Paralelo entre la Isla de Cuba y algunas colonias inglesas," in Saco, *Colección de paples*, Vol. III.

[59]Anthony Trollope, *The West Indies and the Spanish Main*, p. 188.

[60]Spanish officials complained to the American government of British abolitionist societies planting secret agents in Cuba. The Count de Ofalia, minister of foreign affairs, of Spain, to John H. Eaton, United States minister to Spain, February 22, 1838. William R. Manning (ed.), *Diplomatic Correspondence of the United States: Inter-American Affairs 1831–1860*, XI, 307–309. When the Count noted that the Laws of the Indies gave the most adequate protection to the slaves, Eaton responded by saying that the United States also had no need for British abolitionist activities since slaves were well taken care of, the proof being the fact that

Creoles were plotting an independence movement. But apparently this did not worry the Spanish government. The Spanish minister, Calatrava, was reported as saying in 1837 that the existence of slavery in Cuba was worth an army of 100,000 men for maintaining Cuban loyalty to Spain.[61]

In this same year of 1837 Saco again protested against the undiminished current of the slave traffic.[62] He debated the question of whether abolition of the traffic would ruin or endanger the agriculture of the island. He addressed the question directly to the Creole proprietors, and began by examining the three most common arguments employed by them to justify the slave trade: first, that only African slaves could withstand the hard labor on sugar plantations; second, that only Africans could resist tropical climes and infirmities; third, that free labor was too expensive in Cuba. Saco answered each of these arguments in turn, giving appropriate examples. Whites could, and had in some instances, become accustomed to the hard work in question; whites born on the island could and did withstand the heat and diseases of tropical lands; white labor could and did prove less expensive when compared with the cost, mortality, and maintenance of slave labor. After all, was not the slave trade doomed to disappear before the demands of universal opinion? The proprietors should awaken to that fact, and make the necessary adjustments now and with foresight.[63]

But Saco's labor went for naught. The pamphlet aroused little positive response among the proprietors and since there was no way for Cuban reformers to bring the matter to the Spanish Cortes, the reformer's disillusionment was complete. He could see no immediate change in the spirit of the monarchy under Isabel II. Spain was too preoccupied with the Carlist War at this time to think about colonial policy or about the special laws promised to Cuba and Puerto Rico.

---

they multiply as rapidly as the whites (Eaton to the Count of Ofalia, March 10, 1838, *ibid.*, XI, 310–313).

[61]Callahan, *Cuba and International Relations*, p. 173. Turnbull, *Travels in the West*, p. 171.

[62]According to Aimes, the number of Africans imported in 1835, the year of the new treaty revision, was 9,500. This number rose to 12,240 in 1837, *History of Slavery*, Appendix II, "Slaves Imported into Cuba."

[63]José Antonio Saco, "La primera pregunta: ¿La abolición del comercio de esclavos africanos arruinará o atrasará la agricultura cubana?" (1837), *Colección.* Vol. III.

Saco could not return to Cuba, nor would he remain in Spain, not only because of the hostility of both governments but also because of his determination to protest by his lonely exile the injustice of Cuban exclusion from the Cortes and the continuance of the slave trade. He decided that perhaps his exile might be permanent,[64] and at the end of the year 1837 he took up residence in Italy and then France, where he remained for many years. For the moment he abandoned all polemical activities, while he began work on his monumental history of slavery.

Cuba prospered under Tacón. The first railroad in Latin America was built in Cuba in 1837 by an American engineer with English capital. Law and order reigned; Creole political agitation was silenced. Abolitionism and republicanism were no longer feared by the slave interests. Spain apparently had an iron grip on the Ever Faithful Isle. At this point the abolition cause seemed quite dead.

The British, despairing of the treaty of 1835, no longer delivered emancipados captured in Cuban waters to Havana authorities of the mixed court, since in Cuba "they are treated little better than slaves." Beginning in 1836 emancipados were transferred to British colonies because, to cite Palmerston's words, "their removal to any British colony would certainly be an act of benevolence." Also, the emancipados, like East Indian laborers and Chinese coolies, were to compensate British planters for the abolition of slavery in 1833 by satisfying their demands for cheap "free labor" in Jamaica and British Honduras, where emancipados were requested on a sixteen-year contract.[65] One wonders how free or benevolent this new arrangement was?

[64]Letter of José de la Luz Caballero. Cited by Fernando Ortiz, Prologue of Saco's *Contra la anexión*, I, lxx.
[65]Circular to the Governors of the British West Indies Colonies. Viscount Palmerston, Downing Street, January 1836. *BFSP* (1835–1836), XXIV, 79.

5. Britain Grows More Aggressive 1840-1848

> Her majesty's functionaries here continue to suffer the indignity of having their communications returned with a denial of their rights of interference. The treaties were violated under our very eyes . . .
>
> Crawford, consul general in Cuba[1]

We have seen that the treaty of 1835 was for various reasons a failure, nor did the fact that Britain had recently abolished slavery in the British West Indies have any appreciable effect on the Cuban slave trade, except to stimulate it. A British naval commander stated that slave ships were still fitting out in Spanish ports and landing cargoes in Cuba, assisted by government officials, who received the accustomed payoff.[2] In view of these facts, and following the advice of the English consul in Cuba, David Turnbull, the British gov-

[1] Consul General James F. Crawford to Lord Aberdeen, February 20, 1845, *Slade Trade* No. 4, A.H.N. Estado, Leg. 8040, L. 9, N. 3.

[2] According to Commander Tucker, the Spanish governor received $16.00 for each slave landed, the commander of the Spanish naval force $4.00, the collector of customs $7.00, and lesser officials lesser amounts. Since slaves were bought cheap in Africa and sold for over $300 apiece in Cuba, the slave trader could afford the payoffs. Commander Tucker to Mr. More O'Ferrall, H.M.S. "Wolverine," at Sea, September 29, 1840. (*Correspondence with Spain, Portugal, Brazil, the Netherlands, Sweden, and the Argentine Confederation Relative to the Slave Trade, from January 1 to December 31, 1841*, Class B, p. 90.)

Governor Valdés, reputed to be personally honest, vigorously denied the charges of connivance and payoffs, asking where is the proof? Are Spanish ships the only ones? "No, the greatest part are foreign and sail under foreign flags" (Captain General Gerónimo Valdés to M. González, Havana, May 31, 1841. *Ibid.*, pp. 149–150).

ernment decided to press a radical measure. Accordingly, at the end of 1840 Britain proposed that Spain formally agree to a new treaty that would amplify the faculties of the mixed commission so that a census of all slaves illegally introduced since 1820 could be determined. Suspected slaveowners would be called before the tribunal and examined under oath, and if slaves of "trans-atlantic origin" were found in their possession they would be immediately placed at liberty by order of the commission. If after three callings, the suspected slaveowner did not appear, the commission would proceed to declare the slaves free.[3]

The British proposal could not have been more offensive to Spanish dignity, for in effect it would have authorized the intervention of British officials in the administration of slave-trade agreements. The Spanish Council of State rejected the suggestion absolutely, declaring that its acceptance would signify "the renunciation of authority by the government of a nation free and independent and a public confession of its impotence." The Council in justifying its rejection did not hesitate to lay hands on thread-worn arguments. Had not the incapacity of the white man to work in the tropics caused all the colonizing nations to import slaves, but with the difference that the "situation of slaves in Spanish colonies had always been better than in other colonies?" The Council then falsely asserted, as will be seen, that the increase of slaves in Cuba was derived not from the African trade but from the marriage and raising of slaves "as in the United States." Furthermore, the Council contended that if the Negroes in question were liberated and abandoned to themselves, ignorance and laziness would result as in Santo Domingo and Jamaica, and this "would ruin the production of sugar." Finally, the British were reminded that slavery existed in the United States and yet England did not attempt a similar action there. "We view with sadness," concluded the Council, "such a suggestion from our old ally and friend."[4]

In any case, the Council knew that even if such a proposal was accepted it could not be enforced, for it was virtually a project to abolish slavery, since most slaves had been illegally imported after 1820. According to the captain general, Gerónimo Valdés, all the slaveowners, illustrious men, and corporations consulted were unani-

---

[3]Resumen de la comunicación del Ministro de Inglaterra, Madrid, 27 de diciembre de 1840, A.H.N. Estado, Leg. 8040, L. 70.
[4]Ibid.

mously opposed. Furthermore, they demanded the recall of Turnbull, the zealous abolitionist consul who had proposed the idea.[5]

The corporations referred to—La Junta de Fomento, La Real Sociedad Patriotica, El Consulado Real, El Ayuntamiento de la Habana, El Tribunal de Comercio de la Habana—and various officials presented a core of common arguments. In essence, they alleged that they all wanted the cessation of the slave trade because it was a source of continual embarrassment and threat to the security of the island; in the words of the Consulado Real, prohibition of the traffic was necessary "not only because the national dignity compromised by a treaty requires it, but because it is the means for reducing our enemies."[6] More to the point, the corporations argued that no law could be justly made retroactive to liberate slaves purchased in good faith by the proprietors; the result would be black vagrancy, economic ruin, and the loss to Spain of millions of revenue from the Pearl of the Antilles.

The Ayuntamiento of Havana threatened that if Spain signed a convention with Britain giving the latter power to establish a tribunal in Cuba with authority to decide the status of illegally imported slaves, then rebellion would be likely and the island would be irretrievably lost to the mother country.[7]

Among other slave arguments advanced at this time were those that enlarged upon the ideas of Saco. Bernardo María Navarro expressed the patriotism of the "enlightened Creole" when he assured Madrid that the mass of Cubans wanted the closing of the slave trade, that Spain should adopt the means to close it, but that the new treaty, if applied, would threaten the future of a white Cuba. It is a delirium to believe, said Navarro, that free Negroes would continue working for a modest salary. "Left to themselves, free Negroes, in the ignorance and stupidity in which we maintain them for our convenience, would retrograde naturally to a savage state." The natural indolence of the Negro, his aversion to work, was proven by the economic decadence of the island of Española.[8]

[5]Comunicación del Captain General Gerónimo Valdés, La Habana, 3 de noviembre de 1841, A.H.N. Estado, Leg. 8040, L. 70.

[6]"Informe reservado del Real Consulado, emitido pro la misma Comisión que redactó la anterior exposición," Saco, *La historia de la esclavitud de la raza africana en el Nuevo Mundo y en especial en los países Américo-Hispanos*, IV, 125.

[7]"Exposición del Illustre Ayuntamiento de la Habana, 1841." *Ibid.*, IV, 127–135.

[8]"Informe del Licenciado don Bernardo Navarro, residente en Matanzas,

Furthermore, according to Navarro, slaves were exceptionally well treated. No other people in an area where slavery had existed could point to laws which so limited the power of the master (*potestad dominica*) over the slave. Navarro conveniently assumed that all features of the paternal slave code were in full effect, and that the slave's rights to marry, to have a family, to acquire personal property, to purchase his own freedom, and to complain to the government against his master were sufficient reason in themselves for rejecting British intervention.[9]

No doubt, many well-meaning, intelligent, and otherwise liberal men joined with the slave interests in opposing the greatest threat thus far to the very institution of slavery in Cuba. In the precise words of the Tribunal of Commerce of Havana concerning the British proposal of 1840:

> This Tribunal does not consider itself destitute of liberal maxims, or principles of philanthropy and humanity. On the contrary, in the name of these very same we ask of the Regency [of Isabella II] for a status quo in the island of Cuba on this particular; because it would not be just, nor equitable, nor human to sacrifice 400,000 whites for a measure that would make even unhappier 500,000 colored people . . .[10]

Continuing this same line of thought:

> The present inhabitants of this island did not create domestic slavery. They received this unfortunate gift from their ancestors which was conceded to them with all its fatal consequences by the laws. One of these [consequences] is the brutality and ignorance inherent in the slave class, and the demoralization of the freemen; thus the terrible dilemma of the latter: either command or die, and the no less odious alternative of the former: slaves or criminals.

The Spanish intendent advised Madrid as to what should be said to the British:

> If we had our fleet of former days the answer we would give would be as follows: you have deceived and cheated us with your trifling indemnity of

---

acerca del proyecto del convenio sobre emancipación propuesto por Inglaterra." *Ibid.*, IV, 164–165.

[9]*Ibid.*, IV, 165.

[10]"El Tribunal de Comercio de esta plaza de la Habana, representaba a la Regencia del reino contra la emancipación de los esclavos de esta Isla, 30 de marzo de 1841, extendida por el Sr. Intendente don Wenceslao de Villaurrutia." *Ibid.*, IV, 152.

400,000 pounds sterling. . . . You did not teach your slaves, as we do, the holy faith of Jesus Christ . . . These and a thousand other reasons . . . the Spanish government might assign for contemptuously rejecting the new treaty.[11]

Another eloquent voice expressing peninsular interests was that of Mariano Torrente, a notable Spanish patriot and prominent defender of the slave economy, who for many years was a collector of customs revenues in the port of Havana: "The fanaticism of the antislavery society has been carried to such a vicious extreme, that they would sacrifice the interests and future of nations to the idols of Africa."[12] Torrente had especially in mind the recent rising in Cuba (1841), attributed to the abolitionist activities of Consul Turnbull and various Quaker missionaries.

Torrente's arguments that the condition of Spanish slaves was "much more favorable than that of the peasants of Europe" and of their brothers in Africa was common enough, but more important, the Collector of Customs reminded the Spanish people that "this is precisely the moment when Cuba is enjoying her greatest epoch of prosperity."[13] In three years sugar production had risen from 700,000 boxes to 1,500,000. And had not coffee and tobacco shown similar increases? "What right has Britain," asked Torrente, "having paid so little recompense to Spain [400,000 pounds sterling] to demand the destruction of the huge investment of blood and money made by Spain in the Antilles?"[14] And he did not fail to add that Britain, having destroyed her own prosperity in Jamaica, was determined to destroy the same in Cuba.

In the face of such strong opposition from the slave interests, the Madrid government again reassured Governor Valdés that, in respect to the latest pretension of Great Britain, it would not consent to any measures threatening property.[15] But apparently the slave interests were justified in their profound mistrust of the weak metropolis, for suddenly Madrid did a *volte-face* under relentless British pressure

[11]"Report of Don Wenceslao de Villa Urrutia [sic] on the Draft of the Treaty Proposed by Great Britain to Spain, Havana, October 21, 1841." *Correspondence with Spain*, pp. 388–409.
[12]Mariano Torrente, *Cuestión importante sobre la esclavitud*, pp. 4–7, 20.
[13]*Ibid.*, pp. 4–7, 20.
[14]*Ibid.*, pp. 27–28.
[15]Ramiro Guerra y Sánchez, *Manual de la historia de Cuba (económica, social y política)*, p. 402.

and issued alarming orders to Valdés to prepare for the emancipation of all slaves introduced fraudulently since 1820, orders which Valdés did not dare to publish, fearing a dangerous commotion.[16]

The pugnacious Palmerston would not be balked so easily. A squadron of English ships soon arrived in Havana harbor with instructions to help the captain general provide the means for carrying out the register! Vice-Admiral Parker, however, after a series of secret conferences, apparently agreed with Valdés' analysis of the situation. The matter was postponed until further communication with the respective governments.[17]

There were signs, meanwhile, that the slaves were more restless. Insignificant uprisings had occurred in 1838 and 1840, while in July and in September of 1841 minor insurrections were reported at two different plantations. These events, together with the high tension produced by British abolitionist proposals and the aggressive efforts to free the emancipados, were largely responsible for the promulgation of the slave code of November 14, 1842.[18]

The new code was very similar to that of 1789 in its provision for religious instruction, recreation, and care of the slave. It provided for more elaborate working regulations, however, and imposed greater controls over the activities and movements of slaves. Slaves of one plantation could not visit slaves of another without a written license from their owner or overseer. Any individual of any class or color was authorized to detain a slave found without such a license. Slaves were also to be obliged to show greater obedience to constituted authorities, to evidence respect for white persons, and to live in harmony with their fellow slaves. Any slave discovering and reporting a conspiracy was promised liberty and a reward of five hundred pesos.[19]

---

[16] Jacobo de la Pezuela y Lobo, *Historia de la isla de Cuba*, IV, 359.

[17] *Ibid.*, IV, 361.

[18] Reglamento de esclavos, agregado y publicado con el bando de buen gobierno de la Isla de Cuba, 14 de noviembre de 1842," José Zamora y Coronado (ed.), *Biblioteca de legislación ultramarina*, III, 137–139. Also given in José Ferrer de Couto, *Los negros en sus diversos estados y condiciones; tales como son, como se supone que son y como deben ser*, pp. 68–73.

[19] Zamora (ed.), *Biblioteca de legislación ultramarina*, III, 137–139. In the new code an ordinary working day was defined as ten hours, but in times of harvest as sixteen hours (Art. 12). Slaves of advanced age or infirmity were to be maintained by their masters (Art. 15). If a slave mother was purchased, her children under age three had to be purchased with her (Art. 31). Other obligations were placed upon owners as in the code of 1789, for example, an owner could not refuse to

During this time the question of David Turnbull's activities in Cuba dominated diplomatic correspondence. Turnbull was the most outspoken abolitionist England ever sent to Cuba. Turnbull, who took over British consular duties in Havana in November, 1840, had traveled in the West Indies in 1837 as agent of the English Anti-Slavery Society, and had formerly served on the Havana mixed commission. His book, *Travels in the West: Cuba, with Notices of Porto Rico and the Slave Trade*, revealed his intimate knowledge of Spanish duplicity in "closing" the traffic and "freeing" the emancipados. Palmerston decided that Turnbull, who proposed that the mixed courts be empowered to investigate and liberate illegally possessed slaves and emancipados, was just the man to play watchdog in Cuba.[20] Governor Valdés soon regretted that he ever allowed this notorious abolitionist to take office as British Consul in Havana.

Turnbull was quickly accused by Spanish authorities of exaggerating the facts in his reports to London, provoking the danger of a slave insurrection in 1841, encouraging emancipados to present their claims through the English consulate, inciting his Creole friends to declare an abolitionist republic under British protection, and, in general, abusing his lawful powers as consul. In short, Turnbull's presence in Cuba was considered "incompatible with its tranquility and preservation."[21]

Palmerston answered such protests by reminding Madrid that since Spain's orders are looked upon in Cuba "as mere waste paper" Spain had little right to demand Turnbull's dismissal, rather Great Britain had the right to demand the dismissal of all Cuban officials, from the governor down! Did not Valdés publicly declare that all his predecessors had protected the traffic and that he would do the same for at least six months? After all, Mr. Turnbull's opinions "are shared by the

---

accept payment made by a slave toward his emancipation, according to the system of coartación. The master who mistreated a slave, morally or physically, was obliged to sell the same to another master (Arts. 32, 34, and 35). Also as before, a slave could not be punished except by his owner or overseer, or by the authorities in more serious cases. Fines were to be imposed on owners who did not abide by the regulations (Arts. 41, 42, 43, and 44).

[20]Basil Rauch, *American Interest in Cuba: 1848–1850*, pp. 38–39.

[21]Comunicación del Capitán General Gerónomo Valdés, 3 de noviembre de 1851, A.H.N. Estado, Leg. 8040, L. 9, N. 6. Also, Capitán General, El Principe de Anglona (Valdés), to Mr. Turnbull, Havana, December 22, 1840. *Correspondence with Spain*, pp. 213–214.

whole British nation," and it would be difficult to find someone who did not share his opinions.[22] Even if Mr. Turnbull was withdrawn as Consul he would still continue as superintendent of liberated Africans (emancipados), an office "not subject to any instrument of confirmation by the Spanish Crown."[23]

Enrique José Varona said of Consul Turnbull that he was "a man of iron, active and vigilant as few men were, he knew all that went on in Cuba"; on the least rumor of an expedition, or the least infraction of the treaties, he went methodically with his preemptory claims to the captain general.[24]

In a fine example of British understatement, Turnbull said to Palmerston: "When your Lordship did me the honor to appoint me to the Consulate it must have been foreseen that I was not exactly the person whose presence would be most welcome to the local authorities."[25] Meanwhile, the reports that Turnbull sent to London could not fail to heat up the abolitionist ardor of Victorian England.[26]

The slave interests had Turnbull expelled from the Economic Society, of which he had been a member since 1838.[27] Turnbull was

[22]Viscount Palmerston to M. Flores, Foreign Office, August 17, 1841, *BFSP* (1841–1842), XXX, 801–807.

[23]Viscount Palmerston to Mr. Arthur Aston, Foreign Office, March 6, 1851. *Ibid.*, XXX, 770–774. The American chargé d'affairs in Madrid wrote (December 28, 1841) that the Spanish cabinet had demanded that Britain remove Turnbull, remove the mixed court to Puerto Rico, and remove the British ship *Romney*, where the superintendent of liberated Africans accumulated emancipados under protection of the British flag. Aaron Vail to Daniel Webster, Secretary of State, December 28, 1841, William R. Manning (ed.), *Diplomatic Correspondence of the United States: Inter-American Affairs 1831–1860*, XI, 329–330.

[24]"El caso de Mr. Turnbull," in Saco, *Historia de la esclavitud de la raza africana*, III, 92.

[25]Mr. David Turnbull to Viscount Palmerston, Havana, December 30, 1840, *Correspondence with Spain*, p. 210.

[26]In report No. 168 Turnbull reported that Maria, an African girl about thirteen years of age affirmed that "the Captain of the *Jesus Maria* held her nose and mouth to keep her from screaming and had connection with her, she was hurt at the time . . ." No. 171: Mamber, Chela, Mattu, et al., all young girls, ". . . reported by Dr. Richardson as being diseased by gonorrhea," and so on. "Examinations," Mr. Turnbull to Colonel Cockburn, Havana, January 20, 1841, *ibid.*, pp. 76–83.

[27]Some of Turnbull's influential Creole friends, liberals and abolitionists concerning the slave trade, such as José de la Luz Caballero, Juan Poey, Bachiller Morales, Martínez Serrano, Domingo Delmonte, and others, had Turnbull's name reinstated. Saco, *Historia de la esclavitud de la raza africana*, III, 193–194.

undaunted. Soon the Spanish government accused him not only of organizing the emancipados and illegally possessed slaves to claim their freedom but also of urging the disaffected Creoles to strike for an abolitionist republic. In deference to Madrid's protests, Lord Aberdeen, who had replaced the crusading Palmerston as foreign secretary, ordered Turnbull's withdrawal. Before leaving the island, June 8, 1842, Turnbull fired a parting shot at Valdés, predicting that the degrading spectacle of slavery in the Spanish Antilles and Brazil would be swept away by an overwhelming torrent of public indignation. Valdés replied that such a humanitarian and liberal spirit might give attention to the unfortunate people of Ireland and India.[28]

The quixotic Turnbull returned to Cuba in October, 1842, accompanied by some free British Negroes. As superintendent of liberated Africans Turnbull ostensibly planned to tour the island and free certain Negroes that had been re-enslaved. He was now accused of openly organizing a rebellion. Valdés had his companions shot and Turnbull imprisoned, and then deported, with a grim warning never to return. Aberdeen abolished the troublesome office of superintendent of liberated Africans.[29] Nevertheless, for better or worse, Turnbull's ghost would still hover over the island.

At this time the first of the "black hysterias" began to seize the United States. The aggressive abolitionist efforts of British agents in Cuba and the slave unrest there gave substance to the rumors that Britain was attempting to abolish slavery and establish a "Black Republic" under her protection. Cuban planters such as Domingo Delmonte urged the American government to frustrate British policy. Little prodding was needed. Already jumpy about British expansion in Central America, and British machinations to abolish slavery in the Republic of Texas, Washington was moved to defend its established Cuban policy: Cuba must be Spanish . . . that is, until such time as Cuba could be incorporated into the great American Union. Daniel Webster, secretary of state, who had recently signed an agreement with the British to help suppress the slave trade on the African coast, made a fervent promise to defend Spain's sovereign rights in Cuba:

> The Spanish government has long been in possession of the policy and wishes of this Government in regard to Cuba, which has never changed,

[28]Philip S. Foner, *A History of Cuba, and Its Relations with the United States*, I, 210.
[29]*Ibid.*, I, 211.

and has been repeatedly told that the United States never would permit the occupation of that island by British agents or forces, upon any pretext whatsoever; and that in the event of any attempt to wrest it from her, she might securely rely upon the whole naval and military resources of this country to aid her in preserving or recovering it.[30]

The Spaniards could easily see through *Tío Sam's* paternal concern for Spanish Cuba, but for the moment American concern, backed up by American ships in Cuban waters, was a useful foil against Palmerston's irate abolitionism.

After Webster resigned (May, 1843) proslavery Southern Democrats carried the fear of a Black Republic to a further extreme. Would not the spectacle of free black labor at the very doorstep of the United States undermine the slave system of the Southern states? And would not a future slave state be lost forever to Southern expansionists? Abel P. Upshur and John C. Calhoun, successors to Webster, continued a vigilant watch over the rights of Spain. Calhoun, who assumed the post of secretary of state on March 6, 1844, charged that the British in seeking the abolition of slavery in the Republic of Texas and in Cuba were preparing to attack slavery in the United States, so as to destroy all slave-labor competition with the British colonies.[31]

Nor would the United States offer effective cooperation with Great Britain in the closing of the African slave trade. Since Britain would not abandon the right of impressment, the United States would not concede the right of search. By the Webster-Ashburton Treaty of 1842 the United States promised only to station a force of eighty-eight guns on the African coast. At the same time the American minister to France, Lewis Cass, was instrumental in causing that country to repudiate in 1845 an earlier agreement giving Britain the right to search French vessels.[32] The situation was intensified by British utterances. For example, Macauley, February 26, 1845, denounced the United States in Parliament as the "patron and champions of Negro slavery all over the world."[33]

In the meantime, the menacing reactions of the American expan-

---

[30]Daniel Webster, Secretary of State, to Robert B. Campbell, United States Consul at Havana, Washington, January 14, 1843. Manning (ed.), *Diplomatic Correspondence*, XI, 28–29.

[31]Rauch, *American Interest in Cuba*, pp. 44–45.

[32]Hugh G. Soulsby, *The Right of Search and the Slave Trade in Anglo-American Relations 1814–1862*, see Chap. III.

[33]Amos Aschbach Ettinger, *The Mission of Pierre Soulé*, p. 25.

Britain Grows More Aggressive, 1840–1848

sionists, together with a change of ministry in London, Lord Aberdeen replacing the crusading Palmerston, had already caused the danger of a registry of illegally possessed slaves to vanish. A note of February 12, 1842, to Madrid from Aberdeen promised that the British government would not press the matter further for the moment.[34]

Not all abolitionist exertions had been in vain, however, for beginning with Captain General Valdés the first conscientious efforts of the Spanish government in Cuba were made to fulfill treaty obligations in respect to the emancipados. Trollope, who had said the captains general will allow no Africans to be imported into Cuba, "except for a consideration," said that "Valdés would take nothing, and he is spoken of as the foolish Governor."[35] According to figures presented to the Spanish government in June, 1841, British warships had captured thirty-five slave ships between the years 1824–1841; 9,000 slaves, including 2,474 women, were found aboard. Of the first number, 977 had been carried away by the British, 3,216 had died as emancipados in Cuba, and a few had found liberty by other means, leaving a total of 4,773 emancipados when Valdés took command in 1841.[36]

In a letter of October 31, 1842, Valdés claimed that he had given liberty to 837 emancipados "in the past nine months." At this rate, said he, overoptimistically as it proved, all the emancipados would be free in five years. Nevertheless, said the Governor, the subordination of these individuals must be maintained. The emancipados must be made to understand that they owe their liberty not to the intervention of a foreign power but to the Spanish government.[37]

In Spain the revolution of 1843 produced a change in policy and a series of new ministries, more opposed to British abolitionism. And they could count on United States support. One result was that the temperate Valdés was succeeded by Leopoldo O'Donnell, whose reign in Cuba (October, 1843–May, 1848) was devoted to strengthening Spain's grip on the island by protecting and encouraging the slave economy.

The golden age of Cuban prosperity, further stimulated by the abolition of slavery in British Jamaica (1833–1838), continued. A grow-

---

[34]Guerra, *Manual de la historia*, p. 404.
[35]Anthony Trollope, *The West Indies and the Spanish Main*, p. 140.
[36]Cuenta de buques mercantes españoles, A.H.N. Estado, Leg. 8040, L. 9. N. 6; see Appendix for a list of slave ships captured off the coast of Cuba.
[37]Comunicación del Capitán General Gerónimo Valdés, 31 de octubre de 1842, *ibid.*

ing number of North American and European merchants came to Havana for Cuban sugar products. More than ever there was a need for slave labor. An economic survey of the first half of the nineteenth century would make manifest the profitable nature of the Cuban economy. According to the Cuban Feijóo de Sotomayor, the value of Cuban exports rose rapidly:

Exports through the Port of Havana in 1771,	2,069,294 pesos
Exports through the Port of Havana in 1811,	19,048,243 pesos
Exports through the Port of Havana in 1851,	35,000,000 pesos

The number of sugar plantations rose from 510 in 1827 to 1,500 in 1846. The value of the internal trade of the island rose from 31,542,943 pesos in 1830 to 60,080,000 in 1852.[38] From the notes of Humboldt and Thrasher one can see how the number of land holdings had increased through the years:[39]

	1817	1846
Sugar mills (ingenios)	625	1,442
Coffee plantations	779	1,670
Tobacco plantations (vegas)	1,601	9,102
Cattle farms (all kinds)	2,127	9,830

The slave trade during Valdés' administration diminished slightly, but still the over-all picture showed an increasing volume of importations. In the period 1820–1827, an estimated total of 28,915 slaves had been illegally introduced; in the period 1827–1841, 120,489; and in the period 1841–1846, 98,450.

During the first years of his administration O'Donnell, unlike Valdés, was known to be more an accomplice than an opponent of the slave trade.[40] Everyone knew in the Havana of those days that the authorities of the island accepted money from the slave traders and

---

[38]Urbano Feijóo de Sotomayor, *Isla de Cuba. Inmigración de trabajadores Españoles. Documentos y memoria*, pp. 34–35.

[39]Alexander von Humboldt, *The Island of Cuba*, p. 280. These figures do not show the large number of farms and laboring sites of a miscellaneous kind (*sitios de labor*), which Thrasher calculates to be some 25,000 in 1846, nor are the small number of cocoa and cotton plantations shown.

[40]Washington Irving wrote: "It seems beyond a doubt that under the new Captain-General O'Donnell slaves are again admitted in great numbers. Under Valdés, the former governor, who faithfully carried into effect the laws and treaties ... the traffic in great measure declined." Washington Irving, U. S. Minister to Spain, to J. C. Calhoun, Secretary of State, April 23, 1844, Manning (ed.), *Diplomatic Correspondence*, XI, 339–340.

the great slaveowners. O'Donnell could rationalize that the true colonial interests of Spain justified the importation of more slave labor. But the turn of events changed this attitude rather abruptly.

Shortly after O'Donnell arrived on the island the slave insurrection of March 27–28, 1843, occurred in the jurisdiction of Cárdenas. The fact that several haciendas were involved indicated that it had been better planned than any previous uprising. It is true that the insurrection never got much beyond the stage of some emancipated Negroes vociferously asking other slaves to join them in a bid for freedom. But such was the nervous fear of rebellion in Cuba after the events of Haiti and Santo Domingo that O'Donnell employed cruel methods of repression. Suspected Negro leaders were hurriedly executed or banished. A year after the event Negroes were still being seized and tried.[41]

Torture, meanwhile, had revealed the existence of a similar plot, La Conspiración de la Escalera, centered in the province of Matanzas. Since a number of Creole leaders—some of them friends of David Turnbull—were suspected of encouraging Negro emancipation as a means to ending Spanish control of the island, O'Donnell "rounded out his policy by removing Cubans from all public offices and by encouraging the slave trade," thus virtually extinguishing the Creole independence and abolition movements until the American Civil War.[42]

David Turnbull, former consul, was blamed by the Spanish government as the prime mover of the insurrection. A military commission investigating the insurrection came to the conclusion that there was no doubt that he was not only the cause but also the one who conceived the destructive idea.[43] This charge has been sustained by Cuban historians.[44]

For the first time a number of planters openly questioned the continuance of the slave trade. The fact that the slaves now outnumbered

[41] Kennedy, the British judge of the mixed commission, wrote that: "It is truly distressing to hear the account of cruelties and oppressions committed on this unhappy class of persons during the last year." Communication, February 24, 1845, found in "insurrección esclava," A.H.N. Estado, Leg. 8040, L. 9, N. 3.

[42] Rauch, *American Interest in Cuba*, p. 42.

[43] Expedientes acerca del ex-Consul inglés David Turnbull, A.H.N. Estado, Leg. 8057, Comunicaciones 1844–1845.

[44] See "Reafirmación del Régimen colonial" by Emeterio S. Santovenia in *Historia de la nación Cubana*, Ramiro Guerra y Sánchez et al. (eds.), IV, 71–73, or Guerra, *Manual de la historia*, pp. 415–420.

the whites in Cuba—overwhelmingly so in the country districts—led to a number of petitions against the slave traffic.[45] But since Spanish dominion in Cuba depended on the slave trade the solution could only be harsher regulations. The decree of May 31, 1844, added rigid qualifications to the slave code of 1842.[46]

Another of the unfortunate consequences of the "insurrection" was that it worked against the British case for the emancipados. The Cuban government was less than ever disposed to set them free according to treaty terms.

Palmerston, who had returned as foreign secretary, repeatedly accused O'Donnell of scandalous conduct in regard to the fate of the emancipados delivered to Spanish authorities before 1835. The flavor of these accusations can be gathered from one of Foreign Secretary Palmerston's letters to the British minister in Madrid:[47]

Foreign Office
August 3, 1846

Sir:

By Despatch recently received from her Majesty's Commissioners at Havana . . . it appears that the practice of reselling Emancipados, which has been going on for some time past under the sanction and direction of the Captain General of Cuba was the public topic of conversation . . .

It is also stated that upwards of 5,000 of these unfortunate persons have been re-sold at rates varying from 5 to 9 ounces of gold (for example, 50 emancipados were sold to the Gas Company of Havana for a period of five

---

[45] Proprietors of the jurisdiction of Matanzas, where there were sixty thousand slaves feared to be infected with ideas from Haiti and Jamaica, said that it was time the contraband traffic ceased to threaten "all our hopes of security and future well-being." "Importante exposición de los hacendados de Matanzas al Gobernador General pidiendo la supresión de la trata" (29 de noviembre de 1843), Saco, *Historia de la esclavitud de la raza africana*, III, 195–201.

[46] Slaves were now even more restricted in their movements and faced severe punishment for treasonable or disturbing activities. See Ferrer de Couto, *Los Negros esclavos*, p. 105.

[47] Lord Palmerston to Sir Henry Lytton Bulwer, August 3, 1846, A.H.N. Estado, Leg. 8040, L. 9, N. 6. In later testimony Palmerston said that although the condition of the emancipados was "very bad," yet "by way of compensation these Negroes are not principally employed in hard field work but, in work about the town of Havannah in lamp-lighting, sweeping the streets and things of that kind . . . of late years no captured slaves are delivered to the Spanish government in Cuba; they are now sent to a British colony," *First Report from the Select Committee on the Slave Trade Together with the Minutes and Evidence and Appendix*, pp. 12–13.

years to serve as lamp-lighters) by which means a profit of upwards to six hundred thousand dollars has been made by persons in the Government House ... and that 400 Emancipados have been transferred to the Marqués de las Delicias, Chief Judge of the Mixed Court, and the greatest slave proprietor on the Island, to be held by him for the benefit of the Countess Guerega, wife of General O'Donnell ... a direct and flagrant violation of the treaty engagements ...

You will express the confident hope that the Government of Spain will give positive and preemptory orders to General O'Donnell to obtain ... full and complete liberty for these nominally emancipated Negroes ...

Palmerston

The few who would liberate Cuba from the embarrassing problem of the slave trade could only lament the prevailing state of opinion. In 1845 the exile Saco published his "La supresión del tráfico de esclavos en la isla de Cuba," in which he again argued against the internal and external dangers of a continuation of the slave trade, and in which he again suggested the need for increasing the number of whites in Cuba through immigration.[48] This work provoked a cry from the slave interests that Saco was in the pay of the British. It was obviously unpatriotic to abolish the slave trade. The Spaniard Ramón de la Sagra complained (1845) that for twelve years he had been preaching the abolition of the slave trade after the manner of Britain and France but that he was met on all sides "with silence and indifference, if not with calumny."[49]

[48]José Antonio Saco, "La supresión del tráfico de esclavos africanos en la isla de Cuba, examinada con relación a su agricultura y a su seguridad," found in collected works of Saco, *Colección de papeles científicos, históricos, políticos y de otros ramos sobre la isla de Cuba*, III, 85–155. The two main arguments were racial and economic. Saco played upon the dread of a race war. Cuba, preponderantly African and surrounded by three million more Africans in adjoining islands, must balance this terrible influence by increasing the moral and numerical power of the whites (pp. 101–103). The slave insurrections of 1842–1843 were proof that the slaves were better organized. It would not be necessary that the Negroes rebel all at once, sporadic movements would suffice to destroy credit and confidence, and to force an emigration of people and capital, ruining the island economically. "Cuba in order to face the future must not only instantly and forever terminate all slave traffic but also protect the colonization of whites" (pp. 131–133).

[49]Ramón de la Sagra, *Estudios coloniales con aplicación a la isla de Cuba*. It is curious that the learned Sagra, representative of peninsular culture in Cuba, and Saco, representative of Creole culture, were symbolic of the division between peninsulares and criollos, but on the question of the slave trade were in basic

Meanwhile, Spain had reason to believe that Creole slaveholders would betray her. Spain's weakness in the face of British abolitionism produced so much alarm and disgust in Cuba at this time that an increasing number of slaveowners considered annexation to the slaveholding United States as the only safeguard for the continuance of the slave institution. This fear, together with effects produced by the recent slave risings, caused officials in both Spain and Cuba to reconsider the slave problem. They began to see Saco's point that the continuance of the slave trade endangered the security of the island, to say nothing more. Given the international situation of Cuba before aggressive imperial powers, all pretexts for intervention must be removed. These considerations, together with constant British pressure, the ending of the first Carlist War, and the terror caused by the late slave insurrection, brought about a favorable climate for a new measure against the slave trade.

In Madrid, Martínez de la Rosa succeeded in presenting to the Cortes the measure that had been promised since the treaty of 1835. Thus, "The Law of Abolition and Repression of the Slave Trade" was approved on March 4, 1845. In Cuba "all classes" expected a fatal blow to slavery; some proprietors began to sell their ingenios.[50] The

agreement, a proof that the most enlightened and informed men of the time, whether Spanish or Cuban, were against the slave trade. Sagra, who spoke in moderate and rational tones, was one of the first abolitionists, but he was incapable by nature of agitating the problem.

Sagra made one of the early attempts to condemn forced labor on economic grounds. He did not say that slave labor was unprofitable, but he did claim that free labor could be just as profitable. Sugar production in Cuba was no more profitable than in countries where free labor was used. With machines such as were used in the United States, the whites could work in the tropics, and profitably. The abolition of the traffic was inevitable; universal sentiment and the treaties demanded it. Like Saco, Sagra wanted Cuba, and also the metropolis, to face this fact squarely in order to build Cuba's economy on the solid basis of free labor. Cuba must follow the new labor system by which the Dutch prospered in Java. Cuba would produce all her own sugar and tobacco. The planter would no longer own or control both the industrial and agricultural side of sugar production, but would concede the latter process to free or independent cultivators, who would sell their products to the mill owners (pp. 70–86).

Sagra, who made extensive economic and political studies on Cuba, for example, *Historia física, política y natural de Cuba,* foresaw the economic reform arguments of the 1860's, and the evolution of the Cuban sugar industry toward the great specialized mills (*centrales*).

[50]John Glanville Taylor, *The United States and Cuba: Eight Years of Change and Travel,* p. 194.

Spanish government, however, soon made it abundantly clear to the slave interests that it was definitely not a measure giving Britain greater powers of intervention in Cuba. On the contrary, Britain had promised to minimize the intervention of her consuls in the future. According to Martínez de la Rosa, the object of the law was only to stop the slave traffic and not to threaten the existing institution of slavery in any way. In order to make the law more palatable to protesting slaveholders, they were to be informed that it was really intended for their own security. The abolition of the slave trade would remove the danger of slave rebellions, as well as the possibility of foreign intervention.[51]

The first five articles of the law subjected pilots, captains, and other major ship personnel engaged in the slave trade to six years in prison, and eight years if they resisted arrest. This would be reduced to four years or two years depending on whether the ship was on the high seas or at the point of departure without slaves aboard. Sailors and other crew members were subjected to half the above-cited punishment, but shipowners, cargo owners, and those who organized the voyage were subjected to the same punishment as the major ship personnel; they could, like the former, be subjected to exile at more than fifty leagues from their homes, and to fines of from one to ten thousand pesos.

Articles Six, Seven, and Eight provided for the confiscation and destruction of the ship and all articles found aboard, punishment for any abuses practiced on the bozales found aboard, and stiffer penalties in case the crime was repeated.[52]

Provisions for enforcing the treaty promised punishment to any authorities who received proved knowledge of a disembarkation but took no action to stop the ship. All proved connivance of officials with the traffic was punishable by loss of suspension from their position; this included the higher authorities, members of the tribunals, ordinary justices, the *fiscal* (public prosecutor), and *escribano* (notary). The law was to go into effect three months after publication.

A serious reservation in the means of enforcement, however, vir-

[51]Francisco Martínez de la Rosa, Sr. Ministro de Marina, Comercio y Gobernación de Ultramar al Capitán General de la Isla de Cuba, Leopoldo O'Donnell, 28 de diciembre de 1844, A.H.N. Ultramar, Leg. 4655 (1844–1845), N. 181, Expedientes 1 y 2.

[52]La Ley penal contra los traficantes en esclavos del 28 de febrero de 1845, A.H.N. Estado, Leg. 8040.

tually nullified the effect of the treaty articles. Article Nine prohibited the pursuit of contraband slaves within the bounds of the ingenios. Notice that a slave expedition was being prepared or that a slave expedition had landed obliged the officials to take action, "but in no case, nor at any time, shall it be possible to proceed against or disturb slave proprietors in their possession of slaves under pretext of their origin."[53]

The significance of this reservation was that once the bozales had been quietly introduced into the plantations there was no legal way to recover them or to proceed against their new owners. Article Nine would prove to be a gaping hole in the blockade against the traffic, since it considered private property a sacred asylum.

The law of 1845 caused the usual drumbeat of alarm in Cuba, and the usual cry against humiliating concessions to the British. In a series of communications O'Donnell made manifest his belief that the law of 1845 would ruin the economy of the island and lead to its defection from the mother country. White immigration, encouraged since 1817, had already proved itself a failure; the committee on white immigration had in the last few years introduced only 1,673 individuals, 600 of whom were Asiatics. The government did not have sufficient financial resources for promoting the annual introduction of from 20,000 to 30,000 colonists, the number which O'Donnell thought necessary. Furthermore, it was an established fact that the whites could not bear the climate of Cuba, the tropical diseases, or the work in the cane fields.[54]

In ten years, said O'Donnell, Cuba would experience a vast shortage of labor. There would be no way to replace those slaves now working the plantations. It would not be possible to breed more slaves, because even on plantations of from four hundred to seven hundred slaves there existed not one female slave. Most females were employed domestically in the cities. If this situation continued, O'Donnell warned, the whites would outnumber the Negroes. And when this happens, "The guarantee of conserving the integrity of the territory and its dependence on the Metropolis will come to an end."[55]

The Spanish government was alarmed by O'Donnell's dire predic-

[53]*Ibid.*

[54]O'Donnell al Secretario de Estado, comunicación de julio de 1846, suelta, *Ibid.*

[55]O'Donnell al Secretario de Estado, comunicación reservada del 15 de febrero de 1845, suelta, *Ibid.*

tions, and appointed a committee of military men experienced in Cuban affairs—Juan Bautista Topete, Gerónimo Valdés, Conde de Espeleta, and others—to examine the subject further.

The Colonial Section of the Royal Council repeated the charge that England, out of envy for Cuban sugar production, was attempting to destroy Cuban prosperity by championing the cause of emancipation. The proof of this, reasoned the Council, was in the fact that Britain did not make similar demands on slaveholders in Brazil, the United States, or other nations: "These considerations are of a reserved character, and so must be all dispositions that emanate from them."[56]

It was estimated that an addition of eight thousand slaves annually would be needed into Cuba in order to supplement the labor supply of the island. In connection with this, the Council agreed with O'Donnell that the conservation of Spanish dominion in the island would depend on maintaining a ratio of four whites to six colored. The problem was to maintain this proportion by supplementing the labor supply.

Unlike O'Donnell, the Council did not feel that the law of 1845 made the problem irremedial. In the first place, the annual slave imports of twelve thousand to fifteen thousand would not stop at once. It was inevitable that some slaves would be introduced, in which fact "will be found a secret alleviation for the fear that now afflicts Cuba." Secondly, by propagating slaves after the manner of the United States the shortage of black labor could be offset. In order to encourage slave breeding, the proprietors who would increase the number of females on their plantations to 10 or 20 per cent or breed from 2 per cent to 5 per cent of slave-labor needs would be exempt, wholly or in part, from capitation taxes on slaves.

Some other measures suggested were a higher tax to be levied on domestic slaves in order to force them into the fields, and a reduction in the hours of labor "in order to conserve for a longer time the life and health of the slaves." These new measures were to remain confi-

---

[56]Informe de la Sección de Ultramar del Consejo Real, 22 de diciembre de 1846, suelto, *Ibid*. Probably Palmerston gave a fairer reply when answering the parliamentary committee, which asked if the British government was suppressing the traffic out of self-interest, as charged by other nations, or out of a "sense of duty, apart from the interests of humanity." Palmerston answered that in the narrow view of it great injury would be done to British West Indian planters using free labor if the slave trade to Cuba and Brazil were permitted to continue. *First Report from the Select Committee*, pp. 18–19.

dential and to be verbally communicated to the slaveowners, "because it would be very dangerous if the slaves understood that it was necessary to restrain the cupidity of their owners, and because the abolition societies would give to these regulations the interpretation most convenient to them."[57]

The suggestion was made that congregations of clergy be founded for the express purpose of teaching Christian doctrine to the slaves on the plantations. Since a large number of slaves were incapacitated for reasons of insubordination, robbery, homicide, suicide, and other crimes, it was thought that moral education could diminish this loss of slave labor.

Once more, the immigration of free laborers was counseled. Yet-untapped sources of free labor were in the islands of Fernando Po and on the mainland of Latin America, but primary emphasis was placed on Oriental labor, "the good qualities of the Chinese have already been proven in the Philippines."

Finally, in order to maintain the balance of four to six required by the plantation economy, the Council suggested that all free blacks under fifty be exiled or forced to go to work on a sugar plantation. This would also diminish the number of potentially dangerous slaves.[58]

Hubert S. Aimes has claimed that O'Donnell vigorously enforced the treaty, that in 1845 probably not a single cargo was run; and in 1846, not more than two.[59] No doubt the treaty reduced the traffic somewhat, sending prices of slaves higher; and as always happens immediately after the passing of a new law, there was a period of watchful waiting on the part of the slavists.

On the other hand, British officials continued to charge O'Donnell with the most flagrant abuses of the emancipados, and to suggest that no slave cargoes were said to be landed because O'Donnell would not admit the fact. Documents presented to the British Parliament, however, generally sustain the view that in the years immediately following the law of 1845 the traffic did diminish notably. A reported

[57]Informe de la Sección de Ultramar del Consejo Real, 22 de diciembre de 1846, suelto, A.H.N. Estado, Leg. 8040.
[58]*Ibid.*
[59]Hubert S. Aimes, *A History of Slavery in Cuba, 1511 to 1868*, p. 170. Aimes based his affirmation on *Accounts and Papers*, 1846, Vol. XV from the British archives.

10,000 bozales arrived in 1845, but this number had diminished to 1,350 in 1846, to 1,700 in 1847, and to 1,500 in 1848.[60]

The slave economy of Spanish Cuba, meanwhile, received a boost from its potential enemies. In 1842 the United States had increased the tariff against Spanish sugar in order to favor Louisiana planters. But in 1846 Congress, in order to favor mutual trade, exempted Cuban and Puerto Rican products from discriminatory duties.[61] The measure also seems to have reflected a temporary rapprochment between Spain and the United States due to British aggressiveness in the Caribbean region. At the same time the British Parliament in a celebrated move toward free trade repealed the Corn Laws that had protected British agriculture both in England and her colonies. Slave sugar from the Spanish Antilles could now, ironically, undersell Jamaican free sugar in the important English market as a result of the Sugar Duties Act of August 18, 1846. British planters, however, would now more than ever demand an end to slave-labor competition in the Caribbean and, of course, Brazil.[62]

Unfortunately for British abolitionists, just when the flow of Africans to Cuba seemed reduced to a trickle a breach occurred in the Brazilian dike. The convention of 1826, according to Brazilian interpretation, would expire on March 13, 1845, and with it the British right to search and seizure of ships engaged in the Brazilian slave trade. The Brazilian government refused to sign a new convention, in spite of the repeated efforts of the British legation in Rio de Janeiro.

In 1845 nearly 2,500,000 African slaves were in Brazil in a total population of about 6,000,000, as compared to about 350,000 slaves in Cuba in a total population of about 900,000.[63] Supposedly the slave trade to Brazil had been closed from 1826 to 1845, but, according to

---

[60]Documents presented to the English Parliament by Mr. Hutt, given in Francisco de Armas y Céspedes, *De la esclavitud en Cuba*, pp. 120–122. Palmerston testified that in spite of O'Donnell's reputation there was an "undoubted diminution" of the traffic during his administration. *First Report from the Select Committee*, p. 8.

[61]Rauch, *American Interest in Cuba*, p. 46.

[62]Roland T. Ely, *Cuando reinaba su majestad el azúcar. Estudio histórico-sociológico de una tragedia latinoamericana: El monocultivo en Cuba, origen y evolución del proceso*, p. 428.

[63]Cuban census figures are inaccurate due to the interest of the proprietors in hiding contraband slaves. The census of 1846 gave 252,534 slaves, that of 1852, 323,897, whereas an Englishman, long resident in Cuba, gave an 1850 estimate of 436,100. If the Cuban traffic decreased from 1845 to 1850, one can only assume

one conservative estimate, an average of at least 16,000 slaves were imported annually during this period.[64] Such knowledge strained British patience, but the great leap in the Brazilian traffic after 1845 proved intolerable, as may be appreciated from these figures:[65]

1845	19,453
1846	50,324
1847	56,172
1848	60,000
1849	54,000

There was also the burning question of the emancipados but on a much larger scale than in Cuba. According to the Brazilian law of November 7, 1831—to be sure, a most unpopular law resulting from British pressure—all Africans imported after that date were to be declared free, and even returned to Africa.[66] Yet about 1,000,000 slaves were to be imported into Brazil after the law had been passed. In theory, all were liberated Africans. Little wonder that the British government was even more incensed over the emancipado "hypocrisy" in Brazil than in Cuba.

The foregoing explains why the British took more aggressive action against Brazil than against Spain. As Palmerston said, the Brazilian government was wholly destitute of the power, if indeed it had the will, to suppress the prohibited traffic.[67] Parliament passed the Aberdeen Act, August 8, 1845, authorizing the High Court of Admiralty and Courts of Vice-Admiralty to search, seize, and adjudicate all Brazilian vessels engaged in the slave trade without recourse to any mixed court whatsoever.

The Emperor of Brazil loudly protested this unilateral action. The dictatorial reply was that the Aberdeen Act could be exchanged only

---

that the census of 1846 was inaccurate. A discussion of the census question is found in Charles W. Davis, United States Special Agent to Cuba, to William L. Marcy, Secretary of State, Washington, May 22, 1854, Manning (ed.), *Diplomatic Correspondence*, XI, 789–792.

[64]"Report for the Year 1888 on the Trade of the Consular District of Rio de Janeiro," *Diplomatic and Consular Reports on Trade and Finance*, No. 501, p. 39.

[65]*Ibid.*

[66]*Ibid.*

[67]Viscount Palmerston to Lord Howden, Foreign Office, June 4, 1847, *BFSP* (1846–1847), XXXV, 602–603.

for a new and more stringent Anglo-Brazilian convention against the traffic. Palmerston left the Emperor no choice:

> As the Government of Brazil objects to the Act, Her Majesty's Government would be willing, in deference to the wishes of the Imperial Government, to accept the Treaty of which I send you a draft, in exchange for the Act of 1845 . . . upon no other condition whatever can Her Majesty's Government recommend Parliament to repeal the Act of 1845.[68]

Spain, at least, in passing the law of 1845 against the traffic avoided, or postponed, the extremes of British interference and retained full control of Cuban internal affairs.

[68] *Ibid.*, XXXV, 603–604.

6. The Status Quo Reaffirmed in the Face of New International Threats, 1848-1851

> Emancipation would be the ruin of the proprietors and merchants of the island. It would put an end to the only means for preventing the island's falling to the English or American annexationists.
>
> Captain General Alcoy, 1848[1]

If one had to choose the typical military governor of this period in Cuban colonial history perhaps it would be the Count of Alcoy, who formed a solid but undistinguished link in the chain of Cuban government (February, 1848, to November, 1850). His administration mirrored faithfully what was then the settled role of the colonial governor: to comply with the expectations of the slave interests while assuming an insulted look at British charges of connivance. And he enriched himself along the way, something which was understood at the time to be more a customary right than a reward.

The Count, who replaced O'Donnell as governor, continued the precedent of Tacón in favoring the Spanish party, and in demonstrating the same obstinate resistance against British abolitionist efforts. Alcoy, like his predecessors, maintained that the English consuls, following motive of self-interest, were seeking excuses to intervene in the Cuban slave problem and that their absurd charges concerning slave landings were based on nothing more than café rumors.[2]

[1]Oficio del Conde de Alcoy [Federico Roncali] al Excmo. Sr. Secretario de Estado, La Habana, 9 de julio de 1848, A.H.N. Ultramar, Leg. 4628 (1848).

[2]For example, the accusation of the British Commissioner Kennedy that five slave landings had taken place in 1848 and twenty in 1849 was termed "absurdly

Blissfully or willfully ignorant of the slave landings taking place in Cuba, Alcoy wanted to abolish the mixed court of Havana on the alleged ground that no Spanish ship had been found engaged in the slave trade since 1835. As for the fate of the emancipados, he repelled all English charges on that score, claiming that these Negroes were not sold, and the treaties were faithfully observed. In proof, he submitted the statement that 1,931 emancipados together with 462 children had received certificates of liberty. Also, why not remind the British that the emancipados of Jamaica received worse treatment; for one thing, were they not employed at miserable salaries?[3]

Alcoy's explanation of the bold efforts of intervention made by British officials in Cuba may have been partially true; the British government was unable to stop the departure of certain slave ships from the African coast, and in order to silence critics in the British parliament the blame was shifted on to the authorities of Cuba.[4]

In England grave misgivings had arisen about the success of British efforts to abolish the slave trade. It had been over thirty years since England had established this as her goal at the Treaty of Vienna. Much effort and treasure had been spent in maintaining the ships that guarded the coasts of Africa, Cuba, and Brazil, and in incessantly bringing diplomatic pressure to bear on those countries that had signed agreements with England. Yet the slavers sailing under different flags avoided capture. The slave merchants still found the American flag and American equipment most useful because the United States government continued to deny Britain the right of search, and continued to issue, as a favor to the American shipping industry, sea letters to American ships purchased in foreign ports.[5] Palmerston testified: "The American vessels, I believe, are a good deal employed in conveying to the coast of Africa equipment for the slave trade . . . and at a particular moment she [the American ship] is often sold to a

---

false." Oficio del Conde de Alcoy al Secretario de Estado, 4 de abril de 1848, 2⁰ sección: Opinión de la Sección del Estado, A.H.N. Estado, Leg. 8043, N. 325.

[3]Oficio del Conde de Alcoy al Secretario de Estado, 4 de abril de 1848, A.H.N. Estado, Leg. 8040, N. 12.

[4]Ibid.

[5]For a full treatment of the problem of the right of search, Hugh G. Soulsby, *The Right of Search and the Slave Trade in Anglo-American Relations 1814–1862*. Also, Lawrence F. Hill, "The Abolition of the African Slave Trade to Brazil," *HAHR*, XI, No. 2 (May, 1931), 169–197.

Brazilian, or Spaniard or Portuguese." The latter flags were the "great coverers of the slave trade ... by 'flag' one means papers."[6]

Public criticism in England demanded results or abandonment of the abolitionist policy. The London *Times* (August 4, 1850) published the calculations of an English employee of Sierra Leone, who indicated that the slave trade was again on the increase, mainly because of the Brazilian breach already described:[7]

Year	Slaves exported from Africa	Slaves seized by cruisers
1840	64,114	3,616
1841	49,097	3,966
1842	28,400	3,950
1843	55,102	2,797
1844	54,102	4,577
1845	36,758	3,519
1846	76,117	2,788
1847	84,356	3,967

Earlier, a commission of the House of Commons investigated the slave-trade question and came to a dismal conclusion: "Long experience has demonstrated that it is impossible to extinguish the traffic by means of naval forces." The commission recommended the prohibition of Cuban and Brazilian "slave-sugar," the punishment of all slavers as pirates, and the emancipation of all slaves imported illegally. "But even supposing Great Britain ... adopted these measures ... their execution would not be supported by the opinion of other countries."[8]

---

[6]*First Report from the Select Committee on the Slave Trade Together with the Minutes and Evidence and Appendix*, p. 7.

[7]The *Globe*, August 17, 1840, on the other hand, supported the government policy, saying that—and these were Palmerston's words—the high price of slaves was proof of its effectiveness. Press articles found in A.H.N. Estado, Leg. 8042 (1848–1850), L. 10, N. 4.

[8]Parliamentary report prepared by the House of Lords (London), The *Times*, August 19, 1850, A.H.N. Estado, Leg. 8042, L. 10, N. 4. The recommendation to stop the importation of "slave-sugar" must have been influenced by testimony such as that of Henry J. Matson, commander of a "naval police" squadron, who said to the Parliamentary Committee: "I might here remark that I was in Havannah when the news of the change in the sugar duties, the admission of slave-grown sugar [into England] arrived; and the value of slaves ... the price of estates and sugar rose 15 per cent, and rather more ... that was in 1846." *First Report from the Select Committee on the Slave Trade*, p. 104.

The means hitherto employed by Great Britain in suppressing the slave trade were (1) the negotiation of treaties with the various civilized states for prohibition and suppression of the trade, (2) the negotiation of pacts with the chiefs of Africa prohibiting the exportation of slaves from their territories (from 1840 to 1849 the English government had signed forty-two such treaties with African chieftains), (3) the maintenance of certain forts on the African coasts, and (4) the maintenance of armed cruisers on the coast of Africa to enforce the treaties. It was hoped also that Christian missionaries would contribute to suppressing the traffic.[9]

When asked by the Select Committee of the House of Commons whether failure to gain French or American cooperation in the mutual right of search would be fatal to British efforts, Palmerston answered: "My opinion is that if the Spanish government and the government of Brazil would honestly fulfill their treaty engagements . . . the slave trade would be practically extinct."[10]

A Select Committee of the Lords examined the same question. Fortunately for the policy of Palmerston and the abolitionists, the Lords' report was favorable. They concluded that the annual expense, estimated at 500,000 pounds by the *Times*, was justified. "Any concession toward modifying the system would be impractical and disgraceful."[11]

Public criticism had the effect of moving the British government to make new demands of Brazil and Spain. Proposals were made in Parliament that Spain should cede Cuba to Britain as compensation to British holders of defaulted Spanish bonds, and as a means of checking further expansion of the slave interests of the United States, which had just annexed Texas. Relations were already strained with Madrid for another reason. On May 19, 1848, the abolitionist Sir Henry Bulwer, British ambassador, was expelled from Spain by General Narváez because of alleged complicity in Spanish political reform movements at a time when the Spanish monarchy trembled at the news of the French Revolution of February, 1848. Also, facing new threats to Cuba, which will be described later, the Spanish court was in no mood to suffer further British abolitionist demands. The captains general were instructed not to receive any communications from English consuls in Havana unless strictly confined to legitimate objects. In October, 1850, the Spanish government again flatly refused to

[9]London *Times*, August 15, 1850.
[10]*Ibid.*
[11]*First Report from the Select Committee on the Slave Trade*, p. 8.

take a census of illegitimately acquired slaves, and to declare the slave trade piracy.[12]

As always the Spaniards suggested that if British officials wanted to end the traffic why did they not do so first in Brazil, where it was greater? As a matter of fact the British were doing just that, since at this time Brazil more than any country frustrated Britain's world-wide abolitionist crusade. On April 22, 1850, London announced that British cruisers would enter Brazilian territorial waters and take any suspected ship. Guardships were stationed in Rio harbor and emancipados collected therein, as formerly in Havana harbor. Brazilian forts exchanged shots with British ships. A complete break in diplomatic relations was avoided when the Emperor, hinting at resignation, succeeded in inducing the Brazilian Parliament to accept the law of September 4, 1850, which again declared slave trading a crime of piracy, as in 1826, but now the law provided for strict enforcement. A bond was required of all shipmasters and captains trading on the African coast, and offenders were remitted to courts of admiralty. Resistance was so strong that in order to enforce the law Emperor Dom Pedro II, who favored abolition, allowed British cruisers to seize suspected ships in Brazilian waters.[13]

The year 1850 was a turning point in Anglo-Brazilian relations. Rapidly thereafter the slave trade declined, and gradually a movement arose among the Brazilians themselves, many of whom were of mixed blood, to end the traffic and eventually slavery itself.[14]

Now Lord Howden, the new British ambassador in Madrid, could triumphantly advise the Spaniards, May 23, 1851, that "as the Spanish Government has quoted the example of Brazil, the British Government hopes that that example may be followed and with corresponding success in regulating the slave trade in Cuba and Puerto Rico."[15]

On hearing of several notorious landings of slaves in Cuba, the imperious Palmerston, fired up by his Brazilian success, decided it was high time to stop Spanish procrastination. In a note to the Spanish minister in London he delivered an ultimatum brushing aside the

[12]Primera Secretaria de Estado, Nota de la Sección, 2⁰ Sección, octubre de 1850, A.H.N. Estado, Leg. 8040, L. 9, N. 6.
[13]Percy A. Martin, "Slavery and Abolition in Brazil," *HAHR*, XIII, No. 2 (May, 1933), 151–196.
[14]*Ibid*.
[15]Lord Howden, Plenipotenciario inglés al Gobierno español, Madrid, 23 de mayo de 1851, A.H.N. Estado, Leg. 8044 (1849–1851), L. 11, N. 13.

explanations of the captain general and Spain's insistence on her treaty rights:

My Lord:

His Majesty's Government is desirous of coming to a plain understanding with the Government at Madrid, and to make that Government comprehend that Great Britain will no longer consent to be baffled in regard to the Spanish Slave trade as it has hitherto been, by unsatisfactory excuses and by unperformed assurances given at Madrid, while the Spanish authorities in Cuba have continued systematically and notoriously to set at nought the stipulations of treaty and to violate the enactments of law. It is high time this system of evasion should cease. His Majesty's Government demand from the Spanish Government a faithful and honorable fulfillment of the treaty engagements of the Spanish Crown and His Majesty's Government throw upon the Government of Spain the whole responsibility of any consequences which may arise from a longer continuance of a breach of faith in this respect . . . [16]

Such direct and forceful language could scarcely be misunderstood. The fact was that during the years 1848–1851 relations between Britain and Spain had been verging on war, and yet the final showdown would never come, for in the meantime a series of events occurred that were to distract the course of Anglo-Spanish diplomacy by placing the United States in the role of the major aggressor. Although fear of American designs on Cuba was not new—such a fact had helped shape Spain's Cuban policy since the 1820's—it was not until the war with Mexico that the United States assumed the same importance as Britain in the foreign relations of Spain.

Before the war with Mexico a stream of Cuban exiles had established themselves in the United States and had begun to make active propaganda in favor of the annexation of Cuba to that country. They started newspapers in New York, New Orleans, and the port cities of Florida,[17] and found sympathy among Southerners, who eyed Cuba as

[16] Lord Palmerston to Isturiz, Foreign Office, London, September 11, 1851, to Her Catholic Majesty, A.H.N. Estado, Leg. 8044, L. 11, N. 8.

[17] The most important early leaders of the Cuban exiles were Gaspar Betancourt Cisnero (*El Lugareño*), José Aniceto Iznaga, and Cristóbal Madan, a planter who later abandoned the cause of annexation. Madan, who claimed American citizenship, typified the confused revolutionary ideology among certain planters. Betancourt, the supreme voice of the annexationists, and Iznaga founded the propaganda organ *La Verdad*, which first appeared in January, 1848, and continued to be a source of embarrassment to the Spanish government until December, 1853. Later, others joined the annexationists in exile, including Do-

a potential slave state. No doubt the exiles had some influence in President Polk's effort to buy Cuba in 1848.[18]

As already indicated, since 1841 Cuban proprietors were considering annexation to the United States as a means of protecting slavery against British abolitionist proposals.[19] For this reason the exiles believed it possible to attract American imperialism to Cuba; the result was a network of conspiracy. As the war in Mexico drew to an end, well might Spanish authorities fear that a blue horde of Yanquis would swoop down on Cuba next. The Spanish representatives in the United States reported wild rumors of imminent expeditions against Cuba. In a sense, victims of their own system of political distrust, espionage, and censorship, the authorities were unable to separate fact from fiction. The Cuban revolutionaries, realizing this, played mercilessly on this credulous tendency of the Spanish government.

Also in circulation were rumors of the plans of American and British abolitionists to liberate Cuba through bases in Jamaica and Haiti,

---

mingo Goicouria, Spanish-born merchant and zealous annexationist, associated with projects for promoting white immigration, and El Conde de Pozos Dulces, another outspoken reformer of the planter class. Following the example of Texas independence and annexation to the United States, this group organized the secret Order of the Lone Star for the same purpose (Herminio Portell Vilá, *Narciso López y su época 1848–1850*, pp. 8–42).

[18]After the close of the Mexican wars Secretary of State Buchanan instructed Romulus M. Saunders in Madrid, June 17, 1848, to offer $50,000,000 or more for the voluntary cession of Cuba by Spain. The main arguments were (1) that the United States feared that Britain, whose ambassador Bulwer had just been expelled from Madrid, would seize Cuba, as she was seizing Central American territories; (2) that possession of Cuba was vital to America's internal interests as well, since it would serve to heal the controversy on slaves between North and South; and, furthermore (3), that it would pay Spain to sell Cuba, since it was known that the Creoles hated Spanish dominion and would start an insurrection at any time. But notwithstanding these arguments and several others, the Government of Narváez refused to entertain the offer. (James Morton Callahan, *Cuba and International Relations: A Historical Study in American Diplomacy*, pp. 207–215.)

[19]The annexationists in the United States were in intimate contact with conspirator movements in Cuba, including *la conspiración de la mina de la Rosa Cubana*, discovered by the government near Cárdenas in July, 1848. The leader, Narciso López, had been planning a revolt among the criollos since 1842. After discovery he fled to New York, September, 1848, to organize an annexationist invasion with his fellow exiles. An attempt was then made to coordinate this invasion with the plans of another group of Creole conspirators in Havana (El Club

and through the cooperation of various Cubans secretly organized in Masonic societies. Referring to British and American abolitionists, the Spanish government said that without a doubt "the principal focus of those plots, cautiously protected by the British government, existed in London, but that from both English and Americans came thousands of pamphlets exciting Cuban slaves to rebellion."[20]

In view of these threats, it was easier to justify the despotic system of Cuba and to deny all abolitionist measures. As the Spanish Ambassador in Washington warned: "If the present system is not maintained the island will be lost and the colored race will triumph."[21]

The situation was made even more complicated by the French Revolution of 1848 in Europe, the first news of which reached Havana by the English steamer *Arrow* on March 28, 1848. Following the settled policy of strict censorship, the Cuban government attempted to confine the news within the circles of official interpretation. But soon news of the Revolution in Paris and the dramatic abolition of slavery in the French West Indies was common talk on Havana's sidewalks. Newspapers published by Cuban exiles in the United States, *La Verdad* of New York, for example, somehow always managed to penetrate the wall of censorship. Such publications exploited the French abolitionist example and argued that Spain must follow the course of the civilized world and free the slaves; this propaganda, together with reports of debates on the European Revolution in the American Congress, "[has] not failed to cause some effect and misgivings in the minds of many inhabitants," as Governor Alcoy admitted. The Cuban conspirators thus played upon the proprietors' fear that the French Revolution would also triumph in Spain and thereby abolish Cuban slavery. As a result annexationist feeling assumed an ominous shape, and a worried governor elaborated on the need, now greater than

---

de la Habana), who since the ending of the Mexican War were negotiating for American troops for the purpose of annexing Cuba. Leading members of this group were famous names in the Creole reform movement: Miguel de Aldama, José Antonio Echeverría, Manuel de Carrera, José Luis Alfonso. There were thus two conspiracies underway. The problem was to coordinate them—a difficult task, since the Havana group were more concerned with protecting the slave economy (Portell Vilá, *Narciso López*, pp. 83–91; Robert Granville Caldwell, *The López Expeditions to Cuba 1848–1851*, pp. 40–45).

[20]Correspondencia, Nota de la Sección de Gobernación. Mayo de 1847, A.H.N. Ultramar, Leg. 4628 (1845), N. 37.

[21]O'Donnell cartas, informes del Capitán General al Ministro de Gobernación, 29 de abril de 1847, A.H.N. Ultramar, Leg. 4628, N. 37.

ever, to keep the island, "submissive, faithful and united to the Metropolis; to this I will respond with my life."[22]

Thus far Spain had followed a policy of enforced silence on the slave question—a policy of "hush" as some called it. But now the mere mention of abolition should be anathema. According to Alcoy, every Spaniard, regardless of party, must consider it a matter of national honor and interest to sustain slavery in Cuba and thereby Spanish dominion:

> Your Excellency knows very well that the existence or the emancipation of the slaves . . . is the most serious question that could arise . . . a matter of life or death for the interests of all the inhabitants, because slavery constitutes the principal property and the only productive element . . . It made the island prosperous and causes envy among foreigners.
>
> Emancipation would be the ruin of the proprietors and merchants of the island. It would put an end to the only means for preventing the island's falling to the English or American annexationists.[23]

Alcoy would employ the threat of abolition in case the island was threatened by political insurrection:

> As for myself, Your Excellency, I maintain the conviction that this terrible weapon [a decree of emancipation] could in the last extreme prevent the loss of the island, and if the inhabitants convince themselves that it will be used, they will tremble and renounce every illusion before bringing upon themselves such an anathema.[24]

In the face of the annexationist threat, Spain received rather unexpected help from the long-suffering José Antonio Saco. His *Ideas on the Incorporation of Cuba into the United States*, published in Paris in November, 1848, attempted to arouse a patriotic conscience among the Cubans in order to reject annexation. Saco pleaded with his countrymen not to sell their birthright for the chimera of American incorporation. If Cuba were a small, sterile, insufficient island, he would not object to its pacific annexation, ". . . but an island that is one of

---

[22]El Capitán General El Conde de Alcoy da cuenta de haber recibido noticias de la revolución francesa, La Habana, 28 de marzo de 1848, *ibid.*, N. 40.

[23]El Conde de Alcoy al Excmo. Sr. Secretario de Estado, La Habana, 19 de julio de 1848, *ibid.*

[24]Conde de Alcoy al Ministro de Estado, 9 de septiembre de 1849, cited by Raúl Cepero Bonilla, *Azúcar y abolición: Apuntes para una historia crítica de abolicionismo*, p. 45.

the largest of the globe and has within itself so many elements of power and greatness is an island that can have a brilliant future."

Referring to the hopes that had sustained him through fifteen years of exile, Saco protested that it would be a greater sacrifice to live as a foreigner in his own country under the American flag. "The day that I throw myself into a revolution . . . it will be for my own country." This appeal to the "true interests" of Cuba by the patriarch in exile undoubtedly caused many to reconsider the ultimate meaning of annexation, especially when it was suggested that an invasion might ignite a slave rising.[25]

In the same manner in which he lectured the Cubans on erroneous thinking, Saco addressed himself to Spain. The concession of long overdue reforms would be the only way to conserve Cuba, he warned. Saco still believed that Spain would listen to Creole complaints.

Nevertheless, the annexationists in the United States marched forward with their plans, insisting that the Cubans were ready to throw off the yoke of Spain. The López expeditions to Cuba (1850–1851) confirmed the worst fears of the Spaniards. The first attempt was blocked by President Tyler's strong proclamation of August 11, 1849.[26] But López continued to find encouragement in the Southern states. In April, 1850, López, accompanied by American filibusters, set sail from New Orleans with the idea of liberating the island from Spain and annexing it to the United States.[27]

Few inhabitants would dare openly to receive the filibusters, even though López insisted that Cuban slave institutions would be protected.[28] After a narrow escape the expedition returned to Key West.

[25] Saco's argument that some of the annexationists would inevitably seek the support of the Negroes against Spanish government added to the fears of the proprietors that an annexationist invasion—unsupported by the power of the United States government—would set off a slave insurrection. (*Ideas sobre la incorporación de Cuba en los Estados Unidos* [pamphlet] in *Contra la anexión*, I, 33–67). Saco was supported, even led in these arguments, by Domingo Delmonte, who believed Spain was capable of conceding the desired reforms to the criollos. Leading annexationists Cristóbal Madan, Pedro de Agüero, and José Alfonso, all reflecting the planter psychology, were soon converted to this point of view. Through the years 1848–1852 Saco and Delmonte engaged in a polemic war of pamphlets and epistles with Betancourt Cisneros and other resolute annexationists, who could never trust Spain to concede reforms.

[26] Caldwell, *López Expeditions*, pp. 54–55.

[27] *Ibid.*, p. 59.

[28] In this last expedition, López carried the following decree guaranteeing slavery to the proprietors, from whom he expected cooperation, eventual or im-

López was now a more popular hero than ever in the South. He would not be dissuaded from a third attempt, and in August, 1851, eluding the authorities again, he headed for Cuba with the "immortal 400."[29] The entire expedition was captured by the tough General José de la Concha, who had replaced Alcoy as governor of Cuba. Colonel William S. Crittendon of Kentucky and fifty Americans were shot before foreign consuls intervened to save some of the expeditioners. The dauntless López was executed, *muerte en garrote vil*, on September 1, 1851, after his calm prophecy that his death would not change the destiny of Cuba.[30]

Riots broke out in New Orleans and Mobile upon the news of the executions. Spanish citizens were attacked in the streets and the Spanish consulate threatened. Upon receiving news of these insults to the flag of Castile, the Spanish government demanded reparations or a break in diplomatic relations.[31]

Calderón, the Spanish ambassador, wisely counseled his government to postpone any rash action until President Fillmore sent his annual message to Congress (December 2, 1851). Calderón found the

---

mediate: "Don't be frightened, Cubans, of the scarecrow of the African race that has served so often the tyranny of our oppressors. Slavery is not a social phenomenon exclusive to Cuba, nor incompatible within the liberty of citizens. Modern and ancient history shows us this, and nearby you have the example of the United States, where three million slaves do not prevent the flourishing of the most liberal institutions in the world . . . We will respect and we will defend property such as it exists today." Vidal Morales, *Iniciadores y primeros mártires de la revolución cubana*, I, 165.

[29] But no concerted plan had been achieved between López and the Creole planters or the conspirators of El Club de la Habana. The planters, even the most radical, feared that a revolutionary invasion would arouse the slaves. They could not confide in López as much as they could in Captain General Alcoy to preserve slave institutions. The risk to achieve a new political order was not worth the economic sacrifice involved. El Club, once it was realized that the American government would not support the invasion, did not want a revolution, but only wanted to place pressure on the Spanish government in order to achieve reforms. López, in moving ahead with his plans, was forced to break with both groups—in essence they were the same—and to place his hopes on the rising of the Creole masses in the interior, although he still counted on the cooperation of the planters after the initial success of the invasion (Portell Vilá, *Narciso López*, pp. 58–72, 150–162).

[30] Caldwell, *López Expeditions*, p. 118.

[31] Instrucciones al Ministro español sobre los incidentes de Nuevo Orleans, 1 de octubre de 1851, A.M.A.E., Leg. 1466 (1843–1852).

message on the whole satisfactory, especially Fillmore's words condemning Cubans who abused the hospitality of the United States, and his statement that "our true mission is not to propagate our opinions but to teach by example." Nevertheless, Spain continued suspicious.[32]

The boldness of American filibusterism threatened to upset the balance of power in the Caribbean and alarmed France and Britain, who in 1852 suggested that the United States government agree to a joint proposal guaranteeing Spanish sovereignty over the island of Cuba. But the American government haughtily refused a proposal that would limit its manifest destiny. Said the *Daily Union* of Washington on October 26, 1853: "That silent life in death existence, known as the *Status quo* in nations is abhorrent to nature, to God, to the progress of mankind ... and to the great American law which has created our existence."[33] The *Baltimore Clipper*, October 21, 1853, saw a sinister abolitionist plot behind the joint proposal.

During these turbulent years the slave trade waxed rather than waned. True, it had tended to decrease after the law of 1845 until the end of O'Donnell's administration, but beginning with the government of Alcoy (February, 1848–November, 1850) there was a rise in the number of slave importations. As already indicated, Alcoy pretended ignorance but there is reason to believe that he was protecting the trade. In the first place, he could say that it was necessary to conserve the island against revolutionary threats, and secondly, it was known that he was very popular with the slave merchants and slave buyers and that he had made a fortune in Cuba. On the occasion of his leaving the island the merchants and proprietors gave him a gift of fifty thousand pesos so that he could continue to protect their interests in Madrid.[34] It was said that under Alcoy the Queen Mother's share of each "sack of coal" delivered to Cuba was protected by gov-

[32]Calderón underlined the following passage of Fillmore's as dangerous: "The deep interest which we feel in the spread of liberal principles and the establishment of free governments, and the sympathy with which we witness every struggle against oppression forbid that we should be indifferent to those in which the strong arm of a foreign power is invoked to stifle public sentiment and repress the spirit of freedom in any country." Mensaje del Presidente de los Estados Unidos al Congreso, *ibid*.

[33]Calderón in reporting the mood of the American Congress said that it could be summarized in those two resolutions of Cromwell: "Resolved: 1. that the saints inherit the earth: and 2, that we are the saints." Artículos de la prensa Americana, A.M.A.E., Leg. 1467 (1854–1855), N. 151.

[34]Portell Vilá, *Narciso López*, p. 442.

ernment officials.[35] This court revenue may have been one of the reasons why the Narváez government opposed the negotiations to sell Cuba in 1848.

It is not surprising that the Spanish Court should derive revenue from this source, if such were the case. It was always easy to dignify the slave trade as a patriotic duty and to secretly defy the arrogant, self-righteous British. According to English officials, the great body of the people of Havana were not easily scandalized; they had no sense of any injustice in the trade.[36]

The new master of the island, General Concha, did little to please the British. In the first of his three commands in Cuba (November, 1850–April, 1852) undertaken after Alcoy's failure to prevent the first landing of López, he made it emphatically clear that he had come mainly to defend the island militarily and to crush Creole conspiracies. Though he was a terror to the disaffected Creoles the slavocrats were soon at ease with him, for he was disposed like Alcoy to regard slavery as an ally to Spanish dominion, although like Alcoy he carried the usual formula of instructions for closing the trade.

Concha also used the threat of invasion for arbitrarily exercising emergency faculties. Under Concha there were administrative reforms but no political concessions to the Creoles. Those planters who had followed Saco's and Delmonte's argument that Spain was capable of reforming her colonial policy without resort to rebellion were suffering their disillusions.

The exiles, meanwhile, had learned from the López failure that slavery was the obstacle to a unified movement. The slave business, disguised as Spanish "patriotism," served to divide and morally undermine the unity of the Creole class, who, although detesting Spanish tyranny, were incapable of risking material interests. As Rauch put it: "The slave-owners in their complaints against Spain turned against the slave-trade, but they did not stop buying *bozales*."[37]

Naturally, the Spanish government knew that the key to conserving Cuba was a prosperous slave economy. Under Concha's severe but efficient administration sugar production expanded, and more high-

[35]See footnote to letter of Gaspar Betancourt Cisneros to Saco, August 14, 1849, José Antonio Fernández Castro (ed.), *Medio siglo de historia colonial de Cuba, cartas a José Antonio Saco de 1823–1879*, p. 125.

[36]Accounts and Papers, *BFSP*, XIX, cited by Hubert S. Aimes, *A History of Slavery in Cuba, 1511 to 1868*, p. 172.

[37]Basil Rauch, *American Interest in Cuba: 1848–1850*, p. 37.

ways and public works, the sweet fruits of Roman despotism, embellished the island. Concha, satisfied with his first command in Cuba, could still insist that slavery was the only basis of this prosperity, and that slavery, if not the slave trade, should be protected and not tampered with.[38] Thus Cuba moved into the second half of the nineteenth century.

[38] José Gutiérrez de la Concha, *Memoria sobre el estado político, gobierno y administración de la isla de Cuba*, pp. 258–260.

7. A More Serious Effort To Suppress the Slave Traffic, 1851-1860

> The prosecution of the slave trade brings us the friendship and consideration of England . . . As for the defense at all costs of existing slavery, even England, convinced that we can do no other thing to keep our colony, does not reject it . . .
>
> Captain General Pezuela, 1854[1]

In spite of the rising importations of bozales under Alcoy and Concha, the government at Madrid manifested a more consistent desire, if not policy, to reduce the slave trade to a tolerable minimum, largely because it was proving to be a source of continuous international embarrassment and a threat to the internal security of the island. Again the colonial officials went through the motions of applying alternative plans, some suggested by the proprietors themselves, for the readjustment of the Cuban economy as if they thought that some day the annual flow of from ten thousand to fifteen thousand Africans would cease.

As we have already suggested, there is a long history of Spanish efforts to promote free white labor in Cuba. Every time the supply of slave labor was threatened the government took a new interest in this subject. That had been the meaning of the immigration act of 1817, which followed the first abolition treaty. Following the law of 1835 against the traffic the government recommended an investigation of

---

[1]Capitán General Pezuela al Sr. D. Leopoldo A. de Cueto, Plenipotenciario español en Washington, La Habana, 1 de julio de 1854, A.H.N. Ultramar, Leg. 4648, N. 3.

the means for remedying the lack of field laborers. It was said that in 1839, 240 laborers were contracted from the Canary Islands and that in 1840 the planter Miguel Estorch made one of the earliest experiments with free contract labor on his plantation (La Colonia), contracting 90 laborers from Cataluña.[2]

Before the terror produced by the slave risings of 1840–1843, a few people like Saco, for example, preached the economic utility of free white labor. The law of 1845 in pursuit of the traffic stimulated a number of recommendations. Saco's work of 1845 condemning the traffic and favoring free labor has already been mentioned. In the same year Vázquez Queipo produced a memorandum in which he discussed the pros and cons of free labor. He estimated that slave labor cost 70 pesos a year per unit and free labor around 140 pesos, but observed that the rising cost of slaves, due to the measures against the traffic, together with the high degree of mortality to which they were subject, tended to favor free labor.[3]

Of the various remedies suggested, the government found that the simplest to put into effect was a tax on domestic or household slaves. With the object of forcing this class of slaves into field work, a capitation tax of one peso was decreed on July 29, 1844, and amplified on December 18, 1849, and March 22, 1854. If an owner employed more than one slave in household service he had to pay a progressively higher tax; for the first slave two pesos, for the second three pesos, and so on.[4]

The inactive Junta de Población Blanca, established in 1817, was abolished in 1842. The decree of 1844 consigned the funds derived from capitation taxes to the Junta de Fomento, now charged with promoting white immigration. Then followed the royal order of February 8, 1845, which directed Spanish consular agents abroad to prepare passage for immigrants. Domingo Goicouria, commissioner of colonization of the Junta de Fomento, expressed the hopes of the government's plan. Within a year five hundred Spanish and European agricultural colonists, aged eighteen to forty, were to be brought to Cuba under contract at government expense, the colonists to repay half of the expenses within a term of three years after being placed in em-

[2]Julio J. Le Riverend Brusone, "Historia económica," *Historia de la nación cubana*, Ramiro Guerra Sánchez et al. (eds.), IV, 189.
[3]Vicente Vázquez Queipo, *Informe fiscal sobre fomento de la población blanca en la isla de Cuba*.
[4]*Colección de disposiciones sobre esclavos, 1840–56*.

ployment. The plan was to shift more slaves into the canefields and make tropical labor more attractive for the whites, who were to be employed in tobacco and coffee cultivation, in the industrial side of sugar production, in administrative work on the haciendas, or as artisans.[5]

But since nothing immediately materialized from these plans, it occurred to the Junta de Fomento, as it already had to the Council of State, to look elsewhere for the solution to the labor problem. In 1847 the first Chinese were introduced on a contract-labor basis for a period of eight years, the contract subject to voluntary renewal if desired. A number of prominent planters subscribed for the laborers, hoping that they would prove as efficient as Negroes and less costly.[6]

In 1849 the first contingent of Yucatecan Indians, numbering 135, arrived in Havana, contracted by the merchant Carlos Tolmé. They were acquired at a cost of twenty-five pesos and sold at around one hundred pesos, but they were never imported in large numbers because they did not prove satisfactory. They were treated as cruelly as slaves, and at one point the Mexican government momentarily prohibited this commerce.[7]

At first the Chinese proved almost as disappointing as the Indians. Feeling that they had been deceived, they not only were difficult to manage but also fell victims of the diseases of Cuba and imported some of their own (Asiatic cholera, for example). The initial cost of a Chinese laborer was from one hundred to two hundred pesos, while that of a good African slave was six hundred pesos; but allowing for sickness, fatalities, and salaries of four pesos per month, the planters soon discovered that during a contract period of eight years Chinese labor could be just as expensive and less efficient, unless employed in

[5] Elías Entralgo, "Historia social," *Historia de la nación cubana*, Guerra (ed.), III, 328–329.

[6] The Chinese immigration was organized like the slave trade, asientos being given to companies which brought coolies from Hong Kong and Macao. The firm of Villoldo, Waltrop y Cía was conceded a contract in 1852 to introduce six thousand Chinese, for example. The price of each coolie laborer was fixed at 125 pesos; they were, in this case, to serve a minimum of four years. During this period they could be bought, sold, and transferred like slaves. *Ibid.*, III, 334–335.

[7] The first Yucatecs came from prisons, to which they had been condemned after the terrible Caste War ending in 1848. They had been sold on the pretext that it would improve their condition and relieve Yucatan of dangerous enemies of the white race. Their numbers never exceeded 2,000. The census of 1861 listed 1,047 "Mexicans." Le Riverend Brusone, "Historia económica," pp. 192–193.

household service or given lighter work in the sugar mill. Coolies tended to flee the plantation, to find shelter in the cities, and to enter upon a small business.[8]

According to Sagra, Chinese labor gave disappointing results because the proprietors did not know how to use or manage a more intelligent labor force. The coolies, who had "voluntarily obligated themselves" to perform any labor task, were governed at first by the same system applied to slaves. The regulations of April 10, 1849, authorized the use of the whip, irons, and imprisonment for a coolie who resisted labor duties or the commands of his superior.[9] Suicides were frequent. Some Chinese, as did some Africans, believed that death freed their spirits to return home. Later on, more humane controls—partly due to British protests—were placed on coolie labor. And some hacendados, like Fernando Diago, using a method of persuasion and rewards, proved that coolie labor could be very satisfactory.[10]

One planter, Feijóo de Sotomayor, who experimented with Chinese laborers, contended that slaves were preferable, since at the end of eight years the planters still retained an investment in them. Even white contract labor for a period of five years would be better, he declared, and to prove it he set about organizing a colonizing company for the purpose of attracting free laborers from Galicia.[11] Several hundred *gallegos* were thus introduced. But these workers soon rebelled against the working conditions, the climate, and breach of contract, and ensuing judicial action ruined both the company and Feijóo.[12]

The general failure of schemes for promoting contract labor, together with increasing pressure against the slave traffic, led some to reconsider the idea already expressed by the Council of State on several occasions, that is, the reproduction of slaves, and the importation of "free African labor." Torrente, that consistent defender of the status

---

[8]Urbano Feijóo de Sotomayor, *Isla de Cuba. Inmigracion de trabajadores españoles. Documentos y memoria*, pp. 27–45.

[9]Ramón de la Sagra, *Cuba en 1860, o sea cuadro de sus adelantos en la población, la agricultura, el comercio y las rentas públicas, suplemento a la primera parte de la historia política y natural de la isla de Cuba*, pp. 43–44.

[10]*Ibid.*

[11]Feijóo de Sotomayor, *Isla de Cuba*, p. 54.

[12]Years later, in 1861, other gallegos were employed in the hacienda of the Count of Pozos Dulces, another experimenter in free labor. Le Riverend Brusone, "Historia económica," p. 191.

quo, also argued in favor of conserving slave numbers by more humane treatment.[13]

For various reasons Cuban proprietors showed little interest in raising slaves commercially.[14] And the British naturally opposed "free African labor." Once more attention shifted to schemes for promoting yellow, red, and white contract labor. The decree of March 22, 1854, opened a two-year period during which Chinese and Yucatecan labor, as well as white European, could be contracted.[15] In the meantime, an estimated thirty thousand Chinese laborers had entered through the port of Havana in the period of 1847–1853.[16] And the cost of a coolie had gone up considerably, along with the price of contraband slaves.[17]

It is already abundantly clear that while the government was attempting to sporadically promote alternative solutions to the labor problem, the slave traffic flourished. Betancourt Cisnero, a Cuban annexationist, claimed that it was a notorious fact that the traffic had

[13]Torrente also argued in favor of free African labor to be imported with or without British permission. Mariano Torrente, *Bosquejo económico, político de la isla de Cuba*, pp. 420–425. In another work Torrente went into more detail in explaining a plan for free African labor based on a contract system of eight years as in the case of Chinese labor. The contract would also pay the passage, and provide medical assistance, food, clothing, and a wage of four pesos per month. "I am in favor of every kind of immigration," said Torrente, "because I know they need labor in Cuba," *Política ultramarina que abraza todos los puntos referentes a las relaciones con los Estados Unidos, con la Inglaterra, y las Antillas y señaladamente con la isla de Santo Domingo*, pp. 171–172, 209.

[14]Roland T. Ely, citing several sources, discusses why slaves were not reproduced commercially in Cuba as in Virginia and Kentucky. Among the reasons: a large, acclimated Negro population in the American South at the time of the closing of the traffic in 1808, whereas in Cuba most slaves at that date were fresh importations; better living conditions for Southern slaves, and the nature of cotton cultivation, which found female labor useful, whereas in Cuba sugar production favored the sale of male slaves, and the relentless competition in this business did not favor investments of time or money in slave-breeding farms; and, probably the most important reason of all, the laws against the traffic were rigidly applied by the United States government, whereas in Cuba the proprietors could always count on Spanish leniency.(*Cuando reinaba su majestad el azúcar. Estudio histórico-sociológico de una tragedia latinoamericana: El monocultivo en Cuba, origen y evolución del proceso*, pp. 488–491).

[15]Le Riverend Brusone, "Historia económica," p. 191.

[16]Entralgo, "Historia social," p. 334.

[17]Richard Henry Dana reported that the cost of a coolie had risen to $340. This suggests that planters valued coolies for certain types of work. *To Cuba and Back: A Vacation Voyage*, p. 212.

been reorganized under the Duchess of Rianzares, mother of Isabel II,[18] and that merchants and officials like Antonio Parejo, Manuel Pastor, and José Forcade were importing thousands of African slaves and claiming that they came from Brazil.[19] True or not, few bothered to raise a doubting eyebrow at such accusations.

In any case, the transient nature of Spanish ministerial government still permitted the slave interests to defy the orders of the government against the traffic, and even when and if the authorities in Cuba had the good intention to suppress this commerce, they found that they lacked the legal instruments for enforcing the laws and confiscating illegally acquired slaves. But, at the same time, from motives of national pride, real or alleged, Spain consistently refused to let the British take a further hand in the problem.

Britain's exasperating position remained unchanged. Fearing that the Americans would seize Cuba, she could but come to Spain's aid by underlining the status quo in the Caribbean. But at the same time could the British government, under great abolitionist pressure at home, cease to demand a halt to treaty violations?

The continuation of the slave trade and the abuses practiced on from three to four thousand emancipados could not fail to aggravate a government whose jaded ministers tired of insisting that the same was an intolerable breach of faith. We have seen that at the time when Britain and France were attempting to commit the United States to a pledge guaranteeing the possession of Cuba to Spain, diplomatic relations between Spain and Britain teetered on the brink of hostilities. In January, 1853, Lord John Russell wrote ominously to Lord Howden in Madrid that whatever might be the interest of England in not seeing Cuba in the hands of any other power (namely the United States), yet if such a transfer could terminate the slave trade, a large compensation would be gained. "For such an exhibition of public feeling the government of Spain should be prepared."[20] The year 1853 was, in fact, the high-water mark of British abolitionist pressure and Spanish resentment. At one point the Spanish Council of State concluded that if Spain was prepared to go to war with the

[18]Carta a José Antonio Saco, Nueva York, Agosto 30 de 1848, José Antonio Fernández Castro (ed.), *Medio siglo de historia colonial de Cuba, cartas a José Antonio Saco de 1823–1879*, p. 88.

[19]Carta a José Antonio Saco, Nueva York, Agosto 7, 1849, *Ibid.*, p. 121.

[20]*Report on the Slave Trade*, cited by Thrasher, Alexander von Humboldt, *The Island of Cuba*, pp. 34–35.

United States concerning her rights in Cuba, ". . . it is necessary to adopt the same resolution with regard to England."[21]

Yet both nations were moved to make concessions, and, as previously indicated, the conciliating factor was a mutual fear of the United States. Britain, wanting to believe in the promises of each new ministry, returned to a more sympathetic attitude. Spain, completely unprepared for a showdown with Britain and needing the moral support of the British lion against the yanqui annexation threat, decided on—it may come as a surprise—a bold new course of action calculated to please allies and confound enemies.

As the new Prime Minister, the Count of San Luis, explained to the Queen, ". . . a system of new measures" was needed to close the trade, and yet provide for an adequate labor supply. Spain was resolved to fulfill "solemn treaties" with England, but no measure would be proposed that would undermine the discipline of the slave system. The solution would consist of liberty for the emancipados and a slave registry, as originally provided by the law of 1845. All slaves found unregistered after a certain date would be freed. The proprietors would not thereafter risk buying bozales, and would "forever abandon so unworthy a traffic." Aside from removing the British pretext for intervention, and gaining her good will, the registry would actually serve "to secure for proprietors a legitimate title to their slaves."[22] The object of the registry, therefore, was not to liberate all contraband slaves, but only to put an end to future purchases of contraband slaves.

At the same time, as we have already seen, the planters would be guaranteed a sufficient labor supply if (1) domestically employed slaves were forced into the field by means of a capitation tax, (2) Negro marriages were encouraged; and (3) immigration was promoted and properly regulated. By immigration the government meant Spanish, Yucatecan, and coolie contract labor.[23]

The dissident Creoles would protest, but Spain would create a loyal Negro militia to overawe them and help defend the island against filibusters. Also, Spain held as a reserve weapon for maintaining the loyalty of annexation planters the hint of complete abolition, such as Alcoy had suggested. Such a threat would also give the yanqui im-

[21]Opinión de la Sección de Estado, Secretaría de Estado, Palacio, 9 de abril de 1853, A.H.N. Estado, Leg. 8048, L. 15, N. 10.

[22]Exposition to Her Majesty from the Count of San Luis, Madrid, March 22, 1854, *BFSP* (1854–1855), XLV, 1083–1089.

[23]*Ibid.*

perialists the message loud and clear: Spain would turn over the island to the Africans sooner than to the Southern expansionists. In the words of Rauch:

> The plan was ingenious as it seemed to satisfy perennial British demands ... provided for a new labor supply made necessary especially after the epidemics swept away 70,000 slaves in the summer of 1853, and, if carried out, would make Cuban annexation anathema to the American South. On the other hand, it entailed a risk that it would provoke intervention ... The fact that preoccupation of Britain and France with the Near Eastern crisis reduced their ability to support Spain in Cuba gave Spanish daring the quality of desperation.[24]

The man chosen for this difficult mission, Juan de la Pezuela, son of one of the last viceroys of Peru, was known to be an austere, incorruptible servant of the Crown. During his two-year command as governor of Puerto Rico (1849–1851) Pezuela had made a reputation as an enemy of slavery. In the smaller island he had vigorously persecuted the slave traffic (never a great problem in Puerto Rico) and befriended the slaves in many ways, rigorously inspecting their condition, fining cruel masters, and dictating other humanitarian measures. With the exception of the usual slavist complaints, the work of Pezuela was generally appreciated in Puerto Rico, where slavery never had had the hold that it did in Cuba,[25] and where miscegenation of races had blurred the distinctions between black and white castes.

But if the Spanish government thought that Pezuela would have a similar success in Cuba, they little understood the basic differences between the two islands. In Cuba the slave trade was engrained into a flourishing sugar and tobacco economy. Creole planters, Spanish merchants, and conniving officials, who socially formed distinct and even mutually hostile castes, were nevertheless bound together by a common bond of business interests. These groups all joined in professing "unconditional loyalty" to the mother country but *only on condition* that Spain protect the economic interests of the Ever-Faithful Isle.

Success was doubtful from the start, for Pezuela's reputation preceded him to Cuba. Fully aware that British diplomats were exercising the strongest pressure upon the Madrid government, the slave

---

[24]Basil Rauch, *American Interest in Cuba: 1848–50*, pp. 277–278.
[25]Marqués de Rozalejo, *Cheste o todo un siglo 1809–1906: El Isabelino tradicionalista*, pp. 161–162.

An Effort To Suppress the Slave Traffic, 1851–1860

interests feared the worst. Rumors had it that Pezuela was arriving with orders to abolish not only the slave traffic but also the institution of slavery itself; and that the Count of San Luis had made a secret agreement with the British to abolish slavery for an unstipulated sum of money.[26] On arriving in Cuba, December 3, 1853, therefore, Pezuela was coldly received.

The worst fears of the *negreros* were realized when Pezuela, contrary to the usual pattern (that of his immediate successor Cañedo, for example), refused to be bribed into complicity. He gave orders to seize not only all Negroes fraudulently introduced but also the owners and organizers of the expeditions as well. His stern procedure forced his subordinates to take a similar attitude. Not only this, but Pezuela made common cause with the Bishop of Santiago, Padre Antonio María Claret, who had been fighting a lonely campaign to improve the material and moral condition of the slaves.[27] Pezuela took special interest in the case of the unfortunate emancipados, and at the request of the Bishop dictated a decree permitting the marriage of a white man with a colored woman, which the slavists claimed was forbidden by the law of the Indies.[28] He also established a militia, into which he would admit free blacks as well as whites.

These measures of "Africanization" alone would have sufficed to alarm the slaveholders. But it appeared that Pezuela intended to do much more, and this gave credence to the charge that he had come upon an abolitionist mission. Pezuela ordered that all emancipados introduced since 1835 should be set free. This was soon followed by a decree giving freedom to all emancipados, with no exceptions.

Before Pezuela's day the slave question had never been discussed in the press. Now, however, at the instance of Pezuela, the *Diario de la Marina*, organ of the government, began to print a series of articles attributed to the Captain General, in which the previous policy of the government was condemned. The new position called for the fulfillment of treaty obligations.[29] The *Diario* also began to stress the advantage of a free-labor system as demonstrated by the Northern States of the American Republic. The language was alarming, and excited

[26]*Ibid.*, p. 178.
[27]*Ibid.*, pp. 176–177.
[28]*Ibid.*, p. 179.
[29]*Diario de la Marina*, 6, 7 y 8 de diciembre de 1853, Biblioteca Nacional Madrid.

the greatest fears.[30] To make matters worse, Pezuela's circulars repeated the same ominous and exciting language. He spoke of the government's plan for permitting the introduction of free Negro apprentices from Africa, as well as Indian, Chinese, and Spanish contract labor as substitute for slave labor.[31] Such measures led the slave interests to fear the worst, or in the words of American Consul William H. Robertson: "It cannot, in my opinion, escape an intelligent mind that the object of these preparations is the liberation of all the Africans imported in the Island since 1820."[32]

Of course, Cuban exiles in the United States, and certain dissident planters, seeking to revive annexationist hopes, seized the occasion and gave further currency to the rumor that Spain had secretly promised to abolish slavery in Cuba in exchange for British aid in maintaining the Spanish flag over the island—a rumor also calculated to arouse the Southern states into insisting on immediate annexation of the island. The expansionist elements in the United States were particularly sensitive to Cuban affairs after the disaster of the López expeditions. A series of disagreeable incidents involving American rights and Spanish territorial jurisdiction in Cuba had already threatened to precipitate war: the detention of the *Crescent City*; the rifling of American mails; the imprisonment of an American consul. More important, the Kansas-Nebraska Bill for adding free states to the Union could be made more acceptable to the South if Cuba could be acquired as a slave state. The Pierce administration hoped to purchase or acquire Cuba by diplomatic means, and sent the Louisiana expansionist Pierre Soulé to Madrid for this purpose.

Soulé from Madrid and Consul W. H. Robertson from Havana, a fast friend of Cuban annexationists, sought every means to precipitate a crisis favorable to American annexation and the dream of a Southern slave empire. They sent a steady stream of alarming reports to Washington. In March, 1853, the expansionist Secretary of State Marcy sent Charles W. Davis as a special agent to Cuba to investigate Robertson's urgent communiqué that Spain was attempting to Afri-

[30]*Ibid.*, 26 de diciembre de 1853.

[31]Juan de la Pezuela, *Circular*, 23 de diciembre de 1853, Biblioteca Nacional Madrid.

[32]W. H. Robertson, Acting Consul of the United States at Havana, to W. L. Marcy, Secretary of State, Havana, April 21, 1854, William R. Manning (ed.), *Diplomatic Correspondence of the United States: Inter-American Affairs 1831–1860*, XI, 764–766.

canize Cuba under a secret agreement with the British, and that the slave interests, Spanish and Cuban, had formed a united front and were daily expecting the Great American Eagle to fly to their aid before Cuba was lost forever to the white race.[33] Robertson thoughtfully prepared an invasion "Proclamation" addressed to the inhabitants of Cuba and recommended that President Pierce use it word for word: "The Eagle will protect your lives, your families, your property, and the social condition of your country."[34]

While Davis went about preparing an "objective report" in company with Robertson, the Consul himself wrote:

> The cry is *Revolution*—arms are being procured as fast as possible. A fusion has taken place between the Old Spaniards and Creoles, which only the most imminent danger could have brought about. There is a spirit among them that I have never given them credit for . . .
> I do not relate to you the accounts of the growing insolence of the negroes. They speak of the Marquis de la Pezuela as "tití Juan," or "Papa Juan," the Patron of Liberty and Equality.[35]

Pezuela's circular concerning the introduction of free Negro "apprentices" and the sailing of Spanish ships to Africa for this purpose was, of course, attributed to British influence, even though the British opposed African apprentices and Yucatecan Indians as a disguised form of servitude. Nevertheless, Secretary of State Marcy wrote to Buchanan on July 2, 1854, that the United States did not complain against Britain enforcing her treaty stipulations in regard to the emancipados, but that if it should prove true that she was using her influence to fill Cuba with emigrants from Africa so that when Spanish rule was over it should become an African colony given over to barbarism, ". . . she ought to be conscious that she is concurring in an act which in its consequences must be injurious to the United States."[36]

Rumors were now so widespread about a secret treaty of abolition with Britain that the Spanish government was forced to make official denials. Adding his indignation to that of the metropolis, Pezuela

---

[33] William H. Robertson, Acting Consul of the United States at Havana, to William L. Marcy, Secretary of State, Havana, May 11, 1854, *Ibid.*, XI, 785–787.

[34] As cited by Philip S. Foner, *A History of Cuba and Its Relations with the United States*, II, 80.

[35] Robertson to Marcy, May 11, 1854, Manning (ed.), *Diplomatic Correspondence*, XI, 785–787.

[36] William L. Marcy, Secretary of State, to James Buchanan, U.S. Minister to Great Britain, Washington, July 2, 1853, *Ibid.*, VII, 84–95.

stated that Spain did not need the aid of a foreign power to sustain her interests in Cuba, and called the rumor a "detestable invention ... false in every way."[37]

At the same time Pezuela attempted to enforce the law of 1845. The major defect of that law had been constantly brought to the attention of the Spanish government by British diplomats, namely, that the authorities of Cuba were not empowered to enter the plantations in pursuit of contraband slaves, and that the lack of an effective registry of slaves made it impossible to tell which were contraband and which were legal. As Pezuela pointed out, once the slave ship had succeeded in landing its cargo on an obscure inlet, it was virtually impossible to pursue the matter further. It was said that a Negro bought in Africa for forty duros was sold in Cuba for seven hundred; and since many leagues of coastline made it extremely difficult to prevent landings, the huge profits involved encouraged slavers to defy British and Spanish squadrons.[38]

As already suggested, Pezuela removed some officials, for example, the governors of Trinidad and Santo Spiritus, because of their failure to prevent the landing of bozales in their jurisdiction.[39] But he soon realized that he did not have sufficient authority to pursue the slave traffic in the interior of the island, and was forced to admit that he could not carry out the registry. As an outcome of the complaints of Pezuela and the British, the Spanish government decided to add one more measure to the "new system of measures."

The celebrated decree of May 3, 1854, for the first time authorized Spanish officials to enter all plantations under suspicion of contraband practices, and to carry out Article Nine of the law of 1845 concerning the registration of all slaves. Again, careful emphasis was put on maintaining the discipline of existing institutions; registration officials were not to commit any act that "could lower the prestige of the master or administrator in the eyes of the slaves." The law provided for an annual registration of slaves after the August harvest, in which

[37]Prologue to the decree of May 3, 1854, *Diario de la Marina*.

[38]Testimony of the abolitionist deputy Pastor, debate on the inefficiency of the law of 1845, April 18, 1866. *Diario de las sesiones de las Cortes, generales y extraordinarias 1810–1898, Senado* (1865–1866), I, N. 50, 595.

[39]Lord Howden, British minister in Madrid, expressed his profound satisfaction at this action. Howden to Calderón de la Barca, Madrid, 11 de abril de 1854, A.H.N., Estado, Leg. 8047, L. 13, N. 12.

age, name, sex, and origin of the slave would appear, as well as all information concerning the acquisition, loss, or alienation of the same. Article Three declared free all contraband slaves thus discovered. Article Four warned all civil and military authorities that they would be separated from their employment if on hearing of a disembarkation of slaves they would fail to notify the government within twenty-four hours. Article Five applied the same penalty to any lesser officials involved, "since it is not possible to effect an embarkation without the connivance of minor officials." Article Six subjected all those proved to be occupied in the slave trade to a two-year exile.[40]

"Now," said Pezuela concerning the new decree, "the spectacle of an impotent authority must come to an end. Avaricious interests that place private gain above the national honor can no longer be tolerated."[41] Noble words, but so powerful and so universal was the opposition in Cuba to this new law that it could not be enforced. The slave interests talked openly of revolting against the government, and at the same time, as noted in another place, the revived annexationist movement took on a more portentous significance. The Creole proprietors would not permit the authorities to enter the plantations, nor supervise the registration of slaves, claiming that this was a gross violation of the rights of private property.

On May 22, 1854, Davis presented a written report to Secretary of State Marcy.[42] Not surprisingly, it confirmed all of Robertson's dark warnings. Speaking of Pezuela's measures, Davis said: "The conclusion is irresistible that the emancipation of the Slaves and consequent Africanization of the Island is the true object had in view, and to which the March is as rapid as circumstances will allow." As to a secret treaty with England, "... the new policy must be the result of a Treaty—for on any other ground the conduct of both nations is inexplicable."

The report then went on to give an excellent summary of the complaints of disaffected Creoles against a cynical Spanish regime that

---

[40]El Marqués de la Pezuela, Decreto del 3 de mayo de 1854, *Gaceta de la Habana*.

[41]*Ibid*.

[42]Charles W. Davis, United States Special Agent to Cuba, to William L. Marcy, Secretary of State, Washington, May 22, 1854, Manning (ed.), *Diplomatic Correspondence*, XI, 789–795.

used slavery and the slave trade to hold them in subjection. The United States cannot stand idly by, wrote Davis:

> Should emancipation be carried out (as it undoubtedly will be) of Slaves imported since 1820, its inevitable immediate result will be . . . a disastrous bloody war of the races, a step backwards in the civilization of America—and, in a commercial view, an immense loss to the United States . . . should the United States remain passive spectators of the consummation of the plans of the British Ministry the time is not distant in which they will be obliged to rise and destroy such dangerous and pernicious neighbors.

Meantime, the menacing wave of reaction in Cuba forced Pezuela to a sudden retreat. On May 30, 1854, he proclaimed that the government would not interfere with the social institutions of the island and in a desperate effort to be conciliatory, he reversed the gist of previous affirmations, making the surprising admission that the slave in Cuba was a thousand times more happy placed among civilized men and protected by laws and religion than other classes in Europe which had freedom in name only.[43]

How much Pezuela was deterred from his abolitionist course by the implicit threat of intervention by the proslavery Pierce administration is difficult to say. It would be the greatest disgrace, he had said, referring to the grumblings in North America, and the preparation of a new filibuster expedition under General Quitman, to change this policy for frivolous causes.[44]

In "Africanizing Cuba" and in detaining the *Black Warrior* (February, 1854), Pezuela directly challenged the proslavery, proannexationist Pierce administration. In the *Black Warrior* affair Soulé presented exorbitant demands, which the Spanish government simply ignored. Spain could not be forced to sell Cuba, nor could Soulé and Marcy directly force the removal of Pezuela. In a last desperate move Soulé put a hand to the Ostend Manifesto (October 18, 1854).[45] This crude public threat designed to intimidate Spain into selling or giving up Cuba only hardened Spain's determination to hold the Pearl of the Antilles at any cost.[46]

[43]Pezuela, *Circular*, 30 de mayo de 1854, Biblioteca Nacional Madrid.
[44]Pezuela al Sr. D. Leopoldo A. de Cueto, 1 de julio de 1854, A.H.N. Ultramar, Leg. 4648, N. 3.
[45]The Manifesto was signed at Aix-la-Chapelle by James Buchanan, John Y. Mason, and Soulé, American ministers to Great Britain, France, and Spain, respectively, with the unwitting encouragement of W. L. Marcy, secretary of state.
[46]In a confidential dissent the United States secretary of legation at Madrid,

The decisive factor forcing Pezuela's retreat from partial abolitionist measures, and then his removal, was the unexpectedly firm union of Spanish mercantile interests and Creole planters, who threatened to welcome the American filibusters with open arms. Pezuela was either unable to explain the limits of the "system of new measures," or he was unable to play one group off against the other, and he certainly could not rule the island with the support of a Negro militia. The charge was that Pezuela was ruining the prosperity of the Ever-Faithful Isle for peninsular and Creole alike. Too weak to sustain the Governor, and probably feeling that in his zeal he had exceeded orders, Madrid decided to replace the abolitionist governor (December, 1854).

Pezuela's administration at least marked the first conscientious effort by the Spanish government, no matter what the motives, to extinguish the slave trade, to liberate the emancipados, and at the same time to follow a new tack in foreign policy that now sought to win the good will of Great Britain. The British government expressed profound satisfaction with Pezuela's efforts.[47] But Spain was by no means about to try another noble experiment in "Africanization."

Pezuela's measures concerning the mass liberation of illegally introduced slaves and the right of investigating officials to enter plantation boundaries were, of course, abandoned. Nor was this the only setback to British abolitionist hopes.

The following countries had upon English insistence and example declared the slave trade to be piracy and deserving of the death penalty: the United States, Brazil, Portugal, Mexico, Russia, Argentina, Nueva Granada (Colombia), Venezuela, and Ecuador. No better proof of a lack of a secret treaty with England was Spain's consistent refusal to declare the slave trade piracy. While Pezuela undertook his dangerous program, Lord Howden proposed the measure several

---

Horatio J. Perry, called Soulé's policy "a complete failure." As a diplomat, Soulé "has mistaken his career." Then Perry added: "Cuba will be ours, not by threats but by peaceful promotion of commerce and geographical advantage," Perry to W. L. Marcy, Secretary of State, Madrid, September 6, 1854, Manning (ed.), *Diplomatic Correspondence*, 685–695.

[47]According to Sedano the British government relaxed abolitionist pressure on Spain after the Pezuela administration had won British sympathies, *Cuba desde 1850 á 1873. Colección de informes, memorias, proyectos antecedentes sobre el gobierno de la isla de Cuba, que ha reunido por comisión del Gobierno D. Carlos de Sedano y Cruzat, ex-diputado á Cortes*, pp. 178–179.

times. On one occasion Spain answered (October 29, 1854) that the enemies of Spain were already falsely claiming Africanization in order to drive the slaveholders into the arms of the United States, and that Spain would not give them another pretext.[48] Howden answered obstinately that if Spain declared the slave trade piracy it would be showing her enemies that she was not trying to flood Cuba with Africans.[49] Even as Pezuela faced defeat in Cuba, Howden persisted (December 23, 1854), "It must be indescribably painful to an honest and energetic Captain-General to find that he is unable to carry out his purposes." The trouble was, said Howden, that the laws were inadequate. If piracy was declared, "it would fill all England with joy from one end of it to the other."[50] One can only imagine what Spain uttered in reply.

Foreign abolitionists continued to pelt the Spanish government with remonstrances devised to shame the Spaniards into keeping their promises. One exposition in particular, that of the British and Foreign Missionary Society, dated March 2, 1855, and sent to General Espartero (Duque de la Victoria), at that time head of the Spanish government, was notable for its use of calculations taken from the Spanish authorities themselves. Quoting figures from the *Memorias* of José de la Concha, former captain general of the island, the abolitionists asserted that 150,000 slaves should be free, that is, if Spain would abide by the treaties of 1817 and 1835. They reminded Spain of her promise of the sixteenth of March, 1853, to free all slaves illegally imported since 1817, as well as all slaves imported since 1835 who had completed five years of apprenticeship.[51]

Speaking for the Spanish Council of State on British abolitionist demands, Isidro Díaz de Argüelles responded that nothing more could be done to solve the slave problem until opinion in Cuba asked for it. "For my part," he said, "it will not be possible to extirpate this cancer until public opinion comes to reject it as prejudicial to the in-

---

[48]Señor I. F. Pacheco to Lord Howden, Madrid, October 27, 1854, *BFSP* (1854–1855), XLV, 1116–1119.

[49]*Ibid.*, October 29, 1854, XLV, 1120.

[50]*Ibid.*, December 23, 1854, XLV, 1121–1122.

[51]*Exposición al General Espartero por la British and Foreign Missionary Society*, London, December 21, 1855 (written in Spanish), A.M.A.E., Leg. 1467 (1855).

terests of the Island, and as immoral and reprehensible in itself."[52] Evidently Spain and Cuba had yet to develop an abolitionist conscience.[53]

Pezuela meanwhile was succeeded by José de la Concha, who for the second time took command of Cuba (December, 1854–December, 1859). Thus returned the terror of the filibusters: the man who had shattered the López expedition of 1851, and dictated peace in the island. Concha, who by now had made it his peculiar destiny to save Cuba for Spain, again threw himself into the work of thoroughly stamping out annexationist sentiments. He followed with consuming intensity the activities of the Cuban exiles in the United States, and not in vain, for his discovery and crushing of the Pintó conspiracy, which was connected with annexationist plans, proved to be a mortal blow to filibuster aspirations. The much heralded Quitman expedition never sailed. The Cuban exiles, who now were plunged into fraternal quarrels, could not raise another expedition.

Concha could write the filibuster epitaph on February 27, 1855: "I believe, in effect, that I have dominated the internal situation completely; not only will parties in favor of filibusters not arise, but in case the filibusters come again they will be met with more hostility by this country than was the López expedition."[54]

Opinion in the United States, especially in the North, meanwhile had veered against filibusters, Cuban exiles, and the authors of the Ostend Manifesto. The *National Intelligencer* of Washington (April 14, 1855) observed that, after all, Spain had refused to sell Cuba, and

---

[52]Opinión de la Sección de Estado, Secretaría de Estado, Palacio, 4 de julio de 1855, A.H.N. Estado, Leg. 8048, L. 15, N. 15.

[53]During this period of fervent criticism Mariano Torrento continued to defend Spanish honor in London through a series of letters to the British press: the reports of slave introductions were, of course, exaggerated; the captain general could not fully employ the army and navy in the suppression of the traffic because he must hold them in reserve for filibuster threats; the slave trade controversy could be settled with less cost to England if the latter would permit Spain to import free blacks on the same conditions as Chinese labor; Lord Carlisle and the Bishop of Oxford exaggerated when they said England would withdraw support for Spanish dominion in Cuba unless Spain harkened to the wishes of British abolitionists (*Slavery in the Island of Cuba, with Remarks on the Statements of the British Press Relative to the Slave Trade*).

[54]Concha a L. A. de Cueto, Plenipotenciario Español en Washington, La Habana, 27 de febrero de 1855, A.H.N. Ultramar, Leg. 1467 (1854–1855), N. 2.

that the people of Cuba had demonstrated that they did not want to be annexed to the United States.⁵⁵

During his first administration (November, 1850–April, 1852) Concha had not distinguished himself as a castigator of the slave trade.⁵⁶ He seemed rather to have condoned it as necessary to maintenance of Spanish dominion in the island and essential to a governor's popularity with the Spanish party. But, like Pezuela, Concha now arrived with strict orders to suppress the traffic. He later claimed that this had been his only reason in assuming command: "The obligation to fulfill treaties made with England . . . with this idea I came to take command over this island."⁵⁷ Indeed, immediately after arrival he began to issue a series of decrees against participation in the traffic. The explanation of this zeal lies partly in the fact that the well-informed Concha was one of the first to realize that the Cuban exiles would raise the standard of abolition.

The final breaking point of the annexationist movement occurred in 1855, when the Cuban Junta of New York was dissolved and the outstanding leaders, Valiente, Betancourt Cisneros, and El Conde de Pozos Dulces, disheartened, took up residence in Paris, and more important, in the same year (June 10) Domingo Goicouria, another exile, issued to all Cubans a manifesto which had the effect of clearing the air after the manner of Tom Paine's *Common Sense*. Events had proved, cried the manifesto, that the Americans had failed the Cubans. Rather than beg for American aid, the price of which was annexation and Negro slavery, the Cubans must confess their error and adopt as their ideal both independence and the emancipation of all slaves.⁵⁸

Whereas the Cuban exiles had once sought to attract Cuban slave proprietors by representing annexation as a safeguard for Cuban slavery, they now sought to attract the rank and file of Cuban criollos. And whereas the Cuban exiles had once sought to interest the South in Cuba by flattering it with the vision of another slave state, they now sought to attract the abolitionist North with the vision of a Cuban Republic in which slavery would be abolished. The idea of Goicouria

---

⁵⁵*Ibid.*

⁵⁶Rozalejo, *Cheste o todo un siglo 1809–1906*, p. 179.

⁵⁷Debate in the Cortes on the projected law in suppression of the slave trade of 1866, April 18, 1866, *Diario, Senado* (1865–1866), I. N. 50, 594–595.

⁵⁸Ramiro Guerra y Sánchez, *Manual de la historia de Cuba (económica, social y política)*, pp. 528–529.

quickly took root in the minds of Cuban revolutionaries, even though annexation would still have its dogged supporters till the end of the nineteenth century.

Concha readily understood the dangerous implications of an appeal to the abolitionist North, to world liberal opinion, and to the Creole masses in Cuba. He solemnly warned the Spanish government (July 12, 1855) that the Cuban rebels, defeated militarily and despairing of help from the Southern states, would raise the flag of abolition of slavery "in order to find support in the Northern States, and above all in England."[59]

The Spanish government, learning from the Pezuela failure, decided to publicly reassure Creole proprietors as to the limits of Concha's policy. As previously indicated, Cuban officials were to castigate the slave trade but the slave institution itself was not to be touched. The Spanish Minister of State, Luzuriaga, asked the Cortes to approve a status quo policy:

> The Government of Her Majesty entertains the inmost conviction that slavery is a necessity and an indispensable condition for the maintenance of landed property in the Island of Cuba, and has sought to anticipate the sentiments of the Honorable Deputies by giving these property-holders assurances ... never to meddle with the system in any manner whatsoever.

The Cortes approved the proposal unanimously.[60]

Also concerned about Concha's true aims, and still hoping to get another slave state, the Pierce administration sent August Caesar Dodge as American minister to Spain (August, 1855) with instructions to impress upon Spain the American concern that Pezuela's policies would not be revived, since they were instigated by British abolitionists and other enemies who were seeking through Cuba to undermine slavery in the South. Spain had no difficulty in sincerely replying that there was no secret abolition treaty with Britain and that Spain regarded slavery as an indispensable element in Cuban prosperity.[61]

[59]Comunicaciones de Concha referentes al estado político y reformas que convendrán hacer para evitar el éxito de las tentativas de rebelión. Carta de 12 de julio de 1855, A.H.N. Ultramar, Leg. 4645 (1850–1855), N. 8.

[60]Claudio Antón de Luzuriaga to Horatio J. Perry, United States Chargé d'Affairs ad interim at Madrid, Palace, March 12, 1855, Manning (ed.), *Diplomatic Correspondence*, XI, 854–857.

[61]Dodge to Marcy, August 26, 1855, State Department, Diplomatic Des-

Spain wisely refrained from provoking further incidents involving American rights on the high seas. When James Buchanan, one of the authors of the Ostend Manifesto, ascended to the presidency in 1856, Spanish-American relations had taken a more pacific turn. The abolitionist question in the United States would soon deflect Buchanan's interest from Cuban affairs.

Concha's efforts to suppress the traffic were only partially successful. Like Pezuela, he failed in the attempt to enforce a census against the opposition of the slave interests. Concha attempted to invent an alternative system for checking on illegally introduced slaves, namely, personal identification tags (*cédulas personales*) to be placed about the neck of every slave. However, this system fell to earth because neither slave owners nor officials would cooperate, and so Concha reluctantly had to abandon it, except in the case of Yucatecs and coolies, who could not be disguised as slaves.

Judge Crawford of the mixed court wrote that at least 6,408 slaves were landed in 1855, of which only 125 had been captured. Since 3,012 coolies and 416 Yucatecs had also been imported, Cuba had received almost 10,000 new field hands.[62] The following year Crawford reported that 5,478 slaves had been landed with only 54 captured. In spite of Concha's efforts, "the slave trade continues to be carried on ... almost with impunity." Concha's system of cedulas was so imperfect that it actually protected purchasers of contraband slaves, since owners could buy false registration tags.[63] Almost all slave ships were being fitted out in the United States with the help of Portuguese agents, who simply refused to give up slaving activities. Crawford wondered if steamships would be the answer to speedy slavers.[64]

Finding the laws and authority of the government ineffective in stopping the traffic, and painfully aware of new expeditions in preparation, Concha proposed that the Cuban government be empowered to exile by decree anyone suspected of being involved in a slave expedition. This stark proposal caused the peninsular government to sit

---

patches: Spain, XI, N.A. Cited by Philip S. Foner, *A History of Cuba and Its Relations with the United States*, II, 105.

[62]Her Majesty's Acting Commissary Judge Joseph T. Crawford to the Earl of Clarendon, Havana, January 14, 1856, *BFSP* (1855–1856), XLVI, 928–931.

[63]Her Majesty's Commissioners to the Earl of Clarendon, January 31, 1857, *Ibid.*, XLVI, 850–851.

[64]Her Majesty's Commissioners to the Earl of Clarendon, September 29, 1857, *Ibid.*, XLVI, 1085.

up in alarm and, after hasty consultation with the Superior Tribunal of Justice, it disallowed the measure as being too arbitrary. Concha, thus balked in his determination to stop the traffic, resigned the governorship in disgust and abandoned the island on December 12, 1859.[65]

Thus the metropolis continued with a policy that can only be termed weak and inadequate. If Madrid wanted to stop the slave trade because it was a continual source of international danger and embarrassment, it was obviously incapable of taking the necessary drastic measures and facing up to the arrogant slavocrats. It refused to declare the slave trade piracy, and, now in Concha's case, it refused to exile suspected slavers. If Concha's solution seemed extreme and arbitrary it was because higher Spanish authorities were unwilling to provide an adequate alternative solution for a colonial governor charged with putting an end to the slave trade.

Nor, as we have seen, was the Spanish government willing to accept proposals of foreign aid in the suppression of the traffic—proposals that were again occasioned, it must be confessed, by Spain's own weakness in the matter. Lord John Russell, successor to Palmerston's policies, proposed a conference (1860) to be held in London and to be attended by representatives from Spain, France, England, Portugal, the United States, and Brazil. The object of the conference would be adoption of convenient measures for "putting an end to an increasing traffic, and to finally assure its complete abolition." Russell bluntly told the Spanish government that the slave trade in Cuba was expanding partly because American ships and capital were increasingly engaged in the deplorable business. Among the nations agreeing to suppress the slave trade, said Russell in a burning accusation, "only the government of Spain had continued to conceal and protect it."[66]

According to the Spanish government, such accusations were unfair. Did not Spain's efforts and sacrifices in keeping the English

[65] José Gutiérrez de la Concha, *Memoria sobre la guerra de la isla de Cuba y sobre su estado político y económico, desde abril de 1874 hasta 1875*.

[66] Nota, Sección de Estado, 2 de mayo de 1860, A.H.N. Estado, Leg. 8048. Russell reported on September 10, 1860, just before Lincoln's election, that eighty-five slave ships had been fitted out in North American ports in the last eighteen months, that twenty-six of these vessels had landed from twelve to fifteen thousand slaves in Cuba. In spite of American protests, Britain again began detaining American ships off the African coast (Hugh G. Soulsby, *The Right of Search and the Slave Trade in Anglo-American Relations 1814–1862*, pp. 152–159).

treaties deserve more consideration? Had not the price of slaves tripled in Cuba? Spain was insulted by the repetition of old charges. The Spanish Ministry of State felt that such "bad sounding words" could only have an effect on Spain contrary to that intended by Russell. The agreements with Britain, as they stood and as they were interpreted by the British government, had already prejudiced the interest of Spain sufficiently. Spain, now playing United States support against Britain, flatly rejected the proposed conference, insisting that she would not permit other powers to examine a treaty that existed only between Spain and England.[67]

At this point the abolitionist picture seemed dismal enough. Over four decades had now passed since the treaty of 1817; yet little progress had been made in eliminating slavery and the slave trade in the Spanish West Indies. The seeds of new developments, nevertheless, had already been sown, and, as will be seen in subsequent chapters, more would be accomplished abolitionwise in the next decade than in all the previous ones.

[67]Nota, Sección de Estado, 2 de mayo de 1860, A.H.N. Estado, Leg. 8048. Tassara, Spanish Minister in Washington, conferred with Secretary of State Lewis Cass on the matter of the conference proposed by Russell. Cass saw a sinister motive behind the proposal, namely that the British wanted to reassert their claim to visit foreign ships. The Americans had the same complaint as the Spanish: the British were overbearing in exercising their right of search. This claim to search the Americans had never been admitted, and would not be. Cass agreed with Tassara that the slave trade was not on the increase. He was reported as saying: "In this policy of the English there is something of fanatic self-interest." What was necessary in Cuba was a firmer policy on the part of Spain, said Cass; this would best solve the slave-traffic problem there (Tassara al Secretaria de Estado, 24 de abril de 1860, *ibid.*, N. 54).

8. Signs of Change, 1855-1865

> I found on returning to the Island . . . a Creole abolitionist party that went everywhere crying against slavery, condemning it as immoral and barbarous, the remarkable thing being that . . . the majority live directly from slave labor . . .
>
> Here everyone knows that the idea that explains this abolitionism—is not what it seems—it is the death of Spanish dominion in the Antilles . . .
>
> Barras y Prado, 1864[1]

In spite of rigid censorship, the inhabitants of the Spanish Antilles were surprisingly abreast of world affairs, and more responsive to international currents of thought than Spain herself. This was due partly to commercial intercourse with the United States and Britain, partly to the feeling of kinship that Cubans and Puerto Ricans had with the republics of South America, and partly to some very remarkable men of arts and letters, Creoles, born on the islands, like José Cipriano de la Luz Caballero of Cuba, and Rafael Cordero of Puerto Rico, who taught younger generations a liberal credo.

As the Creoles grew conscious of themselves as Cubans the cultural schism between Spain and Cuba gradually widened through the years. Not only was it possible for the sons of the Creole slaveholders to find liberal educators in the islands, but they often traveled to the United States and Europe in search of wider horizons. Cuban stu-

---

[1]Antonio de las Barras y Prado, *La Habana a mediados del siglo XIX: Memorias de Barras y Prado publicadas por su hijo Francisco de las Barras y Aragón,* p. 252. Barras y Prado was a Spanish merchant who lived in Havana for a number of years, returning to Spain for the last time in December, 1862.

dents and travelers in Spain usually suffered disenchantment with the political situation there and the gross ignorance concerning the colonies. Culturally, they tended to compare Madrid unfavorably with New York, London, Paris, or Berlin. Some of them regretted profoundly that their own destinies should be limited by affiliation with a decadent power.

Physically close to the United States, sending the bulk of their export trade there, the Cubans were especially infected by the "go-ahead spirit" of American merchants and politicos.[2] Judge Robert Madden, of the mixed court, said in 1849 that Cuba was slowly but steadily becoming Americanized.[3] Concha observed in his *Memoria* of 1851 that changing customs due to contact with the most democratic and anti-Spanish part of the New World would necessarily produce a change of ideas; "... naturally, these ideas must be unfavorable to Peninsular interests."[4]

Add to this, said Concha, students who emerge from the law and medical schools of Havana with exaggerated pretensions, and finding no place for themselves in the system, "are so many malcontents." The notorious corruption of the colonial administration was another factor. A people thus governed, concluded Concha, would naturally turn to any means in order to separate themselves from a society that oppressed them.[5]

Concha's first administration in Cuba (November, 1850–April, 1852) coincided with the first reform hopes in Cuba and Puerto Rico, and Concha's famous *Memoria* of 1853 was the first important recognition by a Spanish official of the justice of many Antillian demands. The *Memoria*, which was widely read in Madrid, caused some Spaniards to view colonial problems — especially the division between the peninsulares and the criollos — in a different light.

[2]*Ibid.*, p. 70. In 1850 the United States shipped an estimated eight million dollars of goods to Cuba and bought in return twelve million worth of Cuban goods, 84 per cent of which were sugar products. A Spanish traveler in 1859 was surprised to find Singer sewing machines in the most remote corners of the island (Felipe Pazos y Roque, "La economía cubana en el siglo XIX," *Revista Bimestre Cubana*, XLVII, No. 1 [enero-febrero, 1941], 83–106).

[3]James Morton Callahan, *Cuba and International Relations: A Historical Study in American Diplomacy*, p. 201.

[4]*Cuba desde 1850 á 1873. Colección de informes, memorias, proyectos, antecedentes sobre el gobierno de la isla de Cuba, que ha reunido por comisión del Gobierno D. Carlos de Sedano y Cruzat, ex-diputado a Cortes*, p. 17.

[5]*Ibid.*

Salustiano de Olózaga, a Progressive Party leader, raised the question of Cuban participation in insular affairs in the Cortes in December, 1854. His action and Concha's recommendations led to the petition of December 26, 1854, in which merchants and proprietors of Cuba requested, among other things, representation in the Cortes that had been denied in 1837. The unity of merchants and proprietors on this question was partially due to the fact that an increasing number of Spanish merchants were becoming landholders in Cuba.[6] Many of the peninsulars in Cuba saw the necessity of political and economic reforms, at least.

But this reform stir produced few results as yet. For one thing, not even Concha's liberal views went so far as to include political reforms. In common with the most reactionary Spaniards, Concha feared that political reforms would lead ultimately to independence. He thought administrative reforms sufficient to cure the rampant corruption of insular administration and to pacify the complaining Creoles.[7] But some cognizance was now shown of the dangerous division between peninsulars and Cubans, especially since other men versed in Antillian affairs, like O'Donnell and Pezuela, supported Concha's affirmations. Cautious administrative reform might allow a greater voice to the Creoles in insular affairs.

General Francisco Serrano, who succeeded Concha as governor of Cuba on November 24, 1859, carried instructions from Madrid "not to close the doors on reform hopes, but on the contrary to keep them alive and satisfy them in so much as they do not become dangerous."[8]

An important factor in the failure to achieve political reforms in the 1850's had been the lack of any organized reform party in the island. However, under the liberal policy initiated by Serrano it became possible to organize such a party.

Serrano's administration (November 24, 1859–December 10, 1862)

---

[6]Ramiro Guerra y Sánchez, *Manual de la historia de Cuba (económica, social y política)* p. 536. Also, *Información: reformas de Cuba y Puerto Rico*, I, Introducción, xxx–xxxiv.

[7]"Now is not the time to touch upon any political question," said Concha. "Any concession made suddenly would give him [the Cuban] a motive for believing that he had a right to demand more, and who knows where the pretensions of the majority of these inhabitants would stop? . . . What is urgent is to fully enter upon administrative reforms." "Memoria de 1851," *Cuba desde 1850 á 1873*, p. 21.

[8]*Ibid.*, p. 94.

fortunately corresponded with one of the longest and most stable Spanish ministries, that of the Liberal Union composed of Moderates and Liberals. Headed by O'Donnell, former governor of Cuba, this ministry lasted from June, 1858, to March, 1863. The new stability permitted a more vigorous foreign policy at the time when the United States was entering upon civil war. Buchanan's offer to buy Cuba was summarily rejected in 1859; the Moroccan War, 1860–1861, was carried to a successful conclusion; Spain participated in the intervention in Mexico; and the Dominican Republic was annexed to Spain (1862).

Since the United States was now preoccupied, the force of the annexationist and independence sentiment in Cuba subsided and the O'Donnell ministry felt free to begin a policy of *atracción* toward the disaffected elements in Cuba. This is what Serrano, married to the daughter of a rich Creole family, began to implant.[9]

Encouraged by his instructions, Serrano secretly proposed (November 12, 1860) to Madrid that Cuba be governed by an "organic law," which would serve as a kind of charter of rights for the Cuban people. Basing his project on the theory of *asimilación*, Serrano felt that Cubans were entitled to the rights and obligations of Iberian Spaniards. The rights of petition, of freedom from arbitrary arrest and illegal confiscation of property, of protection under the civil, commercial, and criminal codes of Spain — all these were to be granted.[10]

The omnipotent faculties of the captains general were to be curtailed and Cuban representatives were to be heard previous to action on important legislation or decisions. Representation in the Cortes was to be granted on the basis of one white representative for each 75,000 white taxpayers. Article Nine of this project would guarantee to the inhabitants their property in slaves. "This is a necessity," said Serrano, "... the fear that Spain might arbitrarily dispose of this property without previous consideration of any kind has had more influence, perhaps, than was believed in political events in this island after 1848."[11]

Serrano, affable and liberal by nature, made headway in winning the good will of the Cubans. He conceded to them the same privilege

[9]Guerra, *Manual de la historia de Cuba*, p. 547.
[10]"Proyecto de ley orgánica de la isla de Cuba," *Cuba desde 1850 á 1873*, pp. 235–237.
[11]*Ibid.*

Signs of Change, 1855–1865

enjoyed by the peninsular party since 1834, that is, the privilege to meet informally and to advise the insular government on matters of policy.[12]

Domingo Dulce (December, 1862–July, 1865), who succeeded Serrano as governor of Cuba, continued the same *política de atracción* toward the Creole party. Dulce, like Serrano, was an exceptionally liberal military man; he did not abuse the arbitrary powers with which he was invested as governor but sought to rule the island in concord and harmony. He was equally aware that the idea of separation was gaining ground rapidly in Cuba, for the causes previously mentioned, and he understood that Spanish dominion could not be preserved under an antiquated colonial system.[13] This he knew had cost Spain the loss of the mainland colonies. In order to arrest separatist tendencies, Dulce followed Serrano's lead — apparently both were influenced by the English colonial system — by inviting the participation of the Creoles in government affairs.

The reformers took advantage of this extended period of tolerance and founded a controversial newspaper, *El Siglo*, in May, 1863. Saco, who had returned for a brief visit to Cuba in 1861 after twenty-six years of exile, was offered the editorship of the proposed paper. He refused, however, believing that it was more important to have a Cuban paper in Madrid.[14] The editorship was therefore taken over by the enigmatic Conde de Pozos Dulces, a Cuban with a Castillian title, who had once been an annexationist. This was a highly significant step because it enabled the Count, Morales Lemus, José Manuel Mestre, José Antonio Echeverría, Miguel de Aldama, and other liberal leaders to diffuse their reformist ideas — cautiously, to be sure — on social, political, and economic problems. One consequence was that *El Siglo* could now challenge the more conservative reform leadership of Saco, who hitherto had been the major spokesman for the reformist Creoles.

[12]The residences of José Ricardo O'Farrill and Miguel de Aldama, prominent criollo reformers and slaveholders, became the centers of these informal meetings. José Morales Lemus, José Manuel Mestre, José Luis Alfonso, José Silverio Jorrin, Nicolás Azcárate, José Antonio Echeverría, José Valdés Fauli, and other hacendados and business and professional men were participants. Guerra, *Manual de las historia de Cuba*, p. 551.

[13] See the interesting report presented by Domingo Dulce (El Marqués de Castel-Florite) to the Colonial Minister Alejandro Castro, *Informe al Ministro de Ultramar*.

[14]Luis M. Pérez, *Estudios sobre las ideas políticas de José Antonio Saco*, p. 50.

Under the astute direction of Pozos Dulces the new periodical rapidly gained popularity, and it soon became the recognized voice of the Creole reform movement. As such it engaged in head-on discussions with *El Diario de la Marina,* organ of the Spanish party and the slavocrats. During the administration of Serrano, the so-called "unconditionally Spanish party" was formed to combat the growing influence of the reformers in the Cuban government. Each side sought desperately to ingratiate itself with the Captain General, the Cubans to seek more liberty, the peninsulares to repress those liberties which threatened privilege. As long as the Captain General tolerated the *siglistas* (Creole supporters of the reformist newspaper *El Siglo*), as they were called, the reform group could breathe freely.[15]

The Creole literati set about publicizing a program which included all the political and administrative reforms suggested by Serrano. In addition, they wanted a gradual solution to the slave problem. They took up Saco's old cry that the slave trade should be absolutely prohibited. All nonwhite immigration was to be suppressed and all obstacles to white immigration removed. This provision reflected acute dissatisfaction with Oriental and Yucatecan contract labor. Furthermore, the reformists proposed to study the question of existing slave institutions and to try resolving it by harmonizing the solution with the interests of the proprietors.[16]

The above program represented a remarkable evolution of thought among the criollos. The reformist group could not speak for all Creole interests in Cuba, of course, but it did represent a growing trend of opinion among the proprietors themselves on the slave question. These statements perhaps require further explanation.

The agricultural economy had in the past few years suffered periods of prolonged crisis. The causes were several. The relation of Cuban sugar to the world market was certainly one. In 1855, for example, prices of cane sugar rose; Cuban production expanded accordingly, but so did European beet sugar. The result was the depression of 1856–1858. The fact that credit had been overextended also contributed to the crisis. Since competition in sugar production required more-efficient methods for extracting and crystallizing, greater investments followed in steam-engines, chemicals, railroads, and other

---

[15]Miguel Blanco Herrero, *La política de España en Ultramar,* p. 381.
[16]The complete list of reforms is given in Guerra, *Manual de la historia de Cuba,* p. 555.

Signs of Change, 1855–1865

related items. In turn, this led to a precarious extension of credit on the part of Spanish merchants and bankers to the planters. As we have said, this process helped solidify the interests of the money-lenders and the proprietors, and gave rise to the conservative wing of the Cuban bourgeois.

The inescapable fact was that, in spite of technical improvements made in the refining end of the sugar industry, there was no method of improving the efficiency of slave labor, and no satisfactory method, as we shall see, of replacing it. Yet the price of slave labor continued to rise, thereby diminishing the profit margin. The prime factor here was the gradual closing of the slave market. Until the law of 1845 the price of a bozal was approximately 300 pesos; by the period 1855–1860 the average price had risen to 1,250 to 1,500 pesos.[17] The high cost of labor helps to explain why during the period 1850–1860 an estimated 385 ingenios disappeared.[18]

Reducing the traffic was related to other factors which forced prices upward. The slave population increased by only 43,470 from 1849 to 1860, whereas in the period of 1828–1841 it had increased by 149,000.[19] The white population, on the other hand, increased 135,828 in the five-year period 1856–1859.[20] The increasing white population caused a demand for more slaves, if only for household purposes. The process of manumission, although slowed down, served further to deplete labor resources, while the relatively unsettled interior encouraged runaways, who added to Cuba's old problem of vagrancy. Economic pressures forced proprietors to work slaves harder and this, too, accentuated the depletion of the labor force. Add to this the fact that slaves frequently fell victims to virulent diseases.

At the time of the adoption of the law of 1845, as we have seen, an awareness of these problems was shown. More-humane labor regulations were recommended in order to preserve the existing number of

---

[17]Hubert S. Aimes, *A History of Slavery in Cuba, 1511 to 1868*, Appendix I, p. 268.

[18]Julio J. Le Riverend Brusone, "Sobre la industria azucarera de Cuba durante el Siglo XIX," *El Trimestre Económico* (Mexico), XI (abril 1944–marzo 1945), 63. Cited by Roland T. Ely, *Cuando reinaba su majestad el azúcar. Estudio histórico-sociológico de una tragedia latinoamericana; El monocultivo en Cuba, origen y evolución del proceso*, p. 595.

[19]Ely, *Cuando reinaba su majestad el azúcar*, pp. 245–248.

[20]Julio J. Le Riverend Brusone, "Historia económica," *Historia de la nación cubana*, Ramiro Guerra y Sánchez et al. (eds.), p. 299.

slaves, efforts were made to force domestic slaves into field work, and incentives were offered for encouraging the commercial breeding of slaves on the ingenios, but we have already concluded that the latter effort was never successful.[21]

Nor had the importation of free white labor fulfilled expectations, not only because the government did not consistently support it but also because the whites refused to accept the "degrading work" of slaves, or found that slave labor depressed wages. Perhaps there was something to the slavist argument that unacclimated whites could not do manual labor in the tropics. Certainly it seemed to prove the abolitionist argument that labor could never be dignified in a slaveholding society. In any case, the white immigrant preferred to enter into business or commerce, or to become independent cultivators of coffee, sugar, or tobacco, or merely to return home again.

As a result of the above, it became profitable since the 1840's for smaller planters to rent their slaves to larger plantations. Also, an increasing number of white Creole laborers were being employed on the plantations.[22] In fact, white Creole production was always an important factor in the Cuban economy. The census of 1862 revealed that 41,661 whites, most of them peasant Creoles, were employed as cane workers, and that of 700,000 whites, 400,000 were working on agricultural tasks of one form or another.[23]

But none of the alternative sources of labor could fully supply the needs of the sugar planters. And since the contracting of free African labor, frequently suggested, was not allowed by the British, the planters in desperation turned again to Oriental and Yucatecan labor, even though they added to Cuba's race and vagrancy problems. At least 60,000 Chinese laborers were imported from time to time under a policy made sporadic by misgivings and uncertainties.

The great planters, who were most in need of labor resources, were the ones who experimented most with technical improvements and various forms of labor, especially Chinese laborers. On the great ingenios of Julián Zulueta, the richest planter, and Juan Poey, who knew, perhaps, more than any other man about the plantation prob-

[21] Aimes, *History of Slavery*, p. 255.

[22] According to Raúl Cepero Bonilla, slaves rented for twenty-five to thirty pesos per month, and for thirty to forty pesos at harvest time, *Azúcar y abolición: Apuntes para una historia crítica de abolicionismo*, p. 54.

[23] From the census of June, 1862, given by Fermín Figuera, *Estudios sobre la isla de Cuba: La cuestión social*, pp. 20–21.

lem, Chinese were employed in great numbers. The Las Cañas of Poey had 480 slaves and 44 coolies; the San Martín, 436 slaves and 348 coolies; the Pontifex, 289 slaves and 379 coolies.[24]

During the second command of Concha, 1856–1859, who left no doubt as to his intention to eradicate the slave trade, the government once more permitted the introduction of Chinese contract labor. In the meantime, during the period 1853–1859, more than 42,000 Chinese had been admitted to Cuba. The attitude of the Cuban reform group concerning coolies was expressed by Francisco Frías y Jacott, better known as El Conde de Pozos Dulces. Pozos Dulces, like Saco, felt that already there were too many disparate elements obstructing Cuba's cultural and economic progress. When, in another fluctuation of policy, Governor Serrano forbade Chinese immigration (1860), El Conde and the reformists covered him with felicitations.[25]

According to Pozos Dulces, Cuba wanted neither more slaves nor more Orientals, but rather a system of incentives that would attract white colonists disposed toward labor. For example, said El Conde, the white worker should be given a share of interest in the sugar industry, "... and, therefore, white colonization will not be a failure as it has been before."[26] Such preaching was in vain. By the end of the year 1860 the importation of coolie labor was again reopened at the demand of the proprietors. At the same time regulations were issued like those of 1854 that attempted to humanize the working conditions

---

[24]Julián Zulueta, born in Spain, was a wealthy Havana merchant and slave-owner. He was one of the first to experiment with coolies and to install modern machinery in his ingenios. One of his several estates was valued at $1,500,000 in 1873. He organized his own slaving expeditions. Zulueta was, perhaps, the wealthiest representative and most influential man in Cuba during this period. As a representative of banking, commercial, and planter interests he was one of the leaders of the Spanish party in Cuba, and one of the great defenders of the status quo.

Juan Poey, half-Creole, half-French, was not as wealthy as Zulueta, but politically and economically he was an influential figure not only because of the experiments worked on his plantations but also because by his writings on the economic problems of Cuba he reflected more the liberal Cuban spirit (see Aimes, *History of Slavery*, pp. 211–212).

[25]El Conde de Pozos Dulces, *La cuestión del trabajo agrícola y de la población en la isla de Cuba*. This book is, in fact, a collection of articles written by Pozos Dulces in the reformist press of Havana, 1858–1860.

[26]*Ibid.*, p. 40.

of the coolies.[27] No matter what was done for the coolie, Saco insisted that he was a plague on the island and cited the fact that according to the crime statistics for 1862, the Chinese were the most delinquent of races.[28]

The labor shortage, therefore, was giving rise to a mixed system of agricultural labor, which included slave labor, contract labor, and free labor. At the same time, the incipient process of separation between the industrial and the agricultural sides of sugar production gave emphasis to the independent cultivator, and further served to undermine the slave economy of the traditional ingenios, which combined the raising and refining of sugar cane.

Owing to the labor crisis some planters began to specialize in refining sugar. They would buy from smaller planters or independent producers part or all of the sugar cane required for the mill. Experiments of this type began in the 1840's and came to be regarded by the reformers, especially Pozos Dulces, as another possible substitute for slave labor.[29] Such experiments were stimulated by the American Civil War; Fernando Diago, for one, conceded land to colonists (1863–1864) then paid them two pesos for each one hundred arrobas of cane delivered to his mill. But these experiments were not very successful.[30]

The centralization of sugar production was still premature, since

[27]The regulations of 1860 required that contracts specifically mention the duration, the salary, the food, the medical assistance, and the number of working hours. But the fact was that the coolies were treated like slaves. They were denied all civil rights, nor could they marry without the permission of their patrons. As in the regulations of 1854, the patron could impose discipline consisting of arrest up to ten days, and loss of salary. The coolie could acquire personal property, however, and dispose of the same so long as it did not infringe upon his contract. He could approach a delegated protector and ask for a change of contract from a cruel master. At the end of his contract the coolie could not remain in Cuba unless he signed another one.

Toward the end of 1864 the immigration of Chinese coolies was legalized by the Treaty of Tientsin between Spain and China (see Elías Entralgo, "Historia social," *Historia de la nación cubana*, Guerra [ed.], Vol. III).

[28]José A. Saco, *Los Chinos en Cuba*, published in *La América* (February–March, 1864), cited by Pérez, *Estudios*, p. 54.

[29]According to Ely, the Count's brother José began such an experiment in 1836, *Cuando reinaba su majestad el azúcar*, p. 602.

[30]Riverend Brusone, "Historia económica," *Historia de la nación cubana*, Guerra (ed.), IV, 208.

Signs of Change, 1855–1865

it would require the building of more railway trunk lines and the development of more-efficient refining methods in order to offer remunerative prices to the independent planter. Capital incentives toward complete mechanization were not yet fully present in the economic situation. The majority of ingenios tended to conserve their own small mills *(trapiches)* and to supervise their own planting. It was not until a later period that the process of centralization was carried to an extreme in the founding of great central sugar refineries (centrales) that served surrounding planters. In spite of the incipient decline of the slave economy, the great majority of planters were still thinking in terms of servile labor.[31] To solve the labor crisis they frequently proposed, if not more slave labor, then, at least the importation of free African labor or coolies. José Suárez Argudín could say in 1866 that what Cuba and Puerto Rico wanted were strong African laborers — humble, peaceful, and without turbulent aspirations.[32]

Competitive conditions widened the division between large and small planters. Both were suffering from a diminishing margin of profit, and often both were in debt, but the small planter was hurt more especially in the isolated Eastern provinces.[33] The latter was less able to pay the high cost of slave or coolie labor, and since it was impossible to lower prices by reopening the traffic, he was more inclined to close it entirely, since only the wealthy planters could patronize it.

The economic crisis, therefore, coupled with the growing sense of a national destiny among the Cubans, first clearly expressed by Saco, was gradually working against the Cuban slave market. The impact of the American Civil War hastened the search for some gradual means of closing the market. The government of Serrano found

---

[31]It was evident, too, that most planters lacked the capital needed to mechanize agriculture. Cepero, *Azúcar y abolición*, p. 16.

[32]José S. Argudín testifying before the Reform Commission of 1866–1867, *Información*, I, 161.

[33]The development of large plantations did not immediately reduce the number of small holdings. The interior of Cuba offered much open land, where emancipated slaves and poor whites could live poorly but independently, preferring this existence to that of laborers on the plantations. This was one factor contributing to the reduction of the available labor force (Ramón de la Sagra, *La historia física, política y natural de la isla de Cuba*, I, xli, cited by Aimes, *History of Slavery*, p. 261).

among the planters increasing support concerning the enforcement of measures against the traffic.[34]

In 1860, according to Sagra, Cuba was producing about 26 per cent of the Western World's consumption of cane and beet sugar, Puerto Rico about 3 per cent. The Spanish Antilles supplied 20 per cent of the British market (Brazil but 10%), and about 75 per cent of the American market (Louisiana the remainder). In 1860 the total population of Cuba was given as 1,179,713, Havana having 150,000 residents, and the next city in size, Matanzas, 30,000. The free colored population was about 200,000, and the slave population was given as 367,356, of whom 40 per cent were females. The eastern end of the island (Oriente) had only about 30 per cent of the total population.[35]

Although the outbreak of the American Civil War in April, 1861, contributed to the growing realization that slavery was a doomed institution, others still could hope, in the first indecisive years of the struggle, that a victorious Southern Confederacy would serve to prolong existing slave institutions and assure Spain's hold on Cuba. In this respect the war caused a deeper rift between the criollos and peninsulares.

Formerly, the leaders of the Cuban reformist party, Pozos Dulces and others, sympathized with the annexationist movement, which was antiabolitionist. But this did not mean that they were necessarily *esclavistas*, that is, defenders of slavery. Though they depended on slave labor, the liberal leaders of Cuba identified themselves with the abolitionist Lincoln, claiming that they were on the side of civilization and progress.

But why? If the Creole leaders were still predominantly conservative on the slave question, how could they sympathize with Lincoln the Emancipator, whose example threatened the Cuban slave economy? The Cuban Marxist-historian Raúl Cepero y Bonilla has an ingenious materialistic explanation. Citing articles written by Pozos Dulces during the war, Cepero shows that the reformers feared a Southern victory, since such a victory would have radically changed the relation of Cuba to North America, for a victorious South would

---

[34]Francisco Serrano (Duque de la Torre), *Informe al Sr. Ministro de Ultramar*. In this report Serrano describes the rising sentiment against the slave traffic in Cuba.

[35]Ramón de la Sagra, *Cuba en 1860, o sea cuadro de sus adelantos en la población, la agricultura, el comercio y las rentas públicas, suplemento a la primera parte de la historia política y natural de la isla de Cuba*, pp. 9, 19–21, 128–131.

1. Julio L. de Vizcarrondo y Coronado. Photo by Don Keillor, Río Piedras, Puerto Rico.

2. Harriet Brewster de Vizcarrondo. Courtesy of Lic. Francisco Vizcarrondo Morell, San Juan, Puerto Rico.

3. Henry John Temple, Third Viscount Palmerston.
Courtesy Radio Times Hulton Picture Library, London.

4. José Antonio Saco. *Courtesy Biblioteca Nacional, Madrid.*

5. Domingo Dulce y Garay. *Courtesy Biblioteca Nacional, Madrid.*

6. Juan de la Pezuela, Marqués y Conde de Cheste. *Courtesy Biblioteca Nacional, Madrid.*

7. Francisco Serrano y Domínguez, Duque de la Torre. *Courtesy Biblioteca Nacional, Madrid.*

8. José Gutiérrez de la Concha, Marqués de la Habana. *Courtesy Biblioteca Nacional, Madrid.*

9. Antonio Cánovas del Castillo. *Courtesy Biblioteca Nacional, Madrid.*

10. Juan Prim y Pratts. *Courtesy Biblioteca Nacional, Madrid.*

LA SOCIEDAD
ABOLICIONISTA ESPAÑOLA

TIENE POR OBJETO

Propagar el principio de la Abolición INMEDIATA de la esclavitud de los negros;

Discutir los medios de llevarla á cabo sin agravio de ningun derecho, evitando perturbaciones en el órden así moral como material, de nuestras Antillas;

Dar todos los pasos oportunos para conseguir su pronta realizacion,

Y volver por la honra de nuestra Pátria, única nacion de Europa que conserva aquella afrentosa institucion.

Forman la *Sociedad* todas las personas que se inscriban como sócios, dirigiéndose á la Oficina central de Madrid—Balmes, 25 y 27, tercero, derecha; Secretaría general de la Sociedad Abolicionista.

Los sócios contribuirán, *por lo menos*, con dos reales vellon mensuales (pagados cada dos meses adelantados), á los gastos de la *Sociedad* y tienen derecho á recibir el pe-

11. Abolitionist literature bearing the signature of Rafael María de Labra y Cadrama. *Courtesy Biblioteca Nacional, Madrid.*

12. Rafael María de Labra y Cadrama. *Courtesy Biblioteca Nacional, Madrid.*

13. Segismundo Moret y Prendergast. *Courtesy Biblioteca Nacional, Madrid.*

14. Emilio Castelar. *Courtesy Biblioteca Nacional, Madrid.*

impose higher tariff barriers on Cuban products, even perhaps prohibition.[36]

Admittedly the South was a rising competitor of Cuban sugar. In 1825, Louisiana, for example, produced only 30,000 bocoyes of cane sugar, but in 1861 this production had increased to 459,419. The Creole planters could hope that a disastrous civil war would ruin their Southern rival, and that the victorious North would not raise the old customs barriers.[37] According to the Count, the victorious North would prefer to sell manufactured goods to Cuba in exchange for sugar, which after all could be produced more cheaply in Cuba.[38]

According to Cepero, the Count must defend slavery if Cuba were to sell sugar abroad at lower prices, thus regretting Lincoln's Emancipation Proclamation, in spite of his admiration for the American President. "We regret," he said, "that the necessities of war had to precipitate a catastrophe that we believe must be everywhere a work of time and economic and social progress."[39] Again, the Count assured his readers and critics, who might interpret his sympathy for the North as a sign of an abolitionist stand by *El Siglo*, that property "should be duly protected and guaranteed no matter in what form it should happen to present itself."[40]

The Cuban historian Ramiro Guerra and others had interpreted the reformers' admiration and sympathy for Lincoln and the Union as evidence of an abolitionist inclination in the Cuban reform leaders.[41] Cepero, basing his judgment on what was said by *El Siglo*, calls this an error and argues that, on the contrary, the reformists were determined to protect property in all forms. Their love for human liberty, due to class interests, could not have been more than "abstract love." "Social classes," as he said, "do not commit suicide," even though there is no longer an economic basis for supporting them.[42]

---

[36]Editorial (Pozos Dulces), *El Siglo*, año II, No. 351 (4 de noviembre de 1863), Cepero, *Azúcar y abolición*, pp. 83–84.

[37]*Ibid.*

[38]Editorial (Pozos Dulces), año III, No. 206 (12 de octubre de 1864), *ibid.*, p. 83.

[39]Editorial (Pozos Dulces), año III, No. 163 (23 de agosto de 1863), *ibid.*, p. 82.

[40]Editorial (Pozos Dulces), año III, No. 24 (28 de enero de 1864), *ibid.*, p. 82.

[41]Guerra, *Manual de la historia*, p. 561.

[42]Cepero, Azúcar y abolición, p. 91.

The trouble with the forceful thesis of Cepero is that it leans too heavily on the Marxian theme of economic determinism; that proof leans too heavily on the editorials of one man; that the conservative tone of these editorials was not interpreted in the light of the semi-free press; that it fails to define the term esclavistas; that it overlooks other statements by reformists in which they recognized the abolitionist significance of the Civil War and began to consider cautiously the means to replace gradually the slave system; and, finally, that it minimizes other reasons why the Creoles wanted the North to win. A Southern victory, as the oppressed Cubans knew, would serve to guarantee Spain's grip about their throat.

To emphasize this latter point, according to the Spanish merchant Barras y Prado, in the midst of the Civil War it was the hated peninsulares who were the most fanatical defenders of slavery, since they "are more rational than the Creoles because they firmly believe that slavery is tied to the prosperity of the island ... that European colonists can't substitute for Negroes [one of Pozos Dulces' suggestions for gradual abolition], where yellow fever causes a mortality rate among immigrants of from 26 per cent to 46 per cent."[43] But the Spaniards had even more important reasons for wanting a Northern defeat, "... a divided United States would assure Spanish domination for a long time."[44]

As Barras y Prado pointed out, Creole abolitionism was not what it appeared to be. It was inspired more by hatred of Spanish domination than by humanitarian love for the slave. Little wonder that Creole reformists who lived on slave labor could embrace the Union cause even though it symbolized an abolitionist one — anything to oppose the Spaniards, who were cynically using slavery to hold the criollos in subjection. As the near future would prove, the cause of abolition and cause of independence would become as one.

No matter how self-interested, the fact was that as a result of the American Civil War a growing abolitionist sentiment was taking root among the Creoles. The war created a feeling of imminent change to the point that some peninsulars and planters began sending money to Spain, as if abandoning a sinking ship. Yet the unique thing, to quote José A. Echeverría, one of the Creole reformers, was that no one expected slavery to be abolished suddenly; although

---

[43]Barras y Prado, *La Habana a mediados del siglo XIX*, p. 251.
[44]*Ibid.*, p. 252.

Signs of Change, 1855–1865   143

everyone accepted the word *abolition* without the terror of former years.[45]

At this point attention must be called once more to the slave-trade question because, despite a growing feeling against the traffic in Cuba, the problem of suppressing the business remained unchanged. The English consul in Havana estimated that 16,000 Africans had been landed in 1858, and 15,000 in 1859. American newspapers mentioned eighty-five vessels engaged in slaving, twenty-six of which had landed slaves in Cuba in the latter years.[46] In 1860 Crawford, the most eager English official in Cuba since David Turnbull, reported that a shareholding company was being formed in Cuba to introduce 150,000 or more bozales.[47] Britain had already proposed a new international treaty to France and Spain to join in naval efforts against the traffic, including a cordon of Spanish ships around Cuba. Madrid was evasive. What then did Spain propose to do about the problem? The British Ambassador announced: "The present state of things, therefore, as regards Great Britain and Spain, is one of embarrassment and uneasiness."[48]

Madrid explained that because of exorbitant profits slavers took any risk; that reports of slave landings were exaggerated, in any case; that the refusal of the United States to cooperate in the mutual right of search shielded the traffic; that the limitations on contract labor supply such as African "apprentices," and East Indian coolies (which the British consistently opposed) was another factor; and finally that there was a certain lack of integrity in some Cuban officials. The O'Donnell government promised the usual "vigorous measures" against the traffic.[49]

The year 1862 saw estimated slave imports rise to 23,964.[50] Even

---

[45] José A. Echeverría a José A. Saco, La Habana, 6 de junio de 1865, José Antonio Fernández Castro (ed.), *Medio siglo de historia colonial de Cuba, cartas a José Antonio Saco de 1823–1879*, p. 329.

[46] Sir A. Buchanan to Sr. Collantes, Madrid, October 17, 1860, BFSP (1860–1861), LI, 1053–1054.

[47] Consul General J. T. Crawford to Lord J. Russell, Havana, May 24, 1860, *Ibid.*, LI, 1058–1059.

[48] Buchanan to Collantes, *Ibid.*, LI, 1053–1054.

[49] Sir J. Crampton to Earl Russell, San Ildefonso, August 25, 1861, *Ibid.*, LI, 708–711.

[50] "Tráfico de Esclavos," A.H.N., Leg. 3547 (1859–1865), N. 20. These figures conflict with Aimes, who said that only 9,000 slaves were imported for the period

allowing for exaggeration, the fact is that after the opening of the American Civil War a large number of slaves was being successfully imported into Cuba in part by "unemployed" American slavers. No doubt, some proprietors, fearing the future consequences of the American conflict, wished to stock up on slaves. Between the years 1860 and 1862 freshly imported Africans were selling from 555 pesos to 774 pesos each.[51] This represented a drop in value over previous prices, but it may have been due to the greater number of slaves imported as much as to the fears aroused concerning the outcome of the North American conflict.

The Spanish government claimed that Spanish ships had ceased to participate in the slave trade. Between the years 1845 and 1861 only twelve ships bearing the Spanish flag were captured on the coast of Africa. In the years 1857 to 1861 no Spanish slave ships were reported in African waters.[52] This did not mean, however, that Cubans or Spaniards had ceased to engage in the traffic. According to the Spanish consul in Sierra Leone, in the period 1845–1861 a total of 187 slave ships sailing without a flag had been captured in African waters. Of this number 184 were condemned as slavers, and 19,993 Africans were set free. "Of said ships, three fifths were Spanish property or of Spanish origin, with Spanish captains and crews prepared in the Antilles, the Canaries, Brazil, and the United States, and even in Great Britain."[53]

British exasperation with Spain on this matter was boundless. An abolitionist petition of 1862 addressed to the Spanish people who would come to the Industrial Exposition in London decried the "insolent shamelessness and shocking bad faith with which the government of that nation had conducted itself concerning the treaties.... If Spain continues to maintain such a horrible commerce she will attract the hatred of all nations."[54]

1856 to 1859, and only 600 in the year 1862. It is doubtful that Aimes had reliable information (see *History of Slavery*, Appendix II, p. 269).

[51]Carta del Capitán general remitiendo datos sobre el valor de esclavos, 27 de mayo de 1863, A.H.N. Ultramar, Leg. 3547 (1827–1869), N. 20.

[52]Ministerio de Estado, 16 de junio de 1862, "Noticias de Sierra Leone," *Ibid.*

[53]*Ibid.*

[54]*España y el tráfico de negros, observaciones que dirige la Sociedad Británica y extranjera contra la esclavitud a los Señores Españoles*. This interesting manifesto was translated to Spanish and signed by such prominent British abolitionists as William Allen, Robert Alsop, Joseph Cooper, and others.

Signs of Change, 1855–1865

It was common for British statesmen to explain to Parliament that the slave trade had virtually ceased but for the infernal market of Cuba. Lord John Russell, like Palmerston, insisted that the only solution was for Spain to declare the slave trade an act of piracy and punish it accordingly. But even the outbreak of the American Civil War would not, as yet, force Spain to consider more-drastic measures. The same vested interests still controlled Cuban policy.

Serrano had been charged with suppressing the traffic, and he was determined to do so, but soon he was explaining to Madrid exactly what the British officials had always maintained: that the captain general lacked the means for closing the traffic. Serrano said that three things impeded his success: (1) the lack of complete authority in the matter, (2) the lack of strong penal laws, and (3) the lack of cruisers for patrolling the coast.[55]

Concha had resigned when the Madrid government refused to sanction his plan for exiling the slave dealers from the island. In a decree similar to that of Concha's, Serrano (June 2, 1861) gave notice that the authors and accomplices involved in any slave landings would be sent to Spain under arrest. The metropolitan government, apparently uncertain as to a response, answered that it was confident the decree would not be enforced unless there was clear and indisputable proof of the criminality of the accused.[56] This amounted to a rejection of the decree.

Serrano confided to the English consul that he was in favor of declaring the slave traffic piracy, and of punishing offenders by martial law. Madrid on receiving this suggestion from Serrano gave the usual Spanish negative. "Piracy," said the colonial minister, in a burst of indignation, "is against the principles of morality and justice that everywhere serve as a basis for penal legislation, and therefore, definitely not!"[57]

It is hard to disagree with the conclusions of a Spanish merchant living in Havana at this time:

For many reasons, Spain would gain with abolition of the slave trade, generally speaking, but the government recognizes, as does everyone here, that

---

[55]Informe de la Secretaría de Estado, Dirección Política, 31 de agosto de 1858, A.H.N. Ultramar, Leg. 4655, carta reservada N. 154.
[56]*Cuba desde 1850 á 1873*, p. 70.
[57]"Comunicación del Ministerio de Ultramar," 5 de abril de 1862, A.H.N. Ultramar, Leg. 3547 (1827–1869).

the economic problem is connected with the existence of slavery since the island's wealth depends on slave labor. Thus the benignancy and leniency that is employed in dealing with such an infamous trade.[58]

According to the census of June, 1862, there were 368,550 slaves in the island of Cuba. This number constituted approximately one fourth of the population of the island:[59]

White	728,957
Asiatic	34,050
Yucatecan	743
Emancipados	4,521
Free Blacks	221,417
Slaves	368,550
	1,358,238

Slaves were employed according to the following general categories:

In the cities (largely servant class)	75,977
On sugar plantations	172,671
On coffee plantations	26,942
In other agricultural occupations	92,960

As noted before, the percentage of slaves in Cuba was declining. An over-all view of the trend shows that the whites were multiplying faster than the combined colored population, free and slaves:[60]

Year	Percentage Of Whites	Percentage Of Blacks
1775	56.2	43.8
1811	45.5	54.5
1827	44.2	55.8
1841	41.5	58.5

[58]Barras y Prado, *La Habana a mediados del siglo XIX*, p. 152.

[59]Figures based on census of June, 1862, as given by Fermín Figuera, *Estudios sobre la isla de Cuba: La cuestión social*, pp. 20–21, and Rafael María de Labra, *La abolición de la esclavitud en las Antillas españolas*, pp. 55–57.

By comparison, in the slaveholding states of the North American republic there was a total population of 12,315,333, of which 3,953,760 were slaves, a proportion of approximately one out of four. There were only 250,000 free negroes in the slave states. Ownership of slaves was confined to 384,884 proprietors (Richard B. Morris, "The Measure of Bondage in the Slave States," *Mississippi Valley Historical Review*, XLI, No. 2 [September, 1954], 219–240).

[60]Figures based on Fernando Ortiz Fernández, *Hampa afro-cubana: Los negros esclavos. Estudio sociólogo y de derecho público*, pp. 20–21.

1846	47.4	52.6
1855	47.8	52.2
1859	52.2	47.8
1861	56.8	43.2

Under the administration of Domingo Dulce, who replaced Serrano on December 10, 1862, another vigorous effort was made to contain the slave trade. Since it was also necessary to preserve existing labor resources, further steps were taken to ameliorate the conditions of the slave, as for example, the regulations of January 22, 1863.[61] The fact that Dulce's administration coincided with a turn of events in the American Civil War explained why Madrid was now very determined to close the trade. Spain feared that in the event of a Northern victory a hitherto protective policy toward slavery in Cuba might become abolitionist.[62]

American resistance to British efforts to exercise the right of search in closing the traffic — resistance typified by former Secretary of State Lewis Cass — for years had shielded the Atlantic slave trade. This trade had been declared a crime of piracy by the American government in 1820, but it was not until 1862 under the abolitionist government of Lincoln that the first man was executed for this crime. This did not deter the slavers because the Federal Navy was now preoccupied with war duties. The slave trade was actually on the increase. Between 1839, when American cruisers began a half-hearted effort to patrol the African coast, and 1859 only two slave cargoes were seized, but in 1860 seven were captured.[63]

Finally, Lincoln and Secretary of State Seward, needing to avoid British recognition of the rebellious South, agreed to mutual right of search for a ten-year period, as well as to other effective measures.[64] The new agreement was the death blow to the Atlantic slave trade, and undoubtedly stimulated Spanish abolitionist efforts.

The least excuse would serve the Americans for justifying inter-

[61]"Reglamento para las sindicaturas de esta ciudad a la presentación de los esclavos en queja de sus amos," La Habana, 28 de enero de 1863, Domingo Dulce, found in José Ferrer de Couto, Los negros en sus diversos estados y condiciones; tales como son, como se supone que son y como deben ser, pp. 97–101.

[62]Ministerio de Guerra al Ministro de Ultramar, 11 de julio de 1865, A.H.N. Ultramar, Leg. 3547 (1827–1869).

[63]Warren S. Howard, American Slavers and the Federal Law, 1837–1862, p. 64.

[64]John R. Spears, The American Slave Trade: An Account of Its Origin, Growth, and Suppression, 216–217.

vention in Cuba. On July 11, 1865, a new royal order authorized the captain general to remove any governors or military commanders or any other officials suspected of connivance or indifference in respect to slave landings.[65] Positive proof of connivance was now no longer needed in order to justify the removal of suspected personnel. The emergent abolitionist feeling in Cuba, of which we have spoken, also influenced this stern policy.

Earlier, in February, 1864, the Madrid government was asked by Dulce for authorization to exile all persons who had repeatedly endangered the peace of the island by their conduct. The request was granted on August 20, 1865, with the provision that the offender be exiled to Spain, or any other point he might choose abroad. Thus, in principle, the policy of Pezuela and Concha was finally admitted. This authorization did not apply strictly to questions of the slave traffic, but the captain general was now free to proceed against the slave merchants on the grounds that their conduct endangered the peace of the island.[66]

Dulce did much to improve Anglo-Spanish relations. When Robert Bunch of the mixed court called upon the Governor he reported: "It is impossible that anyone should express himself more strongly against this infamous traffic than General Dulce did." In rare tones of cordiality the English official admitted that he might occasionally be deceived by false reports and entreated the Governor's indulgence. His Excellency replied that he was often deceived himself, and as Bunch was taking leave: "Send in all the information you can get, be it true or false, we will do our best to sift it."[67]

Dulce attacked the great leaders of the slave commerce, including the rich Spanish planter, Julián Zulueta, who previously had always been influential in winning Cuban officials to a policy of tolerance for the traffic. Dulce used the terrible emergency powers of his office, conceded in 1825, in order to exile the great Zulueta and others.[68] The Spanish party, defender of arbitrary power, decried this action as "arbitrary," and demanded Dulce's recall, but to no avail. No doubt existed about Spain's intention to close the traffic, but there still re-

[65]"Ministerio de Guerra al Ministro de Ultramar," 11 de julio de 1865, A.H.N. Ultramar, Leg. 3547 (1827–1869).
[66]*Cuba desde 1850 á 1873*, p. 71.
[67]Her Majesty's Commissary Judge, Robert Bunch, to Earl Russell, Havana, November 28, 1864, *BFSP* (1865–1866), LXI, 1194–1195.
[68]Guerra, *Manual de la historia*, pp. 561–562.

mained the problem of arming the captains general with specific penal legislation against slave traders.

The violent drift of the American conflict suggested that perhaps gradual abolition would be better than immediate. A number of Cubans, several of them slaveowners, took the initiative of airing plans for gradual abolition, with indemnities for all liberated slaves, except those fraudulently introduced from Africa. Francisco Serrano, then governor of Cuba, had written as early as June 30, 1862, that talk of abolition was inspired by the American Civil War. He advised Madrid that perhaps it was time to consider abolition before events precipitated the matter.[69]

A flood of abolitionist plans followed the Northern victory.[70] In August, 1865, an anonymous author published a plan for abolition in eight years after the manner of the British tutelage system in Jamaica. Calixto Bernal proposed the liberty of all new-born slaves. López de Letona proposed a similar plan.

The distinguished peninsular, Don Francisco Montaos y Robillard, presented a plan to the governor of Cuba suggesting a cautious approach to emancipation "without disturbing the habits of subordination and respect instilled in the slaves ... nor introducing great disturbances in the labor system."[71]

Another Cuban, Fermín Figuera, writing in 1866, submitted a twenty-five-year plan of gradual abolition. The problem cannot be hidden for a long time, he said. Like most abolitionists Figuera referred to the success of gradual abolition in Brazil and the disaster of immediate abolition in the United States. "Look at the example of the United States," he cried, "a disastrous civil war was not necessary. A plan of gradual emancipation with compensation was possible and much more intelligent."[72]

A demand that Spain declare the slave traffic a crime of piracy appeared consistently in abolition plans. Also, as a necessary corollary, the abolitionist authors, in the manner of Figuera, considered in de-

[69]Francisco Serrano, Governor General of Cuba, communication to Leopoldo O'Donnell, Minister of War and Colonies, June 30, 1862, A.H.N. Ultramar, Leg. 3547 (1827–1869).

[70]For a summary view of abolition projects, Eugenio Alonso y Sanjurjo, *Apuntes sobre los proyectos de la abolición de la esclavitud en las islas de Cuba y Puerto Rico*.

[71]*Ibid.*, pp. 50–51.

[72]Figuera, *Estudios sobre la isla de Cuba*, p. 90.

tail the solution to the labor problem. They made the usual recommendations for encouraging immigration and settlement of new workers on the plantations as a compensation for the loss of forced labor. The idea of importing free black labor from Africa, which Great Britain always distrusted, was again suggested. The plan of José Suárez Argudín, Cunha Reis, and Fernández Perdones for importing sixty thousand free Africans aroused considerable interest. Saco, still speaking for a white Cuba, vigorously condemned the plan.[73] The hapless Africans, said he, would be placed under contracts and treated like coolie labor, but, even worse, Cuba would still have to suffer the consequences of Africanization: "The introduction of Africans is one of the principal causes which has enchained the progress of the white population ... and which has expelled from the land many whites who would have made honorable laborers."[74]

At this time Spain's position in the Antilles was positively more precarious. She was suffering a humiliating defeat in Santo Domingo, and in Cuba the spectre of abolition was not the only threat to the old colonial regime, for meanwhile the reform aspirations of the Cubans had reached a new and perilously exciting pitch. Serrano, after returning to Spain, gave a resounding speech in the Cortes (January, 1865) in behalf of Cuban reforms. He defended the right of Cuba to have representation in the Cortes. Serrano was feverishly congratulated by the hitherto-neglected Creoles. A memorandum (May 12, 1865) signed by 24,000 persons, claiming to speak for a cross section of all interests throughout the island, was addressed to Serrano and asked him to present their demands to the Cortes.[75]

The memorandum listed three basic demands: (1) the reform of the tariff system (especially on flour imported from the United States); (2) the representation of Cuba in the Cortes and other political reforms; (3) the extinction of the slave traffic. The traffic, incidentally, was condemned in no uncertain terms: "The commerce

[73]Pérez, *Estudios*, pp. 53–54.

[74]José A. Saco, "Introducción de colonos en Cuba y sus inconvenientes," publicado en *La Revista Hispano-Americano* (marzo-mayo, 1865), cited by Pérez, *Estudios*, p. 54.

[75]Carta al General Francisco Serrano, 12 de mayo de 1865, *Cuba desde 1850 á 1873*, p. 267. The Cuban reformists sent a second memorandum to the government of Leopoldo O'Donnell, who assumed power for a second time in July 1865. Serrano was charged with delivering this letter to O'Donnell. Guerra, *Manual de la historia*, p. 569.

Signs of Change, 1855–1865

in Africans continues . . . a repugnant and dangerous cancer of immorality . . . Private interests here have proven themselves more powerful than the honor and conscience of the nation."[76]

The Spanish party protested to the queen in an exposition of June 28, 1865. The signers of this document were not against administrative or tariff reforms but for reasons of "ignorance" and "factions" in Cuba they opposed all political reforms, as well as the assimilation of Cuba into the Cortes. Furthermore, political assimilation would be dangerous because of the existence of "a patronage system that cannot yet be suppressed," and the diversity of races. The metropolis was reminded, of course, that political reforms given to an ignorant and factious people had facilitated the separation of the continental American colonies from Spain.[77]

These two petitions mirrored the colonial dilemma. The Creoles would not be satisfied with mere administrative reforms. They were demanding political and civil rights equal to those of the metropolis. The Creole reformers were assuming that political reforms could be harmonized with existing slave institutions, and that civil rights for the whites did not necessarily involve civil rights for the blacks. They also were assuming that political reforms could be harmonized with the division between peninsulares and criollos. On the other hand, the Spanish party insisted that political reforms, no matter how meager, might awaken dangerous appetites. The tendency of the Spanish government, liberal or conservative, to believe in the "patriotism" of the Spanish party and in the "separatist tendencies" of the Creoles complicated the question.

[76] *Cuba desde 1850 á 1873*, p. 267.
[77] *Ibid.*, p. 277. Also, Blanco Herrero, *La política de España*, p. 382.

9. Abolitionism Invades Spain, 1863-1866

> The war in the United States is finished, and being finished, slavery in the whole American continent can be taken as finished. Is it possible to hold Spanish provinces . . . while keeping this institution in the dominion? I don't think so . . .
> Antonio María Fabié, May 6, 1865[1]

Spain was not wholly indifferent to the slave question. At least after the modest triumph of a liberal movement in Spain (la Unión Liberal) in 1855, the first lonely voices dared to raise the slave question in the Cortes. These were the voices of a new generation of Spanish liberals, Nicolás María Rivero, Emilio Castelar, and Laureano Figuerola among them, men destined to play a leading role in the arousing of the Spanish conscience. As early as 1857, *La Discusión*, edited by Rivero, dared to advocate the abolition of slavery.[2] Not just the slave problem but the whole colonial question, both inside and outside the Cortes, was raised with increasing frequency during the 1850's, largely because the López expeditions and the threat of annexation awakened a new interest in the Antilles, especially among the liberals.

But during the years from 1855 to 1864 these men were as a voice in the wilderness of Spanish politics. Had the question of colonial reforms depended solely on a handful of Spanish liberals speaking to ephemeral ministeries nothing could have been done. In 1864 the

[1]*Diario de las sesiones de las Cortes, generales y extraordinarias, 1810–1898*, Congreso (1864–1865), III, No. 79 (6 de mayo de 1865), 1700–1701.
[2]Rafael María de Labra, *La abolición de la esclavitud en las Antillas españolas*, p. 23.

ministeries of Miraflores, Arrazola, Mon, and Narváez filed by. That of Narváez lasted from September, 1864, to June, 1865, when O'Donnell once again returned to power. Yet each in turn seemed reluctant to face the significance of the Southern defeat. One did not have to be a liberal to realize that some measures of abolition in Cuba and Puerto Rico would be almost universally expected—as we shall see in a subsequent chapter, enlightened Spaniards of all political stripes could concede that much—but, in keeping with a recurrent pattern, it was not from the Peninsula that the dynamic impulse to action came.

Unheralded, the Puerto Rican Julio Vizcarrondo arrived in Madrid sometime during the year 1863. He immediately set to work to give the first cohesive expression to the nascent abolitionism of the metropolitan liberals by organizing the first meeting of the Spanish Abolitionist Society (Sociedad Abolicionista Española) on December 7, 1864. The Society was formally constituted on April 2, 1865, in La Academia de Jurisprudencia, including among its original members some of the brightest stars in the liberal firmament: Emilio Castelar, Félix Bona, Laureano Figuerola, Salustiano de Olózaga, Antonio María Segovia, el Marqués de Albaida, Juan Valera, Fermín Caballero, Mateo Práxedes Sagasta, Gabriel Rodríguez, Segismundo D. Moret, Manuel Becerra, Calixto Bernal, and Nicolás Salmerón.[3]

Also among the original founders were two other Puerto Ricans, Joaquín Sanromá and José J. Acosta, who were both to play a leading role in the emancipation movement (Sanromá for a brief period in 1879 became president of the Abolitionist Society). Later, other Puerto Ricans, such as Román Baldorioty and Mariano Quiñones, would also make important contributions to the abolitionist crusade. In a word, the Puerto Ricans in Madrid would become the spearhead of the emancipation movement, writing a bright chapter in the humble history of that island and making a unique contribution to the human race in general.

Is it not a remarkable fact that a small colony produced men of the slaveholding Creole class who came to the metropolis to ask for the liberty of slaves? A purely economic explanation would scarcely suffice, for the causes of the rise of abolitionist sentiment in Puerto Rico were more complex. On this subject study is yet to be done on the

[3]See the brief biographical sketch of Vizcarrondo, "Puertorriqueños ilustres" Cayetano Coll y Toste (ed.), in *Boletín histórico de Puerto Rico*, Vol. 8, pp. 131–135.

diverse influences that brought colonial reformers to a passionate agreement on the need for emancipation.

However, we can attempt a sketch of the major causes of abolitionism in Puerto Rico. Like Cuba, Puerto Rico was infected by the revolutionary currents of Europe and America. Seductive concepts of nationalism, independence, republicanism, the rights of man, and free thought made subtle inroads among a small group of Creole intellectuals. Nor were the brief triumphs of the Spanish liberals of 1812, 1822, and 1836 forgotten. The censorship of the captains general and their efforts to close liberal schools (a small academy in which young Acosta planned to teach was closed by Governor Pezuela in 1846) were ineffective.[4] Again as in Cuba, commercial relations between Puerto Rico and the United States led to an interplay of mind. Wealthy families and commercial societies (though on a much smaller scale than Cuba) began sending able young men abroad for higher education. They returned with a vision of a more liberal society.

However, the *ambiente* of Puerto Rican liberalism was not quite the same as that of Cuba, even if the same sources of ideas were drawn upon. It is true that in both Cuba and Puerto Rico a liberal reform movement was maturing among the Creoles, dividing this group into right and left wings. In both islands the right wing generally opposed all abolitionist talk. The left wing persisted in reform plans, including emancipationism. But at this point, important differences must be noted. In Cuba at this time, as we have seen, left-wing liberal sentiment did not go beyond the abolition of the slave trade or the advancement of cautious projects of gradual abolition that rarely got beyond the captain general's office. In Puerto Rico, on the other hand, the same movement had a much more emphatic abolitionist character. Why? Again one might tread on highly speculative ground. But we will not do so without first listing some of the basic facts upon which Puerto Rican historians are in general agreement.

Of course, the economic fact is foremost. Slavery did not strike deep roots in Puerto Rico; this has already been mentioned. Slavery in Puerto Rico by the time of the American Civil War was, in fact, a dying institution. The best proof of this was that the slave trade had virtually ceased in Puerto Rico after 1835.[5] Puerto Rican proprietors,

[4]For details concerning the education of José Acosta and his companions, Angel Acosta y Quintero, *José J. Acosta y su tiempo*.
[5]Luis Díaz Soler, *La historia de la esclavitud negra en Puerto Rico*, pp. 136–137.

unlike Cuban proprietors, could not afford the high price of slaves after the treaties with Britain because the productivity of the smaller island did not warrant it.⁶ In fact, Cuban proprietors began importing slaves from Puerto Rico. British complaints against this trade led to the prohibitory decree of 1848, later repeated in 1854; thereafter this trade was reduced to negligible proportions.

The truth is that the smaller island, more isolated and more limited in natural resources, only partially shared the fabulous prosperity of Cuba after 1790. In 1765 Puerto Rico had a population of 45,000, of which number 5,000 were slaves. Sugar production then was scarcely 250,000 pounds per annum.⁷ Like Cuba, Puerto Rico enjoyed an economic boom during the first decades of the nineteenth century, but it was in no sense flooded with Africans. By 1860 slaves numbered only 41,746 in a population of 541,445.⁸ By the latter date the approximate proportion of slave to free in Puerto Rico was only one to thirteen, while in Cuba, with 368,550 slaves in a total population of 1,359,238, it was one to four. Thus slavery was never profitable enough to prevent the steady mixing of races that had begun early in the colonial period and continued uninterrupted in the nineteenth century. More so than in Cuba miscegenation served to break down caste and class lines and to encourage manumission. These socioeconomic facts help explain the growth of a powerful equalitarian sentiment that penetrated all social classes, as in Brazil. As early as the 1840's this equalitarianism began to manifest itself, accentuated by the liberal ideology then in vogue among Puerto Ricans like Vizcarrondo. Some of the Puerto Ricans who later carried the abolitionist fight to the Cortes were mulattoes.

In the lives of Puerto Rican reformers we see in operation the cultural forces previously mentioned. Vizcarrondo, Acosta, Baldorioty, and Sanromá were all intimate friends and members of that same lonely brigade fighting for colonial reforms in Madrid. All were teachers, writers, and reformers sharing the same commitment to liberal ideas. Baldorioty and Acosta traveled to Spain together and studied on fellowships in Madrid. In such men a distinctly Puerto Rican conscience began to emerge as they traveled widely over Spain, Europe, and America. In Madrid, significantly, Baldorioty and Acosta, together with other Puerto Rican students, founded "La Sociedad Pro-

⁶*Ibid.*, pp. 194–195.
⁷Salvador Brau, *Disquisiciones sociológicas y otros ensayos*, pp. 136–137.
⁸*Información: Reformas de Cuba y Puerto Rico*, pp. 215–216.

tectora de Documentos Históricos de Puerto Rico."[9] They returned to Puerto Rico (1854) with the purpose of contributing to the cultural and economic uplift of their society.

Unlike Acosta and Baldorioty, Vizcarrondo (once a student of Acosta's in San Juan, about 1845) continued his higher education in the United States, though exactly where remains unrecorded. His liberal and humanitarian inclinations, which had caused his exile from Puerto Rico (about 1850), and the abolitionist crusade then going on in the North American Republic, led him to embrace fully the abolitionist cause. "In the land of freedom, in the United States," said a contemporary, "the spirit of a great rebel mingled with ideas. There he studied, there he learned, there he lived. Who could now recount all the evolutions that took place in the conscience of that fighter?"[10]

While in the United States, Vizcarrondo married an American woman, Harriet Brewster of Philadelphia. Undoubtedly, she influenced his abolitionist ideas, but to what extent remains a mystery. She was probably a Quaker. Labra described her as "intelligent," and as having taken "a brilliant part" in the abolitionist campaign in Spain.[11]

In 1854, when Vizcarrondo returned from the United States, he immediately began emancipating his slaves, and what must have been even more astounding, he began denouncing before the tribunals of justice abuses practiced on slaves. Here, at last, after three centuries was a man who seemed worthy of the mantle of Las Casas. Vizcarrondo soon provoked the concern of the authorities and the slave interests who called him a filibuster, a label applied to all those who disagreed with the established order.[12]

Like other builders of Creole culture, Vizcarrondo plunged into educational and social work. In 1862 he wrote a book for use in schools: *Elementos de Historia y Geografía de Puerto Rico*. In the previous year he and his wife founded a house of charity for poor children: Casa de Caridad de San Ildefonso.[13]

Frustrated in his abolition work in Puerto Rico, where rigidity of colonial government prohibited a free press, Vizcarrondo—by nature

[9]Acosta y Quintero, *José J. Acosta;* also see Coll y Toste (ed.), *Boletín histórico*, Vol. 5.
[10]Juan Arrillaga Roqué, *Memorias de antaño, historia de un viaje a España 1887-88.*
[11]Labra, *La abolición de la esclavitud en las Antillas españolas*, p. 23.
[12]Coll y Toste (ed.), *Boletín histórico*, Vol. 8, pp. 131–135.
[13]*Ibid.*

a spirited journalist—decided to carry the argument to Madrid where, after all, the issue would have to be decided. As we have said, sometime in the year 1863 Vizcarrondo and his wife arrived in Madrid and shortly thereafter the Spanish Abolitionist Society was launched. That Spanish abolitionism owed much to Vizcarrondo can scarcely be doubted. Sanromá said of Vizcarrondo's abolitionist work that he "was the soul . . . he began the movement, organized it, united us, encouraged us, he looked after the meetings and the publications of pamphlets and the *Abolitionist*, and he did all this with a zeal, a diligence, and a practical sense that betrayed his Anglo-American education."[14]

As an interesting sidelight, Vizcarrondo later, after religious liberty had been briefly established in Spain in 1869, attempted to found a Protestant sect of Lutheran inclinations. But he lacked funds and soon, anyway, religious liberty ended.[15]

The Abolitionist Society, with the usual symbol of a Negro on bended knee, his chained hands raised in an attitude of supplication, had obtained within a year of its foundation some seven hundred members of varied social and political influence. Under Vizcarrondo's direction, the Society launched the newspaper *El Abolicionista Español*, and sponsored a series of great meetings in theaters throughout Spain to dramatize the cause. They founded branch societies in Seville, León, Valencia, Saragossa, Barcelona, and other peninsular cities.[16]

The activities of the Society were guided by the following principles:[17]

1. To propagate the principle of the immediate abolition of Negro slavery. To discuss the means to carry this out without infringing on the right of anyone, and to prevent disturbances in the moral and material order of our Antilles.
2. The Spanish Abolitionist Society is absolutely above all party interests . . . exclusive doctrines and Church obligations.
3. Its mottoes are: free labor
   moral redemption of the slave
4. The Society is formed of all persons who inscribe themselves as members . . .

[14]Joaquín Mará Sanromá, *Mis memorias 1828–1868*, I, 333.
[15]Zoilo Ruiz García, *Nuestros hombres de antaño*, p. 141.
[16]For more details see Labra, *La abolición de las esclavitud en las Antillas españolas*.
[17]*Ibid.*

Some liberal papers, *La Discusión*, *La Democracia*, and *La Propaganda*, opened their columns to the abolitionists. Poetry contests attempted to arouse compassion for the plight of the slave. One poet, for example, in sixty-two pages of dismal cadence, pictured the doleful journey of the slave from Africa to the plantations of Cuba. The emotional appeal of the poem can be judged from this extract describing the landing of the hapless Negroes on the dark shores of Cuba:[18]

> A man broke the silence with these brief words:
> "Ho! the living ashore; the dead to the water!"
> ... they threw a female body still breathing to the waves,
> A slave saw this and fearlessly dove back into the sea,
> ... at last, saving the dying victim.
>
> Amidst a flow of tears, his trembling finger
> Touched her cold hands, while the woman
> In her native tongue moaned repeatedly:
> Mother of my soul!
> Said the crowd of Negroes: "the woman is his mother!"
> Then turning, the miserable band
> Continued its doleful march.

A feminine chapter of the Spanish Abolitionist Society soon took form. Here, again, Harriet Brewster de Vizcarrondo played a little-known but very important role. Included in the feminine committee were prominent ladies in Spanish society: la Condesa de Pomar, la Condesa de Priegue, and the Señoras Saéz y Melgar, Matamoros de Tormo, Ayguala de Izco, and Mrs. Brewster de Vizcarrondo.[19]

The Society also tried to enlist international support. An interesting example of this effort is the letter Vizcarrondo wrote to Victor Hugo on June 28, 1866. The Puerto Rican wanted the French writer, who had fought valiantly for the abolition of the death sentence and the liberty of man, to publicize before the world the terrible tale of two slaves in Puerto Rico who made a suicide pact in order to escape from an unbearable servitude. The one killed the other, then surrendered,

---

[18]E. Silio y Gutiérrez, "El Esclavo," leyenda en verso in *La cuestión social, Antillas: Colección de Justo Zaragoza de varias exposiciones de la Sociedad Abolicionista Española, discursos de sus miembros en el Congreso y Ateneo, etc., 1868-73.*

[19]"Puertorriqueños ilustres," Coll y Toste, *Boletín histórico*, Vol. 8, pp. 131-135.

knowing the authorities would put him to death. Despite protests of a defense lawyer, the death penalty was carried out.[20]

But Vizcarrondo did not build the Abolitionist Society singlehandedly. A number of influential names were to be counted among the founders, and one name in particular came to acquire an abolitionist fame greater than that of Vizcarrondo's. Rafael María de Labra more than shared the honor of building a solid abolitionist organization in Spain, and the sum total of his services to this cause was even greater than that of Vizcarrondo.

Labra (1840–1915) was born in Cuba of a Creole mother. The father, a Spanish army officer, soon moved the family to Spain, where young Labra was educated.[21] Thereafter Labra spent his life in the Peninsula, but he never forgot the fact that he was born in the Antilles.[22] Beginning an active political and journalistic vocation in Madrid in 1865 at the age of 25, Labra spent the next thirty-three years fighting for the neglected interests of Cuba and Puerto Rico, within and without the Cortes, till the day of disaster in 1898.

Of the same liberal school as Vizcarrondo, Labra believed on principle that the slaves should be free in a democratic society, and that emancipation was for the best interests of both the colonies and the mother country. For Labra, who was also a charter member of the Abolitionist Society, the preservation of slavery was the most disgraceful characteristic of Spanish colonial policy. Labra fought not only for emancipation but also for every possible reform that would liberalize the colonial administration of the Spanish Antilles.

Labra would prove to be the Wilberforce of Spain, the stoical untiring champion of what would seem to be for many years a lost cause. Labra's character fitted the circumstances, for he was a determined but patient man, a prolific but empirical writer, and a persuasive but

[20]The Frenchman replied that he was touched to the heart with the story but, being very busy with so many worthy causes to defend, he would have to postpone the appropriate moment before taking up his pen in behalf of such a cause; "Carta de Vizcarrondo a Víctor Hugo," Madrid, 28 de junio de 1866, and "Contestación de Víctor Hugo a Vizcarrondo," Hautville, 23 de octubre de 1866, Coll y Toste (ed.), *Boletín histórico*, Vol. 6, p. 200.

[21]It is worthy of note that Labra, who studied law, presented as his doctoral thesis: "El Congreso Internacional de Vienna en 1815." For further details on his political life and legislative influence see Juana H. Oliva Bulnes, "Labra en las Cortes españolas," *Revista Bimestre Cubana*, LXV, Nos. 1, 2, 3 (1950), 190–262.

[22]Rafael María de Labra, *La política colonial y la revolución española de 1868*, p. 16.

unemotional speaker who backed his arguments with statistical facts. Labra was the finest type of Spanish liberal, and a man of moral stature seldom found anywhere. Perhaps no man knew more about colonial affairs than he did; his numerous and informative publications on the subject are proof of this. Both Cuba and Puerto Rico later elected him to the Cortes, and both could claim him as their own. In the words of an admirer, Labra's entire life "was dedicated to the study of the great problems of Spanish policy . . . above all, a recognized authority among the most eminent men in colonial affairs."[23] The name became a legend overseas, and when he died in 1915 the lost colonies could still sigh long and mournfully at the passing of the Spanish colonial conscience.

Under the guiding hands of Vizcarrondo and Labra, the Society set about the task of building up an abolitionist will in Spain. The success of the movement, however, cannot be understood without another reference to events in North America, where the future of human slavery was being decided before a wide audience. The approaching defeat of the slave-holding Confederacy meant that the Bastille of Slavery in the Americas was about to fall. As the American Civil War had precipitated abolitionist expressions in Cuba, so it produced the same effect in Spain. Sentiment heretofore indifferent or timid was now emboldened to speak out on the problem of slavery in Spanish colonies. Vizcarrondo's arrival in Madrid had coincided with the decisive year of battle.

Until the Battle of Gettysburg (July, 1863), Spanish diplomats contemplated the Southern Confederacy as serving as a moral and political bulwark for slaveholding Cuba against the forces of international abolitionism. But after Gettysburg, informed Spaniards, like informed colonials, realized that the South was doomed, and that slavery in the New World must eventually perish. What was more to be feared was that the expansionist yanqui would use abolitionism as a pretext for intervening in Cuban affairs. That is why Gabriel Tassara, Spanish minister in Washington, like General Serrano before him, fearing the future direction of American foreign policy, advised Madrid (July, 1865) "to consider in one form or another the means for initiating the

---

[23]Arrillaga Roqué, *Memorias de antaño*, p. 54. When news of Labra's death (April 18, 1915) reached Puerto Rico, Coll y Toste wrote with great feeling: "No matter how much the Puerto Ricans do for the memory of Labra, it is little," *Boletín histórico*, Vol. 5, p. 378.

abolition of slavery."[24] Thus the pretext would be denied the Americans.

The general effect of the American struggle on Spanish public opinion was readily acknowledged by the Abolitionists: "The American Civil War," said Gabriel Rodríguez, "influenced opinion in Spain giving tremendous support to the hitherto isolated efforts of our abolitionists."[25]

Even before the founding and extension of the Abolitionist Society, there were concrete indications that at last some Spanish citizens were moved to discuss the abolition question. In 1864 two societies, the Free Society of Political Economy and the Academy of Jurisprudence and Legislation, publicly discussed the slave question for the first time.

In the Cortes, at this date, the slave question seemed to rise spontaneously. The impending Northern victory caused such anxiety that some deputies dared to press the government on the subject of abolition. On June 15, 1865, León Galindo suggested that the government take opportune steps toward complete abolition. However, the government as yet would not dare permit an open discussion of the motion. A minister of the O'Donnell Government, Agustín Ulloa, in the most solemn tones, immediately put the matter to rest: "The Congress understands the gravity, the immense gravity of the question presented by Sr. Galindo."[26]

Again, the final victory of the North moved some deputies to defy the long-standing taboo not to introduce the slave question in the Cortes. It had been twenty-eight years, said José Modet (May 6, 1865), since the question had been spoken about in the Cortes. "We must solve the problem ... before a cataclysm strikes here as it did in other countries."[27]

Antonio María Fabié, a conservative long interested in colonial reforms, arose to second the words of Modet:

> The war in the United States is finished, and being finished, slavery on the whole American continent can be taken as finished. Is it possible to

---

[24]Gabriel Tassara, Spanish Minister in Washington, to the Spanish Department of State, July 19, 1865, A.H.N. Ultramar, Leg. 3547 (1827–1869).
[25]Gabriel Rodríguez, "La idea y el movimiento antiesclavista en España durante el siglo XIX" (pamphlet) in *Las España del siglo XIX*, Vol. III.
[26]*Diario, Congreso* (1863–1864), V, No. 149 (15 de junio de 1864), 2608.
[27]*Ibid., Congreso* (1864–1865), III, No. 79 (6 de mayo de 1865), 1700.

keep Spanish provinces . . . while keeping this institution in the dominions? I don't think so, and therefore I say the question is urgent, that the Government must comply with great obligations . . . I hope that the enlightenment necessary to solve this problem will be sought for in cooperation with the Cortes. I won't say more on this question.[28]

The American Civil War, in effect, tore the lid off a suppressed question. One might think that at this point Spain would be forced to some gesture of abolition, but this would be to underestimate the powerful network of commercial and property interest linking Cuba to Spain. In fact, the public airing of the slave question was just beginning and the defenders of slavery were not idle. The abolitionist talk touched off by the Civil War aroused them as never before to a reasoned defense of slavery. The slave interests found numerous allies among halfhearted reformers, who would not go beyond a gesture of abolition to the civilized world, and among the patriots, who would hold onto Cuba at any price. Such people were forced to find that Spanish slavery after all was not so bad; in fact, it was quite good.

A large number of Spanish writers had always assumed on good faith—ignorant and antiempirical as they were about colonial affairs —that black slavery in the Spanish colonies was an eminently humanitarian practice compared to other empires. If one wished to read the Laws of the Indies one could find wondrous provisions for spiritual and physical health of Indians and Africans. Even some who argued abolition, like Labra and Fabié, occasionally felt obliged to confess that Spanish slavery was always less cruel.

As we have seen, Fabié addressed himself to the Cortes (May 6, 1865) on the necessity for abolishing slavery. But before reaching this conclusion—and Fabié was one of the first to reach it in the Cortes— the speaker performed the usual eulogy on slavery in Spanish dominions: "In all the history of slavery, from classical times to the present, no country has known how to organize it like Spain, no country has made the situation of the Negro race more elevated, more tolerable, or at times more sweet . . . this explains why we have preserved the institution longer than other countries."[29]

Similar assertions can be found in a number of contemporaneous works. Perhaps Spanish slavery was more humane because it was less efficient than other forms. Suffice it to say, a people with a proud his-

[28]*Ibid.*, p. 1701.
[29]Antonio María Fabié, *Mi gestión ministerial respecto a la isla de Cuba*, p. 14.

tory did not readily humble themselves before the demands of foreign and colonial abolitionism.

The most systematic defense of slavery in the Spanish colonies was made by the illustrious Spaniard, José Ferrer de Couto, an untiring defender of Spanish interests everywhere, a distinguished historian, and a bemedaled bearer of royal honors. As such, Ferrer was an influential man in Spain's Cuban policy, and he overlooked no argument in defending slavery. He despised abolitionists, "the promoters of civil wars." *The Diverse Nature and Condition of the Negro* was written under the influence of the American Civil War and published in New York in 1864. In that city Ferrer was the editor of *La Crónica*, a paper that defended the interests of Spain against the incessant attacks of Cuban exiles living in the United States.

Ferrer was not the first, but he was the most thorough, in defending Spanish slavery on classical and biblical grounds. "And furthermore, it is well known that in the Politics of Aristotle the slavery of savage peoples was proclaimed as a civilizing principle." The author cited several biblical justifications for master-slave relationships, the letter of Paul to the Ephesians, for example.[30]

In a chapter entitled "The Calamities Produced in the World by the Obstinacy of the Abolitionists," the author painted a frightful picture of Haiti and Santo Domingo sunk in anarchy and voodoo following the abolition of slavery. Spanish slaveowners had always trembled in their boots at the thought of a Haitian-like slave rising.

Ferrer de Couto, half-mockingly, proposed an "International Treaty" for legalizing slavery. Article One would declare the forced labor of Negroes to be Christian, civilizing, and legal in all nations. Article Three would prohibit calling the *redemption of slaves* slavery. Article Ten would repress in Negroes any exaggerated ideas regarding their future rights.[31]

The benevolent ordinances composing the "Slave Code" of the Spanish Antilles were listed by Ferrer in order to demonstrate that the regulations of 1789, 1842, 1863, and other years were models of humane concern for the slave.

Ferrer's work was to become a textbook for the defenders of the slave interests in the Cortes. He provided the slavists, who up to this

---

[30] José Ferrer de Couto, *Los negros en sus diversos estados y condiciones; tales como son, como se supone que son y como deben ser*, pp. 48–49.

[31] *Ibid.*, pp. 295–301.

time had made no sustained ethical defense of slavery, with a reservoir of facts and arguments.

The book provoked an indignant cry from the abolitionists. Fermín Hernández answered Ferrer point by point in *Slavery and Mr. Ferrer de Couto* (1866). Hernández re-examined the slave code, extracting various regulations concerning forced labor, whippings, and prison that suggested the harshness of the system. He cited Francisco Arango's *Report on Fugitive Slaves* (Havana, 1796), which concluded that all measures up to that time in favor of Negroes were ineffective. The mortality of the slave was another proof. According to Hernández, the Negro population of Cuba increased by only 64,000 in the years 1811 to 1825, ". . . although it is certain that 185,000 slaves were imported."[32]

Hernández quoted the classical world, the Bible, and the popes (Pius II, Paul III, Urban VIII, Benedict XIV) against slavery and the slave trade. He asked that Spain, following the "illustrious and unfortunate Lincoln," would decree, "in the name of God, the abolition of slavery in all Spanish dominions."[33]

The most powerful work against the theme of the sweet, Christian nature of slavery in the Spanish Antilles was written by the Cuban Francisco de Armas y Céspedes: *On Cuban Slavery* (1866). In a chapter called "Brief Reflections on our Legislation," Armas said: "The motive [of this chapter] is due to the fact that the supporters of the *status quo* greatly eulogize our legislation in this matter, limiting themselves to citing only the most favorable prescriptions in favor of slaves." After a summary view of this legislation in favor of the slave, Armas concluded with Hernández that "the greater part of the laws are not in use." Armas y Céspedes quoted an article published by a Cuban priest in *The Catholic Truth* to the effect that only one case had been known of a slave proprietor asking for a priest to instruct his slaves in Christian doctrine.[34]

The most frequent argument brought to bear against the slave interests by the abolitionists was in reference to the scandalously cruel fate of those "emancipated Negroes," who according to the slave treaties with Britain should have been free. It was commonly known in Havana that Cuban authorities sold these emancipados (Negroes

---

[32] Fermín Hernández Iglesias, *La esclavitud y el Señor Ferrer de Couto*, p. 26.
[33] *Ibid.*, p. 52.
[34] Francisco de Armas y Céspedes, *De la esclavitud en Cuba*, pp. 164–170.

confiscated from slave ships) to slave proprietors, who according to the law, were charged with teaching the hapless Africans a freeman's trade. As we have seen, there were over forty years of Anglo-Spanish diplomacy concerning abuses practiced on "emancipated Negroes" in Cuba.[35] And Spanish abolitionists did not fail to effectively utilize the emancipado argument.

During these slave arguments the clergy were conspicuous by their absence. With rare exceptions, neither in Spain nor Cuba did they take up the abolition cause. One recalls that the dean of the Church of the Conception in Santo Domingo was one of the first to ask for Negro slaves. In America one also recalls the words of Saco:

But there was another reason that caused the demoralization of the clergy ... we have seen that monarchs and other Christians loaded the churches and monasteries with gifts ... From those first acquisitions, the clergy, abbots, and bishops proved themselves devoted in conserving their properties, and with them the slaves who worked the land.[36]

Apparently both proprietors and priests neglected their spiritual duty. The colonial government investigated the alarming number of slave suicides and concluded "that the lack of religious instruction is the major cause."[37] According to law, proprietors were to pay the cost of baptism and instruction, but they did not want to disburse the money, saying that the teaching of Christian doctrine would be dan-

[35] Interesting diplomatic correspondence of the subject of the emancipados during the period 1825–1865 can be found in A.H.N. Estado, Legs. 8040–8059.

[36] José Antonio Saco, *La historia de la esclavitud desde los tiempos más remotos hasta nuestros días*, II, 409. Notable exceptions to the generalization that the clergy were indifferent to the slave question were Padre Félix Varela y Morales, who presented a project of abolition to the liberal Cortes of 1822–1823, and Antonio María Claret, archbishop of Santiago de Cuba, who dared the wrath of the slave interests by promoting the welfare of the slaves during the 1850's. Many priests and some rich nuns had slaves in Cuba. When Madden asked if it was common for the clergy to have slave plantations, Delmonte replied: "Yes, most of them have them, and they treat their slaves the same as the other inhabitants of the island." "Interrogatorio de 120 preguntas que, sobre el estado eclesiástico de la isla de Cuba, me ha hecho, Mr. Roberto Ricardo Madden, Juez de la Comisión Mixta por Inglaterra, Noviembre, 1838", ... por Domingo Delmonte, in Saco, *La historia de la esclavitud de la raza africana en el Nuevo Mundo y en especial en los países Américo-Hispanos*, IV, 325–326.

[37] "Informe de la Junta de Fomento dada en el Expediente sobre suicidios de esclavos," A.H.N. Ultramar, Leg. 4655, N. 152.

gerous for the established order on the plantation. Without pay, the clergy showed no evangelical fervor.

We have said that it was a combination of the Protestant conscience and eighteenth century rational humanitarianism which gave rise to the abolitionist movement in England. In Spain the religious conscience was missing. As Cánovas said, the meaning of Valladolid, where (in the long run) Doctor Sepúlveda's viewpoint would triumph over that of Las Casas, was that doctrinaire Aristotelianism triumphed over the Christian conscience.[38]

According to a well-known Spanish historian the Spaniards, famous for their religiosity, continued observing all the external symbols of salvation, but the inner dynamism of faith was dead. The monks were mostly in charge of education, of libraries, of philosophy, and of nonempirical scholarship, such as it was. The dead hand of scholasticism hung over all.[39]

The last theological words spoken on the rights of subject peoples, it would seem, had been uttered in the sixteenth century, when Spanish doctors and theologians like Vitoria, Soto, Las Casas, Sepúlveda, and others argued the pro and con of Indian rights.[40] It is intriguing to ponder why a nation with precedents of this kind should be so indifferent to the cause of the Negro slave.

Perhaps the answer is that slavery seemed a distant colonial problem of no pressing importance. Not since the days of the Moors and the Jews was slavery a visible, legal, ethical, social, or economic prob-

[38] Antonio Cánovas del Castillo, *Historia de la decadencia en España desde el advenimiento de Felipe III al trono hasta la muerte de Carlos II*, pp. 16–19.

[39] Antonio Ballesteros y Beretta, *Historia de España y su influencia en la historia*, Vol. 8, p. 104.

[40] It is true that the Spanish Jesuit Alonso de Sandoval in the early seventeenth century made a widely circulated plea to his brothers of the Society in the united kingdom of Spain and Portugal asking for more human care of the Negros, who were human and equal in the sight of God, *Naturaleza, policía sagrada i profana, costumbres i ritos, disciplina i catechismo evangélico de todos Etiopes por el P. Alonso de Sandoval, natural de Toledo, de la Compañia de Jesus, Rector del Collegio de Cartegena de las Indias*, Sevilla, 1627. But as C. R. Boxer, who has considered the phenomenon of the Jesuits in Brazil (enemies of Indian slavery but indifferent to or approving of Negro slavery), points out, Sandoval admitted the validity of African slavery under canon and civil law. The Indian was born free, but the Negro was accustomed to slavery as his natural condition. Essentially this was the Aristotelian position of the sixteenth-century Juan Ginés de Sepúlveda.

lem in Spain. Fugitive slaves were to be free on touching foot there.⁴¹ Or the answer might be that the problem was not properly the concern of Spain. Spaniards could reply with some justification that Britain owed her abolitionism to a guilty conscience. The English had carried more slaves to America than had any other nation. Liverpool grew into a great city on the slave trade. But these considerations do not satisfactorily explain the relative lack of abolitionist sentiment in Spain.

Nowhere in the study of Spain's problem of Negro slavery does one find a protest of religious conscience equal to, say, that of the Quakers. As we have seen, the theologian Jaime Balmes was typically occupied in fighting the battles of the medieval church, lauding the redemptionist work of medieval Catholicism, and lamenting the birth of erroneous sects, such as the Quakers, who, meanwhile, had not forgotten that slavery still flourished in the New World.⁴²

Like the English Quakers, the Quakers of Pennsylvania advised their members against holding slaves (1696). In 1774 all members engaged in the business of slavery were excluded. In this same year a society was founded for abolitionist propaganda, Benjamin Franklin being one of the presidents of this society. The following address was typical of those sent by American, English, and Irish Quakers to the government of Spain; the passage is cited at length simply because it illustrates what a vital abolitionist ingredient was missing in nineteenth-century Spain:⁴³

> It having pleased the Lord to bring our fathers to a sense of cruelty and wickedness of the African slave trade, and of the injustice of holding fellowmen in slavery, they were strengthened to act upon the conviction wrought

---

The Jesuit Antonio Viera, adviser to the Portuguese crown, summed up (ca. 1640) the political attitude of the Brazilian Jesuits: ". . . without Negroes there is no Pernambuco," which might be paraphrased: ". . . without Negroes there is no Cuba" (C. R. Boxer, *Salvador de Sá and the Struggle for Brazil and Angola, 1602–1868*, pp. 257–258).

⁴¹The royal cedulas of April and May of 1789 declared free any fugitive slave taking refuge on Spanish territory (the Peninsula), Rafael María de Labra, *América y la constitución de 1812*, p. 133.

⁴²Balmes' apologetic defense of the Medieval Church is found in his *El Protestantismo comparado con el Catolicismo en sus relaciones con la civilización europea.*

⁴³The "Address" of the Quaker societies is contained in A.H.N. Ultramar, Leg. 8043 (1849–1850), L. 10, N. 2.

in their minds: they set at liberty those they held in bondage, and in their faithfulness they enjoyed the answer of a good conscience toward God . . . From that time to the present day we have felt it to be laid upon us as a church to bear witness against the sin of slavery.

We have believed it a Christian duty to represent the wrongs inflicted upon the people of Africa . . .

One God is the creator of us all . . .

The Gospel of Christ is precious to us . . .

May it please the Lord Almighty to bless those who reign. May His wisdom preside . . . Glory be to God in the highest and on earth peace, good will toward men.

Signed in behalf of the (yearly) meeting,
George Macey,
Clerk to the Meeting this year (1849)

When the Spanish abolitionist conscience began to reassert itself in the form of liberalism, it owed little or nothing to scholastic philosophy.[44] As we have indicated, the freethinking Vizcarrondo would go so far as to attempt to found a Protestant sect in Spain. Spanish and colonial abolitionists were motivated not by St. Augustine nor St. Thomas but by French and English rationalists and freethinkers, and by foreign philosophy in general, including German idealism. The names of liberals and abolitionists appeared as the followers of Hegel, or of Comte and Spencer, or of the most influential of all, Karl Christian Krause. Masonry, too, which had taken hold in the eighteenth century, played an important ideological role. General Juan Prim, Manuel Ruíz Zorilla, Nicolás María Rivero, and other builders of the constitutional and republican movement, were either Masons or influenced by Masonry.[45]

Furthermore, these liberals, observing that progressive countries were abolishing slavery, could only conclude that backward countries preserved slavery. The arguments of Labra and Castelar, particularly, emphasized this point. A note of indignation at the hypocrisy of scholastic Christianity and the inertia of tradition-bound Spain was always present.

This indignant feeling is communicated to the reader in the memoirs of the Puerto Rican abolitionist Sanromá. The critics of abolitionism frequently asked why abolitionists engaged in a redundant activ-

---

[44]Antonio Ballesteros y Beretta, *Historia de España y su influencia en la historia*, Vol. 8, p. 104.

[45]*Ibid.*, p. 100.

ity. Had not the Church already abolished slavery? The rationalists, particularly galled by these claims, charged that the Church obstructed abolition. Sanromá tells us that he set himself the task of investigating the claims of both sides.

The Puerto Rican began by comparing the works of two Catholic theologians, Jaime Balmes and the Abbot Bergier, with the works of two anticlerical liberals, Francois Laurent and Patrice Larroque. Both Balmes and Bergier maintained that slavery was incompatible with Christianity: "Apud Deum non est exceptio personarum; non est servus libre: unum estis in Christo Jesu." So went the Latin clichés. But why didn't Christianity immediately abolish slavery?[46] Balmes and Bergier, author of an article *au dictionaire* on slavery, answered that immediate abolition would have destroyed the civilizing influence of the master over the slave. Given the low intellectual and moral level of the slave he could not have enjoyed freedom in any case. Furthermore, immediate abolition would have radically upset the ideas of law, custom, and property. Abolition of servitude had to be the work of time. Prudently but positively the Church moved in the direction of abolition, a step at a time, meanwhile sweetening the lot of slave and serf as the dawn of full liberation approached. The Church customs of manumission, of admitting slaves to ecclesiastical status, of sanctioning slave matrimonies (thus recognizing the civil and religious unit of the family), and of the right of asylum to mistreated slaves were some of these steps.[47]

Sanromá then saw what Laurent and Larroque had to say against the above arguments.[48] If slavery was abolished *ipso facto* in Christian theology, why, asked the rationalists, did it require so many centuries to abolish it in fact? That "abolition must be the work of time" was a worn-out argument used throughout the Middle Ages, and still employed in the seventeenth century by Grotius to defend slave institutions. No, replied the rationalists, there were other reasons, theological if you like, that explained the delay. Did not St. Paul say: "Although they offer you liberty, prefer slavery"? Did not St. Ambrose say: "Slavery is a gift from the Most High"? Did not St. Isidore of

---

[46]Sanromá, *Mis memorias*, pp. 347–348.
[47]*Ibid.*, pp. 348–349.
[48]Francois Laurent (1810–1887) was a Belgian historian and jurisconsult; his most famous work was *Etude sur l'historie de l'humanité*. Patrice Larroque (1801–1879) was a French philosopher and author of many works, including *De l'esclavage* (1857).

Pelusa counsel slaves not to leave their condition? Did not St. Thomas admit every kind of slavery that was founded in natural law according to Aristotle—that it was derived from war and peace pacts according to the lawyer? Did not Bossuet call slavery a just and rational state?[49]

As to the imposing list of papal declarations against slavery and the slave trade cited by Balmes and Bergier, the rationalists pointed out their limited character. Were not most papal declarations against holding Christian slaves and not against slavery in general? And were they not often limited to the slave trade? Did not Julius II, seeking to revenge himself on the Venetians, authorize their reduction to slavery? And, as Saco also suggested, were there not property reasons? Were not slaves possessed by ecclesiastics in the Middle Ages? By religious orders in the New World?[50]

It is evident therefore that Spanish abolitionism was a facet of the anticlerical movement of nineteenth-century Spanish liberalism. The greatest percentage of the abolitionists were freethinking anticlericals who inclined strongly toward a republic or constitutional monarchy, for example, Emilio Castelar, Francisco Pi y Margall, Manuel Ruíz Zorilla, Cristino Martos, Romero Ortiz, and Nicolás Salmerón.[51] Colonial abolitionists like Sanromá and Vizcarrondo were other examples of this school of thought.

At the time of the founding of the Abolitionist Society, however, the liberals were still largely a marginal influence in Spanish politics. For the moment, all along the line, the conservatives were still entrenched in the seats of power. We leave to a subsequent chapter the story of what happened when the liberals finally came to power.

[49]Sanromá, *Mis memorias*, pp. 350–353.
[50]*Ibid.*, p. 354.
[51]These men and others from the abolitionist ranks took part in shaping the decree of June, 1869, which established freedom for dissident religious sects. Ballesteros y Beretta, *Historia de España*, Vol. 8, pp. 104–106.

10. Two Hesitant Steps Forward, 1865-1866

> I am not afraid to speak of the problem of
> slavery as other Spaniards and Cubans ... until
> now the slaves have been peaceful, because the
> problem was never discussed.
>
> Fermín Figuera, 1866[1]

Speaking of the reform aspirations of the Cubans in 1859, Ramón Just, a Spaniard who had resided twelve years in Cuba, lamented Spanish ignorance concerning Cuba. He predicted that Spain would lose Cuba as it had lost other colonies unless attention were soon given to colonial reforms. "I confess that I expect nothing for now," said Just of his warnings, "nevertheless, I believe that I have paid a debt of honor to my country and to my own conscience."[2]

It was not that the government did not care about Cuba, but vested interests simply preferred to let sleeping dogs lie. Previously, the Spanish government had always been able to evade embarrassing questions about Cuban policy: first, because colonial delegates were conspicuously absent from the Cortes; second, because the Spanish public was scarcely aware of the colonial situation—as one deputy admitted in 1866, "... until a very short while ago, only a very small number of people understood colonial problems"[3]—and third, because government spokesmen could always return to the fiction of the "Special Laws" by which Cuba was supposedly governed. This was still the most convenient foil; for example, the Colonial Minister, Manuel Seijas Lozano, when nullifying the petition of the Barcelona

---

[1] Fermín Figuera, *Estudios sobre la isla de Cuba: La cuestión social*, p. 5.
[2] Ramón Just, *Las aspiraciones de Cuba*, p. 64.
[3] Cited from a debate on the Law against the Slave Traffic of 1866, *Diario de las sesiones de las Cortes, generales y extraordinarias, 1810–1898, Congreso* (1865–1866), V, No. 112 (16 de junio de 1866), 2488.

merchants (1865) requesting free entry of flour into Cuba, stated: "I believe that I am able to prove to the Congress that it has no existing legality or competence to discuss a projected law relating to the overseas colonies."[4]

Thus it was an obvious deduction, if one accepted *las leyes especiales*, that the Cortes could be held conveniently incompetent to discuss any aspect of Cuban policy. This field of jurisdiction had belonged exclusively to the colonial section of the Council of State. Nor, by the way, did the creation of the Ministry of Colonies (Ministerio de Ultramar) in 1863 essentially change this arrangement. It was true that a minister was now responsible for colonial policy before the Cortes, but the example just cited of Seijas Lozano suggests the settled inertia of colonial policy.

The truth was, of course, that the problem of reform was much more complicated than it appeared to the critics of colonial policy. The vacillating government knew that foreign and colonial opinion expected action on colonial problems, especially on the slave problem, but government officials knew also that any reform would call into question Spain's whole colonial policy in Cuba, and the slave problem could not be isolated from that policy. The prime considerations had not changed in a half century. The abolition of slavery not only would destroy Cuban prosperity but also, obviously, would cause the mother country to suffer a loss in revenue, and offended commercial and planter interests might, as they had previously threatened, join the revolutionary ranks. It goes without saying that Spanish political dominion rested upon the protection given these interests. Moreover, as we have suggested in a previous chapter, abolition involved the question of civil and political status for the Negro. The conservatives knew that this would lead to the alarming question of civil and political rights for the criollos. From their point of view, therefore, any reform was a hole in the dike that could lead to disaster.

Fortunately for reform hopes, the government of Spain at this time was presided over by the Liberal Union Party (Unión Liberal), from June, 1865, to July, 1866. The president of the Council of Ministers, General Leopoldo O'Donnell, was a liberal in name only, but, at least by Spanish political standards of the day, he was not a reactionary. He had governed in Cuba and he favored some measure of colonial reform. Under this government two able men, Seijas Lozano, and,

[4]*Diario, Congreso* 1864–1865, III, No. 79 (6 de mayo de 1865), 1800–1881.

later, Antonio Cánovas del Castillo, were named colonial ministers. Seijas Lozano was a cautious conservative concerning colonial policy, as we have seen, and so was Cánovas; yet these two men took the first hesitant steps toward a revised colonial policy in deference to rising reform pressure.

According to Saco, Seijas Lozano, like most ministers, was blissfully ignorant of colonial affairs. As an article of the conservative creed, he believed like most good patriots that the loss of Spanish America was due to the reforms of 1812. Furthermore, he was not repelled by the fact that the ever-faithful slave interests were Spain's true interests in Cuba.[5] But with the ending of the Civil War in favor of the abolitionist cause, Seijas Lozano stood up to the fact that Spain must soon make an abolitionist move. Perhaps he was influenced also by British diplomacy which, meanwhile, had renewed its efforts to push Spain into declaring the slave trade an act of piracy.

But the state of opinion in Spain and Cuba was still so overwhelmingly conservative that Seijas Lozano had to move as quietly as a cat. He wrote to Captain General Domingo Dulce asking the latter to promote a meeting of Cuban proprietors to discuss some form of gradual abolition. The great majority of the proprietors received the idea coldly, yet the reform-minded Dulce continued with the project. He authorized a meeting of the Cuban reform circle in the house of José Ricardo O'Farrill, with the object of discussing a plan of gradual abolition even though it was still forbidden to discuss the slave question publicly in Cuba. This plan, to which an earlier reference has been made, was the idea of the peninsular Francisco Montaos, director of *La Prensa*, a Havana newspaper; it divided slaves into five groups, giving value to each slave according to age. The slave would be freed through his own efforts (coartación) or by a fund designed to purchase the freedom of slaves in a gradual manner.[6]

The Creole proprietors could not agree on Montaos' plan. O'Farrill and other Creole reformers joined with the antireformists in a common protest in which they requested Dulce not to permit further dis-

---

[5]José A. Saco, "La política absolutista en las provincias ultramarinas," cartas al Excmo. Sr. D. Manuel Seijas Lozano, Ministro de Ultramar, Abril-Mayo de 1865, cited by Luis M. Pérez, *Estudios sobre las ideas políticas de José Antonio Saco*, p. 54.

[6]*Cuba desde 1850 á 1873. Colección de informes, memorias proyectos, antecedentes sobre el gobierno de la isla de Cuba, que ha reunido por comisión del Gobierno D. Carlos de Sedano y Cruzat, ex-diputado á Cortes*, p. 283.

cussion or publication of the plan. The two groups then attempted to reach an agreement on a political reform program that would exclude the "social question," but the abyss between them was too deep.[7]

In spite of the feelings of the proprietors on the social question, Dulce approved the plan of a young Havana lawyer, Antonio González de Mendoza, for founding an Association against the Slave Trade (Asociación contra la trata). Members, who were to be inscribed in a public register, would promise not to buy Negroes introduced into the island directly or indirectly after November 19, 1865. Leading abolitionist reformists backed the Association and among these were several peninsulars, including the same Montaos.[8]

Seijas Lozano, timid in the face of slavocrat opposition, refused to sustain Dulce's provisional approval, and the Association remained stillborn. The idea of the Association, however, once more indicated to the government the growing force of public opinion against the slave trade.

Cánovas meanwhile succeeded Seijas Lozano as colonial minister (June, 1865). Cánovas like his predecessor was primarily concerned about the slave trade because most members of the government agreed that at least something had to be done, otherwise the government would be seriously embarrassed by foreign demands and by the growing abolitionist voice in Spain itself.

The O'Donnell government, meanwhile, finally answered (October 13, 1865) the notes on the slave trade presented several months previously by the American and English ambassadors in Madrid. The English note had recommended a general statement by the governments of Europe and America declaring the slave trade piracy, and that said governments should propose to their respective parliaments the application of a legal punishment commensurate with the offense of piracy. The American note was more polite, and asked only that Spain apply stronger legislation against the slave trade. As always, Spain, in responding to these notes, circumnavigated the question of declaring the slave trade piracy. However, the O'Donnell government did definitely commit itself to enact a new and more stringent law against the slave trade, with Cánovas promising the American gov-

[7]Guerra, *Manual de la historia de Cuba (económica, social y política)* p. 571.
[8]Vidal Morales, *Iniciadores y primeros mártires*, III, 139, cited by Guerra, *Manual de la historia*, p. 572.

ernment (October 21, 1865) that such a law would be presented to the next session of the Cortes.⁹

For Cánovas the abolition of the slave trade would remove the main source of embarrassment, but like Seijas Lozano he was aware of the need for further measures tending toward gradual abolition of slavery itself. Yet, given the feeling in Cuba, he also had to proceed with great caution. The problem was doubly complicated because something had to be done to pacify the Creole political grievances of Cuba and Puerto Rico. Notwithstanding the delicacy of the colonial question, Cánovas thought it best that the O'Donnell government make concessions on two fronts at once. And so it was that Cánovas not only introduced in the Cortes the long overdue "Law for the Suppression and Punishment of the Slave Trade," but, due to his initiative a royal decree was issued (November 25, 1865) announcing the convocation of a Colonial Reform Commission (Junta de Información de Ultramar) for the purpose of studying reform possibilities. Since these two measures touched off the most serious discussions on colonial policy in the Cortes since 1837, they must be pictured in some detail.

In April, 1866, the Cortes began examination of the proposed "Law for the Suppression and Punishment of the Slave Trade." In the course of the arguments, as the conservative critics feared, the whole question of Spanish policy in Cuba came unavoidably to light. As previously noted, it had been many years since the colonial problem had been discussed so fully in the Cortes, and this fact added drama to the occasion. Some of the most influential dignitaries of the realm participated, including three former governors of the island—el Marqués de la Habana (José de la Concha), el Marqués de Pezuela (Conde de Cheste), and the president of the Council of Ministers (Leopoldo O'Donnell).

It was soon evident that the Cortes was predisposed to accept the law, partly because it was always rather servile to the will of the government, partly because the participants who had had experience in colonial affairs realized that the spectacle of a thriving slave trade in Cuba could not long continue before the critical eyes of world opinion, and partly because the newly founded Spanish Abolitionist Society

⁹"Ministro de Ultramar contesta la nota inglesa y americana," 21 de octubre de 1865, A.H.N. Ultramar, Leg. 3547 (1827–1869).

had already succeeded in creating an air of expectancy. The commission named by the Cortes to prepare the projected law set the tone of the discussion when it called "the infamous slave traffic ... a fact unexplainable to the eyes of Christian civilization."[10] Yet, despite the general unanimity of feeling concerning the need for the measure, Cánovas, as sponsor of the bill, had to speak long and eloquently in order to overcome a small but hard core of opposition representing the Cuban property and commercial interests.

The main spokesman for the slave interests was José Luis Riquelme. Owner of slave property in Cuba and a man who had held high government offices, Riquelme felt that the provisions of the new law permitting agents to enter the plantations in search of slaves would again excite profound disturbances as in 1854. The old law of 1845 would suffice. In a word: leave well enough alone. "On my own plantation," said Riquelme, "I have given liberty to those slaves who asked for it, and they have remained to work on the plantation. This is the way."[11]

Essentially, the opposition argued that the least reform would lead as sure as the law of gravity to the emancipation of the slaves and the consequent destruction of the Cuban economy and Spanish domination. Pedro A. Alarcón supported such arguments with petitions allegedly representing three quarters of the wealth and commerce of Cuba. Nor did other conservatives fail to stress that the new law was another ignominious bow to England.[12]

Cánovas, in defending the measure against this line of reasoning, exclaimed, "I, Señores, do not understand this dilemma: that either we have to admit a more extreme and repugnant form of slavery, or admit the absolute liberty of the slaves." Spain had made, he said, a promise to abolish the slave trade in 1817, and the promise must be honored.[13] The present measure was necessary, continued the Colonial Minister, because previous laws [that of 1845, for example] had been insufficient. In those days the spirit of the times was different:

... there existed the universal belief that the prosperity of the island demanded the existence of the slave trade.

Then slavery could be maintained without any danger to the nation because almost all the most powerful nations then maintained it. Today, as I

---

[10]Preamble, Law for the Repression and Punishment of the Slave Trade, *Diario, Congreso* (1865–1866), IV, No. 108, Appendix 2.

[11]*Ibid.*, V, No. 128 (7 de julio de 1866), 2500–2502.

[12]*Ibid.*, p. 2174.   [13]*Ibid.*, p. 2495.

have repeated more than once, slavery is limited to our territory, and there is no one who doesn't believe that it is indispensable that slavery disappear completely.[14]

Cánovas, however, was obliged to disclaim that his government intended any measures of abolition. He assured the deputies that the government would preserve slavery "such as it now exists." But this admission could in no wise deter the government from its prime objective: "I am obliged," said the Colonial Minister, "to suppress the slave trade . . . and I will not stop at anything in order to achieve this result."[15]

Cánovas had some support from small owners, who not only approved the law but also advocated strict provisions for pursuing the traffic into the plantations themselves. To repeat, the small owners felt that the traffic favored only the great plantations, who could afford the inflated price of slaves. The small plantation became impoverished and gradually died off, and so long as there were slaves available the free man refused to work. The only remedy therefore was the complete extinction of the traffic. "But it is essential that at the same time the Government encourage white colonization and the immigration of Asiatics—Hill-coolies—that have given such good results in the English island of Trinidad."[16]

To return to the fears of the conservatives, the discussion of the slave law led some deputies to propose that it was time to consider other reforms for the Antilles. Since this implied political reforms, and, perhaps, the admission of Antillian deputies into the Cortes, a heated argument followed. Alarcón, in vehemently opposing such reforms, raised the old "beseiged fortress" argument:

Some inhabitants of the Antilles complain that they do not enjoy liberty! This is as if the guards or the inhabitants of a frontier plaza . . . would complain that they can't go out into the fields . . . that they don't have, in summary, all the *privilegios* . . . of the citizens of Seville, of Valencia or Madrid.[17]

[14]*Ibid.*, pp. 2503–2504.   [15]*Ibid.*, p. 2504.
[16]"Exposición presentada al Senado por varios dueños de ingenios con esclavos en la isla de Cuba" (Madrid, 20 de marzo de 1866). This document was signed by several owners, some of whom lived in Madrid, and by Antonio Murúa, a deputy to the Cortes. *Diario, Senado* (1865–1866), Vol. I, Appendix No. 41.
[17]*Diario, Congreso* (1865–1866), V, No. 112 (16 de junio de 1866), 2174–2175.

There was a Spanish party on the island, said Alarcón in a rather simple-minded argument, ". . . from this it is clearly deduced that there is a party that is not Spanish." This anti-Spanish party had temporarily restrained its conduct while awaiting reforms, because, according to Alarcón, this was the simplest method for achieving independence or annexation without wasting blood as in the case of the López expeditions.

López Domínguez, in protest, paraphrased Alarcón's words as "no reforms, no liberty, repression, always repression." Simply why, he asked, does Cuba have to be considered a besieged plaza? As for the reform element in Cuba, were they really anti-Spanish? "There are rich proprietors, some with Castilian titles, that appear on the reform petitions."[18]

"Whenever the political question is mentioned in Cuba," persisted Riquelme, "it is reduced to a question of Creoles and Peninsulars . . . it is impossible to consider these reforms without great complications." Moreno Nieto, answering Riquelme, said, "It is the same old argument that reforms will produce anarchy and the separation of Cuba from Spain. If we give Cuba and Puerto Rico reforms, they won't have any interest in separation."[19]

The discussion of the Cuban political question was, of course, not properly on the agenda. The O'Donnell government was more than aware that in turning from a discussion of the slave-traffic law to a discussion of political reforms there existed the danger that passions would be aroused both within and without the Cortes which could embarrass the government, and might even serve to defer the measure at hand. This danger was, in fact, strategically exploited by the spokesmen of the slave interests in the Cortes. Cánovas, recognizing the danger, hastened to confine the discussion to the measure in question. He regretted that such terms as "Spanish party" and "anti-Spanish party" had to be introduced in every discussion of Antillian problems. In summing up the government's position he once more underlined the fact that the government had no intention at that time of considering further the question of Cuban reforms. What was under consideration was "only the Law of the Suppression and Punishment of the Slave Trade and nothing more."[20]

[18]*Ibid.*, V, No. 128 (9 de julio de 1866), 2518.
[19]*Ibid.*, V, No. 128 (9 de julio de 1866), 2518.
[20]*Ibid.*, V, No. 129 (9 de julio de 1866), 2521-2522.

On July 9, 1866, the Cortes voted their approval of the law as submitted by Cánovas, making only minor changes in the form rather than the substance. Again it is significant that the government was most careful to point out in the preamble that the law in no way threatened the institution of slavery per se: "Slavery has to exist in the islands of Cuba and Puerto Rico as a pre-existing fact."[21]

The Law for the Suppression and Punishment of the Slave Trade of 1866 gave a more precise definition of what constituted complicity in the slave trade than the law of 1845. Now any person connected with such operations in any way was liable to heavy fines and imprisonment. But the death penalty was reserved only for those who resisted arrest, and for those whose cruelty resulted in death or grave injury to the slave.

The highly debated Article Thirty-eight provided for the registration and census of all slaves in Cuba and Puerto Rico "so that at no time can Negroes be taken for slaves when they have been introduced in contravention to this law." Men of color who were not inscribed in this registration were by that sole fact to be considered as free men. Fines and imprisonment were stipulated for any irregularities in the procedure of registration.[22]

London, highly pleased with Dulce's vigorous prosecution of the traffic, mildly protested that the new law said nothing about piracy. Ambassador Crampton from Madrid explained that even so it provided for criminal penalties nearly as severe as those against piracy.[23] At the same time, Britain nodded approval of a Spanish decree declaring the freedom of all slaves arriving in Peninsular territory from Cuba or Puerto Rico.

The Spanish Abolitionist Society attacked the new law as less rigorous than laws in operation in other countries. In accord with the British point of view Society members protested against its failure to consider slave traders as pirates. Furthermore, the law contained the same loophole as that of 1845: the colonial officials could not effectively carry on inspections within the bounds of the plantation. The only lasting solution, said the abolitionists, would be to abolish slavery completely: "We will never tire of saying it, that while slavery

[21]Preamble, Law for the Repression and Punishment of the Slave Trade, *Diario, Congreso* (1865–1866), IV, Appendix No. 129.
[22]*Ibid.*
[23]Sir J. Crampton to the Earl of Clarendon, Madrid, July 5, 1866, *BFSP* (1866–1867), LVII, 1332–1335.

exists all efforts to suppress the slave traffic will prove futile; long and painful experience has proved it."[24]

Neither did José de la Concha, Marqués de la Habana, believe the new law sufficient. He was especially doubtful about registration. Concha, like Pezuela, had failed to carry out the registration law of 1854, because of the resistance of the hacendados and because the tribunals refused to cooperate. "It was an error to believe as the commission does" said Concha, "that conditions in Cuba are more favorable now than in 1854."[25]

The Spanish government, however, assumed that the law of 1866 ended whatever remained of the Cuban slave trade. Officials could point to the fact that no slave ships were captured after this date. True, foreign newspapers continued to publish rumors concerning slave landings in Cuba. *L'opinion nacionale* of Paris recorded (August 18, 1866) that since the departure of General Dulce the slave traffic seemed to have reached greater proportions. One slave dealer was reported to have paid $50,000 for permission to import seven hundred Africans. The New York *Herald*, friend of the Cuban revolutionary exiles, reported (July 10, 1866) that following a slave revolt two thousand Chilean liberators had invaded the island of Cuba, that recently one thousand Africans, or "sacks of coal" had been landed near Jaruco without opposition. "Three hundred of the Negroes were taken by a schooner to Marianao, a summer residence where the Captain General is living ... afterwards to the farm of a wealthy Spaniard ... They were duly provided with the necessary *pases de tránsito*."[26] No doubt, the greater part of these rumors were part of the strategy of the Cuban exiles, who sought to enlist the sympathy of the abolitionist powers and embarrass the Spanish government in every possible way.

But the Spanish government was more sensitive than its critics imagined, especially when foreign ambassadors asked if there was any truth in such rumors. The new colonial minister, Alejandro de Castro, warned Francisco Lersundi, governor general of Cuba, that no complicity of any kind in the slave trade could be tolerated. Ler-

[24]"Exposición por la Sociedad Abolicionista al Senado," *Diario, Senado* (1865-1866), I, No. 52 (20 de abril de 1866), 617-620.

[25]*Ibid.*, p. 622.

[26]Excerpts from foreign newspapers, A.H.N. Ultramar, Leg. 4658 (1856-1863).

sundi replied in anger that he knew of no slave landings, and he threatened to resign unless the government exhibited confidence in him.[27]

Certainly the law of 1866 could be better applied than any previous law against the slave traffic because, as Lersundi said, public opinion, stronger than decrees or threats, was against the traffic.[28] The traffic ceased to be a diplomatic problem after 1866. Aimes, who agreed with British consular agents that no landings had been made during the period 1865–1872, said: "It seems virtually certain that the trade had entirely ceased before the end of 1865."[29] On the other hand, Fernando Ortiz, the Cuban authority, assumed that the trade did not end until 1880, and supplied figures to show that during the period 1850–1880, 200,000 Africans were introduced into Cuba.[30]

Labra reported that as late as 1873 a Havana paper offered for sale Negroes proceeding from Africa.[31] Also, after 1866 complaints were heard in the Cortes that Negro slaves were being imported from Puerto Rico. That the Cubans did not consider the slave trade closed will be made amply evident in the next chapter.

The high cost of slaves and the fear that Spain might follow the abolitionist example of the United States undoubtedly deterred many a prospective buyer from investing new capital in new slaves. On the other hand the island's sugar economy, especially after the Civil War had ruined Louisiana sugar, was more prosperous than ever, as may be seen:

---

[27]"Ministro de Ultramar al Capitán General Francisco Lersundi," 8 de agosto de 1866; "Lersundi al Ministro de Ultramar," 14 de septiembre de 1866, A.H.N. Ultramar, Leg. 4658 (1856–1863).

[28]General Lersundi's Circular relating to the Slave Trade, Havana, December 26, 1867, BFSP (1868–1869), LIX, 974. Lersundi warned: "I do not believe there is anyone acquainted with my former command here, who would be so mad . . . as to attempt the experiment of landing Negroes."

[29]Hubert S. Aimes, *A History of Slavery in Cuba, 1511 to 1868*, p. 312.

[30]Fernando Ortiz Fernández, *Hampa afro-cubana: Los negros esclavos. Estudio sociólogo y de derecho público*, pp. 87–88.

[31]Rafael María de Labra, *La abolición de la esclavitud en el orden económico*, p. 269.

Total value of export-import trade in pesos:[32]

1849	9,832,476
1852	13,407,586
1857	18,813,832
1861	21,108,750
1865	22,085,335

This prosperity indicated that the Cuban proprietors had every reason to continue to depend on slave labor. The continual labor shortage, no doubt, induced some proprietors to patronize a small furtive trade in slaves even after the law of 1866. It will be remembered that there was scarcely a domestic source of slaves in Cuba as there had been in the United States. Cuba could replenish human labor only through fresh imports. One proof of this is that in spite of the pros and cons of Chinese laborers, planters still bought them. An estimated 60,104 coolies entered Cuba in the period 1855–1865.[33]

The first part of the Cánovas program, the law for the suppression of the slave trade, was a measure that for many years had been pending. Spain really had little choice, since the international situation, above all, necessitated approval of the law. As to the second part of the Cánovas program, that of colonial reforms, the problem was positively more complicated.

The fact that Cánovas intended to fulfill the promise of 1837 conceding Cuba the long-neglected "Special Laws," aroused vehement opposition. According to Cánovas this was the first concrete offer of its kind made in Spain since that date, for no one had said until now: "Let us begin work on the Special Laws," and he added: "I will understand that these measures will please no one ... I have needed courage ... to carry such a project forward."[34]

---

[32]Based on data given by Dr. Francisco Rodríguez Ecay, *Compendio de la geografía de la isla de Cuba*, Appendix 17.

[33]According to *Revista Económica* and other sources cited by Roland T. Ely, *Cuando reinaba su majestad el azúcar. Estudio histórico-sociológico de una tragedia latinoamericana: El monocultivo en Cuba, origen y evolución del proceso*, p. 616.

[34]These words are found in a letter to General Domingo Dulce, then commanding in Cuba, December 12, 1865. To cite Cánovas more fully: "My own conviction is that the moment has arrived to do as much as possible ... I well understand that these measures will please no one ...

"Stationary people of which there are many in this country and who almost form the general opinion concerning the government of the Antilles, have taken

Yet, despite vociferous protests, there were, as we have seen, powerful reform agents. Cánovas after all was supported by men experienced in colonial affairs: O'Donnell, now the president of the Council of Ministers, Concha, Pezuela, Serrano, Dulce, and others. Furthermore, the Cuban and Puerto Rican reform parties, and their allies in Madrid, continued to beat the drums of political and economic reform in subsidized newspapers. And, unlike the case of the law against the slave trade, all parties of Creoles in Cuba and Puerto Rico were in favor of political reforms.

On the twenty-fifth of November, 1865, through the initiative of Cánovas, the O'Donnell government decreed the opening of the Colonial Reform Commission (Junta de Información de Ultramar) with the declared object of examining the bases over which the "Special Laws" were to be structured. This was one of the first important acts of young Cánovas del Castillo. Spain would hear much more from this brilliant conservative in the future. And so would Cuba, for Cánovas was fated to die at the helm of Spain's Cuban policy.[35]

On the announcement that elections would be held in the Antilles in order to select commissioners a wave of excitement shot through both islands. The electorate of Cuba and Puerto Rico promptly separated into reformists and antireformists; the latter group of course, represented the Spanish or Peninsular party.

According to government instructions the municipalities of the island were to elect twenty commissioners, sixteen from Cuba and four from Puerto Rico. The government assumed that property qualifications would favor the conservative party, but to make doubly sure General Dulce was instructed to divide the electorate of the municipalities into four groups: property, industry, commerce, and the professions. The division of industrial and commercial interests was arranged in a way that would serve to increase the electoral power of the Spanish party.[36]

---

it very badly that I officially pronounced the word reform . . . This is why I have needed all perseverence in deciding to carry such a project forward." *Cuba desde 1850 á 1873*, pp. 266–267.

[35]In later years Cánovas was responsible for restoring the monarchy (1876), and for sending General Weyler to Cuba. He died at the hands of an assassin in 1897, as the curtain was falling on the tragic drama of the Spanish Antilles. An interesting study of Cánovas' unfortunate influence on colonial policy is that by Enrique Piñeyro, *Cómo acabó la dominación de España en América*.

[36]Guerra, *Manual de la historia*, p. 584.

Although Dulce did the above, in other ways he aided the reformist cause by protecting their propaganda activities from the fury of the reactionaries. The reactionary organ, *El Diario de la Marina*, repeatedly asked the government to suppress *El Siglo*, organ of the reformists. But Dulce, olympiclike, refused to intervene other than to maintain order.

The result was an amazing victory for the reformists in the municipal elections of March 25, 1866. Of the sixteen Cuban commissioners elected, twelve were reformers; in Puerto Rico three out of four were reformers. These results proved again that political reforms were almost uniformly demanded by the inhabitants of the Antilles.[37]

Before the Antillian commissioners could gather in Madrid, revolutionary upheavals (January to June, 1866) inspired by the more radical leader of Spanish liberalism, General Juan Prim, culminated in bloody executions by O'Donnell. (O'Donnell thus reasserted his cruel fame acquired in the suppression of the Negro protest in Cuba in the 1840's.) Apparently the executions, which contravened the *noblesse oblige* principles of Spanish revolution, led to strong criticism against O'Donnell. The Queen, as a result, called upon her favorite, Ramón María Narvaéz, Duke of Valencia, to take command of the government in July, 1866, after which the Cortes was suspended for six months. Soon after, Cánovas was forced to flee Madrid for having presented a memorandum of the deputies (December 28, 1866) asking for the reopening of the Cortes.[38]

The Moderado government of Narváez was hostile to colonial reforms. But unable to stop the ball put into motion by Cánovas, the new ministry had no choice but to issue a decree of convocation (August 11, 1866). From the beginning, therefore, it might be expected that the Commission would not achieve the results desired by Cánovas and the reformers. In order to control the decisions of the commis-

---

[37]Angel Acosta y Quintero, *José J. Acosta y su tiempo*, pp. 163–164. The following commissioners were elected for Cuba: Manuel de Armas and Antonio X. de San Martín (Havana), José M. Angulo de Heredia (Matanzas), José A. Saco (Santiago de Cuba), José Antonio Echeverría (Puerto Príncipe), Calixto Bernal (Puerto Príncipe), Tomás Terry and el Conde de Pozos Dulces (Villa Clara), Juan Munne (Holguín), el Conde de Vallellano (Sagua), Manuel de Ortega (Cárdenas, Nicolás Azcárate (Guines), Agustín Camejo (Santi Espíritu) and Antonio R. Ojea (Guanajay).

From Puerto Rico: José Julián Acosta, Segundo Ruíz Belvís, Francisco M. Quiñones, Manuel P. Zeno, and two more who did not appear at the conferences.

[38]Juan Ortega Rubio, *Historia de España*, VI, 100–102.

sioners the Moderate ministry named twenty-one persons to represent the Peninsula as against the twenty elected in the Antilles.[39]

In the meantime the Moderados suppressed the Spanish Abolitionist Society because it was a "disturbing factor." This should have come as no surprise. As Sanromá said, when the movement first began, ". . . the people of the Peninsula, the well-to-do of Cuba, the politicians of importance . . . called us filibusters, senseless instruments of the Yankees and, naturally, enemies of the fatherland."[40] Moreover, abolitionism was almost wholly the work of colonial and Spanish liberals, and this gave the liberal-hating government an added reason for suppressing the society.

Aside from the reactionary attitude of the Moderados, there was another serious obstacle that bade ill for the reformist cause. Cuban liberalism, as represented by reform commissioners, was badly divided in body and soul. The relation of José Antonio Saco to the Junta de Información occupied an important place. It was naturally thought by both Spaniards and Cubans that one who for so long had epitomized Cuban reform hopes would be numbered among the colonial representatives. So thought General Serrano, who wrote to Saco offering him a government-sponsored seat on the Commission.[41]

But, exhibiting that aloofness characteristic of him, Saco would not commit himself. His alleged reason was that his acceptance of a position on the Commission would be tantamount to a recognition of the legality of the act of 1837, whereby Cubans, including Saco, had been excluded from the Spanish Cortes.[42] Saco may have had other motives, however. Perhaps he wanted first of all to see what form the Commission would take before he would associate his name with it. Saco was not willing to lend his renowned name to any movement,

---

[39]Cánovas, at least, would have been more liberal. The government would have named an equal number of deputies from both the Peninsula and the Antilles, "so that no interest would be excluded." And concerning the Cuban deputies, if the elections "exclude rich Spaniards . . . I would have to name some Peninsulares . . . If, on the other hand, persons of advanced ideas were excluded, those of *El Siglo*, for example, I would not be opposed to naming them." Cánovas' letter to Dulce, December 12, 1865, *Cuba desde 1850 á 1873*, pp. 266–267.

[40]Joaquín María Sanromá, *Mis memorias 1828–1868*, pp. 345–346.

[41]"Carta de D. Francisco Serrano a D. Antonio Saco" (Madrid, 7 de diciembre de 1865), José Antonio Fernández Castro (ed.), *Medio siglo de historia colonial de Cuba, cartas a José Antonio Saco de 1823–1879*, pp. 335–336.

[42]Guerra, *Manual de la historia*, p. 577.

including the Abolitionist Society, unless his own conservative-reform criteria were fully met.

The Saco name was especially important to the Cuban *reformistas*, for it would lend prestige and respectability to their cause. Leaders such as Morales Lemus, Miguel de Aldama, and el Conde de Pozos Dulces, all former annexationists, were tainted with treasonable tendencies in the eyes of the Spanish government. These very men realized that their position in the colonial conferences would be severely compromised unless they had at their head the name of a man who was honored in both Cuba and Spain.

At least one of the elected reformers from Cuba who favored gradual abolition, José M. Mestre, felt that perhaps Saco was attempting to dissociate himself from the abolitionist tendencies of the reformist circle, due to his close relations with the Creole slaveholding class.[43] In any case, on the eve of the elections in Cuba (March, 1866), Saco was still uncommitted. Nevertheless, such was the prestige of the exile that the city of Santiago de Cuba submitted his name in an election that witnessed the overwhelming triumph of the liberal-reformist cause. Saco was thus included among the twelve Creole delegates. But was he still the Moses of his people?

The tendency of Saco to dissociate himself, together with his late arrival in Madrid, gave an undisputable position to Morales Lemus as leader of the Cuban delegation. True, Saco would later work in harmony with Morales Lemus on the economic and political reforms considered by the Commission, but the fact was that Cuban reformism was now moving beyond him.

[43]"Carta de D. José Manuel Mestre a D. José A. Saco" (La Habana, 30 de enero de 1867), Castro (ed.), *Medio siglo de historia colonial*, pp. 355–356.

11. Great Expectations: The Reform Commission of 1866-1867

> *Mr. President:* Are there objections to considering a method for resolving the extinction of slavery? (*Voices:* Yes, there are.)
> Reform Commission, December 4, 1866[1]

On the thirtieth of October, 1866, Alejandro de Castro, colonial minister of the Moderate government, opened the first meeting of the Junta de Información de Ultramar in the salon of the Colonial Ministry. The government insisted that the sessions be held in secret, apparently because the government feared to excite public opinion in the Spanish Antilles. But, in spite of censorship precautions, letters describing the progress of the conferences were sent by colonial delegates to friends in Cuba and Puerto Rico, and there the word got around.[2]

The Cuban commissioners arrived in Madrid carrying an enormous

---

[1]Colonial Reform Commission, Fifth Conference, December 4, 1866, *Información: Reformas de Cuba y Puerto Rico*, I, 80.

[2]Castro, colonial minister, officially opened the Commission, but the discussions were presided over by Alejandro Oliván, named president of the Commission by the government.

The following commissioners, all to some extent having an interest in colonial affairs, were named to represent the government in the Commission: Pedro de Sotolongo, Nicolás Martínez Valdivieso, Ramón Montalvo y Calvo, Alejandro Oliván, Ramón de la Sagra, el Marqués de Almendares, Jerónimo de Usera (dean of the Holy Cathedral Church, Havana), Francisco Corral, Vicente Vásquez Queipo, José Suárez Argudín, Joaquín González Stéfani, José Ignacio Echeverría, Joaquín M. Ruíz, el Marqués de Manzanedo, José de la Cruz Castellanos, Ignacio González Alvarez, Domingo Sterling, Francisco de Paula Jiménez, and Isidro Díaz de Argüelles. *Ibid.*, p. 33.

accumulation of reform demands. They wanted (1) an end to the exceptional state in which Cuba had been governed since 1825, (2) the separation of the military from civil power, (3) constitutional rights for all Spanish citizens, (4) representative government for administering local affairs, (5) representation in the Cortes, (6) tariff, customs, tax, and administrative reforms, and finally (7) efficacious measures for ending the slave trade, with the recommendation that it be declared piracy as was done in Brazil in 1850.[3]

An impressive list, but it remained to be seen how many of these reforms would actually receive a hearing. After all, the Spanish government had not counted on such an overwhelming reformist victory in the Antilles, and it should not be forgotten that according to the royal decree of November 25, 1865, the Junta was to be limited to an examination of the following topics:[4]

1. The bases upon which must be founded the Special Laws which according to Article 80 of the Constitution of the Monarchy [adopted 1836] must be presented to the Cortes for the government of the provinces of Cuba and Puerto Rico.
2. The means for regulating the work of the Colored and Asiatic population, and on the methods for facilitating immigration . . .
3. The treaties of navigation and commerce that should be celebrated with other nations . . . and the reforms in the tariff system and the administration of customs.

Such was the government agenda. The commissioners had been called to discuss this and nothing more; however, in fairness to the government of the Moderates, to Alejandro de Castro, colonial minister, and to Alejandro Oliván, president of the Conferences, this agenda was discussed freely with little or no pressure upon the delegates. To this degree, at least, the spirit of Cánovas' words was carried out:

They will not come to answer, but to discuss . . . they will discuss freely one with another, and the President will do nothing more than direct the discussion. . . . Such is my system . . . and I believe we will do a service to Cuba and to the Nation.[5]

[3]*Cuba desde 1850 á 1873. Colección de informes, memorias, proyectos, antecedentes sobre el gobierno de la isla de Cuba, que ha reunido por comisión del Gobierno D. Carlos de Sedano y Cruzat, ex-diputado á Cortes*, p. 287.
[4]*Información*, I, p. 33.
[5]Letter of Cánovas to Dulce, December 12, 1865, *Cuba desde 1850 á 1873*,

But too much must not be made of the loose reins that the Moderate ministry held over the commissioners. Apparently, the most embarrassing possibilities had not been foreseen. For example, nothing was on the agenda concerning the abolition of slavery. On the contrary, the assumption of the government was that no problem existed other than that of humanely regulating the labor supply. That the government would allow the discussion to take a free and natural course seems due to blissful ignorance. How little the government understood abolitionist sentiment in Puerto Rico, or Creole feeling against the slave trade in Cuba, is yet to be seen.

The government announced on November 6, 1866, a change in the order of agenda. Questions related with slave labor were to be discussed first. Cuban reformists, always more interested in political reforms, protested angrily, but the only alternative was to withdraw from the Commission.[6] Accordingly, in the second conference four committees were named from among the representatives to study problems related to free and forced labor:

Negros esclavos: Ignacio Gonzáles Olivares (president)
Negros libres: José de la Cruz Castellanos (president)
Inmigración: El Conde de Pozos Dulces (president)
Población asiática: Ramón de la Sagra (president)

The interesting government *interrogatorio* on the regulation of labor is perhaps the best indication of the government's intentions in regard to the slave institution. The questionnaire may be paraphrased as follows:[7]

1. Would it be desirable to establish missions to administer the religious needs of the slaves?
2. What are the means for promoting matrimony among slaves? Would it be desirable to establish annual awards for those slave owners who show the greatest number of marriages on their plantations?
3. Since there are, in the town, more women slaves dedicated to domestic service, and since on the plantations they are scarce, what measures are

pp. 266–267. As a further testimony to the friendly atmosphere in which the delegates worked, the Queen affectionately received a delegation of Antillian commissioners, November 29, 1866. Angel Acosta y Quintero, *José J. Acosta y su tiempo*, p. 169.

[6]Ramiro Guerra y Sánchez, *Manual de la historia de Cuba (económica, social y política)*, p. 591.

[7]*Información*, I, 42–43.

desirable for moving these women to the plantations? Should a tax be imposed on those slaves occupied in domestic service?
4. What measures should regulate the following categories of slaves: slaves under fourteen years of age; slaves over sixty years of age; sick slaves?
5. How should the working hours be regulated? Should disciplinary measures be preserved as they now are?
6. Should coartación, the process whereby a slave obtained his freedom on the installment plan, be reformed?

Concerning the class of free Negroes, the government was primarily concerned with two problems: (1) How to utilize the labor of free blacks? (The delegates were asked whether it was convenient to oblige this class to work.) (2) What measures should be taken to stem the vagrancy problem arising from this class of colored? Was it necessary to exile from the island the habitual vagrant?

Concerning the Asiatic laborers, the interrogatorio posed three questions: (1) What measures would assure their good treatment? (2) Should the labor contracts be reformed? (3) Would it be more desirable to punish this class of offender with fines rather than with corporal punishment?

Finally, concerning the effort to encourage white immigration as a possible alternative to slavery, the government presented the following questions: (1) What form should immigration take? (2) Should it be promoted by the government or by private interest? (3) Should foreign immigrants be admitted equally with those from the Spanish Peninsula?[8]

This questionnaire reflected a general sentiment that the slave trade must virtually cease, especially after the adoption by the Cortes of the new law in pursuit and punishment of the slave trade, and so, therefore, "humanitarian" measures had to be taken to conserve the actual slave labor force of Cuba. It also reflected the position, not of the Moderates but of the original architects of the Commission. Seijas Lozano and Cánovas, who, realizing, as we have said, that emancipation was sooner or later inevitable, thought it wise to prepare the slave for eventual freedom through a transitional stage characterized by religious education and a less compulsory work regimen.

As if to prove that the Moderate ministry scarcely understood the full implications of a free discussion on slave-labor problems, the Puerto Rican commissioners, Acosta, Ruíz Belvís, and Quiñones, in

[8] *Ibid.*

the third conference, November 27, caught the government by surprise by refusing to discuss the first part of the questionnaire. Instead, they declared that the moment had arrived to abolish slavery in Puerto Rico. In a bristling resolution read before the astonished members of the conference, they termed slavery a "miserable institution" and demanded abolition with or without indemnification. Another surprise: two commissioners named by the government, Luis María Pastor, eminent Spanish economist, and Domingo Sterling, associated with Cuban planters, came to the support of the three Puerto Ricans.[9]

The Junta was in a state of great agitation. Most commissioners representing the government naturally protested that abolition was not on the agenda, that it was alarming. The other Puerto Rican, Manuel Zeno, a conservative, hastened to place himself on the side of the government, explaining to his companions that he was not anti-abolitionist but that abolition had to come very gradually, that, in fact, abolition was not a pressing issue, since slavery in Puerto Rico was benevolent and offered a "true protectorate" for the Negroes.[10]

The bombshell effect of the Puerto Rican motion upon the conservatives may be imagined from the following excerpt:[11]

Mr. President [Alejandro Oliván]: Now that the motion of Puerto Rico has been presented ... there is nothing to do but discuss and vote upon it.

Echeverría [Cuban]: There is no motion more radical than this one; there is no greater cry of alarm for Cuba; I believe we must soften it.

[9]The resolution read in part: "The undersigned ask for the abolition of the institution of slavery in their province, abolition with or without indemnity if the latter is not possible; abolition without regulation of free labor or with it, if it is considered absolutely necessary ... "Manifestación de los Señores Comisionados de Puerto Rico pidiendo la abolición inmediata de la esclavitud," 7 de noviembre de 1866, *ibid.*, I, 47–48; also given by Acosta y Quintero, *Acosta y su tiempo*, p. 181.

[10]"Manifestación del Sr. Manuel Zeno contra la inmediata abolición de la esclavitud," 20 de noviembre de 1866, *Información*, I, 48–51.

[11]The point of view of the conservative deputies was expressed by Ramón de la Sagra, who felt that the measures proposed by the government for improving the conditions of slavery were designed to bring about gradual abolition and to satisfy two fundamental needs: not to lose the source of labor entirely, and to satisfy the demands of public opinion.

The rude lessons, said Sagra, learned from the abolitionist experience of Britain, France, and the United States confirmed the wisdom of gradual abolitionist procedures. In any case, the slave class was diminishing naturally in the Antilles due to (1) excessive mortality among newborn slaves, (2) the disproportion between

Mr. President: Are there objections to considering methods for resolving the extinction of slavery? (*Voices:* Yes, there are.)

Azcárate [Cuban]: We will not accept immediate abolition [as a motion of discussion] . . .

Acosta now felt it necessary to pacify the fretful assembly; he therefore explained that the Puerto Ricans were not proposing an abolition law after all but only that the means leading to abolition should be studied.[12]

Even the most reformist deputies of Cuba — Pozos Dulces, Morales Lemus, Echeverría, Azcárate, Ortega, Terry, and others — did not dare sign the proposal of the Puerto Ricans. They limited themselves to congratulating the Puerto Ricans that that island found itself in circumstances so fortunate, but that Cuba was less fortunate and its problem more complex. The cautious memorandum of the Cubans read, in part:

The undersigned . . . have heard with satisfaction the Commissioners from Puerto Rico, Señores Acosta, Ruíz Belvis, and Quiñones, and they cannot but approve the solicitude of said gentlemen concerning their province. At the same time, they [the undersigned] applaud the fact that the sister island had succeeded in demonstrating the practical advantage of free labor, the coexistence and cooperation of the White and Negro races in agricultural tasks, the aptitude of this [the white race] for other industries which until now some have thought supportable only by the African in tropical climates. . . .

But Cuba less fortunate in this regard than Puerto Rico is at the moment in very different circumstances which make impossible the realization of immediate abolition. The question there [in Cuba] is extremely complicated. . . .

The undersigned in no way aspire toward the perpetuation of slavery in their province, nor to prolong it one moment more than necessary in order to prevent grave disturbances in the march of civilization and the moral and material progress of their country. But they reserve the right to express all those ideas which bear on the future prosperity and conservation of the

---

male and female slaves, (3) the lesser degree of fecundity in female slaves, (4) the smaller number of marriages among slaves, (5) partial and full manumissions (on the part of the master), and (6) the lottery by which some slaves could buy freedom ("Explanación del voto del que suscribe D. Ramón de la Sagra sobre los negros esclavos," 11 de diciembre de 1866 [signed by the government commissioners], *ibid.*, I, 91).

[12] December 4, 1866, *Ibid.*, I, 26.

The Reform Commission of 1866–1867   195

island, because such ideas must be in harmony with the poltical laws that will be asked for at the opportune moment.[13]

By the words, "in harmony with the political laws," the Cuban deputies meant that the solution to the slave question must be subordinate to political reforms. The Creoles naturally expected to liberate their own class from Spanish oppression before considering the slave.

It has been indicated that Morales Lemus and most of the Creole reformers of wealth and affluence were by their professed liberal principles abolitionists in theory, but they were sustainers of slavery in practice. Their point of view, according to the Puerto Rican Acosta y Quintero, was modeled after the Democratic Party of the United States, which before the Civil War had great influence in Cuba. The achievement of more-democratic autonomy for the island could serve to safeguard the slave economy upon which Cuban prosperity depended.[14]

The point of view of the Puerto Rican reformers provides a striking contrast. They felt that the slave question was primary, partly because Puerto Rican slavery, being less rooted socially and less important economically, permitted them to think so, but also because the Puerto Ricans believed that the existence of the slave institution had always been employed as a reason for sustaining the political status quo of the Spanish Antilles, that abolition of slavery would have to precede the general program of political reforms desired by both islands. The abolitionist Acosta y Quintero pointedly reminded the commissioners that one of the reasons why the Cortes of 1837 had excluded the Antilles from the constitutional system of the Peninsula was the existence of slavery.[15]

Cuban delegates could be opposed to the abolition of slavery and

---

[13]"Contestación al interrogatorio sobre la manera de reglamentar el trabajo," 26 de noviembre de 1866, *ibid.*, I, 73–75. To forestall the effect of the Puerto Rican declaration, the antireformists, Olivares, Sotolongo, Zeno, Armas, and Ruíz, arranged a private meeting with the Cuban reformists. The first party wanted the second to agree upon two things: first, that they would not support the abolitionist manifesto of the Puerto Ricans, and, second, that they would make a statement of their own on the same question, laying the subject at rest. But the Cuban reformists made no commitments to the conservatives. Acosta y Quintero, *Acosta y su tiempo*, pp. 187–188.

[14]Acosta y Quintero, *Acosta y su tiempo*, p. 188.

[15]*Cuba desde 1850 á 1873*, p. 16.

still logically insist on the closing of the slave traffic. Here they were unanimous, and for complex reasons. Cuban liberals and patriots as exemplified by Saco and el Conde de Pozos Dulces, as we have seen, had come to fear Africanization as a millstone around Cuba's neck. If and when Cuba achieved autonomy or independence, the Creole patriots did not want that autonomy or independence burdened with insoluble social problems.[16] They feared that in a free, mixed society the blacks would predominate and that Cuba would come to be only another Haiti or Santo Domingo, a mulatto, half-savage republic.

In one sense, they wanted autonomy or independence to protect themselves from the inundation of blacks, since Spaniards, not Cubans, profited most from this trade and, of course, Spain used the trade to hold Cuba in subjection.

Also, some reformers believed that property interests in slavery could be better protected by abolishing the slave trade. We have seen that it was this fear in the 1850's that moved Creole planters to consider annexation to the slaveholding United States as the best safeguard for slavery against British demands. Disgusted with Spain's halfhearted efforts to stop the slave trade and with the complicity of Spanish officials, they felt that only drastic measures could crush that profitable business. Hence, they were not satisfied with the recent Law for the Supression and Punishment of the Slave Trade. They believed that no law would be sufficient unless it declared the slave trade piracy.

In accordance with a previous agreement among the reformers, the Cuban Angulo de Heredia, in the session of December 6, 1866, asked that the African slave trade be declared piracy. In this discourse, Angulo, citing Concha's words of 1853 that protecting slavery was a positive threat to the conservation of the island, proposed that closing the trade would be a means of gradual abolition, and then added the significant words:

> The Commissioners of Cuba have the duty to manifest in some way that its inhabitants are not opposed to gradual extinction. . . . In this way we

---

[16] As Fernando Ortiz Fernández has said, Saco was vigorously opposed to the slave trade; ". . . yet he never declared himself an abolitionist." "Saco, la esclavitud y los Negros," *Revista Bimestre Cubana* (La Habana), XLII, Nos. 1-2 (julio–octubre, 1938), 37-64.

will calm the execretion and hate of the abolitionist centers of Europe.[17]

Antonio X. de San Martín, Cuban, in support of the motion argued that a declaration of piracy was necessary if Spain was to recover her national honor; that the nation had lost its character before the other nations of Europe; that it had been lying to the face of the world; and that it must be shamefully confessed that the slave trade survived only by the tolerance of the Spanish government.[18]

The President, Oliván, moved by this discourse, proposed that the motion be admitted. In view of the number of commissioners in favor, a committee was appointed to study the subject. *The Committee Report*, dated January 29, 1867, was a bitter indictment of Spanish slave-trade policy. A theory of the "equilibrium of races" was invented, said the report. Since a Spaniard born in America, that is, a Creole, could not be trusted, as proved by the loss of Spanish America, it was necessary to restrain him by increasing the number of blacks. From then on, among Spaniards, "the slave trade raised its head proudly as a patriotic thing and woe to him who would dare to censure it." Such a critic "was undoubtedly a bad Spaniard, a revolutionary conspiring to destroy the *equilibrium* of races in order to weaken and destroy the power of the metropolis."[19]

As to corruption in the slave trade, that was notorious:

The deputies may judge if an authority could resist the owner of a slave expedition who came up to him and said: "Take 10, 15, 20 or 30,000 duros without receipt, without witnesses, you keep it, and I only ask for you that tomorrow at such an hour instead of watching this part of your jurisdiction that you find yourself in another part."[20]

It was notorious, said the *Report*, that Spain had been thus so shamefully occupied since the 1817 treaty with Great Britain. After citing the Declaration of Vienna against the slave trade, as well as the Bulls of Pius II (1482), Paul III (1557), Urban VIII (1639), Benedict XIV (1741), and Gregory XVI (1839) against the same, the com-

[17]*Ibid.*, p. 24.
[18]Acosta y Quintero, *Acosta y su tiempo*, p. 189.
[19]"Informe presentado por la Comisión nombrada para estudiar la moción del Sr. Angulo Heredia relativa a que se declare piratería la trata africana, *Información*, I, 94–119.
[20]*Ibid.*, I, 107–111.

mittee asked that (1) the slave trade be declared piracy, as in the case of the United States and Brazil, where it had proved to be the only effective means for ending this commerce; (2) that organizers of slave expeditions be judged within the first scale of criminality (according to the Spanish penal code); (3) that buyers of slaves be declared accomplices to the crime; (4) that the before-referred-to Association against the Slave Trade, founded in Havana by the Lawyer Antonio González de Mendoza and others in 1865, be permitted legal existence.[21]

Commissioners representing the government immediately protested. Olivares said that it "would permit all nations to persecute the Cuban slave trade . . . and even England does not consider the slave trade a crime of piracy!"[22] Usera, dean of the Cathedral of Havana, in explaining his opposition, stood on grounds of questionable humanitarianism: "There is an unanimity of feeling that the traffic should cease, because it is contrary to humanity . . . equally with the Holy See I condemn it . . . but Negroes are still savages . . ."[23] The Dean felt that a declaration of piracy, though admirable in purpose, was perhaps too severe. He could not sign a declaration as a Catholic priest, since this declaration would imply severe penalties, including death. Díaz de Argüelles, a member of the slave-trade committee, also opposed. Despite opposition, however, the proposal that a recommendation be made to the government to declare the slave trade as piracy carried by a vote of seventeen to ten.[24]

Closely related to the slave-trade problem were other items of the agenda, namely, problems related to *Free Negroes, Asiatic Population* and *Immigration*. Made manifest in the discussions were the principles that free Negroes were to be strictly subject to civil and

---

[21]*Ibid.*, I, 110–111. The following commissioners signed the Report: Angulo Acosta, Castellanos, Azcárate, Morales Lemus, Pozos Dulces, Antonio Rodríguez, Tomás Terry, Echeverría, Quiñones, Bernal, Ruíz Belvís, Agustín Camejo, Manuel de Ortega, Acosta, and Pastor.

[22]*Ibid.* On March 3, 1824, Great Britain enacted that any British subject found guilty of engaging in the slave trade should be adjudged guilty of piracy, felony, and robbery, and should suffer death without benefit of clergy, and loss of goods and property, as pirates upon the high seas ought to suffer. John R. Spears. *The American Slave Trade: An Account of Its Origin, Growth, and Suppression*, p. 102.

[23]*Cuba desde 1850 á 1873*, p. 115.

[24]Acosta y Quintero, *Acosta y su tiempo*, p. 189.

penal codes, that vagrancy should be controlled, that Asiatics were generally undesirable as laborers, and that white immigration should predominate. In this latter regard, Pozos Dulces, president of the Section on Immigration, presented a report (December 20, 1866) which demanded a policy of white immigration only.[25]

This report, which illustrates the point of view of Creole liberalism, previously explained, asked that the decree of 1817 be nullified. This decree, considered a great advance at the time since its purpose was to foment Spanish immigration to the colonies, was now considered obsolete by the Cuban reformers because it placed cumbersome residence requirements on non-Catholic and non-Spanish white immigrants. According to the report, both islands had great need of white settlers: "We want there the predominance of the white race."[26] This was the theme that Pozos Dulces, Saco, and other liberals had preached for years: the need to "whiten" *(blanquear)* the population of Cuba for cultural, economic, and political reasons.[27]

Meanwhile, the taboo of emancipation could not be avoided by the commissioners. The question which now faced them was whether the slave regimen could be softened without radically undermining the forced-labor system itself.

The third conference (November 27, 1866) emphasized the gravity of the problem. The religious education of slaves was under discussion. As the agenda has recognized, there was a great shortage of priests; the religious needs of the slaves were unattended. But was the real purpose of the agenda to preserve slavery by improving the morale of the slave? Or was it primarily designed to prepare the slave for eventual liberty and civic responsibility through Catholic education? The members of the committee began by discussing the pros and cons of establishing missions among the plantations. Those members who opposed the idea said that it would be better to increase the number of parishes in Cuba, letting the parish priest come for a brief visit on Sundays to say Mass, sermonize, and then depart. This dosage would be sufficient. Otherwise, as Sr. Azcárate said, mission establishments on the plantations could not be harmonized with the regimentation of plantation life. The missions "will arouse

---

[25]"Informe de la Comisión nombrada para contestar los interrogatorios referentes a la inmigración," 20 de diciembre de 1866 y 30 de enero de 1867 (signed by the reformist Commissioners), *Información*, I, 155–215.

[26]*Ibid.*, Also, Acosta y Quintero, *Acosta y su tiempo*, p. 193.

[27]*Información*, I, 151–154.

aspirations for liberty in the slaves, and this will give rise to terrible civic disorders."[28]

Sr. San Martín disagreed with Azcárate, saying that slavery was not incompatible with Christianity. The early Christians never promoted rebellions against the terrestrial order: "Give to Caesar the things that are Caesar's and to God the things that are God's." A knowledge of the doctrines of Christianity "makes slaves more submissive and masters more charitable."[29]

Other representatives, however, thought that, owing to the circumstances of the time, education given to slaves should have a different purpose. Sr. Angulo said that education must prepare the slaves for eventual emancipation:

> The abolition of slavery is an urgent question . . . because the whole world is concerned with it . . . look at all the societies, for example, that of Paris composed of such illustrious gentlemen as Guizot, the Count of Montalambert and the Duke of Broglie. . . . It is necessary to educate the slave in order to prepare him for liberty.[30]

According to Angulo, the best method of carrying through this education would be by increasing the number of parishes in Cuba, ". . . and if the state cannot withstand the expense then there are enough rich proprietors in the island to contribute toward this increase."[31] This discussion, which came to an indecisive vote, was terminated by President Oliván, who said it was not yet time to enter in the question of abolition, even though it seemed to come before everything else.

In the same way, the discussion of whether slave conditions could be improved by abolishing corporal punishment, namely the whip, threatened the foundations of servitude. Olivares and the Marqués de Almendares regretted the use of corporal punishment, but felt strongly that discipline could not be maintained without the whip. Pastor and Azcárate protested that such harsh methods were not necessary; the latter gave an example of how the twenty-five lashes allowed by law had been sufficient to kill a man. Pastor and the abolitionist reformers wanted the whip abolished, and if this was not possible, they hoped Negroes abused in this way could be set free. But this latter motion lost by a vote of fifteen to eleven.[32]

[28]*Cuba desde 1850 á 1873*, pp. 10–11.
[29]*Ibid.*, p. 12.   [30]*Ibid.*, p. 13.   [31]*Ibid.*, p. 13.
[32]Seventh Conference, December 11, 1866, *ibid.*, p. 33.

The Reform Commission of 1866–1867

In discussions concerning improvements in the conditions of the slave (Sixth Conference, December 5, 1866) the reformers proposed that slaves aged sixty years or older should be given liberty, and that in honor of the treaties made with Great Britain, all slaves introduced fraudulently since 1835 should be set at liberty.[33]

Again, discussion inclined itself toward the spectre of emancipation. Pastor, a member of the Spanish Abolitionist Society, again raised his voice:

> When morality, religion and public convenience demand this . . . when the United States had just sacrificed the life and well-being of millions of inhabitants in order to achieve the abolition of slavery at the doorstep of our Antilles, it is impossible that we continue with the illusion that we can delay the solution of this problem.[34]

Some tried to stop the abolitionist drift. Argudín rejected all allusions to the American example, saying that Lincoln only wanted the Confederate States to return to the Union and that these would be allowed to retain slavery for many years more. Abolition there had reduced four million Negroes and eight million whites to a beggar's life. "Ah!" exclaimed Sr. Argudín, "if it were only possible for Lincoln to return from the grave, and to return to that horrible instant in which he gave that unfortunate decree, before signing it again he would first consent to the cutting off of his hand."[35]

Finally, on March 1, 1867, Luis María Pastor bluntly proposed that Castro, minister of colonies, name a committee to study the means for extinguishing slavery. Castro, seeing that an increasing number of delegates were in favor, and realizing that the course of the conferences could not be controlled, agreed.[36] The truth was that the atmosphere of free discussion had permitted a handful of devoted abolitionists to appeal to the liberal sentiments, common sense, and enlightened self-interest of their colleagues, thereby, in the course of the discussions, forcing the subject of emancipation upon the agenda.

Even some of the conservative reformers accepted the motion of Pastor when it was agreed that gradual and not immediate abolition would be the subject. Oliván, the president, could say at this point:

---

[33] *Ibid.*, p. 24.
[34] Twenty-sixth Conference, February 25, 1867, *ibid.*, p. 117.
[35] Twenty-seventh Conference, March 1, 1867, *ibid.*, p. 131.
[36] Thirty-sixth Conference, April 28, 1867, *ibid.*, p. 149.

"There is agreement in the thoughts of everyone that slavery has to be abolished gradually, first hearing those who have an interest therein. This unanimity of feeling should be applauded."[37] A committee was then constituted, consisting of ten members.[38] The Puerto Rican delegates and the Cubans thereupon began to prepare separate plans of abolition.[39]

The last days of the reform inquiry were given over to discussion of the emancipation question. At a late hour, when the conference was about to end, the Puerto Ricans—Acosta, Belvís, and Quiñones—submitted a formal plan for the abolition of slavery in Puerto Rico (April 10, 1867). In the preamble to the project they made an extensive examination of the history of the introduction of slaves in Puerto Rico, of their present economic and social condition, and of the results of immediate abolition in other European colonies. Their conclusion was in favor of immediate abolition: "In summary: We want and ask in the name of the honor of our country the immediate, radical and definite abolition of slavery."[40]

The authors recognized that vested interests would have to be compensated and the labor supply protected to some extent. They also believed that a system of labor regulations should accompany the emancipation decree. They preferred indemnity for slaveowners because the government could not deny the species of property that slaves represented to the owners, and because it would prevent an economic crisis. But, "in any case, with or without indemnification, slavery must not endure one day more."[41]

Following the example of the Puerto Rican delegates, the Cuban reformers presented their project on the last day of the conference (April 27, 1867). In daring to present an emancipation project, even

[37]Ibid.

[38]Olivares, Echeverría, Marqués de Manzanedo, Ojea, Zeno, Ruíz Belvís, Jiménez, Ortega, Terry, and Argudín.

[39]Acosta y Quintero, *Acosta y su tiempo*, p. 199.

[40]The Puerto Rican plan of abolition fixed the indemnity value of slaves according to their age. Children of less than seven years and adults of more than sixty years were to be valued at 100 pesos each; those between eight and fifteen years, and forty and sixty years, at 200 pesos each; and those between sixteen and forty at 400 pesos each. The total amount of indemnification was calculated at 11,993,-800 pesos for the 41,000 slaves in Puerto Rico. The plan recommended a foreign loan to finance indemnification ("Proyecto para la abolición de la esclavitud en Puerto Rico," 10 de abril de 1867, *Información*, II, 207-249).

[41]Ibid.

though it was a gradual plan, the Cuban commissioners were exceeding their instructions. Echeverría, who previously had opposed the introduction of the topic for political reasons, prepared the Cuban project of gradual abolition. Again, mixed motives explained the commissioners' action. Some, such as Morales Lemus, who would have preferred not to touch the issue, felt obliged to follow the abolitionist trend of the conferences. The Cubans feared the radical abolitionism of the Puerto Ricans and the rising abolitionist sentiment in the metropolis.[42] Abolitionist or not, they recognized the danger of sudden and disastrous Africanization and foresaw, as in the matter of wanting to declare the slave trade piracy, that perhaps this danger could be offset by opportune concessions. Equally as important, they had to consider the possibility of a boycott of the products of slave labor by the United States. Such recommendations had already been made in the American Congress. Since the United States was now Cuba's major market, this was a weighty consideration. Some Cuban commissioners were therefore choosing the lesser of two evils in favoring gradual emancipation, while other Cuban commissioners might well have thought that the project had token value only, that coming at the end of the Conference it would not be acted upon.

The Cuban plan of gradual abolition, as was customary, included a prologue in which the authors summarized the reasons and persuations that had induced their course of action: Christianity, enlightenment; among other things they asserted: "The immorality of slavery would suffice by itself to make its abolition indispensable.... The emancipation of the serf is the lesson of the nineteenth century."[43]

This forceful language, attributed to José Antonio Echeverría, was qualified by a number of sober considerations. Certain dangers would have to be avoided and these may be paraphrased as follows:[44]

1. That of arousing aspirations for the immediate liberation of the slaves, an aspiration which if later frustrated might lead to disturbances.
2. That of suddenly interrupting the labor system of the plantations.
3. That of the sudden irruption of ignorant and undisciplined hosts upon the towns and public highways, and that of the abuse of a misunderstood right which would lead to vice and crime.

[42]See Raúl Cepero Bonilla, *Azúcar y abolición: Apuntes para una historia crítica de abolicionismo*, pp. 74–76.
[43]Eugenio Alonso y Sanjurjo, *Apuntes sobre los proyectos de la abolición de la esclavitud en las islas de Cuba y Puerto Rico*, p. 283; *Información*, II, 265.
[44]*Información*, II, 286.

4. That of the retreat of freed slaves, born in Africa, into mountains and unpopulated places in which the island abounds, the Negroes thus returning to a savage life and transforming themselves from instruments of production to instruments of intranquility [shades of Haiti!].
5. That of the sudden raising of wages, which would make it impossible to compete with prices obtained by other countries producing the same product.
6. That of the lack of capital by which proprietors would pay wages to workers, and that of interrupting the operations of industry.
7. That of prejudicing creditors who hold mortgages on plantations [namely Spanish merchants].
8. That of the probability of exaggerated fears and alarms which would cause capital to flee the island, thus producing a great financial crisis.

The Cuban reformers recognized the right of the slave to liberty, but they categorically affirmed in the same breath "the right of the white population to defend its existence and to remain in the country conquered by their forefathers." Furthermore, humanity and progress demanded not only that chains be struck from the slave but also that the more advanced race prevent the retrocession of civilization to a barbaric age.[45]

The most important recommendations of the Cuban plan were the following:[46]

1. That the African slave trade should be positively suppressed.
2. That those born of slaves henceforth be declared free [this concept was known as *vientre libre*].
3. That slaves whose name did not appear in the census or register should be declared free.
4. That no plan of emancipation should be decreed without provision for previous indemnification to the owners.
5. That no plan should be adopted without previous consultation with the corporations of the island.

The plan would establish an annual lottery as a means of obtaining funds "in order to improve the condition of the slaves and rescue

[45] *Ibid.*, II, 286–287.
[46] *Ibid.*, II, 287–288. At this time the Conde de Vegamar, a Cuban slave proprietor, presented a plan similar to that of the Cuban reformists: the slave trade would be declared piracy, and through a process of coartación the liberty of all slaves would be purchased in ten years. See Alonso y Sanjurjo, *Apuntes*, pp. 58–59.

them from their present state." The slaves would be divided into groups, depending on their age. Drawings would be held for each of these groups, and a certain number of slaves would thereby have their freedom purchased through lottery funds.[47]

Slaves sixty years and older would be set free, likewise those under seven, but the latter would remain in a state of tutelage until the age of eighteen. Slaves between the ages of seven and eighteen, even though their number be drawn in the lottery, would remain under the patronage until the age of eighteen. Meanwhile, coartación would continue as always, permitting some slaves to work out their own liberty.

Indemnification was figured at 450 pesos for each slave. A certain proportion of slaves, beginning with the older ones, would be set free, until after seven years all slaves over eighteen would be freed. The funds for compensation would be derived from the revenues of the island over a period of fifteen years. The total number of slaves to be liberated between the ages of seven to sixty was calculated at 302,912. The total cost of emancipation was figured at 117,599,000 pesos.[48] The reform commissioners from Cuba signed the document, but the name of Saco was conspicuously absent.

As a matter of record both the Puerto Rican and Cuban plans on being presented to the Commission received the approval of the majority of members. But approval was by means unanimous, even among the reformers. The Commission being at the point of closing, there was nothing else to do but to recommend these plans to the colonial minister along with other memoranda reflecting the viewpoint of the Antillian deputies.[49]

For our purpose, the real drama of the conferences lay in the "social question." However, the reader would have a false impression if he thought this the main subject of the conferences. Again, it must be reaffirmed that for the Cuban reformers the political and economic questions were more important.

Space does not permit a detailed examination of the economic and political questions debated by the commissioners. Suffice it to say that the lengthy reports submitted by the reformers reflected their laissez-faire or anticolonial philosophy and the purpose for which

---

[47]"Plan de emancipación de la esclavitud en Cuba," *Información*, II, 288–292.
[48]*Ibid.*
[49]*Ibid.*

they had come to Madrid. They had asked for free trade between the colonies and mother country. Since this would involve a loss in revenue for the metropolis, the reformers suggested a substitute revenue in the form of a tax of 6 per cent on all income derived from agriculture, commerce, and the professions. In case free trade was not fully possible, then they asked that customs duties be lowered as far as possible, and that articles of prime necessity, such as flour and foodstuffs (which came largely from the United States), be admitted duty-free.[50]

In political matters the Cubans were no less demanding. A committee headed by Morales Lemus prepared a report on the "Special Laws," which had been promised to Cuba and Puerto Rico since 1837. This document gave a complete summary of the Spanish colonial system then in existence, listing its virtues, which were few, and its defects, which were many. An impressively long list of political and administrative reforms—which had accumulated through the years like a log jam—was given a solemn recommendation.[51] If this list had been put into practice immediately, Cuba might have become a second Canada.

Primary among the "Special Laws" requested was one that would admit the Antilles in the Cortes on the basis of one deputy for each 45,000 inhabitants. Furthermore, the reformers were determined to democratize insular institutions from top to bottom. An insular council and insular assembly, popularly elected, would surround the governor; these institutions would have to be consulted on all matters of insular finance and administrative policy. The islands were to be divided into administrative subdivisions, provided with a responsible provincial council and a responsible provincial assembly. Likewise, municipal governments were to be made more numerous and more representative.[52]

Saco, still a nonconformist, opposed representation in the Cortes on the grounds that Cuban deputies would be a powerless minority,

[50]"Oficio remitiendo la contestación al interrogatorio económico," 30 de enero de 1867 (signed by Luis M. Pastor, Pedro de Sotolongo, and others), *ibid.*, II, 232–235.

[51]"Contestación á las preguntas 3, 4, 5, 6, 7, 8 y 9 del Interrogatorio político," 25 de abril de 1867 (signed by the reformist Commissioners), *ibid.*, II, 100–137.

[52]For a summary of these recommendations see "Extracto de las contestaciones dadas al Interrogatorio sobre las bases en que deben fundarse las Leyes Especiales para el gobierno de las provincias de Cuba y Puerto Rico," *ibid.*, II, 2–101.

and a group carefully selected to represent Peninsular not Creole interests. He believed that an autonomous colonial legislature was the only means by which the Creoles could control their own political destiny. But in any case, the disillusioned Saco expected little or nothing from the reform Commission.[53]

As to the rights of the individual citizen, the reformers asked that all rights of the Spanish Constitutions be applied to the Antilles. Many of these rights, such as freedom of petition, press, and association, were not fully enjoyed by Spaniards themselves. The oppressive nature of Spanish colonial government was further exemplified in the demands for the free exercise of any profession without undue restrictions, equality of access to civil employment according to merit and capacity, the right to acquire property and the protection thereof, freedom from arbitrary arrest and seach, and the same civil and criminal codes as in the Peninsula. Also, the governor general's power to suspend civil liberties in emergencies — the emergency had thus far been permanent — was to be subject to control by the proposed insular council and assembly. Arbitrary tribunals were to be abolished and the reduction of any free citizen to servitude for failure to fulfill any law or contract would be forbidden.[54]

"How many of the reformers," asked the historian Cruz Monclova, "were thinking of the slave when they termed the above rights 'inherited by man and the essential condition of his existence'?"[55] Here it is necessary to stress again that, like John Calhoun and the Democrats of the South, the Cuban liberals did not think slavery inconsistent with republican institutions. The metropolis must stop using slavery as an excuse for denying civil liberties to the whites:

It is supposed that slavery is an insuperable obstacle for liberal institutions due to the existence of diverse races and the great number of free blacks, but contemporary and ancient history denies this . . .

Rome from the earliest times and the republics of Greece had slaves and free-men; the North American Federation had them until recently, and this

[53]José A. Saco, "Carta a D. Manuel Solorzano," enero de 1867, Luis M. Pérez, *Estudios sobre las ideas políticas de José Antonio Saco*, p. 59.

[54]"Respuesta al Interrogatorio sobre las bases en que deban fundarse las leyes especiales que, al cumplir el artículo 80 de la Constitución de Monarquía española, deben presentarse á las Córtes para el gobierno de Cuba y Puerto Rico," 28 de marzo de 1867, *Información*, II, 3–8.

[55]Lidio Cruz Monclova, *Historia de Puerto Rico (Siglo XIX)*, I, 518.

had not impeded these countries nor prevented them from having popular institutions...⁵⁶

These were, of course, a multiplicity of other arguments advanced in favor of political reforms. One of the more interesting referred to the unfortunate division of the insular society into the Spanish and Creole parties:

... the two parties that unfortunately exist today in the Antilles will disappear with the establishment of the proposed system, because everyone being equal in rights and their exercise of the same ... that lamentable division will no longer have reason to exist. Other parties will come, perhaps, but these will be true political parties, parties of doctrine and principles.⁵⁷

Finally, there was the veiled threat of the reformers — which would prove not to be an idle one — that reforms in the direction of self-government were the only way Spain could preserve the fidelity of her overseas possessions:

The islands of Puerto Rico and Cuba have anxiously watched the march of events in the mother country. They witnessed and studied with profit the convulsions of the Hispanic-American republics and the struggle in the neighboring Federation of the United States, and neither the upheavals nor the causes of progress and backwardness in one or the other are unknown to them.

The exceptional and anomalous situation that for so many years has grieved these provinces have made the majority of their enlightened inhabitants understand that such a situation could not perpetuate itself, that there would have to come a day in which they would be called to participate in the administration of their own affairs, and that they should prepare themselves in order to exercise their rights when justice would be done to them.⁵⁸

The decree opening the conferences had authorized the colonial minister to consult, apart from the commissioners, all men who had discharged public duties in the islands of Cuba and Puerto Rico, including former governors; Castro therefore requested memoranda from Francisco Serrano and Domingo Dulce. These two generals, as they had previously done, supported the reform claims of the Cubans almost in their entirety. Since these men were respected in both Spain

---

⁵⁶*Información*, II, 40–41.
⁵⁷*Ibid.*, II, 40–41.   ⁵⁸*Ibid.*, II, 34–55.

and Cuba, their opinions offered strong moral support to reform proposals.

Dulce's report, presented in January, 1867, favored tariff and administrative reforms, white immigration, and the amalgamation of the white and African races. Dulce made notable recommendations for progressive extinction of slavery: "The problem of slavery today occupies the first place... neither the will of the government nor the wishes of those inhabitants [in the Antilles] would be sufficient to postpone it indefinitely. There is a superior force: that of ideas and events..." Concerning the slave trade, he thought the law of September, 1866, insufficient. What was needed was authority to pursue illegal slaves anywhere without exceptions. Though not in favor of a declaration of piracy, he did favor exiling the slavers, "... they are very well known in the island, those who prepare slave ships; furthermore, in the Secretariat of the High Civil Government can be found information concerning the most prominent ones occupied in this odious speculation."[59]

At the end of April, 1867, shortly after the last conference, Serrano submitted his opinion on the agenda of the Commission. Like Dulce and the reform commissioners, he was preoccupied with the problem of slavery. The fact that other nations had abolished slavery had left Spain alone among slaveholding nations: "Slavery is today... it hurts to say it, nothing but a Spanish institution, since Brazil... has given her word that she will promptly resolve the problem."[60] Serrano stressed the possibility of North American action against slaveholding countries:

> We all know the cost of so many sacrifices by which in the United States ... four million slaves have gained liberty.... We all know that more than once in the Congress [of the United States] they have talked of prohibiting the introduction of products of slave labor, this would be the complete ruin of the island of Cuba which sells more than half of her products in the United States.[61]

Serrano repeated that the Antilles were always threatened by foreign intervention so long as slavery was maintained. Abolitionist societies in England, France, and Spain were gaining ground in pub-

[59]Domingo Dulce, *Informe al Ministro de Ultramar*, p. 58.
[60]Francisco Serrano, *Informe al Sr. Ministro de Ultramar*, pp. 15–16.
[61]*Ibid.*, pp. 15–16.

lic opinion; abolition should be anticipated so that it could be accomplished prudently.

"In my opinion," said the former governor, "what the government must do is close immediately the two sources of slavery: the slave traffic and the birth of slaves." In agreement with the abolition plan of the Cuban delegates, he recommended that slavery be declared piracy and that the principle of vientre libre, that is, free birth of slaves, be established. In other ways he went further than the majority of reformers in counseling the reduction in the number of lashes and the concession of liberty to maltreated slaves.[62]

Serrano, incidentally, condemned Asiatic colonization in no uncertain terms: "Asiatic colonization, in spite of regulations, is a true form of temporal slavery with all the inconveniences of perpetual slavery ... furthermore, it is now undone the lie that whites cannot resist the climate."[63]

General Serrano also supported the separation of the military from the civil command. Like the colonials, he rested his arguments on the policy of asimilación that supposedly governed Spain's empire. Serrano cited the Laws of the Indies: "Because being of one crown the kingdoms of Castille and the Indies, the laws ... must be as similar and conformable as possible." The complaints of the Cubans were just, he said, their aspirations legitimate: "Today reforms are convenient. The annexationist party doesn't exist and the United States is occupied with internal affairs. Spain can work freely."[64]

On the last day of the conference, April 16, 1867, the colonial minister, Alejandro de Castro, read the royal decree officially terminating the reform inquiry. Concerning the question of abolition, Castro said:

> Soon the commissioners will return to their provinces. . . . I assure the commissioners that there is no one more interested than the government in solving a problem that dominates everything; there is no need to hide or avoid the word: *slavery*. The impulses that compel this [a solution] are not only feelings of humanity, economic motives, and the interest of the state, but also the necessity to prevent foreign complications.[65]

And speaking generally of the work and recommendations of the commission, Castro terminated his discourse with these hopeful

---

[62]*Ibid.*, p. 20.
[63]*Ibid.*, p. 24.
[64]"Código Indias," Ley B. Titulo II, Libro II, *ibid.*, p. 27.
[65]*Cuba desde 1850 á 1873*, p. 150.

The Reform Commission of 1866–1867

words: "Work done by this junta is of such importance that not a moment can be lost in its application."

The felicitious farewell of the colonial minister rang in the reformers' ears. Some delegates, like Morales Lemus, held grave doubts about the outcome of the conferences from beginning to end.[66] But other commissioners, no doubt, under the spell of the moment, revised their cynical opinions of Spanish justice and fell to congratulating one another.

The long tedious conferences, the exhaustive debates, the boring committee work, the scholarly effort spent on gathering economic and social data — all this had come to fruition in a series of reports, recommendations, and projects, surprisingly unanimous in character, addressed to the crown. That the government apparently approved of the spirit of these recommendations was implicit in the words of the colonial minister, Castro, and the fact that half of the conferees had represented the interests of the government. The Antillian reform deputies might be forgiven, if, on booking passage home, they fondly hoped that something good would come of all this. To this point sublimity. How the reform commission of 1866–1867 was turned into one of the farces of Spanish colonial history will now be briefly related.

After the conferences Alejandro de Castro remained seriously impressed with the abolitionist feelings of the delegates. He felt that some preparatory steps toward abolition were now in order. At least he made some declarations to this effect, claiming that this was the spontaneous thinking of the government.[67]

It seemed that Castro actually intended to carry out plans for gradual abolition, but the obstacles were too many. In the first place, he was advised that a social change of such magnitude would arouse the powerful opposition of the slave proprietors. Spain, as he well knew, did not have the financial resources of England for compensating dispossessed slave owners. The only form of compensation would be to remove all exorbitant taxes of a general and local character weighing upon the products of the plantations, thus permitting the planter to sell products produced by free wage labor in the world market at reasonable prices. But it was not likely that the Spanish government could afford to do without any part of Cuba's revenues for such pur-

[66] Guerra, *Manual de la historia*, p. 597.
[67] Alonso y Sanjurjo, *Apuntes*, p. 15.

poses. From this point of view, Spain was too poor to be abolitionist. Furthermore, other members of the Narváez cabinet, as will soon be made evident, were fully on the side of the antireformists. In any case, another minister soon left the Colonial Ministry without having done anything.[68]

The metropolitan government had good reasons for ignoring the abolitionist proposals. The abolitionist recommendations of the colonial delegates were nullified, according to one interpretation, because they had exceeded their instructions. Many of the slaveholding electorate who had voted for these delegates now denounced them because, contrary to the original purposes of the Commission, the slave economy of Cuba and Puerto Rico was now endangered by abolition.

When it was known in Cuba that reform delegates had presented a plan of gradual abolition, there began a new series of attacks by the "good Spaniards" against the "bad Spaniards," who wanted to overturn the economy and social order of the island. The literary war between the reformist voice *El Siglo* and the conservative voice *El Diario de la Marina* again broke out. Even the Creole slave proprietors who were friends of the delegates were divided in their feelings. Like many inhabitants of Cuba, they wanted political and economic reform but not social reforms. They tended now to censure, if not to reject, the abolitionist proposals of the Cuban delegates; only a few could view these proposals as politic concessions to the abolitionist feelings of the Reform Commission.

In Puerto Rico the reception given the work of Acosta, Ruíz Belvís, and Quiñones was even more hostile. Although there was a large party in favor of abolition in Puerto Rico, a small, powerful class of merchants and slaveowners had a dominant influence in the government. Governor José María Marchessi, on a flimsy pretense, declared the exile of several of the reformers. Acosta, who remained in Madrid for some time, did not dare to return home without first securing a safe conduct from the colonial minister.[69]

In this show of slavophile fury, the Madrid government found plausible reasons for delaying gradual abolition. But so far as Cuba was concerned, this was a secondary matter. The Cubans unanimous-

[68]*Ibid.*, pp. 15–17.
[69]Luis Díaz Soler, *La historia de la esclavitud negra en Puerto Rico*, p. 293. An account of the punitive measures taken by Marchessi is also given in Cruz Monclova, *Historia*, I, 560–572.

The Reform Commission of 1866–1867

ly expected political and economic reforms, and in this regard, the government could allege no plausible reasons for delay.

Not only did the Narváez government do nothing about the fond hopes of Antillians for political and economic reforms; even more amazing, it added insult to injury. On the twelfth of February, 1867, the government imposed a new tax on the colonies. A burden of 6 per cent was now levied on the net income of real and industrial properties; moreover, the colonial government was authorized to assess new taxes up to 12 per cent, if necessary, in order to cover administrative expenses. Ironically, the colonial delegates had suggested this tax, but they had done so on the understanding that customs duties would be abolished, as well as a number of other antiquated taxes that restricted commerce. The government abolished some of the latter, it is true, but did nothing about the costly customs duties. Furthermore, the decision had been taken without consulting the island's representatives in any way![70]

A great cry of pain arose from Creole property interests throughout Cuba and Puerto Rico. But outcries availed not. When the reformists attempted to fight the matter publicly in the press, they found themselves driven from the island like Ruíz Belvís in Puerto Rico or silenced in Cuba by the respective colonial governments. As the reformist delegates had forseen, the Spanish party embraced the government's efforts to crush the reformists, because, as of old they saw the doom of privilege in the reform program, and to defeat it they were willing to pay the price of another arbitrary tax.

Morales Lemus, who had first suggested the 6 per cent tax on real and industrial income in return for the suppression of other taxes, was unjustly blamed by the irate Cubans for the oppressive measure. He, along with Pastor and other reformers who were still in Madrid, made an heroic but unsuccessful effort to change the government's mind.[71]

Morales Lemus and other frustrated reformers must have murmured grimly to themselves: "This is the last deception." In any case, from this time on, a number of reformers began to reconsider the independence movement, which was slowly taking root in Cuba. The Republican Society of Cuba and Puerto Rico, founded in New York in 1865, was really an outgrowth of the annexationist movement that

[70]*Ibid.*, I, 558.
[71]See tax tables presented by Morales Lemus, February 7, 1867, *Información*, I, 330–341.

had failed in the 1850's. Now encouraged by Spain's humiliating retreat from Santo Domingo, they thought it possible to conquer independence. In Cuba they gave wide circulation to the inflammatory *Voice of America*. Don't forget, said this kind of literature, that Cuba and Puerto Rico, being a part of the New World, must be free and republican.[72]

In Puerto Rico, Spain reaped a similar harvest. The exiles Ruíz Belvís and Ramón Emeterio Betances began calling upon Hispanic-American nations to help in the freeing of their island brothers. The time would not be long when shouts of "Viva la República" and "Death to the Spaniards" would be heard in the Caribbean. To have suffered thirty years without reform, then to have been lifted to the pinnacle of hopes only to be rudely dropped to earth — this was the effect of the Junta de Información de Ultramar of 1866–1867.

But farce that it was, not all was completely sterile. As a by-product of the Commission's work, not foreseen by the metropolis, the "first harpoon," to use Acosta's words, had been firmly sunk into the whale of slavery, and it must now swim to the distant shore and die; the principle of abolition, whether immediate or gradual, had been pronounced.[73] The slave trade had been roundly condemned, and it was obvious that Spain could not indefinitely postpone emancipation.

[72]Guerra, *Manual de la historia*, p. 581.
[73]Acosta y Quintero, *Acosta y su tiempo*, pp. 197–98.

12. The Glorious Revolution: A New Horizon, 1868-1870

> It awakened in the heart the hope that a ray of sunshine would illuminate those distant colonial regions, small remnants of our vast colonial empire.
>
> Manuel Becerra, 1870[1]

Following the exit of Castro from the Colonial Ministry, the abolitionist cause in Spain fell into a quiescent and despondent period. The Abolition Society, now temporarily outlawed, found it difficult to publicize its cause. It was apparent that the Spain of Isabel II would attempt no such hazardous innovation as abolition in colonial policy. The Queen's favorites, Narváez, Duke of Valencia (August, 1866–April, 1868), and his successor, González Brabo (April, 1868–September, 1868), did not dare offend the planter and commercial classes, who clung to Spain only because Spain could protect their interests. Besides, both Narváez and González Brabo were preoccupied with maintaining order at home.

Little wonder that colonial matters were seldom given serious attention. Men of public affairs were characteristically immersed in political machinations in Madrid, each faction seeking to advance its own interests under the patronage of the crown or through violence. After the French Revolution had invaded Spain, the picture had not changed much. Conspiracies, outbreaks of armed revolt, and another Carlist uprising now and then continued to maintain the chaotic ferment of public affairs.

---

[1] *La democracia en el Ministerio de Ultramar 1869–70: Colección de leyes, decretos, órdenes y otros documentos emanados del Ministerio de Ultramar durante la administración del Sr. Manuel Becerra*, pp. i–iii.

The year 1868, however, was the *año milagroso*. González Brabo had scarcely seated himself comfortably in the prime minister's chair when the thunderstorm struck and the rotten house of Isabel II collapsed. The reactionary policy of González Brabo was the last straw. Dissatisfaction was so intense that the conspiring liberals at last were forced into a temporary unity of purpose. The new conspiracy was the boldest and most imaginative of all. It enjoyed the added advantage that government precautions against conspiracies had become so routine that they had ceased to be precautions.[2]

On the eighteenth of September, 1868, a powerful nucleus of liberals, led by military and naval personalities, assembled forces in Cádiz, and by means of one of those *pronunciamientos*, typical of revolutionary politics in the Hispanic world, proclaimed the downfall of the inept Bourbon monarchy.

The Spanish people, sick with the muddled drift of national affairs, cheered deliriously for the success of the "Glorious Revolution," as it was henceforth called. The Queen, now grown fussy and fat, and assured that all was lost, hurriedly packed her bags and fled over the French frontier. The ground was thus cleared for the building of a new government. But did the revolutionaries have a constructive program? Immediately they asked for a constituent Cortes, popularly elected, that would determine the future nature of the Spanish government. But it soon became apparent that beyond this point, the revolutionaries had no common plan of action. The revolutionaries and their supporters were a conglomerate of the Moderado, Progresista, and Republicano parties, who were held temporarily together more by common grievances than by common objectives.[3]

In the provisional government formed on the eighth of October the real power was held by two generals, Francisco Serrano, president of the cabinet, and Juan Prim, minister of war, who, together with a majority of the revolutionaries, wanted a constitutional monarchy.[4] They began considering such available candidates as the French Duc de Montpensier, or the young Alfonso, Spanish Bourbon heir to the throne, or Francisco of Portugal. The Spanish press began sarcastically referring to this plan as a lottery of kings. There was splenetic

[2]For a brief, pointed description of the causes of the revolution see Juan Ortega Rubio, *Historia de España*, VI, 96–107.
[3]*Ibid.*, VI, 111–113.
[4]Francisco Pí y Margall, *Las grandes conmociones políticas del siglo XIX en España*, IV, 404; Miguel Villalba Hervás, *De Alcolea a Sagunto*, pp. 18–19.

opposition to another Bourbon, and to offer the throne of Spain to a sorry foreign prince seemed ridiculous to the republicans.

A growing republican sentiment forced the provisional government to leave the matter flexible. In a manifesto to the nation the provisional government conceded that "if the decision of the Spanish people were not favorable to the establishment of monarchic form, then it would respect the sovereign vote of the nation duly consulted."[5]

The success of "La Revolución Gloriosa" might well promise better days for the forgotten Antilles. The leaders of the revolt included, aside from Serrano and Prim, men intimately acquainted with colonial affairs, for example, Domingo Dulce, Caballero de Rodas, and Admiral Juan Bautista Topete. Prim, Dulce, and Serrano had already served at one time or another as enlightened governors in Cuba or Puerto Rico, and we have already outlined their views on the need for colonial reform. The outlook for abolitionism was particularly bright. For one thing, Dulce and Serrano favored a more realistic solution to the slave problem, and Figuerola, Sagasta, Ruíz Zorilla, Castelar, and other revolutionaries were either well-known abolitionists or favorably disposed toward the movement.

While preparations were under way for a constituent Cortes, the provisional government kept its reform promises to peninsular Spain by decreeing universal manhood suffrage, and freedom of the press, assembly, association, education, and religion. In the ensuing elections to the Cortes, the Progresistas of General Prim won a majority of seats. The Unionists, headed by Cánovas del Castillo, an inflexible monarchist of a constitutional type, were next in order. The Monarchic Democrats, the Republicans, and the Absolutists, headed by the archbishop of Compostela, formed the smaller minorities.[6]

The Cortes opened on the eleventh of February, 1869. In spite of its ominously mixed nature, nearly every class in Spain, including the colonies overseas, expected remedial legislation. Meanwhile, abolitionists identified with the triumphant liberal revolution found their hands suddenly untied and they immediately took advantage of the fluid situation.

On the first news of Cádiz, a revolutionary junta arose in Madrid and took over the government of the city. Labra, Vizcarrondo, Nico-

[5]Antonio Ballesteros y Beretta, *Historia de España y su influencia en la historia*, VIII, 48.
[6]*Ibid.*, VIII, 149–151.

lás María Rivero, and other abolitionists persuaded the Madrid junta to issue a manifesto (September 19, 1868) recommending that the revolutionary government declare vientre libre, that is, that all those born of slave mothers should henceforth be free. This bold manifesto, attributed to Labra, served to place the issue squarely in the face of the revolutionaries of Cádiz.[7]

"Negro slavery," said the manifesto, "is an outrage against human nature, and an affront against the only nation in the world that still conserves it . . ." Slavery was then termed a "repugnant institution, whose disappearance must not be made to wait." But, continued the manifesto, considering the history and character of slavery, "any sudden blow given without reflection would cause harm even to the Negroes themselves." Intelligent and well-thought-out measures were therefore in order, but, while the provisional government waited for a new Cortes, at least one step, that of vientre libre, should go into effect immediately: *"All those born of female slaves shall remain free beginning from the nineteenth day of September, 1868."* This date was chosen in honor of the Revolution.[8]

The provisional government headed by Serrano actually issued a decree on the twenty-ninth of September, 1868, declaring vientre libre in Cuba and Puerto Rico. This measure was the easier to obtain, since several members of the new government were abolitionists. The decree, however, was not put into effect overseas. Confusion had reigned there since the first news of the Revolution. In Cuba, Governor General Francisco Lersundi remained faithful to the exiled Queen Isabel. Nevertheless, the declaration of vientre libre was a triumph for abolitionism because the principle of abolition at least had been declared by the government. It seemed, as one of the abolitionists later observed, that the cause of abolition, yesterday so remote, had come a long way in a short time.[9]

The new government gave further proof of its liberal and reformist nature when it promised the colonies a political share, so to speak, in the Revolution of September. In a famous circular addressed to the governors of Cuba, Puerto Rico, and the Philippines, October 27, 1868, the new colonial minister, Abelardo López de Ayala, explained that the Revolution: ". . . was not carried through for the sole benefit

[7]Rafael María de Labra, *La república y las libertades de Ultramar*, pp. 22–23.
[8]*Ibid.*; or José Acosta y Quintero, *José J. Acosta y su tiempo*, pp. 330–331.
[9]Gabriel Rodríguez, "La idea y el movimiento antiesclavista en España durante el siglo XIX," in Manuel Escalera, *La España del siglo XIX*, III, 321.

of the inhabitants of the Peninsula, but also for our loyal brothers overseas."[10]

The Revolution of September 18, 1868, was, in its ultimate consequences, one of the most important political events of nineteenth-century Spain. This liberal triumph was, from one point of view, a delayed expression of eighteenth-century rational and republican ideals. That the liberal vanguard were fully conscious of its ideological significance seems evident in the preamble of the new constitution of 1868, wherein Manuel Becerra, one of the revolutionaries, explained that the "Revolution of September more than any previous movement means consecration to the human rights willed to modern history by the Revolution of 1789."[11] And Becerra insisted that the Revolution had the same significance for the colonists.[12]

Again, the Revolution was inspired by the English example of political, material, and imperial progress. Labra, like many liberals, felt that the events of 1868 were a part of the great universal movement of liberalism and free trade, from which followed logically colonial reforms and, above all, the abolition of slavery.[13]

With the provisional government thus ideologically committed to a promise of colonial reforms, the reformists burst forth into a new period of activity. In a "Memorandum of Various Cubans and Peninsulars residing in Madrid to the Provisional Government, October 2, 1868," the undersigned asked, in the name of the Glorious Revolution, that those political, social, and economic reforms proposed by the Colonial Reform Commission of 1866–1867 be carried into effect.[14]

In the same month of October, 1868, the Abolitionist Society held in El Circo Price in Madrid a public meeting in which they clamored for a law of abolition. In another meeting in La Academia de Jurisprudencia, on November 30, 1868, they reaffirmed the demand. The

---

[10]"Circular del Ministerio de Ultramar a los Gobernadores Superiores Civiles de Cuba, Puerto Rico y Filipinas," Madrid 27 de octubre de 1868, A.H.N. Ultramar, Leg. 4933, Vol. I.

[11]Rafael M. Labra, *La cuestión de Puerto Rico*, p. 55.

[12]*La democracia en el Ministerio de Ultramar 1869–70*, p. ix.

[13]*Diario de las Sessiones de las Cortes, generales y extraordinaries, 1810–1898, Congreso y Senado* (1873) I, No. 11 (27 de febrero de 1873), 267. Labra made this statement during a debate on the Puerto Rican slave bill.

[14]The Memorandum was signed by Calixto Bernal, Nicolás Azcárate, R. M. de Labra, José María Lorro y Carpos, Calixto de Toledo, el Marqués de O'gaban, and seven others. A.H.N. Ultramar, Leg. 4933, Vol. I, Mando Lersundi.

Puerto Ricans resident in the capital were especially insistent. Eugenio María de Hostos, Puerto Rican man of letters, brought the matter eloquently to the attention of the government and the public.[15] The Society's short-lived publication, *El Abolicionista*, reappeared. Shortly after, this paper was replaced by *La Propaganda*, another intermittent publication, at first directed by José Luis Giner de los Ríos, then by Labra, who gave it a more vigorous life.[16]

But if colonial reform could be deduced logically from the principles of 1868, then, as Labra frequently pointed out, what was needed was a stout-hearted colonial minister who would dare to defy the protests of the alarmed slave interests. From the tone of official speeches and declarations, they had every reason to fear that the provisional government would declare for the immediate abolition of slavery, and they began to petition the government for a policy of caution.

To counter the alarming activities of the abolitionists, the slave interests organized a Junta Cubana. In a memorandum to the provisional government they insisted on some reforms, of course, but under a system of representation in the Cortes to be determined by special property qualifications.[17] This would, in effect, leave political power in the hands of commercial and property interests.

Immediately after the Revolution, an article by Saco, in which he elaborated Creole fears concerning the evil effects of immediate abolition, appeared in *La Política*, a Madrid newspaper. Once more he emphasized the racist argument. The prompt liberation of 350,000 slaves would menace the security of the island, and, by implication, the ascendency of the white race. "Don't forget," he said, "... if there is black humanity in Cuba there is also white humanity ... remember Haiti ..." For the last fifty years no good tract in defense of slavery in the Spanish Antilles had overlooked Haiti. Saco said furthermore that abolition would be unjust because Spain could not find 140,000,000 pesos for indemnification. He warned that the proprietors were prepared to go to extremes to protect their property. Recalling the lesson

---

[15]"Obras completas de Hostos," I, 90–93, cited by Luis Díaz Soler, *La historia de la esclavitud negra en Puerto Rico*, pp. 296–299.

[16]*Ibid.*, p. 299.

[17]Ramiro Guerra, *Manual de la historia de Cuba (económica, social y política)*, p. 650.

of the annexationist movement, he predicted that a separatist revolt might well be the result.[18] This, incidentally, was written before Saco knew that a separatist revolution was preparing in Cuba.

The Puerto Rican abolitionists were furious with Saco's article because, in effect, the latter was generalizing for Puerto Rico as well as Cuba. Labra, seizing a pen, assailed the arguments of Saco. He called immediate attention to the fact that conditions and sentiments in Puerto Rico were in no wise the same as those in Cuba, but that even in Cuba abolition was just as inevitable. Labra presented numerous social and economic data to prove that a free economy was making progress in both islands. The free colored would present no crime problem, as Saco argued, because they had almost as low a crime rate as the whites, and certainly much lower than slave or coolie labor. An increasing percentage of free colored were learning to read and write, 11.5 per cent according to the figures of 1851. In Spain itself the percentage of literates was, according to figures for 1860, scarcely 25 per cent, and in the Canary Islands only 9.9 per cent.[19]

Since the owners had expropriated the liberty of the black, said Labra, they had no right to indemnification. Spain had been a partner with the slave master in the exploitation of the Negro; for such injustice the slave, not the master, should be indemnified. Labra concluded that, given the evolution of conditions in the Antilles, the "main obstacles to these reforms [abolition] were no longer found in Cuba and Puerto Rico but in the metropolis itself."[20]

Still remembering its promises, the provisional government of Serrano and Prim planned a series of reforms for the colonies. Freedom of the press and of assembly, benefit of the Spanish civil and penal code, municipal reform, religious freedom, and many more of the reforms recommended by the Commission of 1866–1867 were to be extended to the Antilles. Cuba and Puerto Rico were also to be given representation in the Spanish Cortes. Preparations were made for holding elections. Cuba, with a free population of 955,805, was to

---

[18]José Antonio Saco, *La esclavitud en Cuba y la revolución en España*, pp. 2–15. A later edition appeared in French, *L'esclavage a Cuba et la revolución* par José A. Saco.

[19]Rafael María de Labra, *La abolición de la esclavitud en las Antillas españolas*, pp. 50–71.

[20]*Ibid.*, p. 110.

have eighteen deputies; Puerto Rico, with 612,422 inhabitants, was to have eleven deputies.[21]

The announcement of the Reform Commission in 1865 had caused a great current of excitement to run through the Spanish Antilles. The sensation was repeated following the events of 1868. Indeed, it seemed that a ray of sunshine would illuminate the remnants of the empire. But the tragedy of nineteenth-century Cuba had yet many scenes to play.

Hardly had the Glorious Revolution triumphed in Spain when the incredible news arrived concerning the outbreak of a major revolution in Cuba on October 10, 1868. In spite of the near simultaneousness of the two events, they had, in fact, developed independently of one another.[22] The Cuban conspirators had laid their plans well. In his famous "grito de Yara" Carlos Manuel Céspedes and a small group of criollo planters from the eastern province (Oriente) proclaimed the Republic of Cuba. A proclamation listed the causes of the revolt as due to arbitrary government, corrupt administration, exclusion of Cubans from government employment, exclusion of Cubans from the Cortes, unfulfilled reform promises, and excessive taxation. Explicit reference was made to the failure of the Colonial Reform Commission of 1866–1867.[23]

The cry "Independencia y Cuba libre" was picked up and relayed through the interior of the island. In a short time, what at first appeared to be a desperate cry on the part of a few dissatisfied planters became a formidable insurrection as the movement took root among the Creoles of eastern Cuba.

The Cuban revolution at once made the old Creole reform leadership obsolete. In 1850 Saco had persuaded most Creoles to reject annexation and revolution. "What need is there," he had said, "to appeal to arms in order to obtain what can be reached with only the force of opinion, respectfully and energetically expressed."[24] That was

[21]Decree of December 14, 1868, cited by Díaz Soler, *La esclavitud negra*, p. 299.

[22]Earlier, September 18, 1868, a small, insignificant revolt had occurred in Puerto Rico. The Rebellion of Lares, as it is called, proclaimed the Puerto Rican Republic; but the movement was immediately stamped out without important consequences.

[23]The reasons and motives behind the proclamation of Céspedes are fully discussed in Ramiro Guerra y Sánchez, *La Guerra de Diez Años 1868–1878*, Vol. I, Book I, Chap. III, pp. 34–54.

[24]Luis M. Pérez, *Estudios sobre las ideas políticas de José Antonio Saco*, p. 65.

eighteen years before. The revolutionaries had had enough; reforms offered now would prove useless. The revolutionaries were bent on nothing less than a republic. Noting Spain's failure in Santo Domingo, they rejected Saco's argument that Cuba was not big enough to conquer its independence, for was not Cuba destined to join the republics of the New World?

Spain hardly understood and the first news left her stupified, but on reflection the provisional government saw little cause for alarm. Once the Cubans had seen the reform promises of the Glorious Revolution in action they would come to respect the mother country and lay down their arms like good sons. The government of Prim and Serrano therefore hastened the reform program for the colonies. But immediately complications set in.

Spanish conservatives, suffering from an acute complex that the miserable remnants of the empire would be lost, feeding upon colonial data provided by helpful representatives of the Spanish party in Madrid, and, in any case, seeking an issue with which to strike down the new liberal government, raised an irrepressible demand for a reactionary policy.[25] Reforms conceded at this time, they chanted, would be a sign of gross national weakness. Pure emotionalism poured from the press.

The idea that Cuba, famous since the loss of continental Hispanic America as "the ever faithful and loyal isle," should attempt to abandon its weak old mother was looked upon as the height of ingratitude. Columbus had discovered the island; his son had ruled over it. Cuba had been the cornerstone of the empire in America. Cortes had departed for Mexico from Cuba. Countless blueblooded Castilians had died clearing the fever-infested jungles. What had Spain not done to make Cuba rich and prosperous? Had it not beat off the filibuster? And this was Spain's reward! "Oh, ungrateful children!"[26]

Even many educated Spaniards drew only one lesson from New World history — that reform concessions given to the colonies had availed nothing. Force was the only answer. Only when the rebels surrendered could the imperial metropolis in full dignity consider

---

[25]How the Cuban insurrection disastrously affected the colonial program of the provisional government of Spain is indicated in Rafael María de Labra, *La política colonial y la revolución española de 1868*.

[26]The debates in the Cortes on the subject of colonial reforms for Puerto Rico and Cuba were filled with such sentiments; see, for example, *Diario, Congreso* (1869–1870).

reforms. The cry was raised on all sides of the government: No reforms in Cuba while a single rebel stands in arms. The reactionaries attempted to extract a formal pledge to this effect from the government. Many of the liberals joined in the chorus. The provisional government was thus being forced to reconsider its whole reform program in Cuba. This was fatal for a quick termination of hostilities, and it would prove damaging to the international prestige of the new Spanish government.

The Cuban rebels, on the other hand, made a point of moving in a liberal direction. Céspedes, president of the Cuban Republic, declared the abolition of slavery. It mattered not the true motives, nor the fact that the decree was hardly enforced. The important thing was to convince the outside world that the insurrection stood for the freedom of the slaves.

The revolutionary chieftains of Cuba at first had no clear-cut program of abolition. After the pattern of the earlier revolutions in Spanish America, Creoles were the vanguard of the revolution. Naturally, they sought to advance their own interests. Most of the Creole leaders probably had little more republican faith in the Negro than Miranda or Bolívar had in the Indian, while others naturally expressed a paternal attitude. But there were elements in the nature of the situation which inevitably linked the slave problem with the revolution. Céspedes and the republican chieftains had realistically appraised their position; they understood that if the Cuban Republic was to receive moral support, diplomatic recognition, and foreign military aid they would have to take an abolitionist stand.[27]

Creole planters who followed Céspedes could adopt this attitude because the revolution had erupted in the provinces of Oriente, where the slave economy was decidedly poorer. As previously indicated, a number of plantation owners there were struggling to maintain themselves against the competition of the more prosperous western province. More than a billion pounds of sugar were produced in Cuba in 1864, but the eastern provinces of Camaguey and Oriente produced only 9 per cent of this amount. Yet one rich western province, that of Matanzas, alone produced 43 per cent of the total.[28] In addition,

[27]For a critical, almost cynical, appraisal, Raúl Cepero Bonilla, *Azúcar y abolición: Apuntes para una historia crítica de abolicionismo*, Chap. XI, "Los organizadores de la Revolución de 1868 y la esclavitud."

[28]*Guía de forasteros en la Siempre Fiel Isla de Cuba para el año de 1864*, cited by Roland T. Ely, *Cuando reinaba su majestad el azúcar. Estudio histórico-socio-*

arbitrary tax measures, such as the detested 10-per-cent levy on income property that had resulted from the Colonial Reform Commission, weighed heavy on eastern Cuba. A number of revolutionaries were therefore predisposed toward abolition for economic reasons. Also, like Céspedes and Miguel de Aldama, who set their slaves free, some were moved by the logic of their political ideals to respect the abolitionist decrees of the revolution.

The situation demanded caution, for if, on the one hand, emancipation would gain international support, on the other hand, the powerful slaveholding Creoles of the western province, from whom Céspedes also expected support, must not be alienated. This was the dilemma of the revolutionary chieftains in the first days of the struggle, and in this light, perhaps, we can understand better their guarded announcements concerning the abolitionist aims of the revolutionary republic.

Céspedes, in his first manifesto, as chief of the revolutionary junta, October 10, 1868, said only that: "We desire the gradual and indemnified abolition of slavery." In his second proclamation from Barrancas, October 18, 1868, nothing was said about slavery. But in the important proclamation of Bayamo, December 27, 1868, the rebel chieftains proclaimed a very cautious measure of abolition, calculated to please the outside world without alarming the propertied classes of Cuba, upon whom the success of the revolution would ultimately depend.[29]

In the Bayamo proclamation Céspedes publicly recognized "that a free Cuba was incompatible with a slavist Cuba." But he promptly added that only the entire Cuban nation was competent to effect a measure of complete abolition; when in the full use of its powers as an independent nation it could, through free suffrage, decide the best manner for carrying through the measure. Thus, obviously, Céspedes was making abolition contingent upon the final success of the revolution.[30]

The Bayamo proclamation also recognized the principle of indemnity, which, again, was calculated not to alienate property owners from the republic. While the question of slavery was pending solu-

lógico de una tragedia latinoamericana: El monocultivo en Cuba, origen y evolución del proceso, p. 542.

[29] These projects are summarized in Eugenio Alonso y Sanjurjo, *Apuntes sobre los proyectos de la abolición de la esclavitud en las islas de Cuba y Puerto Rico*, pp. 44–50.

[30] *Ibid.*, pp. 44–50.

tion, continued the document, the republic would respect slave property; fugitive slaves belonging to rebel proprietors would not be admitted into the revolutionary army without the consent of the owners. Those rebel owners who voluntarily offered their slaves to the republican government were to receive certificates of indemnification to be honored at the successful conclusion of the war.[31]

Céspedes further subordinated emancipation to the needs of war when he pointed out the convenience of utilizing for the service of the republic all slaves voluntarily freed by the rebels, "... thereby putting off evils that could result from lack of immediate employment." In reality, the revolutionaries had done little more than proclaim the principle of emancipation. Emancipation was limited to slaves confiscated from persons openly hostile to the insurrection.[32]

Even though the proclamations of the rebels hardly constituted a program of emancipation — in the circumstances this would have been impossible anyway — they achieved the effect of attracting large numbers of fugitive slaves from loyalist plantations, while at the same time maintaining the slaves of the rebels under a form of labor control. Furthermore, the proclamations contributed toward attracting sympathy and some voluntary aid from foreign powers, especially from individual citizens in the United States.

On the other hand, rebel hopes for belligerent status were destined to be frustrated. The revolutionary leaders failed to win the support of the majority of the slave-owning class, above all in the prosperous Occidente. The proprietors had too much invested in slave property, and they feared, perhaps, a slave rebellion as a consequence of the revolution. They could not accept gradual abolition at the hands of an untried revolutionary government, nor confide in Céspedes' promises of indemnity.[33]

Yet the Cuban revolt would have profound effects on slavery. First, not only would the war destroy the slave economy in many areas, but also both sides, in seeking to attract the military aid of the slaves, would set precedents of liberty that later could not be nullified (we shall see later how these precedents bore upon abolition measures). And, second, the declarations of the rebels placing the

[31]*Ibid.*, pp. 44–50.

[32]*Ibid.*, p. 49. Cepero, like Alonso y Sanjurjo, also critically analyzes the abolitionist significance of Céspedes' proclamations, *Azúcar y abolición*, pp. 106–122.

[33]See Cepero's discussion of the material and political reasons why the hacendados refused to join Céspedes, *Azúcar y abolición*, pp. 142–156.

insurrection on the side of emancipation, in principle, at least, had the effect of forcing all parties in Spain to face the emancipation problem. This was recognized at the time by Caballero de Rodas, captain general, whose opinion, written in September, 1869, strongly influenced the Madrid government: "Slavery has died with this insurrection; among many evils it has produced this one good thing."[34]

Yet the Madrid government, facing reactionary fury, could only hesitate on its Cuban reform program. Had there been a stouthearted man at the helm of the Colonial Ministry, as Labra wanted, perhaps reforms could have shortened what would prove to be a long and desperate war. On the very day that Céspedes proclaimed the "Republic," López de Ayala, a man famous as a lyrical poet and dramatist, took possession of the Colonial Ministry. As one of the liberal leaders of the Revolution of September he had helped pen revolutionary declarations, including the notorious promise that the Revolution was for the colonies as much as for the mother country. But Ayala's pen was steadier than he was.[35]

Under reactionary pressure Ayala followed a well-established pattern of colonial history. From papier-mâché liberal he reverted to defender of slavery and the old colonial order. Ayala was probably no disappointment to Saco who had once said:

I belong to no party in Spain, nor do I believe in any; I will only begin to believe in that one which begins with deeds. Outstanding men of all parties when they are in opposition clamor against colonial despotism; but later when they come to power, they all march by the same path as their predecessors.[36]

Ayala refused to extend to Cuba the earlier reform promises of the liberal government, and, concerning slavery, he virtually assured the slave interests that the Glorious Revolution intended nothing in the

[34]In this same communiqué Caballero de Rodas urged the government to take some countermeasure to offset the international appeal of the rebel's emancipatory declarations: "The free birth of slaves [vientre libre], this is a measure urgently needed." Caballero de Rodas al Ministro de Ultramar, 25 de septiembre de 1869, A.H.N. Ultramar, Leg. 4933, Vol. IV, Mando de Rodas.

[35]"Carta abierta dirigida al Sr. D. Antonio Cánovas del Castillo," junio de 1866, Perez, *Estudios sobre las ideas*, pp. 56–57. One of Ayala's biographers revealed another side of his character: ". . . no one denies that the apathy, indolence and incurable negligence of Ayala exceeds the incredible." Cited from the work of Manuel de la Revilla by Acosta y Quintero, *Acosta y su tiempo*, p. 391.

[36]José Antonio Saco, *Contra la anexación*, II, xcvii.

way of basic reforms. In a poetic speech before the Cortes he refused to take responsibility for an abolition law for Cuba, thus placing himself on the side of the "defenders of the national integrity":

> In this debate, I would like to be the one to emancipate the slaves because I love glory as a poet, but I love my country more. In me, the stimulus of duty is more powerful than the stimulus of applause. At the same time that I took possession of the Colonial Ministry I received the news of the Cuban insurrection. How could the social problem with its immense conflicts be added to the natural disturbances of war? Yes, I abandoned my own glory in order to come to the defense of the country; yes, I was timid in reform so that I could be more energetic in war. . . . If for this I merit censure, I leave the judgment of my conduct to those men who have some love for the soil on which they were born. I want to carry abolition through without a violent effect for anyone, given the good spirit of the proprietors [of slaves]. The French Assembly of '93 did it with violence, and Lincoln in the Southern States. . . . Are we now going to decree this with violence against the defenders of the country's integrity?[37]

Like the reactionary leaders, Romero Robledo and Navarro Rodrigo, Ayala would give all his support to the Spanish party and the slavists, upon whom, the reactionaries thought, the dominion of Spain in Cuba must ever depend. The opportunity was thus lost for Spain to establish liberal principles as the pole upon which to fly the Castilian flag over Cuba. And the initiative in this regard fell wholly to the Cuban rebels.

In abandoning reform projects for Cuba, Ayala was strongly influenced by the attitude of the Cuban officials. Francisco Lersundi was governor of the island at the time of the Glorious Revolution. On receiving notice of the event, however, he, as hitherto indicated, conducted himself as if the Queen were still reigning. He attempted to conceal from the Cubans the true nature of the revolution in Spain. Speaking for the Spanish interests of the island, Lersundi threatened to resign if such reforms were insisted upon, because as governor he would not take responsibility for the consequences.[38]

Lersundi's attitude made impossible in the first crucial moments of the revolt any hope of reconciliation. He thus forced many wavering Creoles to make the bitter choice between joining the rebellion or submitting to more autocratic colonial rule. In his attempt to stamp

[37]Cited by Acosta y Quintero, *Acosta y su tiempo*, p. 388.
[38]The implacable policy of Lersundi is described by Guerra, *Guerra de Diez Años*, Vol. I, Book III, Chap. XI, pp. 181–198.

out the revolt he alienated Creole sympathies further by denying any reason or justice to the rebel cause. In his uncharitable proclamations he called the insurrectionaries incendiaries, assassins, and robbers, and subjected them to military tribunals as traitors. Nor would he listen to the peace proposals of several prominent Creole planters, including Morales Lemus and Miguel de Aldama. As a result, the latter two placed their talents and wealth at the disposition of the rebel cause.[39]

The liberal government of Spain did nothing at first to remove Lersundi. Its own feet uncertain, perplexed by the Cuban revolt, afraid to alienate the Spanish party, and realizing Lersundi's popularity among the slave interests, Madrid could only confirm Lersundi in power.

Meanwhile, a militia institution called the "Spanish Volunteers" began to assert a decisive role in colonial policy. This organization had been hastily organized by General José de la Concha, who later gave (February 2, 1855) formal recognition to the Volunteer Corps, to meet the threat of the López expeditions. In the principal cities, such as Havana and Santiago de Cuba, Volunteers, who were mostly Spaniards, many of them reckless adventurers who loved to cow the criollos, were organized into infantry batallions and squadrons of calvary. The highest rank among them was that of colonel.[40]

The purpose of the Volunteers was not to sally out to battle but to relieve the regular Spanish soldiers of garrison duty in the towns so that the latter could be free to risk their neck in battle. So important were the Volunteers in the defense of Spanish dominion in Cuba that without this organization it is extremely doubtful Spain could have won what turned out to be the Ten Years' War (1868-1878). When the Revolt of Yara began in September, 1868, Spain had only 7,000 regulars in the island. The Volunteers enabled the Governor to contain the rebellion until reinforcements arrived. More than 73,000 Volunteers were enlisted on the Spanish side during the command

---

[39]Manuel Guerra, *Manual*, p. 656. Though Morales Lemus and Aldama would, in choosing the rebel side, be forced to free or abandon their slaves, this did not mean that they had chosen the revolution for abolitionist reasons; see Cepero's cynical analysis of their maneuvers before openly embracing the rebel cause, *Azúcar y abolición*, Chaps. XII–XIII.

[40]Eugenio Vandama y Calderón, Coronel, *Colección de artículos sobre el Instituto de Voluntarios de la isla de Cuba*, pp. 30–32.

of Lersundi, and 90,000 Remington rifles were purchased in the United States in order to arm them.[41]

Apparently no government that wanted to keep control of Havana could now ignore the claims of the Spanish party enforced by the powerful Volunteers.[42] Concha, who created the Volunteer Corps, would later admit that the Volunteers exploited patriotism in order to advance their own personal interests against the public authority; but, said Concha: "It is not possible to govern that island without the confidence of the Spanish party."[43] But as the rebellion spread rapidly in the face of Lersundi's hostile policy, the Madrid government, underestimating the power of the Spanish party, decided to remove Lersundi and sent to the island a liberal governor, who would better represent the spirit of the Glorious Revolution. The choice fell upon Don Domingo Dulce, who already had a liberal reputation in Cuban affairs as reformer and friend of the Cuban party. Not only this, but Dulce, along with Prim and Serrano, was a member of the revolutionary junta that disembarked at Cádiz proclaiming the liberal revolution in Spain. It seemed fitting and proper that Dulce (the name means "sweet" in Spanish) should be the instrument for inaugurating the new policy.

The new governor arrived in Cuba on January 4, 1869, carrying with him an emergency three-point reform program: freedom of the press, freedom of assembly, and representation for Cuba in the Cortes. Shortly after arriving, he declared a general amnesty for all those who had suffered imprisonment or punishment for political reasons and for all rebels who would surrender their arms within forty days. Dulce also sent two peace commissions to talk with Céspedes, the revolutionary chieftain.[44]

The leaders of the Cuban reform movement who had not yet chosen rebellion, Conde de Pozos Dulces, José Ignacio Rodríguez, José Luis Alfonso, and others, began to rally around the figure of the liberal governor. In January, 1869, a series of decrees gave a more liberal character to the colonial government.[45] These measures, together with the fear that Dulce was in the complete power of the Cuban reform-

[41]Ibid., pp. 32–37.
[42]Willis F. Johnson, *The History of Cuba*, III, 150–156.
[43]José Gutiérrez de la Concha, *La guerra de Cuba y su estado político y económico desde 1871–74*, p. 107.
[44]Guerra, *Guerra de Diez Años*, Vol. I, Book III, Chap. XI, pp. 204–205.
[45]Ibid., p. 203.

ists, caused unspeakable fury in the intransigent Spanish party. Not unreasonably the Volunteers claimed that certain Cuban reformists were working secretly for the insurrectionary cause; for example, the Revolutionary Junta of Havana shortly after Dulce's arrival agreed to send the dangerous Morales Lemus to the United States in order to advance the "traitorous cause" of Céspedes.[46]

Peace negotiations failed miserably. The rebels took advantage of Dulce's peaceful intention to widen their activities by promoting every kind of disturbance. Many of the rich Creole sugar planters, seeing the rebellion worsen, joined in protest with the Spanish Volunteers. Dulce, realizing that he must either resign or change his policy, decided on the latter course. The date for the deposition of arms by the rebels was the twentieth of February, 1869. But already by the twelfth of the month Dulce had suspended all political guarantees. Further to please the intransigents, the governor pressed military activities and began wholesale exportations of persons suspected of being in sympathy with the rebellion. When a boy of eighteen yelled "Viva Cuba libre" at a departing boatload of exiles, Dulce, to satiate the blood cry of the Volunteers, had the boy judged by a military tribunal and shot.[47]

But even if he converted himself into a complete reactionary, Dulce could not have ingratiated himself with the Spanish party, who remembered Dulce as an arbitrary castigator of the slave interests. His prestige and authority had already ebbed away. The Volunteers sent a committee to the Governor advising him to resign, but before Dulce could decide the matter for himself, the Volunteers took matters in their own hands. Holding the real power in the city of Havana, they forced Dulce to embark for Spain the first week of June, 1869. This done, the Volunteers, while awaiting the arrival of the new captain general, Antonio Caballero de Rodas, also a friend of the Glorious Revolution, took advantage of the weak Ginovés Espinar, commanding temporarily, to consolidate their position. They founded the first of the Casinos Españoles at this time, supposedly for social purposes. When Caballero arrived on June 28, 1869, he authorized the Casino plan, little realizing that he was giving the Volunteers a political weapon of great power.[48]

[46]For the mission of Morales Lemus and the diplomatic problems encountered by him in Washington, *ibid.*, pp. 338–355.
[47]*Ibid.*, pp. 329–333.
[48]*Ibid.*, p. 328.

This remarkable act — the expulsion of a captain general — marked the triumph of the reactionary cause in Cuba over the liberal cause in Spain. The Madrid government, incredibly weak in the matter, accepted the expulsion of the governor and the policy of the Volunteers, and thus political reforms were abandoned.

From the Spanish government point of view, the rebels must completely surrender themselves before reforms could ever again be considered. From the rebel point of view, this was tantamount to submission to the old colonial order wherein the Spanish party must, in the nature of things, continue supreme. In a sense, both sides were right; the government had reason to believe that the rebels would accept nothing but independence or death; on the other hand, the rebels had reason to believe that Spain was either insincere in her reform promises or too impotent to impose them over the Spanish party. Thus the desperate war unfolded with both sides setting fire to the earth.[49]

At this point, in the spring of the year 1869, it seemed that the abolition question had been thrust aside indefinitely along with the entire reform program for Cuba. The Spanish government had adopted as a fixed policy the reactionary cry: No reform in Cuba while a single rebel stands in arms. Nevertheless, the slave question could not be entirely pushed aside. Two factors were destined to force Spain's hand.

First, if there was a full-blown rebellion in Cuba, there was none in Puerto Rico. The abolitionists, therefore, argued that there was no reason why the government should not consider a measure of abolition in the smaller island. There was an increasing strength to the abolitionist demand, largely due to the presence of Puerto Rican representatives recently admitted in the Cortes. The Glorious Revolution in Spain had conceded by decree of December 14, 1868, the right of Puerto Rico and Cuba to elect deputies to the Cortes. This privilege had been canceled in the case of Cuba due to reaction following the Revolt of Yara, but in Puerto Rico elections were celebrated in June, 1869. Eleven deputies were thereby chosen to represent

---

[49]Since neither the Spaniards nor the rebels had decisive military power, the war could only degenerate into a series of vengeful atrocities committed by both sides. It is little wonder that the American government would consider intervening for "the interest of humanity and for the benefit of all parties concerned." James Morton Callahan, *Cuba and International Relations: A Historical Study in American Diplomacy*, p. 375.

The Glorious Revolution, 1868–1870 233

Puerto Rico in the Cortes. Of this number, eight were conservatives, and three, Luis Padial, Juan Hernández Arvizu, and José M. P. Excoriaza, were Liberal-Reformists, or abolitionists.[50] But even some of the conservative deputies elected were not completely opposed to some measure of gradual abolition in Puerto Rico. As previously noted, the abolitionist sentiment was quite general in Puerto Rico. What really divided Puerto Ricans into conservatives and liberals was not only the slave problem but also the extent of projected political and economical reforms.[51] In future elections, those of 1870, for example, the Liberal-Reformists would gain more strength. This, in turn, greatly strengthened the abolitionist voice in the Cortes.

The second factor forcing Spain's hand was the sympathetic attitude of the United States toward the rebellion. The American Congress on April 5, 1869, expressed sympathy for the rebel cause and promised that at an opportune moment it would recognize the independence and sovereignty of the Cuban Republic.[52]

In the meantime, the American government sent General Daniel E. Sickles, a good friend of President Grant, to Madrid. On June 19, 1869, Secretary of State Hamilton Fish handed Sickles his instructions. The condition of the Cuban insurrection suggested that it would not end soon, said Fish. Violence, commercial interests, and the political sympathies created by the aspirations of the Cubans for self-government were sufficient reasons to explain the interest of the United States in the destiny of that island, and therefore Fish offered Spain the good offices of the United States in order to terminate the war upon the following four conditions:[53]

[50] Acosta y Quintero, *Acosta y su tiempo*, p. 360.

[51] Abolitionist sentiment permeated Puerto Rican society, but a small "Spanish Party," akin to that in Cuba and often in alliance with a reactionary governor, was frequently able to stifle reform sentiment in Puerto Rico. See the Puerto Rican historians Luis Díaz Soler, *La esclavitud negra*, or Lidio Cruz Monclova, *Historia de Puerto Rico (Siglo XIX)*.

[52] Jerónimo Becker y González, *La historia política y diplomática de España desde la independencia de Los Estados Unidos hasta nuestros días, 1776–1895*, p. 502.

[53] Fish, it seems, was prepared to have the United States guarantee the payment of the indemnity by the Cubans, perhaps assuming that by default Cuba would fall to the United States. Callahan, *Cuba and International Relations*, pp. 375–376. The story of these negotiations is also told in Allan Nevins, *Hamilton Fish: The Inner Story of the Grant Administration*, and in Jerónimo Becker y González, *La historia de las relaciones exteriores de España durante el siglo XIX*, Vol. III.

1. Spain to recognize the independence of Cuba.
2. Cuba to pay Spain an indemnity for the renunciation of her sovereignty in the island as well as for public property of all kinds belonging to the Spanish government . . .
3. The abolition of slavery in the island of Cuba.
4. An armistice pending negotiations.

In the accompanying note Fish added the threat that Spain would fear most: that if Spain did not accept the note and if the state of things did not change soon in Cuba, it would not be just to detain for a longer time the recognition of the right of belligerency of the Cubans.[54] Belligerent status, once conceded, might well have spelled disaster for the Spanish cause in Cuba, implying, as it did, the promise of eventual diplomatic recognition and the free shipment of arms. One might rightly assume that subsequent Spanish diplomacy would be calculated to prevent the fulfillment of the American threat at all costs.[55]

Fish found the first reports from Madrid most encouraging. Paul S. Forbes, the international business man through whom Prim had made the first confidential contacts with Grant, returned to Madrid ahead of Sickles. Forbes called on Prim on July 15, 1869, and the next day he cabled Fish that Prim insisted on $150,000,000 as the price of Spain's withdrawal from Cuba.[56]

On August 15, 1869, Sickles conferred with Prim, now the undisputed strong man of the provisional government. Prim had consulted the cabinet and found inflexible opposition. But the United States offer might still be artfully exploited to end the rebellion. Prim thereupon formulated new and impossible conditions. The Cubans were to be induced to lay down their arms at once. As usual, Spanish pride insisted upon this; otherwise, Spain could not seat her delegates alongside the rebels. During the amnesty an election of Cuban deputies to the Cortes was to be held. Through the Cortes, a plebiscite would then be called in which the Cubans could vote for independence, if they so desired. Fish immediately saw through the ruse. He was fully aware that a "popular election" or referendum in Cuba

---

[54]Nevins, *Hamilton Fish*, pp. 194–197; Callahan, *Cuba and International Relations*, pp. 375–380.

[55]Meanwhile, in order to aid negotiations by conciliatory gestures, Fish urged Federal officers to increased vigilance against filibusters. Nevins, *Hamilton Fish*, p. 197.

[56]Forbes to Fish, Madrid, July 16, 1869; Fish Papers, *ibid.*, p. 199.

would be so administered as to result in a victory for the intransigent loyalists.⁵⁷

Whatever faint hope remained for a diplomatic solution to the war was exploded when Manuel Becerra, acting secretary of state, an enemy of any plan to relinquish Cuba, purposely let the cat out of the bag. The resulting public outcry forced Prim to reject the American offer of good offices. Though some Spanish papers could approve of the sale of Cuba, most Spaniards could not. As one Spanish writer declared, Cuba was only a milch cow for needy Spanish governments, but its loss would cause Spain to sink into a fourth-rate power.⁵⁸

Yet no declaration of belligerency followed the refusal of the American offer. Fish was still sympathetic with the new regime in Spain, partly because Sickles believed that his friends in the Spanish cabinet were "apparently in earnest for a complete accord with the United States."⁵⁹ But Fish was also influenced by the attitudes of France, England, and Prussia, all of which had presented notes to Fish, at the behest of Spain, expressing hope that relations between Spain and the United States would continue in a good state.⁶⁰

Especially important were the *Alabama* claims against Great Britain. At this very time, Fish was building the justice of American claims on the grounds that Britain had without sufficient claim conceded belligerent status to the South during the Civil War, thereby causing the damages inflicted by the Southern ship *Alabama* (built in England) on the Northern merchant marine. Fish could not carelessly undermine the basis of the American claims. Furthermore, since the *Alabama* was a heated question involving perhaps a war and an attack upon Canada, the British would not have hesitated to ally themselves with Spain.⁶¹

Also at this time, Grant and the expansionists were interested in the

---

⁵⁷For these negotiations see Becker, *La historia de las relaciones exteriores de España*, III, 29–35; Callahan, *Cuba and International Relations*, pp. 278–279; Nevins, *Hamilton Fish*, pp. 239–245.

⁵⁸Callahan, *Cuba and International Relations*, pp. 381–383.

⁵⁹Apparently Fish and Sickles were hoping that sympathy rather than threats could yet bring about the sale of Cuba, a difficult game for the impatient Sickles. W. A. Swanberg, *Sickles the Incredible*, Chap. XXX.

⁶⁰*Ibid.*, p. 381. Becker gives a similar version, *La historia de las relaciones exteriores de España*, p. 35.

⁶¹These considerations were fully known to the representatives of Céspedes in Washington. See Guerra's treatment of the question, *Guerra de Diez Años*, pp. 356–359.

annexation of the Dominican Republic. The friends of the Cuban rebels for the most part opposed the Dominican adventure because they realized that two such projects would divide attention.[62] Fortunately for Spain, expansionist pressure remained divided, but still the situation was critical. President Grant favored the Cubans, and Secretary Rawlins became a fast friend of Morales Lemus, now Céspedes' envoy to the United States. Fish himself was not above conversing unofficially with Morales Lemus. And there was no question that American public opinion was in favor of the Cubans. Also, Fish and his policy of nonbelligerency must face a hostile Congress. The reports of further Spanish atrocities in Cuba and the fact that Spain was constructing gunboats in the United States accentuated the crisis. The Spanish minister in Washington, Mauricio López Roberts, feared he would not be able to prevent a declaration of belligerency.[63]

The provisional government of Spain hoped to deter a declaration of belligerency by forceful diplomacy; therefore, López Roberts was instructed to confront Fish with several vital considerations. First, the Federal government was to be reminded of its policy toward the South during the Civil War when European states were expected not to recognize the belligerency of the Confederacy. Second, France and Britain would not accept an American declaration of belligerency. Third, liberal reforms were now being applied in Puerto Rico. Fourth, the same would be done in Cuba as soon as the insurrection was terminated. Fifth, Spain was disposed to sacrifice the utmost in order to maintain her honor in Cuba.[64]

Fish meanwhile was fighting a desperate delaying battle against his colleagues in the Cabinet. The death of Rawlins on the fifth of September, 1869, hardly eased the pressure. Disgusted with Spanish procrastination, Fish told López Roberts that Spain must abide by reform promises made to Cuba. López Roberts, who fully appreciated the situation, sent a coded message to Madrid: "Believe prudent immediate publication of reforms announced for Cuba due to advantageous moral effect for us in these moments.... [Also] Prudence counsels war preparations in Cuba."[65]

[62]Nevins, *Hamilton Fish*, p. 335.
[63]López Roberts al Ministro de Estado Silvela, Washington, 13 de septiembre de 1869, A.M.A.E. *Correspondencia EEUnidos*, Leg. 1472 (1865–1869), N. 152.
[64]Ministerio de Estado a López Roberts, 18 de septiembre de 1869, *ibid*.
[65]López Roberts al Ministro de Estado Silvela, Telegrama, 22 de septiembre de 1869, *ibid*.

The Glorious Revolution, 1868–1870

Prim responded in a note of September 25, 1869, that, although Spain must proceed cautiously, the Volunteers would be disbanded as soon as hostilities ceased, that scandalous executions would be stopped, that slavery would be abolished, and that political reforms would be granted without waiting for the termination of hostilities.[66]

In reference to slavery, it is difficult to say whether Prim was sincere. As we have seen, the Spanish and Puerto Rican abolitionists had already extracted promises from the provisional government in this regard. But Prim had excellent reasons for not wanting to push a question that would arouse the cry of the reactionaries and endanger his own scheme for the restoration of a constitutional monarch. He was too much the opportunistic politician. As he said on the occasion of refusing the American offer, he would leave to the New World the glory of abolishing slavery.[67]

[66]Callahan, *Cuba and International Relations*, p. 388.
[67]Guerra, *Guerra de Diez Años*, Vol. I, Book I, Chap. III, p. 378.

13. The Moret Law: An Entering Wedge, 1870

> Here is what the law is . . . a compromise between the conservative elements and the revolutionary elements . . . that made the Revolution of September possible.
>
> Segismundo Moret, 1870[1]

A new colonial minister was appointed to carry out Prim's reform promises. Manuel Becerra, a man very different from Ayala, of proved liberal principles, now took charge of colonial affairs (September, 1869–April, 1870). While other reactionaries could say that Spain would fight to the last drop of her blood to keep the flag flying over El Morro, Becerra, believing that reforms could save Spanish Cuba, asked the Cortes to adopt a proposition that if Spain could not triumph in Cuba she could at least act so that her descendents could be proud of her: "All who feel Spanish blood in their veins are agreed upon preserving the integrity of the country, bearing at the same time, to the provinces beyond the sea, the reforms which civilization demands."[2]

Becerra gave promise of action on reform pledges made almost a year before by the Glorious Revolution. A committee consisting of a president, a vice-president, and fifteen *vocales* (counsellors) was finally created (September 10, 1869) for studying social, political, and administrative reforms in the colonies. Among the members were found staunch abolitionists like Labra, Luis María Pastor, Joaquín

---

[1]*Diario de las sesiones de las Cortes, general y extraordinarias 1810–1898*, Congreso (1869–1870), XIV (20 de junio de 1870), 8999.

[2]This statement was made before the Cortes on March 17, 1870; James Morton Callahan, *Cuba and International Relations: A Historical Study in American Diplomacy*, p. 393.

Sanromá, and Luis Ricardo Padial. The committee was to render a report within thirty days.³ A few days later, Becerra assured Sickles (September 14, 1869) that the Spanish government was planning abolition measures for both Puerto Rico and Cuba.⁴

Becerra had under consideration two partial measures of abolition for Cuba: (1) A declaration of freedom for all those slaves who had served in the Spanish army in Cuba, or who had rendered other valuable services to the Spanish cause. This had been proposed by the captain general of Cuba as a necessary war measure, for if slaves of loyalist masters could obtain freedom by fleeing to the insurrectionary side and serving there, then, obviously, Spain had better counter this rebel strategy. (2) A declaration of freedom and civil rights for all individuals of both sexes born of slave mothers since September 29, 1868. These children, however, would remain with their masters until they were eighteen years old, or until the mother or father acquired liberty by purchase.⁵

As far as Cuba was concerned, the committee proved to be another vain gesture. After all, the Spanish government was afraid that action on abolitionist promises for Cuba would alienate powerful economic interests, which, if anything, fattened on the war. The rich western half of the island was made secure from rebel incursions, and Céspedes' emancipation proclamations had no effect there. The demand for sugar was as great as ever, and the rich Western planters (perhaps 1,500 in number), whom Céspedes had hoped to win to the revolutionary cause, prospered in a checkmate situation, as did the Spanish merchants and war contractors. The price of slaves, which had dropped to as low as $200 for an adult, now began to climb upward again.⁶

Unfortunately, too, and this was most important, any abolition plan for Cuba hurt Spanish pride. To abolish slavery would only seem to admit the justice of the rebel cause. Moreover, since Spain could not possibly suppress the insurrection without loyalist help, she had no choice but to subordinate all reform demands, abolitionist or other-

---

³For a complete list of the members of this commission, see Luis Díaz Soler, *La historia de la esclavitud negra en Puerto Rico*, p. 301 n.
⁴Callahan, *Cuba and International Relations*, p. 399.
⁵Eugenio Alonso y Sanjurjo, *Apuntes sobre los proyectos de la abolición de la esclavitud en las islas de Cuba y Puerto Rico*, pp. 20–24.
⁶Allan Nevins, *Hamilton Fish: The Inner History of the Grant Administration*, p. 345.

wise, to the need to conquer in Cuba. It was ironical but true; even the Spanish liberals in power were forced to serve reactionary demands, as they reflected on notices from Cuba that the government there, cowed by the Volunteers, could not support Prim's promises of reform measures made to Spanish liberals and foreign ambassadors.

The Spanish liberal leaders — Becerra, Martos, and Nicolás Rivero, president of the Cortes — frequently assured Sickles that as liberals they wanted to be friends of the United States and liberal institutions. But, due to the circumstances mentioned before, these very men often acted like reactionaries. Rivero in a public speech greeted by fervid applause identified himself with Isabel the Catholic and Friar Las Casas. He favored abolition and political reform for the colonies but not at the point of a bayonet. "It must be a spontaneous gift from our hearts."[7] Martos explained naively that Dulce's sad reform experience in Cuba had proved (as if it were a discovery) that the rebels did not want reform but independence, and that Spain could not yield to force.[8] Becerra, too, had his timid side. He admitted that Cubans were better prepared for free institutions than the average man in Spain, although Spain was no longer, so he thought, ruled by the antiquated and reactionary ideas of the Bourbons. Nevertheless, said Becerra, who had entitled the history of his administration as colonial minister "Democracy in Overseas Administration," Spain could concede nothing to Cuba till hostilities ceased.[9]

But if Becerra was forced to abandon reform plans for Cuba, Puerto Rico was a different matter. As the American government and the Puerto Rican abolitionists pointed out, there was no excuse for further delay in Puerto Rico. Becerra and the commissioners forged ahead with Puerto Rican reform plans.

When at length a project for abolishing slavery in Puerto Rico was presented to the Council of Ministers late in 1869, it was the first time such a project had ever been formally presented to, and considered by, the government. Vaguely based on the Laws of the Indies, the project recognized the civil rights of the liberated Negroes; yet, it would oblige them to remain with their masters for six more years under a labor contract which included a small salary and provisions for maintenance. It was, essentially, an attempt to transform

[7] Extracts from the speeches of Sres. Rivero and Martos (November, 1871), *BFSP* (1871–1872), LXII, 1051.
[8] Callahan, *Cuba and International Relations*, pp. 389–390.
[9] *Ibid.*

slavery gradually into a free-labor system without causing unnecessary disturbances.[10]

Still, the government hesitated to publicly present the Puerto Rican plan to those sectors of opinion which insisted that reforms for Puerto Rico contained perilous implications for Cuba.

The abolitionists in the Cortes, after a year of frustrated promises, were understandably restless at the government's kowtowing before the reactionaries. On November 13, 1869, Luis Padial, Puerto Rican deputy, attacked the "hypocrites" who paraded as "liberals" and "patriots," but who were in league with the slavophiles in the obstruction of abolitionist reforms. Padial was supported by Gabriel Rodríguez, who said that "if this Cortes is dissolved without having made the abomination of slavery disappear, we will return to our homes covered with shame."[11]

Abolitionist outcries, combined with the diplomatic threat that hung over the provisional government, achieved some results at least. Toward the end of November, Madrid informed the American government that it would implant a reform program in Puerto Rico, including freedom of the press, impartial suffrage, local government, equal civil and political rights for white and black, and abolition of slavery. This announcement, together with Sickles' faith in the triumph of liberal principles in Spain, was enough to forestall any coercive action by the Grant administration. Grant in his December message to Congress stated that conditions in Cuba did not justify a declaration of belligerency.[12]

Still it was necessary for Fish to press the procrastinating Spaniards. He warned López Roberts (December 23, 1869) that it was "important to have action and results, and not mere promises." He advocated what the abolitionists had already suggested — vientre libre for Puerto Rico immediately, and, furthermore, that this law be extended to Cuba the moment the rebellion there was ended.[13]

In spite of a contracting circle of foreign and abolitionist pressure, the reactionaries, led by Romero Robledo and Cánovas, made a last ditch stand on the question of Puerto Rican reforms. Becerra was forced to defend his reform policy in the Cortes (March 30, 1870),

[10]Alonso y Sanjurjo, *Apuntes*, p. 24.
[11]Cayetano Coll y Toste, *Boletín histórico*, IV, 34–51, cited by Díaz Soler, *La esclavitud negra*, pp. 304–305.
[12]Callahan, *Cuba and International Relations*, p. 390.
[13]Fish's Diary, December 23, 1869, Nevins, *Hamilton Fish*, p. 345.

explaining in reference to Cuba that if it had not been for reform hopes among the loyal Cubans, Cuba would have been lost to Spain. True, while the rebellion still raged in Cuba reforms would be impossible there, but the Revolution of September had made its promises and there was no reason for denying reforms in Puerto Rico, especially since Puerto Ricans were now represented in the Cortes.[14]

On the following day Cánovas, after presenting petitions in support of his position from Valencia merchants, made an extreme speech in an attempt to associate Puerto Rico with the Cuban rebellion. He discovered that the insignificant rising in Puerto Rico called the Rebellion of Lares (October 18, 1868, in which the cry "death to Spain" was heard) was really a major revolt. Speaking like a demagogue, Cánovas claimed that the reform commissioners for Puerto Rico and Cuba of 1866–1867 "wanted nothing except to break the ties that united the Antilles with Spain and destroy the integrity of the fatherland. I who called this commission and gave impulse to the reforms ... owed this judgment to my country."[15]

Becerra met such obstinate opposition to his projected reforms, especially the law governing the constitutional status of Puerto Rico, that he resigned on April 1, 1870. However, this did not help the reactionary cause in the least. The shift in ministerial posts at this time brought a more radical cabinet to power, with Prim still remaining as the dominant personality. The man who succeeded Becerra as colonial minister, Segismundo Moret y Prendergast, vice-president of the Abolitionist Society, was determined to carry out Becerra's reform policy. Moret was a good choice. He would prove himself an able political tactician and a man of strong character. Although not a brilliant Cánovas or Prim, he was steadfast, and, more important, circumstances favored his mission. In a sorry parade of transient colonial ministers, Moret at least would leave a memorable image.

What Moret and the new ministry had to face was the cold, hard fact that Spain could not suppress the rebellion in Cuba and that with each passing day the danger of American intervention grew. This was the key to understanding why Moret was determined on a measure of abolition not only for Puerto Rico but also for Cuba. How concerned Spain was about American intervention can easily be demonstrated. López Roberts was so disturbed that he desperately

---

[14]*Diario, Congreso* (1869–1870), X, No. 251 (30 de marzo de 1870), 6976.
[15]*Ibid.*, X, No. 253 (1 de abril de 1870), p. 6990.

advised Madrid to declare the rebellion virtually at an end. On January 6, 1870, Caballero de Rodas, following Roberts' instructions, announced in the *Gaceta Oficial* that the rebellion was extinguished, and that civil tribunals were again functioning. López Roberts reported that the ruse was "completely satisfactory, the insertion of the announcement [in American papers] having produced a very good impression on public opinion here."[16]

The American government was only briefly deceived by Spanish diplomatic strategy, soon made ridiculous by rebel victories. By April, 1870, López Roberts, after talking with Fish, reported in alarm that Sickles would make a new offer to buy the island on the pretext that it was impossible for Spain to end the rebellion, and that Sickles would again insist on the abolition of slavery in the Spanish Antilles.[17]

Spain was thus, to employ an old Spanish proverb, "... forced between the sword and the wall." She could not end the rebellion, and she could not risk American intervention. She had one alternative: conciliate the American government, or at least win European allies against it. Spain chose the only feasible reform, namely, abolition. The slave interests of the Antilles were to be sacrificed to circumstance. As a second measure of conciliation, Spain promised to remove all causes of American complaints in Cuba, including abuses of life, property, security, and dignity committed on American residents there. All claims were to be settled by an international claims convention.[18]

It was almost as important for Spain to conciliate the British government, whose diplomats had never ceased to work toward abolition in Cuba, even though the strength of these demands had tapered off in the face of American aggressiveness in the Caribbean. But at this point, the British leaders, who were equally concerned over Spain's failure to pacify Cuba, were apparently working in harmony with the Americans. Layard, the British minister in Madrid, proposed cooperation with the United States in the pacification of Cuba through the abolition of slavery and other reforms. Moret, who knew that Britain was still Spain's most important ally against American intervention

[16] López Roberts, Washington, 13 de enero de 1870, A.M.A.E. *Correspondencia EEUnidos*, Leg. 1473 (1870–1872), Despachos N. 5. y N. 7.

[17] *Ibid.*, López Roberts, Washington, 6 de abril de 1870.

[18] For the story of the Convention of 1871 and the events that led up to it, see Jerónimo Becker y González, *La historia de las relaciones exteriores de España durante el siglo XIX*, Vol. III, Chaps. I–III.

in Cuba, might have suggested that Layard take this course. Moret felt, perhaps, that British participation would serve to restrain the Americans.[19]

In any case, what is certain is that Moret wrote the governor of Cuba, May 8, 1870: "Not another day must pass without doing something about this. France and England will not help us while we are slaveholders and this one word [slavery] gives North America the right to hold a suspended threat over our heads."[20]

Moret, as a realist, knew that the abolitionist sentiment in Spain was not strong enough to force a full measure of abolition over the reactionaries; nor could Spain finance any scheme of pecuniary indemnity on a large scale. Moret knew that vientre libre was inadequate. In the letter mentioned above he told the governor that he wanted at least four things: (1) free-born slaves, or vientre libre; (2) the liberty of all slaves that had fought for Spain; (3) the liberty of all slaves confiscated from the rebels and from slave ships (the latter referred to the emancipados about which British diplomacy was so long concerned); and (4) the transformation of slavery into a patronage system to last for ten or fifteen years. The Negro would receive an annual salary while being obliged to remain on the plantation.[21] Thus with the government of Prim firmly behind him, Moret set about laying the foundations for his much disputed law, which, as finally agreed upon, would include, with some qualifications, all four of the afore-mentioned provisions.

On May 28, 1870, Segismundo Moret presented to the Cortes his "Preparatory Law for the Abolition of Slavery in the Spanish Antilles." As already seen, the pressure of American diplomacy, the abolitionist strategy of the Cuban rebels, and the abolitionists in the Cortes were primary influences in forcing the presentation of the Ley Moret. Inseparable from these influences was the new political conscience created by the Glorious Revolution. As Moret recognized in the preamble: "None of the men who belong to the Revolution of September could consent that the poor Negro remain abject and neglected ... while here in the Peninsula we have raised ourselves to the highest state of political liberty in the Constitution of 1869."[22]

[19]According to Callahan, *Cuba and International Relations*, p. 392.
[20]"Sr. Ministro de Ultramar al Gobernador general," 8 de mayo de 1870, A.H.N. Ultramar, Leg. 4881 (1870–1872), Vol. I.
[21]*Ibid*.
[22]"Proyecto de ley preparatoria para la abolición gradual de la esclavitud en

It was in honor of the Glorious Revolution of September 18, 1868, that vientre libre, the most important article of the Moret Law, provided for the liberty of all slaves born on that date and thereafter "so that now no more slaves are born on Spanish soil." The second most important provision conceded liberty to all slaves aged sixty-five or more (later amended to 60). Other important provisions declared the freedom of all slaves who had served under the Spanish flag in the "present Cuban insurrection" and the freedom of all slaves not legally included in the census registrations of Puerto Rico and Cuba.[23] All in all, it was a conservative gesture of abolition. Even vientre libre was hemmed in by serious qualifications.

The free-born Negro was subject to a system of tutelage (*patronato*) until the age of eighteen. The master, now called a *patrón*, was obliged to care for the young Negroes (*patrocinados*), but he had also the privilege of utilizing their labor without pay until they had reached the age of eighteen. From then on, the Negro youth was entitled to "half the wages of a free man." On reaching the age of twenty-two, the free-born Negro was entitled to full civil rights.[24]

The state of patronato was declared transmissible by all the means known to law, but, at the same time, it could be revoked for just reasons. Freedmen could rescue their children from tutelage by repaying the patron any expenses incurred on behalf of the children. The patronato could be declared void in cases where the patron abused his charges contrary to the dispositions of the law, for example, punishing the Negroes severely, or encouraging the prostitution of the females.[25]

Freedmen aged sixty or more could choose to remain in the house of their masters. The patron was obliged by law to maintain this class of libertos and, in return, the old libertos were obliged to work "according to their capabilities" on the plantation or in the house of the patron.[26]

In regard to indemnification, the government was authorized to raise the necessary funds by imposing a tax upon slaveholders for every slave in their possession between the ages of eleven and sixty

---

las Antillas españolas," *Diario, Congreso* (1869–1870), XIII (28 de mayo de 1870), First Appendix No. 292.
[23] *Ibid.*
[24] *Ibid.*
[25] *Ibid.*
[26] *Ibid.*

years. It is obvious that this provision was intended to hasten the voluntary emancipation of slaves on the part of the tax-paying owners.

Any attempt to evade the application of the law was to be punished in accordance with Title XIII of the Penal Code. Punishment by flogging, a highly debated issue, was suspended pending the final enactment of the law. As an added humanitarian provision, it was forbidden to separate children under fourteen from their mothers, or to separate slaves united in matrimony.[27]

Article Twenty-one promised that as soon as peace was restored in Cuba a fuller measure of abolition would be considered. In the debates that followed in the Cortes, abolitionist deputies attempted to amend the Moret measure. Humanitarian sentiment in the Cortes prevailed to the extent of abolishing the whip *(pena de azotes)* pending publication of the regulations for putting the law into operation. However, stocks, irons, and imprisonment, not considered strictly corporal punishment, were to remain in force in spite of proposals to the contrary. In order to conciliate the abolitionists, however, the committee made other minor amendments which, again, were largely in favor of the slaves.[28] Yet in its final form the law remained essentially what it was on leaving Moret's hand. This preparatory law of abolition was appropriately called "the Moret Law."

Of course, Moret's measure fell far below the expectations of the British, the American, and the Spanish abolitionists, but, under the circumstances, was a more radical measure possible?

Moret attempted to ease the measure through the Cortes by claiming that all sections of opinion, including the slaveholders of Cuba, were in favor of the Preparatory Law. Said Moret: "All interests are in agreement . . . the government had the singular satisfaction of presenting this project in accord with the slaveowners themselves!"[29] This was a gross oversimplification, and later developments would prove it so.

The committee named by the government to examine the proposed law and to present its opinion and recommendations to the Cortes, as was expected, did not disagree with the will of the government. In a statement to the Cortes (June 3, 1870) it approved the project, making another oversimplification: "There is no need to say much . . . the

---

[27]*Ibid.*
[28]*Diario, Congreso* (1869–1870), XIV, No. 311 (21 de junio de 1870), 9029.
[29]*Ibid.*, "Proyecto de ley," (28 de mayo de 1870), First Appendix No. 292.

necessity of the measure is in the conscience of everyone without contradiction."³⁰

Sr. Topete, speaking for the government-appointed committee on the measure, added a special defense of the patronato or tutelar system: "I was born in Cuba, reared by Negroes," said Topete, "I love them. The Negro is our equal [*bien*, from the Cortes], but ... can the legislature in one stroke cause three to four hundred thousand men to abandon their work?"

Still, the law was too extreme for the defenders of the status quo, who wanted it thrown out on the grounds that it was unpatriotic and harmful to the Cuban economy. Romero Robledo spoke for the majority of the conservatives when he said that the law was no way to reward the Spanish party of Cuba, who were risking their lives and fortunes to sustain the Spanish flag. It was the rebels who wanted this reform as a means to destroy Spanish dominion in the island.³¹

"No one defends slavery," Romero Robledo said, "but it is a question of means. Do we want the destruction and ruin of Cuba? How, for example, will workers be found to replace those that will be lacking?" Remember, too, said the Romero Robledo group, what happened to Haiti and Santo Domingo.³²

A source of great controversy was an amendment to Article Twenty-one presented by the archconservatives Cánovas and Romero Robledo. Because of the insurrection, the Cubans had been excluded from representation in the Cortes in spite of the promises of the Glorious Revolution. The opposition, therefore, concentrated on winning a guarantee that no further measures of abolition beyond the Moret Law would be taken until the representatives of Cuba were present in the Cortes.³³ By representatives of Cuba the authors really meant the Spanish party.

During the ensuing years the amendment, which was accepted by the Cortes, would become the subject of heated debates. The liberals would interpret it as a government promise to carry abolition further the moment Cuban deputies were admitted to the Cortes. But the future would show that every time a liberal suggested that elections be held in Cuba, he would be shouted down with the conservative

---

³⁰*Ibid.*, XIII (4 de junio de 1870), Second Appendix No. 298.
³¹*El Español*, periódico político, 13 de junio de 1870.
³²*Diario, Congreso* (1869), XIV (17 de junio de 1870), 8913.
³³See the debates of June 17, 1870, *ibid.*

cry, repeated to the point of ineffable boredom: "No reforms in Cuba while one single rebel remains in arms."

The abolitionists in the Cortes struck hard at the timidity of the Preparatory Law. The Puerto Rican Román Baldorioty exclaimed: "My criterion is absolutely abolitionist ... the project of the Colonial Minister does not satisfy my aspirations, and the statements of the committee ... less yet."[34]

Sr. Díaz Quintero expressed a similar dissatisfaction: "I am against the project because it seems to me small, niggardly ... it is not worthy of what we expected of the Revolution of September."[35]

The high point of the debate was reached on June 20. The deputies had presented various amendments, together with speeches in support of them. The committee threw out the majority of them. Emilio Castelar — the greatest orator in nineteenth-century Spain, professor at the University of Madrid, future president of the Republic, and charter member of the Abolitionist Society — arose to defend his bold amendment: "The government will promise to fully abolish slavery in the next session of the legislature." Rodríguez, Padial, Baldorioty, and other abolitionists affixed their names to the resolution.[36]

Taking a simile from the cock fights, the Spaniards called Castelar "golden beak" (el pico de oro), so effective were his words in argument. Castelar had given his first speech against slavery to an indifferent Cortes in 1854. For many years he had studied the history of human slavery in the university and in the Madrid Atheneum. Now, before a receptive audience, Castelar sketched in brilliant colors a universal history of slavery from the time of the Greeks to the present day. He arrived at the Glorious Revolution as if the whole movement of humanity had evolved toward this event. Applying the principles of the Revolution to the Moret project, he termed it sarcastically a "doctrinaire law." "How can a man of the nineteenth century continue to have property in slaves?" asked the speaker indignantly. And where was the humanitarian conscience? "Doesn't the Cortes know that in some years four hundred slaves commit suicide?" Castelar spoke nearly the whole afternoon before an audience spellbound by the emotional appeal of his arguments: "Slavery and fam-

[34]*Ibid.*, XIV (17 de junio de 1870), 8766.
[35]*Ibid.*, XIV (17 de junio de 1870), 8808.
[36]*Ibid.*, XIII (13 de junio de 1870), Sixth Appendix No. 305. This amendment presented to the Cortes lost by a vote of seventy-eight to forty-eight.

ily, slavery and conscience, slavery and morality, slavery and religion are incompatible terms."[37]

Castelar appealed to the figures of Lincoln, Wendell Phillips, Wilberforce, and Toussaint L'Ouverture:

> I will say that we have nineteen centuries of Christianity . . . and still there are slaves. They only exist, Señores, in the Catholic countries of Brazil and Spain. I know more [said Don Emilio] . . . hardly a century of revolution and the revolutionary peoples, France, England, and the United States, have abolished slavery. Nineteen centuries of Christianity and there are still slaves among Catholic peoples! One century of revolution and there are no slaves among revolutionary peoples.[38]

At length, Castelar reached his soaring conclusion; with his arms extended he shouted: "Arise, Spanish legislators and make of this nineteenth century, those who would lay the cap-stone, the century of the complete and total redemption of all slaves. I have spoken."[39]

This gem of nineteenth-century liberal oratory was feverishly applauded by the Cortes. Colonial Minister Moret, fellow member of the Abolitionist Society with Castelar, was now hard put to defend his limited project: "My situation would be grave if I had nothing more valuable to offer than the magnificent eloquence of your Lordship." Beginning thus, Moret struck hard at the emotional arguments of Castelar, reminding the Cortes, as they were to be reminded many times by the conservatives, that "the great Lincoln did not want to abolish slavery till 1900."[40]

> But Sr. Castelar tells the truth [said Moret with irony] when he says that no one will appreciate the work of the colonial minister. The radicals are not satisfied, and the slave proprietors will curse my name, but I don't care. . . . Perhaps, there will come a day when honorable men, to whose judgment I deliver myself, will say that I knew how to prevent great evils such as the terrible war that cost the United States so much.

Moret insisted that the deputies throw out the amendment of Castelar, and by a vote of seventy-eight to forty-eight the amendment was defeated. Having answered the abolitionists, Moret now turned to defend his project against the reactionaries. His frank statement laid

---

[37]*Ibid.*, XIV (20 de junio de 1870), 8987–8990.
[38]*Ibid.*, XIV (20 de junio de 1870), 8992.
[39]*Ibid.*, XIV (20 de junio de 1870), 8992.
[40]*Ibid.*, XIV (20 de junio de 1870), 8994.

bare the innermost motives behind the government's presentation of the law:

> The government has chosen this moment to present the law because it was the last opportunity. Think, sirs, that our enemies [the Cuban rebels], familiar with North American customs and language, in contact with their statesmen, have been able from the first moment to give to the insurrection a special character, presenting it as the flag of liberty against the flag of tyranny, as the principle of colonial autonomy against the principle of oppression by the metropolis, as the principle of independence against the pretensions of Europe.[41]

These words were not only a tribute to rebel propaganda but also a method of emphasizing to the Cortes the possibility that, unless Spain took abolitionist action, the United States would intervene in behalf of the rebels. "In the face of rebel tactics," said Moret, "we could not oppose much more than our promises and deceptions of other epochs. But promises were not enough, the Government understands that it was essential to present the law, and furthermore, to discuss it."[42]

"This," concluded Moret, "would be like saying to Europe [and the United States]: We give you definite proof; here is the project... slavery is dead, and is finished forever in Spanish dominions."[43] The law, with minor changes, was approved by the Cortes and published on July 4, 1870.

The preparation and discussion of the Moret Law coincided with a new and more critical threat to Spanish dominion in Cuba. Pro-Cuban sentiment in the United States, incited by incidents such as the detention of the American ship *Colonel Lloyd Aspinwall* (January 21, 1870) and the judicial murder of the great Cuban patriot, Domingo Goicouria (May 6, 1870), rose like a threatening tide.[44]

It was another crisis for Fish; unless he acted boldly the expansionists would carry the day. President Grant, in his annual message to Congress, was again preparing to attack Spain. Perhaps this would have been enough, given the disposition of Congress, to lead to a declaration of war or a declaration of belligerency in favor of the Cuban rebels. Fish, supported by other alarmed cabinet members,

---

[41] *Ibid.*, XIII (9 de junio de 1870), 8768.
[42] *Ibid.*, XIII (9 de junio de 1870), 8768–8771.
[43] *Ibid.*, XIII (9 de junio de 1870), 8768–8771.
[44] Nevins, *Hamilton Fish*, p. 352.

prevailed upon Grant to change his mind. Congress was amazed when Grant's message of June 13, 1870, declared that there were no conditions in Cuba that would justify the recognition of the rebels as belligerents.[45]

As far as Grant could see (through the eyes of Fish), nothing had changed since the preceding December. The rebels, avoiding major battles, continued to limit their operations to attacking the rear guard of the Spanish troops. Certain Americans, said the President, who were holders of bonds of the Cuban Republic, wanted to compromise their country. There was no *de facto* government in Cuba; furthermore, a declaration of belligerency might disrupt trade, and produce more controversy over the right of search. In the beginning of the war, said Grant, the Spanish government had initiated by executive decrees a system of exile, councils of war, executions of suspected persons, summary expropriation of possessions, and other arbitrary measures. There thus arose the question of the rights of American citizens in Cuba based on the treaty of 1795. These problems had forced the American government to remonstrate with the Spanish government. But the situation had improved. Spain had agreed to the establishing of a joint commission to settle American claims.[46]

On June 16, in the House of Representatives, as a result of Grant's message, Logan's resolution for granting belligerent rights to the Cubans was defeated by a vote of one hundred to seventy. The House then passed a resolution authorizing the President to protest against the barbarities practiced by both sides and to cooperate with either government, if he thought proper, in mitigating the horrors of war in Cuba.[47] This was a tremendous personal victory for Fish. Had the vote carried, Fish would probably have resigned, and this would have been unfortunate for Spanish diplomacy. But if Fish and the cabinet members who stood by him expected thanks from Spain in the form of a more vigorous abolition bill, they were sadly mistaken.

Foreign opinions could not change the limited character of the Moret bill. Fish, for one, instructed Sickles (June 20, 1870), while the bill was still in debate, to state in a friendly but firm manner the American government's disappointment with the bill. In the opinion

[45]*Ibid.*, p. 359.
[46]López Roberts, Washington, 16 de junio de 1870, A.M.A.E. *Política EEUnidos* (1865–1872), N. 129.
[47]Nevins, *Hamilton Fish*, p. 362.

of the President, the failure of the law to meet universal expectations would produce dissatisfaction throughout the civilized world and would also fail to satisfy or pacify Cuba.[48]

Disgusted with the bill, Fish said that it was not an honest bill of emancipation: "It may rather be called a project for relieving the slave owners from the necessity of supporting infants and aged slaves, who can only be a burden, and of prolonging the institution as to able-bodied slaves."[49]

Despite all the praise given by its supporters, the Moret Law signified nothing more than its original title: "Preparatory Law for the Abolition of Slavery." Its conservative purpose was aptly defined by Gallego Díaz, member of the committee:

In summary, the government had as its objective in presenting this law to make certain that abolition will come to be a real and effective fact in the future, and that slavery would tend to its own extinction in the present, so that even if the law promised by Article Twenty-one is not forthcoming, this present law would by itself be enough to achieve complete abolition.[50]

Viewing the law from another angle, one can observe Moret's definition, in which he said that if the law seemed bad to the abolitionists, it was because it was born of conciliation: "Here is what the law is ... a compromise between the conservative elements and the revolutionary elements ... that made the Revolution of September possible."[51]

Reduced to the simplest terms, then, the Moret Law of free birth was a step toward the gradual abolition of slavery. The new law in no way altered the essential nature of slavery, that is, forced labor with threat of physical punishment for the recalcitrant. Although the use of the whip was temporarily withheld, pending the publication of regulations for putting the law into effect, the principle of corporal punishment was still preserved. Moret had said in answering the abolitionists that the committee and the government believed that it was to the interest of the slaves themselves that corporal punishment not be allowed to disappear completely, because otherwise this would

[48]Fish to Sickles, June 20, 1870, No. 65; State Dept. MSS Spain, Diplomatic Drafts, cited *ibid.*, p. 346.

[49]*Ibid.*, p. 345.

[50]Statement by Gallego Díaz in defending the Moret Law in the Cortes, *Diario, Congreso* (1869–1871), XIII (9 de junio de 1870), 8761.

[51]*Ibid.*, XIV (20 de junio de 1870), 8999.

be to abolish slavery in the worst manner possible, thus provoking conflicts. Furthermore, added Moret, as if to say that corporal punishment was hardly used anyway, "Slavery in Cuba and Puerto Rico today has a humane character."[52]

Most Spanish newspapers approved of the law, even though the conservative ones thought it extreme and the radical ones insufficient. Perhaps the fairest judgment was made by *La Independencia Española*, a liberal paper: "We do not believe Sr. Moret has said the last word ... but we believe he has gone as far as certain great interests will permit. Unfortunately, these interests make impossible a more decisive solution."[53]

[52]*Ibid.*, XIV (21 de junio de 1870), 9029.

[53]*La Independencia Española*, 4 de junio de 1870. Comments on the Moret Law by the newspapers of Spain were largely overshadowed by startling events reported from the Franco-Prussian War.

14. Behind the Scenes: Failure To Enforce the Law, 1870-1872*

> The Junta of hacendados. . . . The majority are for gaining time hoping that the delay will profit them.
>
> Governor General Caballero de Rodas[1]

When the slaveowners heard that the liberal government of Spain was preparing a measure of abolition, they went in alarm to Captain General Caballero to ask permission to assemble and study the social question, as it was euphemistically called, and to prepare a new census of slaves. Caballero, in telegraphing this request to Moret (March 27, 1870), expressed misgivings that the rebels might somehow exploit the anxiety of the proprietors: "I believe matter delicate, that enemies would utilize, and public credit would be directly affected . . . depriving government of recourses."[2]

In answering, Moret left the decision to Caballero, and, incidentally, asked the latter how the abolition proposals had been received in Havana. The governor replied on June 11, 1870, that the disturbed proprietors wanted to know the full extent of the projected law, and that not all the proprietors had welcomed the proposition of vientre libre. Earlier a majority of the Junta de Hacendados had expressed

---

*This chapter appeared in modified form as an article: "The Spanish Abolition Law of 1870: A Study in Legislative Reluctance," *Revista de Ciencias Sociales*, Special Issue on the Caribbean. Río Piedras, P. R.: Universidad de Puerto Rico, 1960.

[1]Caballero de Rodas al Ministro de Ultramar, 11 de junio de 1870, "Revista política," A.H.N. Ultramar, Leg. 4881 (1870–1872), Vol. I.

[2]"Remite el acta de la Junta de hacendados, proprietarios y comerciantes para tratar de la cuestión social en la isla de Cuba," 17 de junio de 1870, *ibid.*, N. 3.

[3]Caballero de Rodas al Ministro de Ultramar, 11 de junio de 1870, *ibid.*, Vol. I.

their approval of vientre libre but could not agree on any other provisions; for example, the freedom of slaves of sixty years of age or more. "The majority are for gaining time," said Caballero, "hoping that the delay will profit them."[3] These words are the key to understanding the ineffective application of the Moret Law in Cuba.

The proprietors, merchants, and notables of the island naturally wanted to discuss the Moret proposals. They did not know as yet that Madrid had already decided to push through the Moret program. On Caballero's advice the government decided to explain the Moret provisions to an assembly of the leading proprietors and merchants. The first meeting was held on June 17, 1870, under the presidency of the governor, Caballero. Pedro Sotolongo, favorable to the government side, was elected secretary. The proprietors soon discovered that they were not called to participate in the shaping of abolitionist measures but to approve a *fait accompli*.

In facing the delicate matter of submitting the projected Moret Law to the proprietors, Caballero gave several reasons why they were expected to assent: (1) that slavery was exclusively found in the island of Cuba, and that this placed the nation in an unfavorable light in its relations with other nations; (2) that slavery was one of the causes prolonging the war because the insurrectionaries had obtained sympathy and help from abolitionist opinion in the United States by propagating the idea that the Spaniards wanted to preserve slavery perpetually; (3) that apart from the first two reasons, the government had in the treaties with Great Britain contracted a promise to resolve this problem.[4]

Caballero said he believed that the Moret measures would be the last blow to the rebellion, and would strengthen commercial relations between Cuba and the United States.[5] Since the United States represented the greatest market for Cuban products, no doubt this type of appeal was calculated to produce a strong effect on the proprietors. But it proved difficult to conciliate slaveowners, who previously had scarcely been consulted by the government. Moret now sent an assurance that although the government had abolished certain aspects of slavery, such as servitude of the newborn and the aged, the government would not take another step without Cuban deputies being present in the Cortes.[6]

Few members of the Junta expressed opinions in full accord with

[4]"Remite el acta de la Junta," 17 de junio de 1870, *ibid.*, N. 3.
[5]*Ibid.* [6]*Ibid.*

the government. Juan Poey and several other hacendados approved of freedom for the newborn and the aged slaves but with proper indemnification. (It was Poey who soon proposed that the proprietor should have the right to exchange one freedman for two imported coolies from British East Indian colonies. Poey believed this would compensate slaveholders and speed up emancipation.)[7] Manuel Cardenal thought the government had acted too hastily. Julián Zulueta, the richest slaveholder, said the reform was dangerous while the enemies of Spain still bore arms. José Argudín, who presented a conservative plan of abolition in 1866, rose to speak in favor of leaving abolition not to the abolitionists nor to the government but to the owners themselves. He bitterly attacked the abolitionists, "who have no money for indemnifying the owners ... no respect for the rights of property, they don't see that slaves know nothing of political rights."[8] Several proprietors supported Argudín's proposal that a committee be sent to Madrid to work against the adoption of the measure.

It was the same Argudín who asked for political and economic reforms for the island. The Creole proprietors still believed it possible to separate these demands from the slave question. "If attention is not given to the reforms," said Argudín, "the independence of Cuba will be inevitable ... and the island will not be prepared to govern itself, it will therefore sink into anarchy as the other independent nations of Latin America."[9]

The pugnacious mood of the Junta forced the governor to make some rather spurious explanations. In the second meeting (July 1, 1870) Caballero claimed that the government did not have time to hear the hacendados because of extraordinary circumstances. The government had not taken the initiative but was obliged to do so by members of the Cortes. The proprietors should have been grateful, because if the question had been left entirely to the Cortes a more radical law would have resulted. Had not the government intervened in the proprietors' behalf? Did it not consult a worthy proprietor resident in Madrid, who represented various great proprietors of this island, and modify the project by suppressing radical articles accord-

[7]For the details of the plan designed to conciliate everyone, see "Sr. Juan Poey to the Captain General of Cuba, Havana, February 6, 1871." *BFSP* 1871–1872, LXII, 1058–1059.

[8]"Remite el acta de la Junta," 17 de junio de 1870, A.H.N. Ultramar, Leg. 4881 (1870–1872), Vol. I.

[9]*Ibid.*

ing to his indications? And remember, added Caballero in a sterner tone, if the government had really wanted to prejudice the proprietors nothing would have been easier than presenting a project of one single article, that is, the complete abolition of slavery.[10]

The third session (July 11, 1870) was another effort, this time by the Secretary Sotolongo, to justify the government's decision. He gave a long speech describing the project as the wisest of measures, and tried to comfort the doubtful hacendados with further assurances. The speech is noteworthy in that it attempted to characterize the Spanish solution to slavery, and, with some truth, pointed out its advantages over those forms adopted by Britain and the United States. With this law, said Sotolongo, Spain would conserve the principle of potestad domínica, broken by the English and the Americans. That is why liberated slaves in English colonies had not advanced in civilization under the tutelage of their masters, and why in the United States, where the principle was broken suddenly, the result was a disastrous civil war. "Here in this island under the tutelage system the Negroes are going to assimilate themselves to the culture and civilization of Spain."[11]

The outcome of these meetings was the unanimous resolution, first, that a new census should be made, and second, that a committee of seven important slaveholders[12] should be named to inform Madrid about the opinions and proposals of the hacendados, merchants, and notables of Cuba concerning the cuestión social.

The supreme government hastily approved of a new census, feeling that such a measure was essential to the adequate and just application of the Moret project, since the census of 1867 was not accepted as accurate.[13] But the decision to take a new census in the midst of a war-torn society could only prove unwise. It was to have been completed in December, 1870, but, as might have been expected, numerous problems arose which aided the delaying tactics of the proprietors.

Caballero performed his duty in attempting to gain the approval

[10]*Ibid.*, (1 de julio de 1870).
[11]*Ibid.*, (11 de julio de 1870).
[12]Julián D. Zulueta, president, assisted by Manuel Cardenal, el Marqués de Almendares, José Morales Lemus, Antonio García Rizo, Segundo Reigal, and Juan A. Colomé.
[13]"Remite el acta de la Junta," 17 de junio de 1870, A.H.N. Ultramar, Leg. 4881 (1870–1872), Vol. I.

of the proprietors for the Moret Law, but, in fact, he became increasingly sympathetic to the cause of the proprietors, either because he felt that they had not been justly consulted, or because he was afraid to be the instrument for carrying out a law that was bound to be unpopular.

On his own initiative, Caballero took an extraordinary step and suspended the publication of the Moret Law, which in the meantime had been approved by the Cortes. The governor justified his action to Moret on the grounds that the publication of the law without the regulations for putting it into effect would be *peligroso* (dangerous) because the slave interests would give the law alarming and exaggerated interpretations. The law was therefore to be suspended until the regulations could be decided upon, and the slaveholders could be heard.[14] Moret was partially to blame for the suspension, since he had falsely said, on presenting the law, that it had the previous consent of the proprietors. But Moret, after listening to further explanations from Caballero, including the repetitious argument that nothing could be done until the new census was taken, gave an emphatic answer via telegraph on September 19, 1870: "Suspension of emancipation law is most serious. Minister lacks faculties for approving it. Publish it . . . with enclosed regulations [a provisional regulation] or in the manner you think best. International situation the same."[15]

Moret was acutely aware of the need to make a good impression on international abolitionists, especially since the Moret Law itself was so unsatisfactory to them. Most governments of the Western World had accepted the Moret Law, but with the Spanish assurances that it would soon go into effect. Great Britain, the United States, Liberia, Costa Rica, Haiti, and others sent official letters of congratulations to the Spanish government. The British government, which had worked so long for such a measure, expressed its formal satisfaction on August, 1870. But the measure by no means satisfied the swollen ranks of English abolitionists. Lord Clarendon was deluged by protests demanding that Spain declare, once and for all, the complete and absolute freedom of all slaves in the Spanish Antilles.[16]

The English abolitionists through long experience had come to doubt the pledged word by transitory Spanish governments. Lord

[14]Caballero, La Habana, 24 de agosto de 1870, *ibid.*, Vol. I.
[15]Segismundo Moret, Madrid, telegrama, 19 de septiembre de 1870, *ibid.*
[16]Letters by foreign governments acknowledging the Moret Law are found in A.H.N. Ultramar, Leg. 4882 (1869–1880), Vols. 3 and 4, E-16-70, N. 22.

Clarendon, however, defended the good intentions of the Spanish ministers. With the Yankees hovering over Cuba he could hardly do otherwise. We witness a strange bit of irony when Colonial Minister Moret expresses the thanks of the Spanish government to Her Britannic Majesty for Clarendon's "worthy and dignified defense" of Spain's good intentions.[17]

The abolitionist societies of England, leaving no stone unturned, sent their protests directly to Captain General Caballero, emphasizing the insufficiency of the law and demanding respectfully that imperfect as it was it deserved a better fate than previous measures made in behalf of the slaves. Concerned, as the captains general now were, with the force of abolitionist opinion, Caballero reported to Madrid that he had shown to the Junta of Hacendados of Cuba the complaint of the abolitionists, believing that this would help convince them of the need to accept and apply the Moret Law. In what way this strategy was effective is hard to say. For his own part Caballero promised to do all he could to live up to the benevolent defense made by Lord Clarendon before the abolitionists of Spain's good intention.[18]

The real danger to Spain was, of course, the American expansionists, who for several reasons were not disposed to accept Spanish diplomatic explanations. Ambassador Sickles was impatient to protest against the deficiencies of the Moret Law, and in this he had the backing of American public opinion.

Spanish sources reported with alarm that many influential Americans thought the Moret Law insufficient, that Mr. Sumner, chairman of the Committee of Foreign Relations, who until now had defended the interests of Spain, did not agree with the President's acceptance of the law, and had proposed resolutions in Congress much more radical than those of Representative Banks, a notorious enemy of Spain. The American press also expressed dissatisfaction. Cuban exiles affiliated with the rebel cause of Céspedes were roundly pleased with the measure. In their meetings, newspapers, and proclamations they claimed that the Moret Law was one more proof that Spain continued to sustain slavery in Cuba.[19] By such expressions they hoped to excite the passion of the North Americans, so that President Grant would

[17] Ministro de Ultramar, Madrid, 12 de agosto de 1870, *ibid.*, N. 22.
[18] Caballero de Rodas, La Habana, 12 de septiembre de 1870, *ibid.*
[19] "Comunicaciones del Ministro de Ultramar al capitán general de Cuba," 15 de julio de 1870, A.H.N. Ultramar, Leg. 4880 (1870–1872), Vol. I.

yet be forced to intervene in Cuba, or to declare a state of belligerency in favor of the rebels. Moved by this information, Moret wrote to Caballero in Cuba: "I hope that public opinion in the United States which today is not very favorable to the law will be rectified shortly in the same manner as that of their Government [referring to Fish and Grant]."[20]

Of course, Spanish diplomatic instructions foresaw that the American government would be dissatisfied with the Ley Moret, but the American cabinet must be made to understand that this was all that could be done, given the circumstances of rebellion in Cuba and the fear of alienating the sympathies of the Spanish volunteers and the wealthy loyalist class.[21] After all, the history of this reform showed many delays in Brazil, where the problem was not so complex, ". . . and no one can justly formulate a charge against the Government of Spain because it had not instantly realized this reform."[22]

Furthermore, Moret gave new emphasis to the threefold strategy hitherto employed against the threat of intervention. Apart from the abolitionist promise of the Moret Law, Spain reiterated promises to settle all American claims in Cuba, and again published in American papers the Spanish resolution to pacify Cuba no matter what the cost.[23]

Still Caballero, with that extraordinary autonomy enjoyed by the captains general, delayed, offering more excuses. He had not yet given effective liberty to newborn slaves or to slaves aged sixty or more. Moret replied angrily, on the twenty-eighth of September: "Your delay in publishing the law is without justification. The declaration of liberty for the newborn does not require the previous formation of the slave census, nor does it absolutely require regulations." Moret went on to say that every delay in publishing the law showed public opinion that the Spanish government had not fulfilled its solemn

---

[20]Segismundo Moret, Madrid, 13 de agosto de 1870, *ibid*.

[21]Ministro de Estado al Ministro español en Washington López Roberts, agosto de 1870, *suelta*, A.M.A.E., Leg. 1473 (1870–1872).

[22]*Ibid*.

[23]Segismundo Moret al Ministro Español en Washington, 6 de agosto de 1870, *ibid*. By the eleventh of February, 1871, after difficult negotiations, an arbitration agreement was signed by Spain and the United States. The agreement promised to settle all claims since October 1, 1868. For details, see Jerónimo Becker y González, *La historia de las relaciones exteriores de España durante el siglo XIX*, Vol. III.

promise, repeated many times, that no more slaves would be born in the Antilles.[24]

Caballero now had no alternative. The same day, September 28, he ordered the law published in the *Official Gazette* of Havana, and sent copies to all the lieutenant governors of the island. Moret was informed that the people had received the law with the "best possible order." By the sixth of November, Caballero claimed that the law was operating in regard to the newborn and the aged. But, still trying to postpone matters in behalf of the hacendados, he asked for a delay in the complete application of the regulations until the new census had been completed.[25]

Moret by now realized that the difficulties in taking a new census would, as the hacendados well knew, hold up indefinitely the application of the law. Therefore, Moret ordered Caballero to abandon the new census and to reform the census of 1867. It seemed the most that could be done under the circumstances. Caballero ordered the reforming of the old census, and thereupon resigned. His resignation was accepted immediately.[26]

On the installation of the new governor general, the Count of Valmaseda, Moret sent him firm instructions, dated November 27, 1870, for putting into effect the abolition law without delay. For any such delays "would present the greatest difficulty to Spanish policy . . . foreign governments are disposed to believe the many charges made by the insurrection against the Spanish government that it sustains slavery in Cuba." The one thought of the government on this subject, concluded Moret, "is to remove this stain from our society."[27]

And yet, in spite of these explicit instructions, in spite of mounting foreign pressures, the Moret Law was no better applied by Valmaseda than it had been by Caballero. A great part of the trouble was due to that recurrent problem: the census. How many times in the correspondence of this period we hear the word! While the rest of the world wondered what sinister motives Spain had in delaying the

[24]Moret, Madrid, 28 de septiembre de 1870, A.H.N. Ultramar, Leg. 4881 (1870–1872), Titulo I, N. 36.

[25]*Gaceta de la Habana*, 28 de septiembre de 1870, *ibid.*, N. 131.

[26]"Comunicaciones," 6 de noviembre de 1870, *ibid.*, N. 46. The Count of Valmaseda, meanwhile, was sent to replace Caballero, who remained in power until Valmaseda arrived in the first week of December.

[27]"Instrucciones al Conde de Valmaseda," Madrid, 26 de noviembre de 1870, *ibid.*, Vol. I.

application of the Moret Law, the simple explanation was that the Cuban authorities were largely enmeshed in the census problem.

Since several categories of slaves depended for their freedom on an accurate census, many hacendados did what they could to confuse and falsify accounts. For example, according to Article Thirty-eight of the law of September 29, 1866, in persecution and punishment of the slave trade, it was established that any slave not legally registered in the census of 1867 would be considered by that single fact to be a free man, and would be, in consequence, issued a certificate of liberty. This same principle was incorporated in the Preparatory Law of Abolition of July 4, 1870. But how could these categories of slaves be freed when the census of 1867 had not been satisfactorily completed? And when the new census ordered for December, 1870, likewise was impossible? The Abolitionist Society fought obstinately for the liberation of unregistered slaves, and British diplomacy did the same. Repeatedly the Spanish government decreed the liberty of slaves not included in the census of 1867. But in almost every case, the proprietors made common cause, insisting that such decrees be suspended until a more accurate census was made.

Not all the inaccuracies of the census of 1867, and subsequent revisions, were the fault of the slaveowners. Some of them had just claims as to the legal origins of their slaves. The Cuban authorities, unable to distinguish between the just and the unjust, threw up their hands in despair, and suspended a series of decrees designed to effect the liberation of unregistered slaves. Therefore, a number of illegally acquired slaves, variously estimated at between forty and eighty thousand, remained for several more years in a state of bondage. The result was that, in spite of the good intentions of the Spanish government, it appeared to the abolitionists and to foreign observers that Spain had slipped back to her procrastinating habits in the matter of abolition and that she was by her lethargy actually protecting slave interests.[28]

Yet further proof that, contrary to appearances, the liberal govern-

---

[28] The governor general of Cuba on at least one occasion (June 13, 1878) requested that Article Seventy-one of the regulations of the census of 1867 be suspended. Due to a shortage of labor, made worse by an epidemic of cholera, the giving of liberty at this time, said the governor, would cause the most "extraordinary alarm," "Empadronamiento y Registro de Esclavos, Opinión del Consejo de Estado," 13 de febrero de 1869, A.H.N. Ultramar, Leg. 4882 (1869–1880), Vols. III and IV.

ment of Spain was doing its feeble best to enforce the emancipating measures of 1867 and 1870 is the fact that several times the Council of State reviewed the claims of slaveowners for a suspension of those articles concerned with the liberation of illegally acquired slaves, and then usually decided in favor of the slaves in question; but it was one thing to order their liberty from Madrid, and another to enforce it in Havana.[29]

The longer the application of the law was delayed the better for the hacendados, of course. The situation gave strength to their argument that they must be consulted before the regulations were put into effect. After all, the Moret Law could be no more effective than the regulations; in fact, the hacendados planned to amend the Moret Law by making the regulations to suit themselves. This was their grand strategy.

The Madrid government finally acceded to the wishes of the hacendados, and decided to permit them to formulate the regulations. But Moret wisely insisted that the regulations be formed on certain bases provided by the government.[30] The formulation of the regulations added to the delays. Meanwhile slaveholders like the Marques de San Miguel and Sr. Colomé offered their own set of regulations, which varied in the extent of their concern for the established interests of property.

Exciting political events in Spain, meanwhile, had served to distract the government's attention from the colonial problem.[31] On December 30, 1870, the great General Juan Prim was assassinated. As head of the provisional government he had been a decisive influence in selecting Don Amadeo de Savoy as the future constitutional monarch of Spain. A curious interlude was about to begin.

The young Italian Prince arrived in Spain in time to gaze upon the marble face of his deceased patron lying in state. Inauspicious beginnings were these, for the guiding hand of the strongman now lay beyond the grave. The new monarch, through a show of democratic

---

[29]That the Madrid government was against suspending the liberty of unregistered slaves, for example, is evident in such statements as this: "The Council is of the opinion that the dispositions of the law must be maintained with force and energy . . . certificates of liberty must immediately be given slaves . . . not registered according to the law," "Opinión del Estado," 13 de febrero de 1869, *ibid.*

[30]Caballero de Rodas, La Habana, 25 de noviembre de 1870, A.H.N. Ultramar, Leg. 4881 (1870–1872), Vol. I, N. 46.

[31]For details, Antonio Ballesteros y Beretta, *Historia de España y su influencia en la historia*, Vol. VIII, Chap. II.

manners, tried to ingratiate himself with the Spanish people, who had received him coldly. But this was regarded as a sign of weakness by the masses, who were accustomed to a more haughty bearing both in their rulers and in their bullfighters. Furthermore, Spanish political factions were already straining at the opportunity to exploit the new monarchy to their own particular advantage.

Political parties in Spain had divided sharply on the question of a constitutional monarchy presided over by a foreign prince, and each prepared for a test of strength. The republican group naturally were not satisfied with a constitutional monarchy, the old monarchists wanted the restoration of the Bourbons, and even the defenders of constitutional monarchy were not at all certain that the *Italiano* had been the best choice. In this atmosphere of bickering, no one Spanish ministry was capable of giving adequate attention to the Cuban problem, nor strong enough to control the unruly Spanish Volunteers in Cuba, who opposed even the rumor of reform.

Had Prim lived—and this is one of the most interesting subjects of speculation in nineteenth-century Spanish history—could he have found the solution to the Cuban problem? Prim was by far the ablest leader to emerge from the Glorious Revolution of 1868, and, aside from Cánovas del Castillo (ironically, he too would be assassinated at a critical moment in Cuban affairs), Prim was the only realist among Spanish statesmen. To his last days he wanted to rid the skinny neck of Spain of the Cuban millstone. A month before his violent end he sent Juan Clemente Zenea, Cuban poet and rebel, as intermediary to Cuba to negotiate with insurgent leaders. Zenea carried a safe-conduct from López Roberts, Spanish minister in Washington. But upon Prim's death Valmaseda threw Zenea into prison, and several months later, to the consummate pleasure of the Volunteers, had Zenea shot.[32]

Perhaps, as some have said, the government of Amadeo with Prim to firmly direct it along a constitutional path would have been able to maneuver the sale of Cuba through the inflammable Cortes. But such a possibility would have been extremely remote in view of the facts of the situation. Prosperous slave interests in the Western province of Cuba, privileged mercantile groups, the colonial bureaucracy, military officials and contractors, and above all, the blind pride of a

[32] For these facts concerning Prim's last effort to sell Cuba, see Allan Nevins, *Hamilton Fish: The Inner History of the Grant Administration*, pp. 617–618.

declining empire, would have combined to shout down any merciful solution to the tragic war.

The year 1871 opened with Don Amadeo seated shakily on the throne of Fernando and Isabel; several months went by and no action was taken toward applying the Moret Law. The mounting indignation of the English abolitionists knew no bounds; committee after committee called upon Lord Granville for action; embarrassing questions were asked in Parliament. The Granville ministry seemingly stood pat, but secretly, as early in 1871, British ambassador Layard in Madrid began presenting a series of notes to the Spanish government concerning the fulfillment of promises "publicly made." No better proof could be given of Spain's good intentions, stated the note of April 10, 1871, than Spain's declaring the complete and unconditional liberty of the emancipados, and, secondly, the passing of a law abolishing slavery in Puerto Rico, "where the relatively small number of slaves would make its application relatively easy."[33] British abolitionist policy thus began to resume its old course, just as Brazil was preparing its first law of gradual abolition very similar to the Moret Law.

At this stage of British abolitionist diplomacy, Layard gave the following view of the situation: The English petitioners, he said, appear to assume that Her Majesty's government has not brought to bear a vigorous and direct moral intervention. "I may venture to say that no previous Government has done more through Her Majesty's mission at Madrid, by official and private representations to the Spanish ministers, to advance the cause of abolition." The petitioners further stated that the civil war in Cuba was carried on between the partisans of slavery and the advocates of freedom, and insisted on cooperation with the United States government. This is not the character of the civil war, said Layard, rather "it is simply an effort, encouraged by a powerful party in the United States, to throw off the Spanish dominion." No Spanish statesmen, added Layard, would venture to abolish slavery while the insurrection continued, and any encouragement given to the insurgents would only tend to prolong the war and delay the abolition of slavery. "It is on this account that any intervention on the part of a foreign power is at this moment much to be deprecated."[34]

[33]Sickles' letter to Bancroft Davis, March 7, 1871, Davis Papers, cited, *ibid.*, p. 616.
[34]Mr. A. H. Layard to Earl Granville, Madrid, July 20, 1871, BFSP (1871–1872), LXII, 1034–1035.

Nevertheless, Layard soon received instructions to press harder. Her Majesty's government did not feel justified in maintaining any longer the "silence and reserve they hitherto observed." After all, Spain gave Britain to understand that the Moret Law would be followed by more-complete measures, but even the emancipados were subject to work contracts as if coolies, and Puerto Rican abolitionists' demands were ignored. Two sessions of the Cortes had passed and nothing, except the cry "No reforms until the insurrection ends." Since there was no hope of further spontaneous action by Spain, "we must fall back on our treaty rights."[35]

Specifically, the British government had in mind the thousands of emancipados who should have received immediate liberty, yet British consuls reported that the demands for labor were so great that the freed but ignorant emancipados were being subject to six-year work contracts that scarcely bettered their condition. Crawford wrote his usual disturbing communiqué:

In conclusion, the emancipado has been somewhat bettered by the Law of July 4, 1870, but, as shown by these contracts, he really continued in a modified sort of slavery for six years longer, and slavery in Cuba is of the most degrading character, especially as the use of the lash is quite as much in vogue as ever it was, in spite of Article XXI of the Law referred to.[36]

The threat of British abolitionism, however, was one of Spain's minor worries. The British government, in spite of complaints, supported Spanish dominion in Cuba. The real threat lay elsewhere. The war in Cuba continued in a kind of gruesome stalemate. The rebel guerrillas, the Spanish regulars, and the Volunteers continued to commit atrocities and violate the lives and property of innocent people, but neither side won decisive battles. Under these degenerating conditions, American intervention was always an immediate possibility. American warships hung ominously over Cuba protecting American shipping from Spanish seizures. It would take little more than an incident to generate an international war. The Spanish government, aware of this, continued to make jittery announcements that the insurrection was finished. Sickles said of the new governor: "Valmaseda out-telegraphs De Rodas. The latter put down the insurrection every

[35]Earl Granville to Mr. Layard, Foreign Office, November 24, 1871, *ibid.*, LXII, 1048–1049.

[36]Acting Consul General Crawford to Earl Granville, Havana, July 28, 1871, *ibid.*, LXII, 1064–1065.

month *morally*, the former demolishes it every night *materially*. Yet it still lives and will not die."[37]

The whole bag of Spanish diplomatic tricks was useless so long as the Spanish Volunteers controlled policy in Cuba. For example, on November 26, 1871, eight medical students were summarily shot in Havana and several others condemned to prison for having allegedly profaned the grave of Colonel Gonzalo Castañón, pugnacious loyalist editor and Volunteer hero. The Volunteers forced the colonial government to commit this drastic act.[38]

When the news of the execution reached the United States the reaction was instantaneous. The exclamations "butchers," "uncivilized barbarians," were heard on all sides. López Roberts, on December 2, 1871, counseled his government to prepare for war or a rupture of diplomatic relations.[39]

As was to be expected, the Americans would combine this new atrocity with already existing dissatisfaction over the Spanish slave law. Proposals such as that of Representative Banks echoed in Congress. Resolved, said he, that in view of the shooting of students in Havana, and the failure of Spain to publish the abolition law in Cuba, that the American government re-examine the whole question of Cuba with the view of taking more-definite action.[40] Earlier, on December 4, 1871, Grant's message to Congress, in the part that referred to Cuba, expressed the government's increasing exasperation with

---

[37] Sickles to Davis, Nevins, *Hamilton Fish*, p. 616.

[38] The Volunteers had seized the students for having "profaned" the grave of Castañón, who had been assassinated, presumably by rebels. Feeling ran high, and a mob led by the Volunteers demanded that vengeance be taken on rebel sympathizers. The students were dragged to the palace of the General Crespo, who was ruling temporarily in Valmaseda's absence. In a scene worthy of the mobs and tyrants of Rome, Crespo came forth upon the balcony to face a crowd screaming for blood. Crespo dared not displease the mob, and so a Council of War was called. After an all-night session, during which it was necessary to reconstitute the Council in favor of the crowd's wishes, eight students were condemned to death, and shot at four o'clock that same morning; two students were absolved and several others were condemned to prison from four to six years. Later, the latter students were pardoned by the Queen, due largely to diplomatic protests. More details are found in the correspondence of General Crespo with the ministers of war and colonies; A.H.N. Ultramar, Leg. 4731 (1871).

[39] López Roberts, Washington, 2 de diciembre de 1871, A.M.A.E. Leg. 1473 (1870–1872).

[40] López Roberts, Washington, 7 de diciembre de 1871, *ibid.*

Spain's cruel and futile effort to quell the rebellion and the unsatisfactory application of the Moret Law.[41]

Remonstrances continued to reach the Spanish government from American societies, and again the Quakers were in the vanguard. On behalf of the Yearly Meeting of Friends of New England, Philadelphia, Baltimore, North Carolina, Indiana, the Western Committee, and the Freedman's Committee of New York and Iowa, the Quakers (May, 1872) informed the Spanish authorities that "for two centuries we have been conscientiously against the slave traffic and holding men in bondage." Abolition in the United States, although sudden, had caused no convulsions, and there is "promise of unprecedented prosperity." One of the largest cotton crops was expected, and former slaves had progressed in education. "The pressure of civilized opinion is heavy against it [slavery], as one of the relics of the dark ages, and we trust the time is near at hand, when, through the prudence of the spirit of Christ, there will not be a single slave in Christendom."[42]

These petitions naturally struck the Spaniards as full of fatuous self-righteousness and occasioned much grumbling among the ministers of the government. Nevertheless, they felt obliged to answer these petitions individually, protesting that the Spanish people were of the same sentiments, and that at the opportune moment the government would complete the abolition of slavery.

Under the circumstances, Fish was at last moved to draw a line on the slave question. Spain must be made to understand that her only hope for preventing intervention in Cuba lay in making some impressive gesture of reform. Even if the Moret Law was put into operation it would be too late. If Fish was to restrain American public opinion —as he so often told the Spanish ambassador—Spain would have to take another step in the direction of reform. But in which direction? The Spanish government consistently maintained that no ministry could carry a program of political reforms for Cuba while the insurrection raged. Like the British, Fish accepted these explanations, but Spain could and must move in the direction of abolition. The Moret Law must be carried out in Cuba, and in Puerto Rico, where there

[41]"Message of President Grant [Third Annual Message to the Senate and the House of Representatives]" December 4, 1871, *ibid.*

[42]"Exposiciones abolicionistas dirigidas al gobierno por sociedades abolicionistas extranjeros," A.H.N. Ultramar, Leg. 4882 (1869–1880), Vol. IV.

was no excuse for delay. Spain must consider abolishing slavery entirely and immediately. The slave question was now the focal point of Spanish-American relations.

The Spanish abolitionist Gabriel Rodríguez suspected Fish of ulterior motives. The Secretary of State really wanted to acquire Cuba, according to Rodríguez, but did not think it was necessary to go to war for it. Once slavery had been abolished in the Spanish Antilles, the islands would no longer be prosperous, and then Spain would be willing to sell them.[43]

As yet Spain could still feel that she could ignore American pressure so long as the power of England stood tacitly behind her. As if in direct response to increased American pressure the British government once more began to accept Spanish explanations concerning the failure to apply the Moret Law. The Spanish minister of state reported on December 9, 1871, the results of a conference with Layard, the British ambassador: "The conference was extremely friendly and my frank explanations left him satisfied."[44]

While extending a sympathetic hand to the distraught Spanish government, the British government employed the other to stay the march of the abolitionists. Thus, the secretary of the British Anti-Slavery Society was politely but firmly dealt with when he read a memorial to Lord Granville, calling attention to the fact that the American government had instructed Minister Sickles in Madrid to make slavery a *sine qua non* in the settlement of the Cuban question. This fact, plus the news that the Spanish abolitionists in Madrid were urging complete abolition in the name of the Revolution of 1868, should have been decisive, according to the memorial, in making Mr. Layard in Madrid take a more decided course. The usual collection of unfilled promises was then listed. Lord Granville listened patiently, concurring in many of the statements made. "But the English government was desirous of exerting its influence on suitable occasions. . . . For the moment," he concluded, "such a delicate question should be put aside."[45]

One of the most newsworthy items of the year was the return of

[43]Gabriel Rodríguez, *La idea y el movimiento antiesclavista en España durante el siglo XIX*, p. 345.

[44]Ministro de Estado al Ministro español en Londres, 9 de diciembre de 1871, A.M.A.E. *Correspondencia EEUnidos*, Leg. 1473 (1870–1872).

[45]The London *Times*, January 24, 1872, A.H.N. Ultramar, Leg. 4882 (1869–1880).

Failure To Enforce the Law, 1870–1872

General Daniel Sickles to the United States to confer with the President. On December 23, 1871, Sickles arrived at the harbor of New York, appropriately enough aboard the *Cuba*, bringing with him his Spanish bride of "black and lustrous eyes." He was met by a host of reporters who hoped that Sickles, given the tense state of Spanish-American relations and the incredible weakness of Spanish policy in Cuba, could throw some light on the situation.

Sickles answered the reporter for the *New York Times* that his return signified nothing in particular. "Our relations" with Spain were going fine. "But are our relations with Spain delicate?" persisted the reporter. The General gave an indirect reply:

The frequent changes in the ministry at Madrid . . . eight since my official residence at that court, combined with unsettled conditions, the establishment of a new dynasty [that of Don Amadeo, the Italian prince], and the introduction of a new constitution have delayed the inauguration of a new and better colonial policy to which the liberal party in Spain is committed by repeated pledges made to the United States through channels. The truth is that with the best intentions on the part of the enlightened statesmen of the Revolution, their tenure of power has been so brief that unsupported as they have been by a working majority in the Spanish Congress, owing to the multitude of factions into which that body is divided, very little has been done in the way of national or colonial legislation, for example, for the past three years no appropriation bill has passed the Cortes.[46]

Perhaps even more important as an obstacle to reform in Cuba was the intransigent attitude of the Volunteers, who associated all reforms with the cause of the rebels. Said Sickles: "It is, perhaps, doubtful whether, as things are in Cuba, any radical measure of colonial reform could be carried out through the Spanish authorities in the Island without provoking a more serious rebellion [among the Volunteers] in Havana than was begun at Yara in October, 1868."[47]

To the question of was the war popular in Spain? Sickles answered, "Oh, yes, 50,000 regular Spanish troops [not counting Volunteers] is proof, and so is the sustaining of 10,000 to 15,000 casualties a year."[48]

The General indicated to the *New York Tribune* that the promised reforms would be better fulfilled if the Liberal Party, represented by

[46]The *New York Times*, December 23, 1871, A.M.A.E. *Correspondencia EEUnidos*, Leg. 1573 (1870–1872), Despacho N. 163.
[47]*New York Times*, December 23, 1871, *ibid*.
[48]*New York Times*, December 23, 1871, *ibid*.

men such as Zorrilla, Rivero, and Martos, should come to power. With the new liberal Cortes soon to be elected, he thought the time would be most favorable for "permanently adjusting vexatious relations." This Liberal Party desired to adopt a colonial policy in accordance with the views of the American government.[49]

But while the Sagasta ministry remained in power, Sickles could do nothing toward influencing colonial policy. In fact, Sagasta was determined to have Sickles recalled. He was tired of Sickles' meddlesome activities, his incautious remarks, and his open friendship with Republicans like Martos and Castelar. Sickles was determined to help establish a republic in Spain. Fish decided that an American minister was not doing any good in Madrid anyway, and so when Sickles set sail for Spain, April 27, 1872, after an extended stay in the United States, he was instructed to present a letter of recall. But before diplomatic relations were broken off the kaleidoscopic political scene in Madrid changed again.[50]

[49]*New York Tribune*, December 23, 1871, *ibid.*
[50]Nevins, *Hamilton Fish*, pp. 620–621.

15. Application of the Moret Law and Abolition in Puerto Rico, 1872-1873

> I am happy to see in the Madrid Journals the announcement that the King has approved the "Regulations." Allow me to congratulate you that you have not permitted your administration to suffer the reproach incurred by your predecessor.
>
> Sickles to Gassett, August 14, 1872[1]

𝕴n June, 1872, the Progressive ministry of Sagasta, which had offered stiff resistance to American policy, fell from power and the Radical Party of Ruíz Zorrilla now took charge. The Radicals, or the left wing of the Progressive movement formerly dominated by the assassinated General Juan Prim, leaned more strongly toward a republic. Now it remained to be seen whether Zorrilla would prove any more liberal than Sagasta in colonial affairs.

Ambassador Sickles' faith that his Radical friends would at least enforce the Moret Law was soon justified. Over two years after the promulgation of that law the regulations for putting it into effect were approved by the Radical government (August, 1872). Sickles, of course, was delighted.[2]

Incidentally, the incredible Daniel Sickles was the cock of the walk in Madrid now that his *compañeros* were in power. In a letter to his friend, Eduardo Artimé y Gassett, the new minister of colonies, Sickles gave a paternal lecture on colonial policy. Concerning Sickles,

[1]Sickles, Baganares der Luchau, Alemania, 14 de agosto de 1872, A.H.N. Ultramar, Leg. 4882 (1869–1880), Vol. IV.
[2]*Ibid.*

the letter is most revealing, but it also reveals the kind of program for the colonies that American diplomacy expected from the Radicals:[3]

> Yesterday, I ventured to suggest to our good friend Martos [Cristino Martos, secretary of state] that he should remember in drafting the King's speech how severely history will regard the present cabinet if it fails to satisfy the reasonable expectations of European and American opinion in ameliorating the government of the Antilles and in advancing yet further the good work of emancipation.
>
> And now with your kind permission, I would appeal to you, my friend, to consider whether it is not easier to pacificate Cuba by magnanimous concessions to the legitimate aspirations of the people than by a continued reliance on mere force. It is a cruel test of allegiance when a population must choose between liberty and loyalty. It is your fortuitous mission by means of higher statesmanship to reconcile these kindred sentiments in your great Commonwealth beyond the seas. England has given you two examples full of instruction. In refusing the full demands of her American Colonies she lost nearly all of them after a seven year's war. She now holds her remaining possessions in America without effort and without force because she has given them free institutions like her own.
>
> With a homogeneous cabinet of democratic opinions, sustained by an ample majority in Congress, you have the opportunity to signalize your administration by restoring tranquillity in Cuba, thus increasing her population and production, expanding her commerce and augmenting her resources and revenues. To this end it is only necessary that the government of Cuba should find inspiration and form in the Spanish Constitution. Let your flag be the symbol of freedom in Cuba as in Spain and its enemies will be powerless as elsewhere.
>
> Faithfully your friend and servant,
[Signed] D. J. Sickles

With the usual delay, the Reglamento for applying the Moret Law of July 4, 1870, was not published in Cuba until November 23, 1872— more than three months after it had been published in Madrid, and nearly two and a half years after the acceptance of the Moret Law by the Cortes. The most important of the regulations, which essentially expressed what the government wanted with some modifications in favor of the hacendados, can be summarized as follows:[4] In accordance with Article Thirteen of the Moret Law, Juntas for the Protec-

---

[3]Sickles, San Sebastián, 7 de septiembre de 1872, *ibid*.

[4]"Reglamento para la ejecución en las islas de Puerto Rico y Cuba de la ley de 4 de julio de 1870," A.H.N. Ultramar, Leg. 4881 (1870–1872), N. 2.

tion of Freedmen (Juntas Protectoras de los Libertos) were to be established in each civil district in Cuba. A Central Junta serving as a court of final appeal would be seated in Havana. In each civil district the Junta members, six in number, were to represent the colonial government, the local government, and the slaveholding and non-slaveholding property interests. Each member was expected to serve a term of two years on a rotation-of-office plan.

The duties of the Junta were mainly, of course, to administer the specifications of the Moret Law, being especially certain that the patrons respected those protecting the *libertos*, for example, working regulations, and provision for salaries, food, clothing, medicine, and the maintenance of the libertos in general. The Juntas were also to make certain that the libertos strictly complied with the law. Accurate registrations and records were to be maintained, and slaves not included in the recent census (completed January, 1871) were to be considered as free by the Juntas. The provisions were generally in favor of the libertos, in accordance with the wishes of the Madrid government, but a few revealed the intervening hands of the hacendados, as in Chapter III of the law.

The libertos were expected to obey and respect their patrons "as if the latter were their own fathers." The liberto, of course, could not leave or change patrons without the consent of his original patron. Also, the provision of the Moret Law declaring the patronato transferable by all known legal means was given re-emphasis. Patrons had also the right to correct the faults of the libertos, although the colonial government, in consultation with the Central Junta, would determine how such corrections should be regulated. The Juntas were responsible for incorrigible libertos. Curiously, the libertos, who were about to receive their final certificate of liberty, were given the choice of remaining in Cuba or returning to Africa. But it is doubtful if enough libertos were so disposed to make a boatload for Africa, and more doubtful even that the boat was available.

Since Puerto Rico did not suffer an insurrection, the same delaying tactics were not possible there. The regulations for applying the Moret Law in Puerto Rico were published on June 23, 1870, and put into effect a year sooner than in Cuba. The pressure of foreign diplomacy can take part credit for forcing Spain to apply the Moret Law in Puerto Rico. But it was the sentiment of the Puerto Rican people themselves that made possible the positive application of the law. The Spanish government recognized this fact when it said of the smaller island: "... there the proprietors have anticipated abolition ... in the question of liberty the slaves owe a lot to their owners, and they should not have to attribute everything to the action of the Government."[5]

It is evident from the correspondence of Colonial Minister Artimé y Gassett and Captain General Francisco de Ceballos that a sincere effort was now being made to put the regulations in force as soon as possible. Continually, on demand from Gassett, Ceballos returned detailed reports on progress made. Emphasis was placed on the immediate establishment of the Juntas Jurisdiccionales de Libertos provided for in Article One of the regulations. Ceballos listed the obstacles that had to be overcome in establishing the juntas: the isolation of certain districts, the lack of communications, and the confusion due to the war.[6]

These obstacles were irritating, said Governor Ceballos, but being "firm in my intention to establish juntas, I have named eleven Jurisdictional Juntas for freedmen; this, together with the sixteen now established and six more to be established soon, will make a total of thirty-three."[7] The United States, said Ceballos in another communication, "has no faith in our fulfilling the laws." But now the colonial minister with such data could prove that Spain was applying the law.[8]

In spite of the enormous complications involved, the government did, from time to time, order the liberty of small groups of unregistered slaves. A reported 5,010 Negroes had by 1871 received their liberty in this way.[9]

The number of unregistered slaves who deserved liberty was estimated at 70,000 more. But, as in the case of the emancipados, the

[5]Comunicación, Ministerio de Estado, 12 de enero de 1871, A.H.N. Ultramar, Leg. 4882 (1868–1880), Vol. IV.
[6]Francisco de Ceballos, La Habana, 15 de diciembre de 1872, A.H.N. Ultramar, Leg. 4881 (1870–1872).
[7]Ibid.
[8]Ibid. An example of the Juntas de Libertos, founded according to regulations, was that of Bahia Hondo. The lieutenant governor of the province and one of the town magistrates were named presidents. Four committee members were then appointed, consisting of two slaveholders, Juan I. Muñoz and Ignacio Sandoval, and two nonslaveholders, Juan Otoala and Manuel Castrillón. *Gaceta de la Habana*, 28 de noviembre de 1872.
[9]"Informe sobre los esclavos no registrados," Consejo de Estado, 15 de marzo de 1873, A.H.N. Ultramar, Leg. 4882 (1869–1880), Vols. III and IV.

whereabouts of many of the unregistered slaves would never be known. It was easy to falsify documents; when a legally possessed slave died, his place was often taken by an unregistered one.[10] The notorious inaccuracy of the census reports aided this kind of deception.

According to the new census completed on January 15, 1871 (revising that of 1867), there were 264,697 slaves in Cuba. But, since the census was carried out in the midst of a widespread rebellion, and since the rebels had declared the liberty of all slaves, the new census was necessarily inaccurate. Only partial registrations could be obtained for the embattled regions near Santiago de Cuba, Victoria de las Tunas, and Morón.[11]

"The actual number of slaves in Cuba," said the British Consul Carden, "has probably at no time been properly known. Whether with the object of concealing infractions of the slave trade treaties on the part of the authorities, or to avoid payment of capitation taxes on the part of the planters, gross misstatements have been constantly made."[12]

Considering the strong feelings of the British government on the subject, it was to be expected that the emancipados would be the first to benefit from the Preparatory Law of 1870. The government of Cuba had been responsible for slaves of this category since the first slave ships had been seized on the coast of Cuba in 1824. Theoretically, as we have seen, these Negroes were free men, but, in fact, they had been sold or placed with the great planters, where their lot differed little from that of the slave. Many of these unfortunates were now dead, or they were rooted to the plantations where they worked, or, in their ignorance, they did not know how to regard their newly acquired liberty.[13]

The emancipados were freed in groups, depending on the year of their capture. For example, 3,929 emancipados belonging to the last

[10]In the Cortes of 1871 the abolitionists, Labra, for example, estimated the number to be 70,000; "Slave Trade Papers" No. 3, 1880, *ibid.*, Leg. 4883 (1879–1880).

[11]"Informe," Consejo de Estado, 15 de marzo de 1873, *ibid.*, Leg. 4882 (1869–1880), Vols. III and IV.

[12]*Report by Acting Consul-General Carden on the Number and Conditions of the Slaves in Cuba*, presented to both Houses of Parliament (London: Harrison and Sons, 1882), *ibid.*, Leg. 4883 (1879–1880).

[13]"Decreto del 30 de octubre de 1870," A.H.N. Estado, Leg. 3548–3549 (1827–1872), Mando de Rodas, N. 30.

nine expeditions captured in Cuba between the years 1862–1866, were conceded liberty by the decree of December 6, 1870. How many of these slaves were still living, or remained on the plantations where they had been assigned, was another question. Proprietors who did not immediately set at liberty this class of Negroes were subject to penal punishment according to Article Eighteen of the law of 1870.[14] An earlier decree of September 21, 1869, set at liberty 1,025 emancipados belonging to seven expeditions captured between the years 1824–1842.[15]

The total number of slaves captured off the coast of Cuba from 1824, when the first cargo was captured, to 1866, when the last cargo was seized, was calculated at 26,026.[16] Perhaps 10,000 of this number eventually found freedom.

According to the regulations, government officials were personally to deliver certificates of liberty to the emancipados, and the governors and lieutenant governors of the provinces were especially charged with investigating the existence of all emancipados not included in this registration. Since ostensibly the free Negro class in Cuba already posed a problem in vagrancy, the emancipados, like other categories of liberated slaves, were subject to work contracts, either with the government or with the former masters.[17] A sample of one of these contracts reads as follows:[18]

Art. 1. I _____[name]_____ promise to work on the railroad between Cienfuegos and Villa Clara.
Art. 2. This contract will last for six years.
Art. 3. I will work according to the terms agreed upon.
Art. 4. As a guarantee I consent that my certificate of liberty remain in the power of my patron until the six years have been fulfilled.

The contractor in the above case was obligated to pay the Negro a salary of twelve pesos a month, to provide him with food, two suits of clothes, and medical care, to give him a bonus of two pesos a

[14]*Gaceta de la Madrid*, 6 de diciembre de 1870.
[15]*Ibid.*
[16]"Documento sobre las expediciones capturadas desde 1824 hasta 1866," La Habana, 12 de diciembre de 1870, El Secretario Cesáreo Fernández, A.H.N. Ultramar, Leg. 4881 (1870–1872).
[17]"Reglamento de emancipados" 16 de septiembre de 1870, A.H.N. Estado, Leg. 3548–3549 (1827–1872), Mando de Caballero de Rodas.
[18]"Disposiciones sobre emancipados de la isla de Cuba," 30 de octubre de 1870, *ibid.*, N. 30.

month if he worked well. The agreements were to be entered into freely by both parties under government supervision. The Negro, or liberto, could complain to government authorities without the intervention of the contractor.

A problem almost as complicated as that of the census question was that concerning the status of slaves captured and confiscated from the rebels. By a decree of November 25, 1870, the Spanish government in Cuba sentenced to death *in absentia* the Republican Junta of Cuba: Carlos Manuel Céspedes, Francisco Vicente Aguilera, Cristóbal Mendoza, Eligio Izaguirre, Eduardo Agramonte, Pedro María de Agüero, and forty-nine more of the wealthy rebel proprietors. Later others were added to this list. The state decreed the confiscation of the property of said rebels, including their property in slaves.[19] Most of the landed property passed into the hands of the Spanish loyalists, or eventually into the hands of foreign purchasers,[20] but confiscated slaves presented a different problem.

The slaves in question could not be returned to their rebel masters —that was obvious—nor could they be set free, since this would greatly prejudice the position of the loyal slave owners. Therefore, the government decided to retain them. But a government that ostensibly stood for the abolition of slavery could only offer embarrassing explanations to the protesting abolitionists in the Cortes, who argued that according to the abolition law of 1870 the colonial government was obliged to liberate all slaves in its possession, and was forbidden to hold them in the future; it mattered not that this provision was originally intended to apply only to the emancipados.[21]

A succession of ministers attempted to justify the matter as a "war measure," or to explain away the fact by refining legal theory: the

[19]"La cuestión de la esclavitud en 1871," documentos publicados por la Sociedad Abolicionista, in *Cuestión social, Antillas: Colección Justo Zaragoza de varias exposiciones de la Sociedad Abolicionista Española, discursos de sus miembros en el Congreso y Ateneo, 1868–73*, Biblioteca Nacional, Madrid.

[20]According to Herminio Portell Vilá, ingenios, vegas, coffee plantations, urban properties, and various business and commercial investments to the amount of one million dollars were confiscated from the rebels and rebel sympathizers, and sold for a fraction of their value to Spaniards and influential foreigners. *Historia de Cuba en sus relaciones con los Estados*, II, 535. No doubt, these confiscations were an important factor in the subsequent rebellion against Spain of 1895–1898. As Machiavelli once observed, a man will sooner forgive the loss of his loved ones than the loss of his property.

[21]*Ibid.*

government did not confiscate the slaves in question, but merely placed an "embargo" upon them. Therefore, the conclusion was reached, to the satisfaction of the government at least, that the government "did not actually possess slaves."

The question was doubly complicated due to the fact that the Cuban revolutionary leaders had declared the freedom of all slaves, and had personally set their own slaves at liberty. Now some of these "liberated slaves" were being held by the Spanish government in Cuba as forfeited property. More embarrassing results followed. In the United States and foreign countries rebel propagandists eagerly exaggerated the whole question. Spain again was made to appear in the role of a cruel, reactionary, slaveholding power.[22]

In time, the volume of protest grew so loud that the Spanish government ordered the release of the "embargoed slaves" in spite of the bitter protests of loyalist slaveowners, who readily recognized the action as another breach in the slave system. But, again, what was ordered in Madrid could not readily be enforced in Cuba.

Captain General Caballero de Rodas, in a communication of July 11, 1870, protested against the general emancipation of rebel slaves captured or confiscated in war operations, claiming that it would encourage rebellion among loyal slaves. This, said Caballero, was a two-bladed sword that, while it deprived the rebels of slave resources, hurt the loyalists, too.[23]

Madrid finally decided that since the insurrectionaries were still attracting the slaves of the loyalists to flee from their labor and take up the cause of independence—a cause that has already promised the complete abolition of slavery upon the successful conclusion of the war—the confiscated slaves should be freed as a counter measure. In a series of decrees the Spanish authorities in Cuba declared that all slaves belonging to the rebels, whether in possession of the govern-

[22]See, for example, the heated discussion between Labra and Salvador de Albacete, colonial minister, on the problem of slaves confiscated by the government: *Diario de las sesiones de las Cortes, generales y extraordinarias, 1810–1898*, Congreso (1879–80), II, 1026–1027.

[23]Caballero de Rodas, La Habana, 11 de julio de 1870, "Expediente general de Cuba," A.H.N. Ultramar, Leg. 4881 (1870–1872). For some years the emancipation of rebel slaves continued to be a source of embarrassment. It seemed unjust to give liberty to those Negroes proceeding from the insurrectionary camp, many of whom had committed every kind of crime during the war, while the slaves of loyal owners remained in slavery. See "Informe" . . . Consejo de Estado, 14 de abril de 1874, *ibid.*, Leg. 4882 (1869–1880), Vols. III and IV.

The Moret Law and Abolition in Puerto Rico, 1872-1873

ment or not, were free. The action was justified on the grounds that the rebels had already declared the liberty of their slaves. It was now hoped that slaves working or fighting for the rebels would desert the rebel cause and cross over to the Spanish side, where their liberty was assured.

Closely allied to the above decrees, and, again, largely due to rebel action, was another series of measures conferring liberty on those slaves of loyal masters who had rendered service to Spain. According to the decree of May 14, 1870, slaves of the rebels as well as slaves of the loyalists were to be set free on the basis of military service rendered under the Spanish flag.[24] As General Valmaseda explained, since the enemy recruited Negroes from both sides by the promise of liberty, Spain could not do less. Loyalist owners of such slaves were promised indemnization.[25]

With the gradual application of the Moret Law, Spain's problem of slavery in Cuba receded into the background; it was evident that the institution faced eventual doom whether a new law was forthcoming or not. In any case, the reactionaries had won their point. No matter how liberal a Spanish ministry might be it would not dare to push further reforms in Cuba. A good example of this was the Radical government of Zorrilla. When British Minister Layard told Martos, the foreign minister, on June 24, 1872, that Britain now agreed with the Americans that Spain should make a specific abolitionist declaration regarding Cuba, Martos could only reply that such a declaration could never be hazarded by any popular government, and that it might lead to an insurrection either by the Volunteers or by reactionary interests in the northwest of Spain. Spain could not be a "traitor" to such interests. It would be better, he replied, to fight the United States, yielding, perhaps, "in the end, to superior forces but we shall have preserved our national dignity."[26]

But if foreign abolitionism could not hasten the end of slavery in Cuba, it could do so in Puerto Rico. The spotlight now shifted to the

---

[24]"Decreto sobre emancipados en la isla de Cuba del Capitán-General Caballero de Rodas," 14 de mayo de 1870, A.H.N. Estado, Leg. 3548–3549 (1827–1872), L. 2. N. 32.

[25]Decreto sobre emancipados del Gobernador General el Conde de Valmaseda," 12 de enero de 1872, *ibid.*, N. 34.

[26]Layard to Granville, Madrid, June 24, 1872: Public Records Office, Foreign Office 11, 536, in Allan Nevins, *Hamilton Fish: The Inner History of the Grant Administration*, p. 619.

smaller island. It is not our proposal to describe how slavery was almost completely abolished in Puerto Rico by the law of March 22, 1873, under the first Spanish Republic; but we cannot avoid pointing out how the Cuban situation greatly influenced that decision.

Immediately following the promulgation of the Moret Law the Abolitionist Society had resumed its propaganda activities, exhorting the public through the press and protest meetings, and showering the government ministers with protests and petitions.[27] The substance of the abolitionist argument at this time alleged the inadequacy of the Moret Law, the failure to apply the law effectively, the continued abuses practiced on slaves in the Antilles (above all, on the emancipado class still not fully liberated), the confiscation of rebel slave property by a government forbidden to hold slaves, the justice of abolitionist demands in the Antilles (especially in Puerto Rico), the disgrace to the Spanish nation before world opinion by the continued maintenance of slavery on Spanish soil, and the obligation of the government by the principles of the Glorious Revolution to abolish slavery completely.[28]

It deserves re-emphasis that the Puerto Ricans were an essential driving force in Spanish abolitionism. The Moret Law was too conservative a measure to satisfy the general abolitionist sentiment of that island. As noted before, Puerto Rico had been conceded representation in the Spanish legislature since 1869, and her elected delegates were becoming increasingly abolitionist. In the Cortes of 1871–1872, for example, eleven out of fifteen deputies were confirmed reformists. From the beginning they did their utmost to convince Don Amadeo, the new constitutional monarch, and his ministers of the necessity of a new measure for Puerto Rico.

Labra and the Puerto Ricans defied the tacit understanding that there were to be no further reforms in either of the colonies while Cuba was in a state of insurrection. A juncture was made between the abolitionists and the Radical Party headed by Ruíz Zorrilla. The Radicals, in seeking allies on the road to power, had promised to abolish slavery in Puerto Rico in its manifesto of October 15, 1871. Thirty

[27] Among the numerous remonstrances: "Manifiesto de la Nación," "Carta al Sr. Mosquera," "Ministro de Ultramar," "Exposición a las Cortes," "Carta al Sr. Topete." See *Cuestión social, Antillas.*
[28] *Ibid.*

prominent reformers, including fifteen Puerto Ricans, signed the document.[29]

When, on June 13, 1872, the Zorrilla ministry came to power, the new Colonial Minister announced that the government was studying the basis for a Puerto Rican abolition law. This meant unavoidable delays, of course, and it soon appeared to the abolitionists that Zorrilla was afraid to keep his promise.[30]

At this point, foreign diplomacy in connection with the Cuban problem came to the aid of the Puerto Rican abolitionists. Four years of military failure in Cuba and a miserable effort to apply the Moret Law, which after all was only a partial measure of abolition, had forfeited Spain the respect and patience of the United States, and, to a lesser degree, that of England. Given the number of disagreeable incidents on the high seas and in Cuba involving American citizens, and given the sympathy of the Americans for the Cuban rebels, who were ostensibly fighting for republicanism and abolition, it seemed that the hour must soon arrive when the United States would recognize the belligerent status of the Cubans, or intervene openly in the Cuban insurrection.

The re-election of President Grant in 1872 meant that a more positive Cuban policy was expected of the administration. According to Don José Polo de Bernarbe, who had replaced López Roberts as Spanish minister to Washington (March 12, 1872), the American people expected two things of the re-elected Grant: one, an active policy of aid to the Cuban rebels with the object of helping them gain their independence; and, two, obliging Spain to emancipate the slaves of the Spanish Antilles completely. It was Bernarbe who said: "The question of slavery is the touchstone of our relations with the United States."[31]

When Polo de Bernarbe showed Fish a letter from Captain General

[29]This understanding between the Radicals and the abolitionists was revealed in the debates on the Puerto Rican abolition bill, *Diario, Congreso y Senado*, I, No. 11 (27 de febrero de 1873), p. 269.

[30]The conservatives led by Cánovas del Castillo protested that reforms for Puerto Rico were dangerous for Cuba. Colonial Minister Eduardo Artimé Gassett also felt this way. The abolitionists, however, applied constant pressure on the Zorrilla ministry; see Lidio Cruz Monclova, *Historia de Puerto Rico (Siglo XIX)*, II, 206–227.

[31]Polo de Bernarbe, Washington, 15 de noviembre de 1872 y 29 de octubre de 1872, A.M.A.E. *Correspondencia EEUnidos*, Leg. 1473 (1870–1872), N. 120 y N. 126.

Ceballos proving that partial abolition was being enforced in accordance with the Regulation, Fish replied that if the law had been applied sooner it would have produced a good effect, but that now it was too late. Many people doubted the sincere intentions of the Spaniards. Furthermore, Fish was not satisfied with the Regulation, saying that "it seemed to offer few guarantees to the slave." Thereupon Fish again insisted that Spain take a further step in the direction of emancipation. This would not only favor relations between the two countries, but, in his opinion, it would also hasten the end of the rebellion.[32]

What the Spanish minister then wrote to the home government must have carried influence:

Concerning the step that Mr. Fish thinks should be taken, I don't know what the Government of Your Majesty believes opportune at this moment, but all the foregoing demonstrates . . . that I am not mistaken when I have the repeated honor of saying to your Excellency that the slave question is a latent danger for the continuation of good relations with the United States.[33]

Nor were other of Polo de Bernarbe's comments less calculated to impress Madrid concerning the urgent need to conciliate the Americans further. Polo de Bernarbe, like López Roberts, was on the scene in Washington and could appreciate the force of public opinion in a democracy, and the tremendous strain undergone by the American Secretary of State in resisting this opinion. Mr. Fish, said the Spanish ambassador, in one of his asides, was a person of uncensurable respectability, "but he must mold himself to the opinion of the country, and he has the merit that on doing it he knows how to keep on middle ground."[34] But President Grant thought in a different way. There was real danger that the cautious Fish would be forced to resign. "I clearly see that this would present a crisis for us."[35] Obviously, if the Zorrilla ministry had to take some step to conciliate the Americans, that step, under the circumstances, could be taken only in Puerto Rico.[36]

---

[32]Polo de Bernarbe, Washington, 22 de octubre de 1872, *ibid.*, N. 128.
[33]*Ibid.*
[34]Polo de Bernarbe, Washington, 6 de diciembre de 1872, *ibid.*, N. 137.
[35]Polo de Bernarbe, Washington, 29 de octubre de 1872, *ibid.*, N. 120.
[36]In an interview between Sickles and Cristino Martos, minister of state, it was decided that if reforms were impossible in Cuba, at least they were possible in Puerto Rico. In this interview, November 30, 1872, Martos replied that reforms

In this same month of October, Zorrilla announced that the cabinet had decided on a four-point reform program for Puerto Rico which it would soon present to the Cortes. The civil authority was to be made separate from and superior to the military authority. The towns were to have local governments, popularly elected. A provincial assembly was to be established with a voice in insular affairs. And, finally, slavery was to be abolished.[37]

It was this last point that caused much agonizing consternation. The cabinet could not readily decide whether emancipation should be immediate or gradual, or whether any measure could be carried against the reactionaries who were insisting that reforms for Puerto Rico were a threat to Spain's hold on Cuba. Consequently there was a very real possibility that the Radical ministry might abandon a second abolition measure for Puerto Rico. Zorrilla, himself, attempted to gain time by involving the Puerto Rican question with that of Cuba.[38]

In order to force Zorrilla to make a definite commitment the Grant administration threatened to boycott Cuban sugar interests. An immediate answer was thereupon obtained (December 2, 1872), by which the Zorrilla government stated that it would send to the Cortes a bill of immediate abolition for Puerto Rico soon after December 15.[39]

During December there was a shifting of positions in the Zorrilla cabinet. Tomás Mosquera, a pronounced reformist who had once represented Puerto Rico in the Cortes, emerged as colonial minister. The change was significant. On December 20, Zorrilla entered the Chamber of Deputies to explain the policy of the reorganized cabinet. Three cabinet members, he said, believed in gradual abolition for Puerto Rico, and five members, among whom Zorrilla had "the honor of counting myself," believed in immediate abolition. "Today, it is enough to know that the present government will propose immediate abolition in Puerto Rico." The announcement made a profound sensation in the Cortes.[40] Reformers who had begun to despair of the Radical government now rallied around.

"But," added Zorrilla, "the government intends nothing, absolutely

would be carried out in the smaller island; Herminio Portell Vilá, II, 371 y 390, cited by Cruz Monclova, *Historia de Puerto Rico*, II, 229 n.

[37]Nevins, *Hamilton Fish*, p. 625.
[38]*Diario, Senado* (1872–1873), XV (15 de octubre de 1872), 145–147.
[39]See Nevins' dramatic account, *Hamilton Fish*, pp. 629–630.
[40]*Diario, Senado* (1872–1873), L (20 de diciembre de 1872), 825.

nothing in Cuba, while there is one single rebel there with a gun in his hand."[41] Zorrilla in this emphatic repetition of the status quo formula for Cuba was simply being politic, if politics is the art of the possible.

The Republican minority added its vote to that of the Radicals in placing the abolition law on the agenda. This was the signal for reactionary protest. Suárez Inclán, who years later was to take a curious pride in affixing his name to a final measure of abolition in Cuba, solemnly warned that it was the Cortes of 1820 that had lost Spain her American colonies.[42] The Spanish newspapers *El Debate*, *La Epoca*, *El Imparcial*, and *El Correo de las Antillas* gloomily foretold the loss of the Antilles.[43]

When a nominal voting taken on the twentieth of December was deceptively in favor of the Puerto Rican proposal, Mosquera, colonial minister, was prompted to say: "No Spaniard defends slavery on principle ... it is only a matter of form." Sanromá would be proved closer to the truth when he said: "Many deny they are slavists, or better said, no one dares to say he is; nevertheless, many attack the abolition law."[44]

The reading of the Puerto Rican bill, which declared slavery abolished forever in that province with due indemnification, soon touched off one of the most exasperating debates ever recorded in the Cortes; it represented the high-water mark of the slave argument, and the first genuine victory for the abolitionists.

On the day before Christmas, Castelar gave one of his stirring speeches in support of the law. "We are brethren with the Americans in the cause of abolition, while 14,000 men died in the battle of Fredericksburg, we said, forward, forward, triumph! and they triumphed." The concluding words were charged with emotional persuasion. Referring to the deputies who had been elected to the Cortes for the first time in relatively free elections, Castelar said:

You are obscure, country people; but this doesn't matter. You can say on returning to your homes: yesterday, we were unknown, today we are immortal. We belong to the race of Christ, Washington, Espartero, and Lincoln because we have fearlessly pronounced the word liberty and the

---

[41]*Ibid.*
[42]*Diario, Senado* (1872–1873), I (20 de diciembre de 1872), 832.
[43]Angel Acosta y Quintero, *José J. Acosta y su tiempo*, p. 429.
[44]*Diario, Congreso*, I (17 de febrero de 1873), 102.

definitive redemption of the slaves. (Great and prolonged applause from the Assembly.)[45]

Minister of State Martos, like the Cortes, was carried away by such oratory. He said excitedly: "Sr. Castelar has said the last word. He has filled our hearts with enthusiasm and our souls with light. The slaves of Puerto Rico are now free." Loud applause and "Viva España!" greeted this announcement.[46]

Unfortunately, Castelar had not said the last word. While the deputies cooled off during a Christmas vacation, and engaged in the pastime of political intrigue, the enemies of abolition had not been idle. They organized a powerful pressure group called the Colonial League (Liga Ultramarina), which followed the tactics of the abolitionists in dramatizing their cause through public demonstrations and speeches. The League represented slaveowners, absentee landlords, rich merchants of Barcelona and Havana, and "many patriotic men," all of whom considered any kind of reform in Puerto Rico as a threatening innovation in the established colonial order. Layard reported that the defenders of national integrity were developing an "unscrupulous opposition" by insisting that abolition was the work of foreign filibusters. Some of the most influential generals had been won over to the cause of "national integrity," including Serrano, Caballero de Rodas, José de la Concha, Lersundi, and others. "It is hoped by the slaveholders that they will carry the army with them."[47] The League had its spokesmen in the Cortes and in the government, even among the so-called Republicans and Radicals.

The League Manifesto of January 10, 1873, summarized classic arguments in denying the need for a new law:

The slave had always the right to purchase his freedom [coartación]. The road had always been open . . . one fourth of the colored population were free. Some of the highest posts in the militia are filled by Negroes. . . . These circumstances have given to slavery in Spain a humanitarian and Christian character that distinguishes it from other forms suffered by the world.[48]

[45]*Diario, Congreso* (1872–1873), IV (24 de diciembre de 1872), 2537–2539.
[46]*Ibid.*, p. 2542.
[47]Layard to Granville, Madrid, December 25, 1872. *BFSP* 1872–1873, LXIII, 496–498.
[48]"Manifiesto de la Liga Ultramarina," 1 de enero de 1873, *Cuestión social, Antillas*. According to Gabriel Rodríguez the activities of the Liga Ultramarina

The abolitionists organized counterdemonstrations demanding the Puerto Rican law for Cuba, as well. *La Nación*, January 13, 1873, described a street parade organized by the abolitionists, in which standards, some borne by Negroes, told the following legends: *Los Comuneros, Las Cortes de Cádiz, La Sociedad Abolicionista, Abolición immediata, Alcocer, Buxton, Lincoln, Wilberforce, Cuba: 363,358 esclavos, Puerto Rico: 31,042.*

The disillusioned Don Amadeo abdicated. The Cortes, in accepting his abdication, declared a Republic, February 13, 1873. By its very credo the Republic was expected to abolish slavery in Puerto Rico. Nevertheless, a small but vociferous opposition was determined to filibuster the measure of abolition, taking advantage of the turbulent political situation. They argued that the law was unconstitutional, since the Cortes had been constituted under the late monarchy and was not qualified to dictate laws of this kind. They drew the usual picture of economic ruin resulting from unpremeditated measures, as in Jamaica, the French colonies, and the United States.

But above all, the opposition tried to prove that the law was forced on Spain by the United States, and that the national honor and dignity made its rejection imperative. In the Cortes, Bugallal, Suárez Inclán, and Romero Ortiz, their hands filled with documents, recited the efforts of the United States to acquire Cuba.[49] Romero Ortiz, quoting American protests against the continuance of slavery in the Antilles, protested that the law was being forced on the Spanish people: "On following this policy of weakness and humiliation," he told the deputies, "you do not represent the opinion of the Spanish people."[50]

Gandara, ex-captain general of Puerto Rico, testified that abolition in Puerto Rico was playing into the hands of the Cuban rebels. The Marqués de Barzanallana reflected the misgivings of many when he warned that certain republican doctrines might coincide with the loss of what yet remained to Spain in America.[51] In this way, the opposition continued to link Puerto Rico with the perilous situation in Cuba.

Unfortunately for the slave interests, the attempt to defeat the law caused great disturbances in the streets of Madrid, *La idea y el movimiento antiesclavista en España durante el siglo XIX.*

[49]*Diario, Congreso y Senado*, I (21 de febrero de 1873), 207–219.
[50]*Ibid.*, I (21 de febrero de 1873), 238.
[51]*Ibid.*, I (22 de febrero de 1873), 231–234, and I (27 de febrero de 1873), 263–264.

by stirring up feeling against the United States was doomed to failure. Several republicans and abolitionists defended the right of the United States to intervene "in a matter that concerned all humanity."[52] A feeling of kinship with the American Republic was evident. Castelar, now secretary of state, made the stirring announcement of American recognition of the Spanish Republic before a rapt audience: "This is one of the greatest satisfactions of my life. . . . The United States of America cannot help but contemplate with feeling and sympathy the conversion of the empire of Fernando and Isabel to a republic."[53]

On February 18 Bugallal resumed his desperate efforts to make the abolitionist movement appear foreign and anti-Spanish. Abolitionist sentiment in Spain, he charged in a desperate argument, was due to German philosophy, above all to Hegelian, anti-Christian thinking.

Instantly Sanromá was to his feet, his voice full of sarcasm, "Well, then, name me one German philosopher who would dare to defend abolition in the name of Christianity." Sanromá, a great Puerto Rican orator, thereupon began an impious discourse. "That Christianity founded the anti-slavery world, I don't know. . . . What I know is that in the name of the Holy Trinity asientos were celebrated that have dishonored our country since the sixteenth century." According to Sanromá, pagans had done as much for abolition as Catholics. The apostles and church doctors had stamped a theological approval on slavery:

> I remember that St. Augustine linked slavery with original sin, that St. Ambrose called slavery the gift of God, that Bossuet affirmed that in war was born the right of slavery, that St. Thomas accepted slavery on the same basis as Aristotle. If you want more proof, remember Padre Puig, named Bishop of Puerto Rico who came here in 1869 to defend slavery from a Catholic point of view. . . . Tell me now that your claim to be abolitionist lies in your claim to be Catholic.[54]

---

[52]On the twenty-first of February, for example, Sr. Rojo Arias defended the conduct of the United States. Having just finished a civil war on the matter of slavery, "they had a natural desire to abolish slavery still flourishing at their doorstep in Cuba." *Ibid.*, I (21 de febrero de 1873), 216.

[53]"We must raise our mind and heart to heaven," added Castelar, "to ask the God of Columbus and Washington to bless our work." *Ibid.*, I (15 de febrero de 1873), 74.

[54]*Ibid.*, I (18 de febrero de 1873), 101–106, 114.

Sanromá was one of the few who referred to the great debates of the Spanish doctors of the sixteenth century. It was his purpose to show that though a majority of churchmen defended slavery, nevertheless some had condemned it. He cited the words of Padre Vitoria: "There is no property possible in either the Indian or the Negro. They and their people have the right to govern themselves."[55]

Pidal y Mon challenged Sanromá's argument that Christianity was no great factor in the abolition of slavery. First in the Roman world, then in the Moslem world the Church performed her redemptive work. "But the pagan Renaissance revived it." Pidal condemned Darwin's theory of evolution which made of the Negro, "no more than the missing link." As if to prove Sanromá's assertions, Pidal ended his defense of Catholicism by asking that the abolition law be voted down. "It is not a question of slavery, but of Spanish colonial policy."[56]

As in Brazil so in Spain. The Church as an institution had little influence on abolition sentiment; yet abolitionists—who tended to be moral reformers—would naturally appeal to Christian sentiments. Carrasco declared to the applause of the Cortes: "I know that in condemning slavery . . . I am a faithful interpreter of the doctrine of Christ Crucified who wrote on the cross the rights of a redeemed race."[57] In abolitionist literature, frequent references to Christian motivation are found. "The cause of abolition," said Acosta, "is the cause of Jesus Christ."[58]

The debate appeared interminable when political circumstances forced a truce between the Colonial League and the reformers.[59] At last, the law was brought to a vote. On the initiative of several Republicans, the law was approved unanimously amid excited cries of "Viva España!" "Viva la República!"[60]

In Cuba notice of the law was received with profound disgust by

[55]*Ibid.*, I (18 de febrero de 1873), 106.
[56]*Ibid.*, I (18 de febrero de 1873), 512–516.
[57]From a speech given in the Cortes by Antonio Carrasco on the fifth of January, 1872, "La esclavitud y el Cristianismo," *Cuestión social, Antillas*, p. 55.
[58]José J. Acosta, "La esclavitud en Puerto Rico," *ibid.*, p. 31.
[59]The Republic, then under the presidency of Figueras, found itself in difficult circumstances. It was necessary to close the debate on the Puerto Rican project so that the Cortes could dedicate itself to the problems of internal order and security. Also, no doubt, the Republicans felt that the sooner the law was accepted the better for the prestige of the first Spanish Republic.
[60]*Diario, Congreso y Senado* (1873), I (22 de marzo de 1873), 250.

the Spanish party, who saw only another sacrifice of their interests. In Puerto Rico, where slavery had never been deeply rooted, both master and slave celebrated with fiestas and Te Deums. This was a great victory for Puerto Rican abolitionists.

16. Epilogue: Last Days Of Spanish Slavery, 1873-1886

[In 1886] slavery was abolished in Cuba. The measure had been so long expected that it seems to have produced no social convulsion. Nor has anyone yet written much upon the subject.

Elizabeth Wormeley Latimer, 1898[1]

Indeed, what happened after the Puerto Rican law of 1873 seemed more in the nature of an anticlimax. It was generally assumed that when the insurrection in Cuba ended, another abolition law for that island would be forthcoming, and that nothing much could be done until then. After the Republic succumbed in January, 1874, and Cánovas, the great conservative statesman, re-established the monarchy under Alfonso XII, the reformist cause declined further. The rebels made no gains in Cuba during these years, and after a final attempt of the Grant administration in November, 1875, to sound out the European powers on the possibility of joint intervention the neutralist policy of Fish came to predominate in American diplomacy.[2] The elevation of Hayes to the American presidency signified a turn from Grant's interest in Caribbean expansion. The Spanish ambassador found Hayes' message to Congress of December 3, 1877, in the paragraph concerning Cuba, "the most temperate, prudent, and favorable in many years."[3]

[1]Elizabeth Wormeley Latimer, *Spain in the 19th Century*, p. 413.
[2]Details of the American proposal for joint intervention are given in: Memorandum, gestiones para justificar la intervención, Fish á Cushing, 5 de noviembre de 1875. A.M.A.E. *Correspondencia EEUnidos*, Leg. 2411 (1875–1877), N. 1.
[3]Ministro en Washington remite copia mensaje de Hayes de 3 de diciembre de 1877, *ibid*.

The British government and other European powers, still fearing American designs on Cuba, continued sympathetic to Spain's problems. The British government reaffirmed its position that foreign abolitionist pressure might embarrass those Spanish liberals and abolitionists working for the cause of colonial reform. From London the Spanish minister reported in July, 1875, that never had the proposals of the abolitionists reached such extremes; but, on the other hand, "never has a British minister [Lord Derby] expressed himself in more considerate terms."[4] Thus encouraged, Spain remained doggedly by her policy of no reforms in Cuba until the insurrection ceased. The government of the restored monarchy discouraged abolitionist activities.

During the remainder of the war, however, the Moret Law continued to be applied with greater or lesser vigor, depending on the disposition of the governor general. According to figures supplied in May, 1875, by the Cuban government, 50,046 slaves had been freed since the promulgation of the Preparatory Law of 1870.[5]

Freed by virtue of being born since the seventeenth of September, 1868	32,813
Freed through service rendered under the flag of Spain	301
Freed by virtue of age, sixty years or more	13,740
Freed as emancipados	3,192
Total	50,046

The above figures do not include from 10,000 to 20,000 unregistered slaves (later incorporated into the Moret Law), who were freed by virtue of the census law of 1867, and approximately 5,000 emancipados, who were freed before the application of the Moret Law.

The effects of war and slave mortality (together with the cessation of the slave trade) reduced the slave population as much as did the effects of the Moret Law. According to the 1869 census, 363,288 slaves were in Cuba in that year; by 1878 only 227,902 were to be found. This represented a reduction of 135,386. The Moret Law, allowing for census errors, liberated about half of this number.

Finally, after ten years of war, General Martínez Campos negoti-

---

[4]El ministro plenipotenciario en Londres, A. Castro, al Ministerio de Estado, 3 de julio de 1875. A.H.N. Ultramar, Leg. 4882 (1869–1880), Vols. III and IV, N. 151.

[5]Documento, Junta central protectora de libertos, La Habana, 11 de mayo de 1875, A.H.N. Ultramar, Leg. 4882 (1869–1880), Vols. III and IV.

ated a peace with the Cuban rebels on February 12, 1878. This Peace of Zanjón opened the final stage in the slave debates, and once more the Abolitionist Society awoke to action. As can be seen from some of the provisions, the Zanjón agreement was the beginning of more than a slave debate: Article One promised the same political concessions to Cuba as Puerto Rico then enjoyed. Other articles promised a general amnesty, and liberty to those slaves and Asiatics found among the insurrectionary forces.[6]

The late insurrection had perhaps done more than anything else to prepare the ground for complete abolition in Cuba. In the districts of Oriente rebels had destroyed almost all loyalist property. Of the one hundred ingenios reported in the district of Santiago de Cuba in 1868, only thirty-nine survived the Peace of Zanjón. In the zone of Puerto Príncipe, the worst hit, only one of a hundred ingenios survived.[7] It is true that many of these plantations were small and already declining before 1868, but the net effect was to diminish further the slave interests of Cuba. A comparison of the census of 1862 also shows a drastic decline, again not entirely due to the insurrection, in the number of coffee, tobacco, and livestock farms, which were chiefly found in Oriente:[8]

Date	Ingenios	Coffee Farms	Tobacco Farms	Livestock Farms	Other Small Farms
1862	1,365	782	11,550	8,834	34,546
1877	1,191	192	4,515	3,172	17,906

On the other hand, it would appear that the slave economy was strongly entrenched in the western end of the island, since most of the 1,191 ingenios reported in 1877 were concentrated in Occidente. Yet, in order to work the plantations surviving the war, and in order to expand and rebuild plantations, it was found necessary to employ a variety of workers at relatively high wages: leased slaves, Creole peasants, free Chinese, and contract Chinese. Some haciendas now had as high as 40 percent free labor. It became more profitable to

---

[6]The complete text of the Convenio de Zanjón may be found in a number of general political histories; a more complete documentation is available in A.H.N., Ultramar, Leg. 4882, Vol. IV.

[7]*Historia de la nación Cubana*. Edited by Ramiro Guerra y Sánchez, et al., III, 152.

[8]*Ibid.*, III, 165.

lease slaves, since they were paid nearly as high as free labor—twenty-one or twenty-two gold pesos per month.[9]

Furthermore, the rhetoric of the war had taught the slaves to expect liberty. Taking advantage of disrupted conditions caused by the insurrection many slaves stole away to live in the cities or to roam the countryside as brigands or vagrants. Still there were over 200,000 slaves. The Junta de Hacendados, representing the rich plantation owners around Havana, together with merchants and officials who had grown rich on war contracts and the confiscation of rebel estates and goods, would not oppose abolition in principle, but the demands of economic expansion, the labor shortage, and the profits made from renting slaves, would cause many of them to resist abolition in practice. These interest groups rightly feared that indemnity would not accompany emancipation, because the Spanish government was hopelessly mired in war debts.

As in former years, however, hacendados and merchants formed no solid conservative front on this question. The old division between Spanish and Creole interests reappeared in a new political guise that would bear heavily on the emancipation movement. The rebellion now over, Cuba, according to the promises of Zanjón, could look forward to electing deputies to the Cortes, as well as to an increased franchise in local government. This novel situation made possible the first organized political parties in Cuban history.

The Liberal-Autonomist Party was born phoenixlike from the ashes of the Creole reform movement of the 1860's. The leaders of the new party, like Pozos Dulces, Miguel de Aldama, and Morales Lemus before them, were men of the planter class. Following Saco's line of thought, they believed that the Creole class could best protect their interests, and Cuba's national interests, under an autonomous government. They believed that Spain, exhausted by war, was ready to concede reforms leading to insular autonomy; and they believed, underestimating the institution of the captaincy general, that in free elections the autonomists could eventually win the electorate of Cuba. They believed further that a solid phalanx of Liberal-Autonomists representing Cuba in the Cortes in alliance with the Liberal Party of Spain, headed by such astute politicians as Sagasta, could press the Cortes to accept their program of insular autonomy and economic reform.

[9]*Ibid.*, III, 180–181.

Meeting in Havana on August 3, 1878, the Liberal-Autonomist Party, headed by José María Gálvez, a slaveholder, addressed itself to the electorate for the first time. In unfolding their banners the members outlined a reform program very similar to that presented to the Colonial Reform Commission of 1866–1867. They asked for a law of indemnified abolition, or abolition with the preservation of the patronato; regulation of free, black labor; moral and civil education for the freedman; and white immigration exclusively.[10]

On the political question the new party wanted recognition of individual rights according to the Spanish constitution of 1876; religious, scientific, and educational liberty; equality of Cubans with Spaniards in public employment; municipal and provincial organization such as those enjoyed in Spain; separation of the civil and the military powers; full application to Cuba of the Spanish penal, commercial, and civil codes; and the greatest degree of decentralization possible within the concept of national unity. On the economic question the autonomists called for suppression of export duties, lower import duties, and an advantageous commercial treaty with the United States.

Returning to the abolition question, aside from a doctrinaire commitment to emancipation, the Liberal-Autonomists had other reasons for waving an abolitionist banner. They understood that slavery was eventually doomed anyway and that its prolongation now would serve only to keep Cuba dependent on Spain, and give the monopolistic Spaniards a reason for putting off economic reforms. Creole abolitionism would show up the privileged Spanish party as reactionary and unprogressive. Also, Creole abolitionism would appeal to the free colored and the mulattoes, who would have voting rights under a widened franchise.

The Liberal-Autonomists were not long in discovering the limits of the Iberian reform spirit. In Cuba the Spanish party, having won a bitter war, was not about to lose the peace to "wolves in sheep's clothing." The members of the Spanish party responded to the challenge by organizing their own political phalanx, which under the circumstances could scarcely bear any other name except "Partido Conservador" (later known as the Constitutional Union Party). Naturally, alliance was struck with the Conservative Party of Spain, headed by Cánovas, who passionately believed that a policy of asimilación was

[10]The Liberal-Autonomist program is contained in the pamphlet *El Partido liberal de Cuba: La política en las Antillas.*

the only means for holding Cuba. The Spanish patriots in Cuba immediately began the offensive by attacking the autonomists, not without reason, as "anti-Spanish," or referring to them jeeringly as "Canadians." The autonomists were accused of being "insurrectionaries" attempting to disguise the independence movement defeated in the late war. Creole abolitionism was explained as a maneuver to ruin Cuba's economy so that Spain would give up the island.

The patriotic party declared that autonomist propaganda was outlawed, since autonomist doctrines had never been legally recognized by the government. The Madrid government, habitually mistrusting the reform motives of the Creoles, again took the side of the patriotic party. The captain general hampered autonomist political activities and censored the liberal press. Election results soon justified the "I told you so's" of the Spanish party.

In the elections of August, 1879, for the bicameral Cortes, the first political election in Cuba since the frustrated event of 1837, the proportion of reformers was much higher than the government anticipated. Out of twenty-four elected deputies seven were pronounced liberals, including the noted abolitionist Labra, who stood for election in Cuba. Supposedly, the sixteen senators were all "men devoted to the government," and to Spanish institutions in Cuba, as were the two senators, Conde de Casa More, chief of the Conservative Party of Cuba, and J. Martín Herrera, archbishop of Cuba.[11] Once more, however, government attempts to control elections had dubious results. Some senators, for example, Güell y Renté, seated for the University of Havana, would prove to be outstanding spokesmen for Creole reform interests in the Cortes.

Madrid directed Havana to be more careful. Suffering from the stigma of illegality, if not treason, and tighter censorship, the Creole party lost three seats in the Chamber of Deputies during the elections of 1881. And so the number of Liberal-Autonomist deputies in the Cortes was reduced to four, but these included Bernardo Portuondo, José Ramón Betancourt, and Calixto Bernal, all eloquent voices in favor of autonomy and abolition. Labra, leader of the abolition movement, was "defeated" in the district of Havana as a deputy, but was elected senator by one of the corporations, namely, the Economic Society of Havana, which on more than one occasion had shown itself

---

[11]Correspondencia del capitán general, Ramón Blanco, agosto de 1881, A.H.N. Ultramar, Leg. 4802 (1881–1882), N. 286, N. 3.

more Creole than Spanish. Moreover, as Governor Ramón Blanco complained, when he looked up from censorship duties, a number of "conservative" deputies were assuming an independent position, and though ostensibly supporters of the government, they did in fact espouse liberal principles.[12]

The policy of the Conservative Party of Cuba regarding abolition was basically the same as that of the Liberal-Autonomist Party. In a statement addressed to the Cortes by Sr. Balaguer, November 7, 1879, Cuban conservatives asked that indemnization take the form of either the patronato or appropriate economic concessions.[13] The difference was that the Liberal-Autonomists in the Cortes had made common cause with Spanish liberals and abolitionists, as well as abolitionist deputies from Puerto Rico. In the meantime, the Spanish Abolitionist Society, encouraged by the presence of abolitionist reinforcements in the Cortes, demanded the right to establish branch societies in Cuba.

Earlier, Cánovas, who would not take responsibility for the promises of Zanjón, resigned. General Martínez Campos, now hailed as the "Pacificator" of Cuba, returned to Madrid to assume the post of prime minister in August, 1879. The slave problem was also reintroduced in diplomatic circles after Zanjón, and the Spanish government began dealing once more with abolitionist petitions. Members of the British Parliament introduced resolutions asking that the British government invite the United States to associate itself with a British demand for immediate abolition, "but that Britain has the right to take the initiative in virtue of treaty violations." Lord Salisbury answered: "We will not fail to call the attention of the Spanish government to their promises."[14] The Spanish minister in Berlin reported that the English Abolitionist Society had presented an exposition to Prince Bismarck asking that the Congress of Berlin accord two resolutions against African slavery, including a declaration against the legality of slavery in those countries where it yet persisted.[15]

The American government showed little interest in Spanish abolition promises following the Peace of Zanjón. There was much less

[12]Ibid.

[13]Nota sobre Sr. Balaguer, 13 de febrero de 1880, ibid., Leg. 4814 (1882–1883), N. 279.

[14]Ministro plenipotenciario en Londres al Ministerio de Estado, 7 de mayo de 1878, ibid., Leg. 4882, Vols. III and IV, N. 249.

[15]Ministro plenipotenciario en Berlin al Ministerio de Estado, 30 de junio de 1878, ibid., Vols. II and IV, N. 251.

pressure from abolitionist societies than in England, and only an occasional voice raised the question in Congress. When Martínez Campos announced, shortly after taking office, that for the moment it was impossible to abolish slavery in Cuba, Cox, chairman of the House Foreign Relations Committee, and an ardent supporter of Cuban independence, introduced a resolution to remind Spain of her promise to abolish slavery as soon as the war terminated. The President was asked to use his good offices, in union with other governments. This resolution did not come to a vote.[16]

As the Spanish ambassadors could explain, their government was already taking preliminary steps toward another emancipation law for Cuba. King Alfonso XII, in his message to the Cortes, on June 1, 1879, stated that the government looked forward to the complete extinction of slavery in Cuba and that abolition had a preferential place among measures under consideration.[17] In fulfillment of the king's words, the ministry of Martínez Campos appointed four subcommissions on August 15, 1879, to study the four interrelated questions of slavery, tariff policy, taxation, and commercial relations of Cuba.

The report of the subcommission on slavery explained why the majority favored caution in the formulation of abolition plans. In no country had the problem of slavery been so complicated as in Cuba, said their report, because of the late war of insurrection. Slavery had been abolished in principle by the law of 1870, and the transition from slavery to freedom had been going on for the past nine years. The commission members believed that gradual abolition should continue, that the slave should be converted into a free worker without upsetting the public peace and destroying the wealth of the island. This lesson was learned not only from Cuban experience but also from the "sad results" of immediate abolition in Jamaica by England, in Santo Domingo by France, and in the American South, and the "good results" of gradual abolition in Brazil, where no convulsions or racial antagonisms were to be noted. Concluded the report: "Modern science counsels this solution by demonstrating that there is no solid progress . . . unless it is through evolutions." The subcommission therefore recommended that the tutelage provisions (patronato) es-

[16]Ministro de España en Washington al Ministerio de Estado, 12 de mayo de 1879 y 14 de julio de 1879, *ibid.*, Vols. III and IV, N. 80, N. 110.

[17]Discurso leido por Su Majestad el Rey en la solemne apertura de las Cortes verificada en 1 de junio de 1879, *ibid.*, Leg. 4760 (1879), N. 110.

tablished by the 1870 law of free birth be retained in any new law, and that the humane slave code remain intact.[18]

No doubt the opinion of the insular government was reflected in the deliberations of the subcommission. From Havana, Governor Blanco, consulted on the question of immediate abolition by the colonial minister, Sánchez Bustillo, responded that after a consultation with the proprietors he was strongly opposed to immediate abolition. Most Negroes were unmarried, had no family obligations, no education; if emancipated suddenly, "they would run off to the woods and live like savages." Blanco favored maintaining the patronato and work regulations for the freedmen.[19]

On November 5, 1879, the government of Martínez Campos presented the long-promised project of abolition. Albacete, then colonial minister, announced that this was a fulfillment of Article Twenty-One of the law of 1870: that the government would present a new abolition law for Cuba as soon as deputies from that island were admitted to the Cortes.

But the law was also necessary, explained Albacete, acknowledging the argument of a revitalized abolitionist society, because the Zanjón agreement gave liberty to slaves of the insurrectionary forces who had laid down their arms. "If some slaves were free for this reason, then other slaves have reasons to be free."[20]

The law in its first article abolished slavery in Cuba. This long-promised measure of "immediate abolition," however, established in the second article an eight-year state of tutelage (patronato) for all slaves liberated as a result of this law. The preamble explained: "In this manner, the production of the island will not be threatened, and fears of social upheaval will be allayed."[21]

But there was a better explanation. Contrary to the promise of 1870, the present law provided no indemnity for slave owners. Therefore, the patronato guaranteeing the continued labor of the Negroes was substituted as a form of indemnity. The Count of Valdosera ex-

[18]The report of the subcommission on slavery is found in *ibid.*, Leg. 4780 (1879–1880), N. 81.

[19]Gobernador Ramón Blanco al Ministro de Ultramar, La Habana, 15 de octubre de 1879, *ibid.*, Leg. 4283 (1879–1880), Vol. V, N. 6.

[20]The preamble of the "Law of abolition of Slavery in the Island of Cuba," *Diario de las sesiones de las Cortes, generales y extraordanarias, 1810–1898*, Senado (1879–1880), I, No. 38 (5 de noviembre de 1870), Appendix.

[21]*Ibid.*, I, No. 38 (5 de noviembre de 1879), Appendix.

plained that, in view of the impecunious circumstances of the government, any scheme of indemnity would weigh on the slaveowners themselves. In Puerto Rico indemnity was possible because there were only 31,000 slaves in 1873, whereas in Cuba there were still 200,000.[22]

The abolitionists were furious with the patronato. A new word for slavery, said Labra; others described it as indemnity paid for by the sweat of slaves. Men in the Cortes lost no time in pointing out the glaring contradiction of a law that abolished slavery in the first article and established a tutelage system in the second. "Does slavery cease or not?" asked Santos Guzmán, pointedly.[23]

The provision permitting the emancipated Negro to buy his way out of the patronato (coartación) by paying a price as high as that of former times, provoked the comment of Sr. Loriga: "A law of abolition, Señores, in which liberty cost more than it did before, I do not understand."[24]

The debates on the law of 1880 are invaluable for an understanding of the Cuban question. Slavery per se was not the issue; that had been decided in 1873. The great success of abolition in Puerto Rico invalidated many fears and arguments. "Fortunately," said Albacete, "there is no problem for anyone in recognizing that slavery cannot continue in Cuba."[25] The form that abolition was to take is what gave a significant character to the arguments. In reading through the discussions one finds a microcosm of the entire problem of Spanish policy in Cuba in the nineteenth century, and the reason why it was doomed to failure.

The last slave debate put in sharp focus the profound economic and political incompatibilities between the interests of the metropolis and those of the colonies. There was added interest, too, because at last Cuba was directly represented in the slave debates. Cuban deputies finally would have their day. Speaking in the Cortes for the first time one of them said appropriately, ". . . let me extend my wings as I can."[26]

The Cubans did not fail to utilize the occasion to lay before the

[22]*Ibid.*, I, No. 50 (12 de diciembre de 1879), 562–564.
[23]*Diario, Congreso* (1879–1880), III, No. 81 (14 de enero de 1880), 1361.
[24]*Diario, Senado* (1879–1880), II, No. 58 (23 de diciembre de 1879), 690.
[25]*Ibid.*, I, No. 38 (5 de noviembre de 1879), Appendix.
[26]Statement made by José Güell y Renté representing the University of Havana in the Senate. *Ibid.*, I, No. 45 (22 de noviembre de 1879), 79–80.

government a huge collection of pent-up claims. They turned the question into a political, an economic, and a constitutional debate. The reformist deputies of Cuba, who spoke for the newly organized Liberal-Autonomist Party, said they would accept the law even without indemnity, so long as the government made economic concessions in the direction of autonomy.

More than anyone, Ruíz Gómez, Cuban liberal, forced the debate onto highly disputed economic grounds. The patronato, he said, was simply another means of stalling the real solution to Cuba's problems. A great advocate of free trade and political autonomy *a la Canada*, a walking dictionary of economic facts, Ruíz Gómez specialized in speaking all afternoon on the tariff situation.

As Ruíz Gómez demonstrated with his eternal figures, the main market for Cuban products lay in the United States. Cheap slave labor had formerly permitted Cuban products to freely penetrate the American tariff wall. But with the abolition of slavery, Cuba would lack the means for competing in the American market. A terrible crisis would follow. The mother country must therefore declare free trade, and negotiate an advantageous treaty with the Americans.[27]

The Conservative Party of Cuba saw eye to eye with the Cuban Liberals on this point. Both parties expected indemnity in the form of economic concessions, including the removal of the burdensome property tax of 1867 and a plethora of war taxes. In Havana, where abolition was now stoically accepted, conservative papers like *El Diario de la Marina* and liberal papers like *El Autonomista* said little on abolition, but had everything to say on the necessity of economic reforms. Spanish newspapers were hotly divided, but some liberal publications found it logical that economic reforms should accompany the abolition law. "The law of abolition," said *El Imparcial*, "is incomplete without the economic reforms; that is evident."[28]

In one attempt at economic conciliation, the Spanish government again promised to promote immigration from the Canary Islands, China, Indo-China, and Annam. The favorite plan of the Cuban hacendados, however, had always been the importation from Africa of free blacks "suited to the climate." Cuban delegates reintroduced the proposal again in the Cortes. The colonial minister at that time, the Marqués del Pozo de la Merced, promised that once slavery had

---

[27]*Ibid.*, I, No. 50 (12 de diciembre de 1879), 573–583.
[28]*El Imparcial*, January 9, 1880, Biblioteca Nacional.

been definitely abolished, the Spanish government could denounce the treaties of 1817 and 1835, and attempt the contracting of free Africans.[29]

It is interesting to note that before presentation of the abolition law of 1880 some contracts had been made between British authorities and the Havana government for the employment of British Negroes in Cuba. But Captain General Blanco feared that, given the smouldering embers of rebellion in Cuba, unidentified revolutionaries might be among them. Hence he invoked the decree of 1843 against the importation of British Negroes. This action was upheld by Madrid.[30]

It seemed to the Cubans that with abolition of slavery, only the inconveniences of the Spanish colonial system remained, with none of the advantages. Said Portuondo, "... suddenly the so-called rich land of Cuba seems very poor." Guerrero and several others threatened that they would not vote for the abolition law unless economic reforms should accompany it.[31]

Meanwhile, the government of Martínez Campos resigned on the question of economic reforms (December 7, 1879). Cánovas, returning to power, refused to consider Cuban demands, stating that heavy war debts made further economic concessions impossible. In the Cortes, Sánchez Bustillo, speaking for the government, told the Cubans that the question of economic reforms "has nothing to do with the law of abolition.... It would disarm our negotiators in front of the United States, forcing Spain to accept a commercial treaty prejudicial to her interests."[32]

As for the slave law itself, Cuban liberals and Spanish abolitionists vigorously attacked it as insufficient. Güell y Renté asked for complete abolition with indemnity. Ramírez and others wanted the Puerto Rican law of 1873 for Cuba.

[29]*Diario, Congreso* (1880–1881), III, No. 88 (22 de enero de 1880), 1586–1587.

[30]Comunicaciones del Consejo de Estado, 13 de julio de 1880, A.H.N. Ultramar, Leg. 4761 (1879–1880), N. 1.

[31]Bernardo Portuondo, Cuban deputy, member of the Liberal-Autonomist Party, *Diario, Congreso* (1879–1880), VI (17 de abril de 1880), 3012–3013. Earlier, Teodoro Guerrero, representing Puerto Rico, asserted: "I will not vote for the law if the Additional Article [introducing economic reforms] is not approved, and I believe the majority of my companions will do the same." *Ibid.*, III (15 de enero de 1880), 1455.

[32]*Ibid.*, III (15 de enero de 1880), 1458–1460.

The Cuban Conservative Party, on the other hand, thought that the Moret Law of 1870 should have been left intact. Fernández de Castro and Ibañez-Palenciano would have altered the law more in favor of the proprietors, for example, extending the patronato from eight to fifteen years. "They call me a slavist," said Fernández de Castro, "but, Señores, I am an eminently practical man." It was Fernández de Castro who best summarized all the old arguments against abolition: Again, Lincoln did not intend to abolish slavery. Again, foreign powers were forcing the issue. Again, agriculture would be ruined as in the American South. Again, anthropological arguments: ". . . the condition and aptitude of the Negro are not those of the whites." Again, the humaneness of Spanish slavery: "This much should be said in honor of Spain and her children, in no part of the world have slaves been treated with so much humanity as in our colonies."[33]

The one notable amendment was made by Dr. Creus. He insisted that the regulations for the law should include Catholic religious instruction, "so that the unfortunate Negroes would be prepared for the transition from slavery to full citizenship." It was a Catholic duty and right to propagate Catholic principles, said Creus (now that conservative monarchists were in power and not liberal republicans). Perier, who supported him, asked, "Isn't it strange that the word Catholic doesn't appear in the preamble?" The Patriarch of the Indies also arose in support: "I ask the Senate that it not be alarmed, I am not going to turn this hall into a Council of Catholic doctors." He then spoke of the redemptive work of the Church. "Muy bien, muy bien," responded the assembly. Noting the feelings of the Senate, the colonial minister admitted the amendment.[34]

On January 30, 1880, the Cortes approved of the law by a large majority. Several colonials voted against the law because it did not attach economic concessions.

[33]The lengthy arguments of Fernández de Castro are best found in the debates of *Diario, Senado* (1879–1880), I, No. 52 (15 de diciembre de 1879), 595–600; and I, No. 54 (17 de diciembre de 1879), 1419–1422.

[34]*Ibid.*, I, No. 56 (19 de diciembre de 1879), 730–735. The very interesting discussion on the "Catholic amendment" indicated that the Catholic hierarchy were finally aroused by the slave question to a point of active interest. It should also be remembered that the Cortes of 1879–1880 under the restored monarchy was a more pious assembly than that of the Glorious Revolution of 1868–1870, or that of the Republic of 1873, and therefore tended more to justify abolition on "Catholic principles" rather than "liberal principles."

Vázquez Queipo, a Cuban liberal, passed a summary judgment on the law of 1880:

> In my poor judgment, this law should be, in view of previous promises, more radical in nature and contain only two provisions, the first declaring emancipation, and the second submitting the Negroes to the regimen of freeworkers.
>
> I believe that instead of calling this a law of immediate abolition ... that it might better be called: the law of abolition more rapid than that of Sr. Moret.[35]

It was expected that the British government would protest the eight years of tutelage established by the law of 1880. But the ministry of Lord Salisbury was disposed to accept the law, such as it was. Good reports coming from Cuba would tend to confirm this position. President Hayes, in his message to Congress, on December 7, 1880, made no mention of the slave question in Cuba.[36] Earlier, on December 19, 1879, the Spanish minister in Washington reported that the publication of the first five articles of the law of 1880 had created a good impression, and that he would give them all the publicity possible. Predictably, La Liga Cubana, an organization of Cuban exiles, attacked the abolition law and urged independence, declaring that Spain would not carry it into effect. But, as the Spanish minister explained, many Americans were tired of the entire Cuban question. One proof was that the *New York Herald,* formerly a staunch supporter of the rebel cause, now believed the Cubans incapable of independence.[37]

Concerning the application of the emancipation measure of 1880, regulations, similar to those governing the application of the Moret Law, went into effect on July 29, 1880. The colonial government, profiting from past experience, began by achieving the most accurate census possible. For the first time Cuban authorities were invested with sufficient power to enforce registration. The law stipulated that every patrocinado be provided with a cedula to be issued by the central committee of Havana on application of the master. If the master

[35]*Diario, Congreso* (1879–1880), III, No. 80 (15 de enero de 1880), 1380–1381.

[36]Nota sobre el mensaje del Presidente Hayes, 7 de diciembre de 1880. A.M.A.E. *Correspondencia EEUnidos,* Leg. 1476 (1879–1881), N. 260.

[37]Felipe Méndez de Vigo, ministro plenipotenciario en Washington al Ministerio de Estado, 18 de agosto de 1879 y 19 de diciembre de 1879, *ibid.,* Leg. 1476 (1879–1881), N. 140, N. 218.

failed to apply before the thirty-first of October, 1881, he forfeited his right to the services of the patrocinados, and the latter were declared free. Inspectors were appointed to visit the plantations and to issue "free papers" to unregistered slaves.

A year after the new abolition measure went into effect, Governor Blanco wrote that the law was being successfully carried out, and that even the *New York Sun*, on April 18, 1881, admitted that harmony reigned between patron and patrocinado.[38] On August 23, 1881, Blanco reported that 116 administrative committees were functioning regularly in the districts of Pinar del Río, Habana, Matanzas, Santa Clara, Puerto Príncipe, and Santiago de Cuba, and that via the 36 committees functioning in the Habana district, 1,813 libertos had been completely freed.[39] In all, according to official calculations, from February 13, 1880, to July 13, 1883, 34,033 slaves were freed. On November 8, 1883, the same authority claimed that only 99,566 registered slaves remained on the island.[40]

As with the Moret Law of 1870, abolition procedures faced many obstacles arising from the ravages of the recent war: registration documents lost, people displaced, and ex-soldiers and runaway slaves living like vagabonds. Proprietors continued to ask for a suspension of the registration law in view of these difficulties. Cuban authorities frequently applied to Madrid for further instructions. But in spite of the difficulties Madrid strictly charged the governors to apply the law to the last letter. English Consul General Crowe could say of the new governor, Luis Prendergast, that he had since his arrival impartially enforced the laws relating to slavery, "and whenever they left a doubt he has declared in favor of the slave."[41]

Crowe's favorable statements were based on such reports as that of Vice-Consul Harris, who wrote, April 2, 1883: "Upon the whole I

---

[38]Gobernador Ramón Blanco al Ministro de Ultramar dando cuenta del estado de la ley de abolición en el primer año de promulgado, 23 de agosto de 1886, A.H.N. Ultramar, Leg. 4884 (1881–1883), Vol. VII, N. 112.

[39]*Ibid.* Vol. VII, N. 112.

[40]Capitán general al Ministerio de Ultramar, 13 de julio de 1883 y 8 de noviembre de 1883, *ibid.*, Vol. VII, N. 273, N. 289.

[41]Consul General Crowe to Earl Granville, Havana, April 20, 1883. *Slave Trade, No. 3 (1883). Reports by Consul-General [A. de C.] Crowe on the Number and Condition of the Slaves in Cuba Presented to Both Houses of Parliament by Command of her Majesty. Ibid.*, Leg. 4884 (1881–1883), VIII, 3.

don't know any Spanish law that is carried out or executed so near to the letter of the law as this Emancipation Act of 1880."[42]

According to Crowe, the parties interested in the slave question could be classified as follows: (1) the rich slaveholder, (2) the poor Creole owner, (3) the autonomists, abolitionists, and opposition press, and (4) the government and the Spanish party in Cuba. The few rich planters had accepted the inevitable and sold their slaves or freed them. Since they possessed capital they were able to pay the price of free labor, thus adapting themselves to the new order. Their interest in slavery ceased. The poor Creole planters wished to retard emancipation and "get the most out of their slaves." By now even the government and the Spanish party wished to see an end to it. Were it not for the problem of vagrancy and what to do with a sudden influx of idle blacks, "they would gladly anticipate the law; but this social problem has to be solved, and a gain of time renders the solution easier."[43]

The process of emancipation was more rapid in and near the towns, where the patrocinados were closer to the local courts. Domestic slaves, who lived in towns, were "lazier, less amenable to control." Their masters had less objection to their liberation. On the other hand, slave labor was more essential in the country districts. Also, slaves there were reluctant to leave the place where they had been born and raised, or to abandon the small plots of land on which they raised vegetables, pigs, and chickens. Sometimes these small plots of land enabled the slave to save enough money to purchase his freedom. Acting-Consul Carden observed that after the law of 1880 few Negroes bothered to purchase their freedom, even though it was in their power. "I am inclined to think, therefore, that the fact of their not doing so more proves they are, on the whole, fairly well-treated."[44]

As to the Chinese, Carden added, their condition had improved so much that they "now practically enjoy the same immunities as other foreigners."[45]

[42] John F. Harris to Consul General Crowe, Sagua la Grande, April 2, 1883, *Slave Trade, No. 3, ibid.*, Leg. 4884 (1881–1883), VIII, 10–11.

[43] Consul General Crowe to Earl Granville, Havana, April 20, 1883, *Slave Trade, No. 3, ibid.*, Leg. 4884 (1881–1883), VIII, 9.

[44] *Slave Trade, No. 2 (1882). Report by Acting Consul General [Lionel] Carden on the Number and Condition of the Slaves in Cuba Presented to Both Houses of Parliament by Command of Her Majesty, ibid.*, Leg. 4884 (1881–1882), VII, 1–3.

[45] *Slave Trade, No. 2, ibid.*, VII, 3.

In the interim, abolitionist and liberal deputies pushed petitions before the Cortes, expressing acute dissatisfaction with the law of 1880. These memorials were solicited from cities and villages in Spain and Cuba, and presented to the legislature by Labra or Güell y Renté. These protestations maintained as always that the "march of civilization," and the national honor demanded the complete cleansing of this "terrible stain" from the Spanish flag. The three most common measures proposed were the immediate liberty of all slaves not enrolled in the registrations of 1867, 1871, and 1877; the abolition of stocks and irons; and, of course, the abolition of the patronato.[46]

The Spanish Abolition Society gathered cases of "notorious abuses" practiced on patrocinados. For example, the Society charged that rarely was the slave given liberty, on grounds that the patron refused to pay the monthly stipend provided by Article Four of the law of 1880. Almost always, the patron could prove the "falsity" of the charge by means of servants and friends, who acted as witnesses, or by the presentation of some specious document.[47]

A more influential argument among reformers was the affirmation that Cuba would never receive economic concessions until slavery was fully abolished. To this end, Labra and several other liberals, including the Cubans Portuondo and Betancourt, presented to the Cortes on June 10, 1882, a formal project to abolish the patronato.[48] The defeat of this proposal in no sense signified the end of such attempts. According to one interpretation, prominent Cuban proprietors, such as the Marqués de Villalva, the Marqués de Calderón, and Tomás Terry, supported the abolition of the patronato, because it was also a bid for political support from newly enfranchised groups, including some colored voters.[49]

The colonial government, still suspicious of the Liberal-Autonomists, prohibited open abolitionist activities. The Havana abolitionists, under the leadership of José Antonio Cortina, protested on one

[46]Exposiciones abolicionistas a las Cortes, 1881–1882, *ibid.*, Leg. 4815 (1880–1882).

[47]Exposición de la Sociedad Abolicionista Española al Excmo. Ministro de Ultramar, 3 de mayo de 1883, *ibid.*, Leg. 4814 (1882–1883).

[48]According to the plan for abolishing the patronato, a three-year work contract would have been substituted and the freedmen would have received the wages and treatment of a free laborer. Full text given in *Diario, Congreso* (1882–1883), II, No. 30 (1 de enero de 1882), Appendix.

[49]According to the newspaper *La Voz de Cuba*, 3 de diciembre de 1881, found in A.H.N. Ultramar, Leg. 4815 (1880–1882).

occasion that they did not wish to engage in public demonstration or political activities but only to raise funds through voluntary subscription for the liberation of patrocinados.[50]

During this time the Liberal-Autonomists were still subject to severe pressure from the Spanish party and the Havana authorities. More than once the Creole party thought of disbanding, but Gálvez's determination in Havana, and Labra's encouragement from Madrid prevented a dissolution.[51] Shortly after, the problem was partially settled when Labra telegraphed the exciting news to Gálvez, on March 30, 1882, that the new liberal ministry headed by Sagasta had recognized in the Cortes the legality of autonomist doctrines and the right to publicize them.[52] The colonial minister, however, soon began hedging this right in typical peninsular fashion. Betancourt and Güell y Renté were told that autonomist activities must not indiscretely conflict with "territorial integrity." The governor general was instructed to combat autonomist ideas "if they seemed to endanger Spanish policy in Cuba."[53]

In spite of the hovering censor the autonomists could now mount an active campaign for political support. *El País* and other Creole papers of Havana gradually grew more outspoken in their demands for abolition and reform concessions.[54]

Meanwhile, the slave question was completely overshadowed by the economic crisis in Cuba. During the years 1880–1886 the economic situation progressed from bad to worse until the colonial government itself could not meet obligations. Whereas in 1878 the Cuban budget had been over 40,000,000 pesos, by 1884 it had been reduced to 30,000,000 pesos, and still all parties complained that tax burdens were excessive. Some insisted that the budget be cut to 24,000,000 pesos. The overhanging war debt and the gradual disintegration of the slave economy, together with lower world sugar prices, were the chief reasons advanced to explain the crisis. Madrid attempted to

[50]According to a newspaper clipping, ca. March 9, 1882, from the reformist paper *Revista económica de las Antillas* (censurado), Editor, Francisco Cepedo (deportado), *ibid.*, Leg. 4811 (1882), N. 148.

[51]*El Partido liberal de Cuba*, p. 41.

[52]Capitán general Luis Prendergast al Ministro de Ultramar, 3 de abril de 1882, A.H.N. Ultramar, Leg. 4811 (1882–1883), N. 130.

[53]Telegrama al Capitán general, Madrid, 9 de abril de 1882, *ibid.*, Leg. 4811 (1882–1883), N. 141.

[54]Revista de la prensa hecha por el Gobernador general Emilio Caneja, 15 de octubre de 1886, *ibid.*, Leg. 4886 (1885–1886), "Partes Decenales."

meet some of the Cuban economic demands. The law of June 23, 1882, established the basis of commercial relations between Spain and the Antilles. Each year, according to a graduated scale of tariff duties, products from the metropolis would pay less duty on entering Cuba, so that, in theory, by July 1, 1891, such imports would enter duty free.[55]

Difficult negotiations with the United States finally led to a *modus vivendi*, confirmed in February, 1884. The American government promised to suppress the 10 percent duty on products imported from the Spanish Antilles. In return, a lower duty was to be charged on flour entering the islands from America. The Cuban reformers were not satisfied. Barcelona merchants were still re-exporting American flour to Cuba under a protective tariff, and the Cubans alleged that they were paying a double tariff as a result of this indirect trade. The attitude of the Creole autonomists was summed up by Güell y Renté: "This system is monstrous," he cried, "Spain wants to live at Cuba's expense."[56]

On November 28, 1883, the Spanish and colonial abolitionists won a decisive victory when the Cánovas government, returned to power, agreed to abolish the punishment of stocks and irons, up until that time still permitted in the slave regulations. The colonial minister, Suárez Inclán, proudly announced that now only the withholding of wages or leisure time were to be used as coercive measures for refractory slaves.[57] The end of forced labor was clearly in sight, for now, indeed, it was only the giving of wages and leisure time that could hold the patrocinado to his job.

Scarcely meeting any resistance, the abolitionists pushed on to final victory. Two years before the eight-year patronato was to terminate, when there remained less than 30,000 Negroes in a state of compulsory labor, the government abolished the tutelage system. The decree of October 7, 1886, that dealt the *golpe de gracia* to slavery in Cuba made the usual apology:

> Unfortunately, it is true that slavery had an asylum on our soil as with the most cultured nations; but our character, our religious beliefs, and other causes too numerous to investigate had established relations between mas-

[55]*Diario, Senado* (1884–1885), I, No. 22 (16 de junio de 1884), 296–298.
[56]*Ibid.*, I, No. 22 (16 de junio de 1884), 299.
[57]Real Decreto de 27 de noviembre de 1883, A.H.N. Ultramar, Leg. 4814 (1882–1883), N. 286.

ter and serf less violent and less unjust than is characteristic of the institution.[58]

Perhaps Spanish slavery was more humane; if so, this very humaneness had reached the proportions of a legend that seemed to have prolonged slavery in Cuba. Labra, speaking years after slavery had been abolished, referred to the extraordinary successful propaganda in favor of the slave interests: "One has to admire, Señores, the nerve by which they propagated the belief that the slaves of the Antilles lived happily and contented.... No one mentioned dungeons, stocks and irons, nor the awful mortality rate among slaves."[59]

If Spanish statesmen were long inclined to listen to the song of the slave interests, perhaps it was because the slave problem could not for one moment be separated from the higher considerations of the imperial conscience. As Labra might have expressed it: one has to admire, Señores, Spain's determination to stay in Cuba, come what may.

Now only Brazil of all the American nations still held African slaves, but after a series of gradual measures similar to those taken in Spain, the monarchy of Brazil approved the final measure of abolition on May 13, 1888. This also signified the end of monarchy in Brazil, just as abolition would signify the end of Spanish dominion in Cuba.

---

[58]Prologue of the decree of the seventh of October, 1886, abolishing the patronato, *La Gaceta de Madrid*, 8 de octubre de 1886, Biblioteca Nacional. Consul General Crowe reported that the "number of slaves now finally freed will not exceed 25,000." Crowe noted further that the only important restriction on the abolition of the patronato was that the freedmen were subject to four years' surveillance, during which period they must show a cedula of identity and that they were earning a living. This restriction was intended to control vagrancy. Crowe observed that such restrictions had hitherto been enforced with leniency, and he added that all parties in the Spanish state were glad to see an end to the slave institution. There was no opposition (Consul General Crowe to the Earl of Iddlesleigh, Havana, November 4, 1886, *BFSP* [1885–1886], Vol. 77, p. 924).

[59]Rafael María de Labra y Cadrana, *La reforma política de Ultramar 1868–1900*, p. 22. The legend of the humaneness of Spanish slavery seems to have been accepted uncritically even by well-known historian Jerónimo Becker y González. Writing in 1920, he said: "We must admit that Spain was the first nation to raise her voice against the slave traffic through her theologians and jurists, so that the Negroes were not the victims of cruel practices common to other colonies. This Spanish race, proud, bold, intrepid and quixotic ... did not fail to practice true feelings of love, brotherhood, and charity inspired by Christianity" (*La política española en las Indias*, p. 422).

It seemed that almost everywhere in the new world the rights of man had triumphed over conservative economic interests.

Of course, the heritage of slavery remained wherever the old system of plantation labor had been destroyed. In Cuba, as in Brazil, plantation owners, as they turned to immigrant labor, complained that the freedman stopped regular work as soon as he earned enough to buy an umbrella, a frock coat, and a felt hat. Or, as Trollope said of the freedmen of Jamaica: "The Negro's idea of emancipation was and is emancipation not from slavery but from work; to lie in the sun and eat breadfruit and yams is his idea of being free."[60] In any case, the new social problems that crowded out the old are not part of our story.

Finally, as to Spain's solution to the difficult problem of abolishing slavery in Cuba, perhaps it was as rapid and as wise as circumstances would allow. Fortunately, the previous existence of a large class of free Negroes and mulattoes, as in Brazil, helped the peaceful assimilation of the former slave into the mass of Cuban society.

[60] Anthony Trollope, *The West Indies and the Spanish Main*, p. 94.

BIBLIOGRAPHY

Bibliographical Aids

Catálogo de la Biblioteca-Museo de Ultramar. Madrid: Impr. de la sucesora de M. Minuesa de los Ríos, 1900.
Jones, Cecil K. *A Bibliography of Latin American Bibliographies.* 2nd. ed. Washington, D. C.: U. S. Government Printing Office, 1942.
King, James F. "The Negro in Continental Spanish America: A Select Bibliography," *Hispanic American Historical Review*, XXIV, No. 3 (August, 1944), 547–559.
Negociado de Ultramar: Registro de documentación de Cuba, Puerto Rico y Filipinas para el Archivo Histórico Militar de Madrid. Madrid: Biblioteca Nacional, n. d.
Pedreira, Antonio S. *Bibliografía puertorriqueña.* San Juan, Puerto Rico: Impr. de la Librería y casa editorial Hernando, 1932.
Sánchez Alonso, Benito. *Fuentes de la historia española e hispano-americana.* 3 vols. 3d. ed. Madrid: Consejo Superior de Investigaciones Científicas, Instituto Miguel de Cervantes, 1952.
Trelles y Govín, Carlos M. *Biblioteca histórica cubana.* 3 vols. Matanzas, Cuba: Impr. de J. F. Oliver, 1922–1924.

Manuscript Collections

Archivo del Ministerio de Asuntos Exteriores de Madrid. *Política EEUnidos* (1855–1882), legajos 2403, 2408, 2409, 2411, 2412; *Correspondencia EEUnidos* (1843–1881), legajos 1466–1476; *Negociaciones EEUnidos* (1854–1884), legajos 19–20.
Archivo Histórico Nacional de Madrid. Sección de Estado: *Subsección de Esclavitud* (1817–1860), legajos 8040–8048, 8057–8059, 8061.
———. Archivo de Ultramar: *Subsección de Esclavitud* (1827–1873), legajos 3547–3558; *Subsección de Gobierno* (1833–1900), legajos 4600–5060. Out of this great mass of unedited documents the following legajos were found to bear more directly on the question of slavery and Spanish policy in Cuba: 3547 (1827–1860), 3548–3549 (1817–1870), 4283 (1879–1880), 4628–4629 (1843–1849), 4635 (1845–1851), 4645 (1850–1855), 4648 (1854–1867), 4655 (1844–1845), 4700 (1866), 4710 (1866–1868), 4716 (1855–1868), 4724–4725 (1869–1871), 4728 (1870), 4731 (1871), 4736–4738 (1873–1874), 4750 (1878), 4760–4761 (1879–1880), 4780 (1879–1880), 4748 (1880–1883), 4790 (1878–1880), 4794–4795 (1881–1886), 4805–4818 (1881–1883), 4880–4889 (1881–1891), 4933 (1867–1869), 4938 (1868–1879).

Documentary Collections

Adams, E. C. (ed.). *British Diplomatic Correspondence: The Republic of Texas, 1838–1846.* Austin: Texas State Historical Association, ca. 1917.

Boletín oficial de Ultramar, 1869–1880. Madrid: Impr. Nacional, 1875–1883.

British and Foreign State Papers. 90 vols. London: Great Britain Foreign Office, 1812–1897. These volumes contain extensive slave-trade correspondence with foreign powers and with British consuls and commissioners responsible for overseeing the administration of treaties against the traffic. Some of this correspondence has been published separately; to give but two examples: *Correspondence Relative to the Slave Trade* [1827: (A) Correspondence with the British Commissioners at Sierra Leone, the Havannah, Rio de Janeiro, Surinam; (B) Correspondence with Foreign Powers. Presented to the House of Commons, April 25, 1828]. London: W. Clowes and Sons, 1828. *Correspondence with Spain, Portugal, Brazil, the Netherlands and Sweden, Relative to the Slave Trade* [from May 11 to December 31, 1840, inclusive]. London: W. Clowes and Sons, 1841.

Colección de artículos sobre el Instituto de Voluntarios de la isla de Cuba. Editado por el Coronel de los Voluntarios de la Habana, D. Eugenio Vandama y Calderón. La Habana: Impr. Militar, 1897.

Colección de disposiciones sobre esclavos, 1840–56. Madrid: Impr. del Gobierno, 1857.

Colección de reales órdenes, decretos, y disposiciones publicados en la Gaceta, 1870–80. La Habana: Impr. del Gobierno, 1880.

Colección de varias exposiciones dirigidas al Excmo. Procer del Reino, Gobernador y Capitán General de la isla de Cuba y a Su Majestad la Reina Gobernadora, de la Colección de Justo Zaragoza. La Habana: Impr. del Gobierno, 1836.

Coll y Toste, Cayetano (ed.). *Boletín histórico de Puerto Rico.* 14 vols. San Juan, Puerto Rico: Tip. Cantero, Fernández & Co., 1914–1927.

Correspondence with Spain, Portugal, Brazil, the Netherlands, Sweden, and the Argentine Confederation, Relative to the Slave Trade, from January 1 to December 31, 1841. Class B. London: Her Majesty's Stationery Office, 1842.

Cuadro estadístico de la siempre fiel isla de Cuba, correspondiente al año de 1846, formado bajo la dirección y protección del Excmo. Sr. Gobernador y Capitán General Don Leopoldo O'Donnell, por una Comisión de Oficiales y Empleados particulares. La Habana: Impr. del Gobierno, 1847.

Cuba. Colección de folletos, 1837–71. Madrid: Biblioteca Nacional, 1837–1871.

Cuba. *Colección de folletos, 1868–70.* Madrid: Biblioteca Nacional, 1868–1870.

Cuba desde 1850 á 1873. Colección de informes, memorias, proyectos, antecedentes sobre el gobierno de la isla de Cuba, que ha reunido por comisión del Gobierno D. Carlos de Sedano y Cruzat, ex-diputado a Cortes. Madrid: Impr. Nacional, 1873.

Cuestión social, Antillas: Colección Justo Zaragoza de varias exposiciones de la Sociedad Abolicionista Española, discursos de sus miembros en el Congreso y Ateneo, etc., 1868–73. Madrid: Biblioteca Nacional, 1868–1873.

La democracia en el Ministerio de Ultramar 1869–70: Colección de leyes, decretos, órdenes y otros documentos emanados del Ministerio de Ultramar durante la administración del Sr. Manuel Becerra. Madrid: Gregorio Entrada, 1870.

Diario de las sesiones de las Cortes, generales y extraordinarias, 1810–1898. Madrid: Impr. Nacional, 1810–1898.

Diplomatic and Consular Reports on Trade and Finance. No. 501. London: Printed for Her Majesty's Stationery Office by Harrison and Sons, 1889.

Donnan, Elizabeth (ed.). *Documents Illustrative of the Slave Trade to America.* 4 vols. Washington: The Carnegie Institution, 1930–1935.

Fernández Castro, José Antonio (ed.). *Medio siglo de historia colonial de Cuba, cartas a José Antonio Saco de 1823–1879.* La Habana: Ricardo Veloso, 1923.

First Report from the Select Committee on the Slave Trade Together with the Minutes and Evidence and Appendix. Ordered by the House of Commons to be printed 18 April 1848. London: Her Majesty's Stationery Office, 1848.

Fragmentos de los discursos pronunciados en el Senado y Congreso de la última legislatura de 1872 y documentos importantes relativos a la cuestión de Ultramar. Madrid: n.p., 1872.

Gaceta de la Habana. Periódico oficial del gobierno de Madrid, 1865–1886.

Gaceta de Madrid. Periódico oficial del gobierno de Madrid, 1865–1886.

Información: Reformas de Cuba y Puerto Rico. 2 vols. New York: Hallet Breen, 1867. (Probably published by Junta Revolucionaria Cubana.)

Manning, William R. (ed.). *Diplomatic Correspondence of the United States: Inter-American Affairs 1831–1860.* 12 vols. Vol. VII: *Great Britain*; Vol. XI: *Spain.* Washington: Carnegie Endowment for International Peace, 1936–1939.

Ministerio de Ultramar: Documentos de la comisión creada por real decreto del 15 de agosto de 1879 sobre reformas en la isla de Cuba. Madrid: Impr. del Gobierno, 1879.

Recopilación de leyes de los reinos de las Indias. 4 vols. 5th ed. Madrid: Boix, 1841.
Slave Trade, No. 2 (1883). Reports by Consul General [A. de C.] Crowe on the Number and Condition of the Slaves in Cuba Presented to Both Houses of Parliament by Command of Her Majesty (pamphlet). London: Harrison and Sons, 1883.
Slave Trade, No. 3 (1882). Report by Acting Consul General [Lionel] Carden on the Number and Condition of the Slaves in Cuba Presented to Both Houses of Parliament by Command of Her Majesty (pamphlet). London: Harrison and Sons, 1883.
Williams, Eric (ed.). *British West Indies at Westminster, Part I: 1789–1823.* Extract from the debates in Parliament. Trinidad, B.W.I.: Government Printing Office, 1954.
———. *Documents of West Indian History.* Port of Spain: P. N. M. Publishing Co., 1963.
Zamora y Coronado, José María (ed.). *Biblioteca de legislación ultramarina.* 6 vols. Madrid: Martín Alegría, 1844–1846.

Newspapers

Unless otherwise noted, the place of publication is Madrid.
Clamor Público (Liberal).
La Crónica (Cuban exiles), Nueva York.
La Democracia (Liberal).
El Diario de la Marina (Conservador), La Habana.
La España (Conservador).
El Español (Conservador).
La Fe (Monárquico y Católico).
La Gorda (Liberal).
La Igualdad (Republicano Federal).
La Imparcial (Liberal).
La Independencia Española (Liberal).
El León Español (Conservador).
La Nación (Progresista-Radical).
La Opinión Nacional (Liberal).
El País (Conservador).
El País (Liberal), La Habana.
La Política (Conservador).
La Restauración (Monárquico-Alfonsino).
Revista Económica de las Antillas (Reformist), La Habana.
El Siglo (Liberal), La Habana.
La Voz de Cuba (Liberal), La Habana.

Books and Articles

Acosta y Calbo, José Julián de. *La abolición de la esclavitud en Puerto Rico* (pamphlet). San Juan, Puerto Rico: Impr. y Librería de Acosta, 1871.

———. *Discurso sobre la esclavitud en Puerto Rico* (pamphlet). Madrid: M. G. Hernández, 1872.

Acosta y Quintero, Angel. *José J. Acosta y su tiempo.* San Juan, Puerto Rico: Impr. Sucesión J. J. Acosta, 1899.

Aguirre Beltrán, Gonzalo. "The Slave Trade in Mexico," *Hispanic American Historical Review*, XXIV, No. 3 (August, 1944), 412–431.

Aimes, Hubert S. *A History of Slavery in Cuba, 1511 to 1868.* New York: G. P. Putnam's Sons, 1907.

Alcazar, José D. *La historia de España en América.* Madrid: J. Quesada, 1898.

Alonso y Sanjurjo, Eugenio. *Apuntes sobre los proyectos de la abolición de la esclavitud en las islas de Cuba y Puerto Rico.* Madrid: Impr. de la Biblioteca de Instrucción y Recreo, 1874.

Amer, Carlos. *Cuba y la opinión pública* (pamphlet). Madrid: H. Gómez, 1897.

Arango y Parreño, Francisco. *Obras de Don Francisco de Arango y Parreño.* 2 vols. La Habana: Ministerio de Educación, 1952.

Armas y Céspedes, Francisco de. *De la esclavitud en Cuba.* Madrid: T. Fontanet, 1866.

Arrillaga Roqué, Juan. *Memorias de antaño, historia de un viaje a España 1887–88.* Ponce, Puerto Rico: Tipografía Baldorioty, 1910.

Balaguer, Víctor. *Memoria redactada por el Ministro de Ultramar, acerca de su gestión en el departamento de su cargo.* 2 vols. Madrid: Manuel Tello, 1888.

Ballesteros y Beretta, Antonio. *Historia de España y su influencia en la historia.* 9 vols. Barcelona: Salvat Editores, 1919–1941.

Ballou, Maturin M. *Due South or Cuba Past and Present.* Boston: Houghton, Mifflin, 1885.

Balmes, Jaime. *El Protestantismo comparado con el Catolicismo en sus relaciones con la civilización europea.* 4 vols. Barcelona: Biblioteca Balmes, 1925.

Bancroft, Frederic. *Slave Trading in the Old South.* Baltimore: J. H. Curst Co., 1931.

Barras y Prado, Antonio de las. *La Habana a mediados del siglo XIX: Memorias de Barras y Prado publicadas por su hijo Francisco de las Barras y Aragón.* Madrid: Ciudad Lineal, 1925.

Becker y González, Jerónimo. *La historia de las relaciones exteriores de España durante el siglo XIX.* 4 vols. Madrid: Impr. J. Ratés Martín, 1924.

———. *La historia política y diplomática de España desde la independencia de Los Estados Unidos hasta nuestros días, 1776–1895.* Madrid: Antonio Romero, 1897.

———. *La política española en las Indias.* Madrid: Impr. J. Ratés Martín, 1920.

Benoist, Charles. *Cánovas del Castillo, la restauración renovadora.* Madrid: Impr. Saez Hermanos, 1931.

Blanco Herrero, Miguel. *La política de España en Ultramar.* Madrid: Sucesores de Rivadenegra, 1888.

Boxer, C. R. *Salvador de Sá and the Struggle for Brazil and Angola, 1602–1868.* London: University of London; Athlone Press, 1952.

Brau, Salvador. *Disquisiciones sociológicas y otros ensayos.* Introducción de E. Fernández Mendez. San Juan: Universidad de Puerto Rico, 1956.

———. *Lo que dice la historia. Cartas al Sr. Ministro de Ultramar por el director de El Clamor del País y Secretario general del Partido autonomista Puertorriqueño.* Madrid: Hijos de M. G. Hernández, 1893.

Brown, Vera L. "The South Sea Company and Contraband Trade," *American Historical Review*, XXXI, No. 4 (July, 1926), 662–678.

Buxton, Sir Thomas F. *The African Slave Trade and Its Remedy.* London: J. Murray, 1840.

Calcagno, Francisco. *Diccionario biográfico cubano.* New York: N. Ponce de Leon, 1878.

Caldwell, Robert Granville. *The López Expeditions to Cuba 1848–51.* Princeton: Princeton University Press, 1915.

Callahan, James Morton. *Cuba and International Relations: A Historical Study in American Diplomacy.* Baltimore: Johns Hopkins University Press, 1899.

Cánovas del Castillo, Antonio. *Historia de la decadencia en España desde el advenimiento de Felipe III al trono hasta la muerte de Carlos II.* 1st ed. 1854. Madrid: J. Ruiz, 1910.

Casas, Bartolomé de las. *Historia de las Indias.* 3 vols. México: Fondo de Cultura Económica, 1951.

Castro, Adolfo de. "La esclavitud en España," *La España moderna* (Madrid), IV, No. 1 (Febrero de 1892), 128–129.

Cepero Bonilla, Raúl. *Azúcar y abolición: Apuntes para una historia crítica de abolicionismo.* La Habana: Editorial Echevarría, 1948.

Christelow, Allan. "Contraband Trade between Jamaica and the Spanish Main, and the Free Port Act of 1766," *Hispanic American Historical Review*, XXII, No. 2 (May, 1942), 309–343.

Clarkson, Thomas. *The History of the Rise, Progress and Accomplishment of the Abolition of the African Slave Trade by the British Parliament* [to 1807]. 2 vols. in one. London: James P. Parke, 1808.

Crespo de la Serna, León. *Informe sobre las reformas políticas, sociales y económicas que deben introducirse en la isla de Cuba* (pamphlet). Presented to the Reform Commission of 1879. Paris: Impr. Hispano-Americana, 1879.

Corbitt, Duvon C. "Immigration in Cuba," *Hispanic American Historical Review*, XXII, No. 2 (May, 1942), 280–308.

Coupland, Sir Reginald. *The British Anti-Slavery Movement*. London: Oxford University Press, 1933.

Cruz Monclova, Lidio. *Historia de Puerto Rico (Siglo XIX)*. 3 vols. San Juan: Universidad de Puerto Rico, 1952–1957.

Dana, Richard Henry. *To Cuba and Back: A Vacation Voyage*. Boston: Houghton, Mifflin, 1859.

Davies, K. G. *The Royal African Company, 1672–1725*. London: Longmans, Green, 1957.

Deerr, Noel. *The History of Sugar*. 2 vols. London: Chapman and Hall, 1949–1950.

Díaz Soler, Luis. *La historia de la esclavitud negra en Puerto Rico*. San Juan: Universidad de Puerto Rico, 1952.

Domínguez Ortiz, Antonio. "La esclavitud en Castilla durante la edad moderna," *Estudios de Historia Social de España*. Madrid: Instituto Balmes de Sociología, 1952. II, 370–428.

Drake, Thomas E. *Quakers and Slavery in America*. New Haven: Yale University Press, 1950.

Dubois, W. E. B. *The Suppression of the African Slave Trade to the United States of America, 1638–1870*. 1st ed. 1896. New York: Social Science Press, 1954.

Dulce, Domingo. *Informe presentado por el Excmo. Sr. D. Domingo Dulce, marqués de Castellflorite, al ministro de ultramar en enero do 1867*. Madrid: Impr. Nacional, 1867.

Edwards, Bryan. *The History, Civil and Commercial, of the British West Indies*. London: J. Stockdale, 1801.

Ely, Roland T. *Cuando reinaba su majestad el azúcar. Estudio histórico-sociológico de una tragedia latinoamericana: El monocultivo en Cuba, origen y evolución del proceso*. Buenos Aires: Editorial Sudamericana, 1963.

Erénchun, Félix. *Anales de la isla de Cuba; diccionario administrativo, económico, estadístico y legislativo*. Año de 1865. 5 vols. La Habana: Impr. La Antill, 1865–1861.

Escalera, Evaristo y González Llana, Manuel. *La España del siglo XIX*. 4 vols. Madrid: M. González Llanos, 1864–1865.

España y el tráfico de negros, observaciones que dirige la Sociedad Británica y extranjera contra la esclavitud a Los Señores Españoles (pamphlet). Londres: British and Foreign Antislavery Society, 1862.

Esquerra del Bayo, J. *Parangón entre el esclavo y el proletario libre en el siglo XIX* (pamphlet). Madrid: n.p., 1856.

Estorch, Miguel. *Apuntes para la historia sobre la administración del marqués de la Pezuela en la isla de Cuba, desde 3 de diciembre de 1853 hasta 21 de setiembre de 1854.* Madrid: M. Galiano, 1856.

Ettinger, Amos Aschbach. *The Mission of Pierre Soulé.* New Haven: Yale University Press, 1932.

Fabié, Antonio María. *Mi gestión ministerial respecto á la isla de Cuba.* Madrid: Asilo de Huérfanos del Sagrado Corazón, 1898.

Feijóo de Sotomayor, Urbano. *Isla de Cuba. Inmigracion de trabajadores Españoles. Documentos y memoria* (pamphlet). Paris: Blondeau, 1852.

Ferrer de Couto, José. *Los negros en sus diversos estados y condiciones; tales como son, como se supone que son y como deben ser.* New York: Hallet Breen, 1864.

Figuera, Fermín. *Estudios sobre la isla de Cuba: La cuestión social* (pamphlet). Madrid: Sordo-mudos, 1866.

Foner, Philip S. *A History of Cuba and Its Relations with the United States.* Vol. I: 1492–1845; Vol. II: 1845–1895. New York: International Publishers, Inc., 1962.

Gallenga, Antonio Carlo Napoleone. *The Pearl of the Antilles.* London: Chapman and Hall, 1873.

García de Arboleya, José. *Manual de la isla de Cuba: Compendio de su historia, geografía, estadística y administración.* La Habana: Impr. del Gobierno, 1852.

Goicouria, Domingo. *Memorial presentado a Su Majestad por Don Domingo Goicouria para el aumento de la población blanca y la producción del azúcar en la isla de Cuba* (pamphlet). Madrid: J. M. Alegría, 1846.

Graham, Richard. "Causes for the Abolition of Negro Slavery in Brazil: An Interpretive Essay," *Hispanic American Historical Review*, XLVI, No. 2 (May, 1966), 123–137.

Griggs, Earl L. *Thomas Clarkson: The Friend of Slaves.* Ann Arbor: University of Michigan Press, 1938.

Guerra y Sánchez, Ramiro. *Azúcar y población en las Antillas.* La Habana: Cultural, S.A., 1935.

———. *La expansión territorial de los Estados Unidos a expensas de España y los países Hispanoamericanos.* La Habana: Cultural, S.A., 1939.

———. *La Guerra de Diez Años 1868–1878.* 2 vols. La Habana: Cultural, S.A., 1950.

———. *Manual de la historia de Cuba (económica, social y política).* La Habana: Cultural, S.A., 1938.

Gutiérrez de la Concha, José [Marqués de la Habana]. *Memoria sobre el estado político, gobierno y administración de la isla de Cuba.* Madrid: J. Trujillo, 1853.

———. *Memoria sobre el ramo de emancipados de la isla de Cuba, formado con motivo de la entrega del mando de la misma al Excmo. Sr. D. Francisco Serrano* (pamphlet). Madrid: M. Moreno Fernandez, 1861.

———. *Memoria sobre la guerra de la isla de Cuba y sobre su estado político y económico desde abril de 1874 hasta marzo de 1875.* Madrid: M. Moreno Fernández, 1875.

Helps, Sir Arthur. *The Conquerors of the New World and Their Bondsmen; Being a Narrative of the Principal Events Which Led to Negro Slavery in the West Indies and America.* 2 vols. London: W. Pickering, 1848–1852.

———. *The Spanish Conquest of America and its Relation to the History of Slavery and to the Government of Colonies.* 4 vols. London: J. W. Parker and Son, 1855–1861.

Hernández Inglesias, Fermín. *La esclavitud y el Señor Ferrer de Couto* (pamphlet). Madrid: Impr. Universal, 1866.

Hill, Lawrence F. "The Abolition of the African Slave Trade to Brazil," *Hispanic American Historical Review,* XI, No. 2 (May, 1931), 169–197.

Historia de la nación Cubana. Edited by Ramiro Guerra y Sánchez, José M. Pérez Cabrera, Juan J. Remos, and Emeterio S. Santovenia. 10 vols. La Habana: Cultural, S.A., 1952.

Howard, Warren S. *American Slavers and the Federal Law, 1837–1862.* Berkeley: University of California Press, 1963.

Humboldt, Alexander von. *The Island of Cuba.* Translated from the Spanish with notes and a preliminary essay by J. S. Thrasher. New York: Derby & Jackson, 1856.

Johnson, Willis F. *The History of Cuba.* 5 vols. New York: B. F. Buch & Co., 1920.

Juderías, Julián. *La leyenda negra.* 2nd. ed. Barcelona: Araluce, 1916.

Just, Ramón. *Las aspiraciones de Cuba* (pamphlet). París: Charles de Mourgues, 1859.

King, James F. "Evolution of the Free Slave Trade Principle in Spanish Colonial Administration," *Hispanic American Historical Review,* XXII, No. 1 (February, 1942), 34–56.

———. "The Latin-American Republics and the Suppression of the Slave Trade," *Hispanic American Historical Review,* XXIV, No. 3 (August, 1944), 387–411.

Klingberg, Frank J. *The Anti-Slavery Movement in England.* New Haven: Yale University Press, 1926.

Labra y Cadrana, Rafael María de. *La abolición de la esclavitud en el orden económico.* Madrid: J. Noguera, 1873.

———. *La abolición de la esclavitud en las Antillas españolas.* Madrid: J. E. Morete, 1869.

———. *América y la constitución española de 1812.* Madrid: Tip. Sindicato de Publicidad, 1914.

———. *La autonomia colonial* (pamphlet), Madrid: A. J. Alaria, 1883.

———. *La cuestión de Puerto Rico* (pamphlet). Madrid: J. E. Morete, 1870.

———. *La cuestión de Ultramar en 1871* (pamphlet). Primer discurso en el Congreso. Madrid: J. Noguera, 1871.

———. *España y América, 1812–1912.* Madrid: Tip. Sindicato de Publicidad, 1912.

——— (ed.). *La experiencia abolicionista de Puerto Rico.* Exposición de la Sociedad Abolitionista al Ministro de Ultramar. Madrid: Sociedad Abolicionista Española, 1874.

———. *El partido liberal de Cuba* (pamphlet). Madrid: J. Alaria, 1882.

———. *La política colonial y la revolución española de 1868* (pamphlet). Madrid: Alfredo Alonso, 1871.

———. *El problema colonial contemporáneo.* Por los Señores Labra, et al. Madrid: V. Suárez, 1879.

———. *La reforma política de Ultramar 1868–1900.* Madrid: Alfredo Alonso, 1902.

———. *La república y las libertades de Ultramar.* Madrid: Alfredo Alonso, 1897.

Latimer, Elizabeth Wormeley. *Spain in the 19th Century.* Chicago: A. C. McClurg, 1898.

López de Letona, Antonio. *Isla de Cuba: Reflexiones sobre su estado social y político y económico* (pamphlet). Madrid: J. M. Ducazal, 1865.

Llorente, Antonio G. *Cuba y el actual Ministro de Ultramar* (pamphlet). Madrid: Andrés Arejas, 1872.

Macinnes, C. M. *England and Slavery.* Bristol: J. W. Arrowsmith, 1934.

MacLachlan, Jean O. *Trade and Peace with Old Spain, 1667–1750. A Study of the Influence of Commerce on Anglo-Spanish Diplomacy in the First Half of the Eighteenth Century.* Cambridge: Cambridge University Press, 1940.

Madan, Cristóbal. *Llamamiento de la isla de Cuba a la nación española, dirigido al Excmo. e Illmo. Señor Don Baldomero Espartero, duque de la Victoria* (pamphlet). New York: Hallet, 1855.

Madariaga, Salvador de. *Spain.* London: Jonathan Cape, 1942.

Madden, Richard Robert. *The Island of Cuba. Its resources, progress, etc., in relation especially to the influence of its prosperity on the interests of the British West India Colonies.* London: C. Gilpin, 1849.

Mannix, Daniel P. *Black Cargoes: A History of the Atlantic Slave Trade, 1518–1865.* In collaboration with Malcolm Cowley. New York: Viking Press, 1962.
María, Jacinto. *Los voluntarios de Cuba y el Obispo de la Habana. Historia de ciertos sucesos por el mismo Obispo, Senador del Reino* (pamphlet). Madrid: D. A. Pérez Dubrull, 1871.
Martin, Percy A. "Slavery and Abolition in Brazil," *Hispanic American Historical Review,* XIII, No. 2 (May, 1933), 151–196.
Mathieson, William Law. *British Slavery and Its Abolition 1823–1838.* London: Longmans, Green and Co., 1926.
———. *Great Britain and the Slave Trade, 1839–1865.* London: Longmans, Green & Co., 1929.
Maura y Gamazo, Gabriel. *Historia crítica del reinado de Don Alfonso durante su menoridad.* 2 vols. Barcelona: Montaner y Simon, 1919–1925.
Mellafe, Rolando. *La esclavitud en Hispanoamérica.* Buenos Aires: Editorial Universitaria, 1964.
Menéndez y Pelayo, Marcelino. *Historia de los Heterodoxos españoles.* 5 vols. Madrid: Victoriano Suárez, 1928.
Montaos y Robillard, Francisco (Coronel de Caballería). *Proyecto de emancipación de la esclavitud en la isla de Cuba* (pamphlet). Madrid: José M. Ducazal, 1865.
Morales y Morales, Vidal. *Iniciadores y primeros mártires de la revolución cubana.* 2 vols. La Habana: Impr. Avisador Comercial, 1901.
Morris, Richard B. "The Measure of Bondage in the Slave States," *Mississippi Valley Historical Review,* XLI, No. 2 (September, 1954), 219–240.
Nevins, Allan. *Hamilton Fish: The Inner History of the Grant Administration.* New York: Dodd, Mead and Co., 1936.
O'Callaghan, Sean. *The Slave Trade Today.* New York: Crown Publishers, 1961.
O'Gaban, Juan Bernardo. *Observaciones sobre la suerte de los negros de Africa, considerados en su propia patria y reclamación contra el tratado celebrado con los Ingleses* (pamphlet). Madrid: Universal, 1821.
Oliva Bulnes, Juana H. "Labra en las Cortes españolas," *Revista Bimestre Cubana,* LXV, Nos. 1, 2, 3 (1950), 190–262.
Olmstead, Frederick Law. *A Journey in the Seaboard Slave States, with Remarks on Their Economy.* New York: Dix and Edwards, 1856.
Ortega Rubio, Juan. *Historia de España.* 8 vols. Madrid: Bailly Bailliere, 1920.
Ortiz Fernández, Fernando. *Cuban Counterpoint: Tobacco and Sugar.* Translated from the Spanish by Harriet de Onís. New York: A. Knopf, 1947.

———. *Hampa afro-cubana: Los negros esclavos. Estudio sociólogo y de derecho público*. La Habana: Revista Bimestre Cubana, 1916.

———. *José Antonio Saco y sus ideas*. La Habana: Revista Bimestre Cubana, 1929.

P. de Arrieta, P. *Cuestión de Cuba: Su salvación o su ruina* (pamphlet). Madrid: F. Nozal, 1879.

Paralelos: Independencia de Cuba 1821–1869 (pamphlet). New York: Hallet Breen, 1869. (Probably published by the Junta Revolucionaria Cubana.)

El Partido liberal de Cuba: La política en las Antillas (pamphlet). Madrid: J. Alaria, 1882.

Pazos y Roque, Felipe. "La economía cubana en el siglo XIX," *Revista Bimestre Cubana*, XLVII (enero–febrero, 1951), 83–106.

Pérez, Luis Marino. *Estudio sobre las ideas políticas de José Antonio Saco*. La Habana: Impr. Avisador Commercial, 1908.

Perojo, José de. *Cuestiones coloniales* (pamphlet). Madrid: Fernando Fe, 1883.

Pezuela y Lobo, Jacobo de la. *Crónica de las Antillas*. Madrid: Rubio, Grilo y Vitturi, 1871.

———. *Diccionario geográfico, estadístico, histórico de la isla de Cuba*. 4 vols. Madrid: Impr. del Mellado, 1863–1866.

———. *Ensayo histórico de la isla de Cuba*. New York: Impr. R. Rafael, 1842.

———. *Historia de la isla de Cuba*. 4 vols. Madrid: Baillière Hermanos, 1868–1878.

Pierson, William W. "Francisco Arango y Parreno," *Hispanic American Historical Review*, XVI (November, 1936), 451–478.

Piñyero, Enrique. *Como acabó la dominación de España en América*. Paris: Garnier Hermanos, 1908.

Pí y Margall, Francisco. *Las grandes conmociones políticas del siglo XIX en España*. 6 vols. Barcelona: Casa Editorial, 1934.

Pons y Umbert, Adolfo. *Cánovas del Castillo*. Madrid: M. G. Hernández, 1901.

Portell Vilá, Herminio. *Historia de Cuba en sus relaciones con los Estados Unidos y Espana*. 2 vols. La Habana: J. Montero, 1938.

———. *Narciso López y su época 1848–1850*. La Habana: Cultural, S.A., 1952.

Pozos Dulces, El Conde de (Frías y Jacott, Francisco). *La cuestión del trabajo agrícola y de la población en la isla de Cuba*. Paris: Impr. Jorge Kugelmann, 1860.

Rauch, Basil. *American Interest in Cuba: 1848–1850*. New York: Columbia University Press, 1948.

Rodríguez, Gabriel. *La idea y el movimiento antiesclavista en España durante el siglo XIX* (pamphlet). Contained in Manuel Escalera, *La España del siglo XIX*. Vol. III. Madrid: A. San Martín, 1886–1887.

Rodríguez, José Ignacio. *Estudio histórico sobre el origen, desenvolvimiento y manifestaciones prácticas de la idea de la anexión de la isla de Cuba a los Estados Unidos de America*. La Habana: Impr. la Propaganda Literaria, 1900.

Rodríguez Ecay, Francisco. *Compendio de la geografía de la isla de Cuba*. La Habana: Miguel de Villa, 1881.

Romero, Fernando. "The Slave Trade and the Negro in South America," *Hispanic American Historical Review*, XXIV, No. 3 (August, 1944), 368–386.

Rozalejo, Marqués de. *Cheste o todo un siglo 1809–1906: El Isabelino tradicionalista*. Madrid: Espasa-Calpe, 1935.

Ruiz García, Zoilo. *Nuestros hombres de antaño*. Mayaguez, Puerto Rico: Mayaguez Publishing Company, 1920.

Saco, José Antonio. *Colección de papeles científicos, históricos, políticos y de otros ramos sobre la isla de Cuba*. 4 vols. Paris: Impr. de d'Aubusson y Kugelmann, 1859.

———. *Contra la anexión*. A collection of Saco's papers with a prologue and commentaries by Fernando Ortiz. 2 vols. La Habana: Cultural, S. A., 1928.

———. *La esclavitud en Cuba y la revolución en España* (pamphlet). Madrid: Impr. La Política, 1868. There exists a French edition, also; *L'esclavage a Cuba et la revolución d'Espagne par José A. Saco*, Paris: E. Dentu, 1869.

———. *La historia de la esclavitud de la raza africana en el Nuevo Mundo y en especial en los países Américo-Hispanos*. Edited by Fernando Ortiz. 4 vols. La Habana: Cultural, S.A., 1938.

———. *La historia de la esclavitud de los Indios en el Nuevo Mundo*. 4 vols. La Habana: Cultural, S.A., 1932.

———. *La historia de la esclavitud desde los tiempos más remotos hasta nuestros días*. 3 vols. Paris: Tipografía la Hure, 1875.

Sagra, Ramón de la. *Cuba en 1860, o sea cuadro de sus adelantos en la población, la agricultura, el comercio y las rentas públicas, suplemento a la primera parte de la historia política y natural de la isla de Cuba*. Paris: L. Hachette y Cia, 1863.

———. *Estudios coloniales con aplicación a la isla de Cuba* (pamphlet). Madrid: D. Hidalgo, 1845.

———. *Historia económica-política y estadística de la isla de Cuba*. La Habana: Impr. de las viudas de Arazoza y Soler, 1831.

———. *Historia física, política y natural de Cuba*. 12 vols. Paris: A. Bertrand, 1838–1842.

Sánchez Albornoz, Claudio. *España: Un enigma histórico.* Buenos Aires: Editorial Sudamericana, 1958.

Sanguily y Garritte, Manuel. *Obras de Manuel Sanguily.* Edited by Manuel Sanguily y Arizte. 7 vols. La Habana: A. Dorrbecker, 1925–1930.

Sanromá, Joaquín María. *Mis memorias 1828–1868.* 2 vols. Madrid: Manuel G. Hernández, 1887 y 1894.

Scelle, Georges. "The Slave Trade in the Spanish Colonies," *American Journal of International Law.* IV, No. 3 (July, 1910), 612–661.

———. *La traite négrière aux Indes de Castille, contrats et traités d'assiento.* 2 vols. Paris: L. Larose & L. Tenin, 1906.

Serrano y Domínguez, Francisco. *Informe presentado por el Excmo. Sr. capitán general duque de la Torre al ministro de ultramar en mayo de 1867* (pamphlet). Madrid: Impr. de la Biblioteca Universal Económica, 1868.

Shafer, Robert J. *The Economic Societies in the Spanish World, 1763–1821.* Syracuse: Syracuse University Press, 1958.

Soulsby, Hugh G. *The Right of Search and the Slave Trade in Anglo-American Relations 1814–1862.* Baltimore: The Johns Hopkins Press, 1933.

Spears, John R. *The American Slave Trade: An Account of Its Origin, Growth, and Suppression.* New York: Ballantine Books, 1960.

Suárez Argudín, José. *Cuestión social* (pamphlet). La Habana: n.p., 1870.

———. *Proyecto de immigración africana. Para las islas de Cuba y Puerto Rico y el imperio del Brasil. Presentado a los respectivos gobiernos por los Sres. Argudín, Cunha Reis y Perdones* (pamphlet). La Habana: Impr. La Habanera, 1860.

Suárez Inclán, Estanislao. *El Gobierno del Ministerio presedido por el Sr. Posada Herrera con respecto a la administración de las provincias de Ultramar.* Madrid: T. Fontanet, 1884.

Swanberg, W. A. *Sickles the Incredible.* New York: C. Scribner's Sons, 1956.

Taylor, John Glanville. *The United States and Cuba: Eight Years of Change and Travel.* London: Richard Bentley, 1851.

Torrente, Mariano. *Bosquejo económico, político de la isla de Cuba.* Vol. I, Madrid: Impr. de M. Pita, 1852. Vol. II, La Habana: Impr. de Barcina, 1853.

———. *Cuestión importante sobre la esclavitud* (pamphlet). Madrid: Viuda de Jordan, 1841.

———. *Política ultramarina que abraza todos los puntos referentes a las relaciones con los Estados Unidos, con la Inglaterra, y las Antillas y señaladamente con la isla de Santo Domingo.* Madrid: Impr. de la Compañía General de Impresores y Libreros del Reino, 1854.

――――. *Slavery in the Island of Cuba, with Remarks on the Statements of the British Press Relative to the Slave Trade* (pamphlet). London: C. Wood, 1853.

Trollope, Anthony. *The West Indies and the Spanish Main.* New York: Harper Bros., ca. 1857.

Turnbull, David. *Travels in the West: Cuba, with Notices of Porto Rico and the Slave Trade.* London: Longman & Co., 1840.

Valiente, Porfirio. *Réformes dan les isles de Cuba et Porto-Rico.* Paris: A. Chaix et Cia., 1869.

Vásquez Queipo, Vicente. *Breves observaciones sobre las principales cuestiones que hoy se agitan respecto de las provincias ultramarinas* (pamphlet. Madrid: n.p., 1873.

――――. *Informe fiscal sobre fomento de la población blanca en la isla de Cuba y emancipación progresiva de la esclava* (pamphlet). Madrid: Impr. de J. M. Alegria, 1845.

Vega Cobiellas, Ulpiano. *Nuestra América y la evolución de Cuba.* La Habana: Cultural, S. A., 1944.

Villalba Hervás, Miguel. *De Alcolea a Sagunto.* Madrid: Victoriano Suárez, 1899.

Wurdermann, Dr. J. G. F. *Notes on Cuba, Containing an Account of Its Discovery and Early History; A Description of the Face of the Country, Its Population, Resources, and Wealth; Its Institutions and Manners and Customs of Its Inhabitants.* Boston: J. Munro and Co., 1844.

Zaragoza, Justo. *Las insurrecciones de Cuba. Apuntes para la historia política de esta isla en el presente siglo.* 2 vols. Madrid: Impr. de M. G. Hernández, 1872–1873.

GLOSSARY

adelantado: a frontier governor
a la moda: fashionable
alcabala: an excise tax
ambiente: the atmosphere
año milagroso: the year of miracles
arroba: a Spanish weight equal to twenty-five pounds
asiento: a royal permit, license, or contract to engage in colonial commerce
asimilación: the theory that overseas territories are not colonies but equal and integral parts of the Spanish kingdom
atracción: attraction or reconciliation
ayuntamiento: the municipal government
blanquear: whiten
bocoy: a large barrel
bozal: a slave proceeding from Africa
buena presa: a fair prize
cabildo: the city council
Casa de Contratación: the Spanish Board of Colonial Trade seated in Seville
Casino Español: the social and political center of Spanish merchants and other elements of the Spanish loyalist party in Cuba
cédulas personales: identification tags or documents
central: a large centralized mill using steam power
coartación: the procedure whereby a slave could purchase his freedom on the installment plan
coartado: a slave purchasing his freedom
compañeros: companions
comunicaciones: communications
Consulado de la Habana: the tribunal of commerce seated in Havana
criollo: a Creole
cuestión social, la: the social question of what to do about slavery
Diputación Provincial: a delegation of colonial representatives
duro: a Spanish coin roughly equivalent to a silver dollar
emancipado: a Negro from a captured slave ship, supposedly free by terms of the Anglo-Spanish treaty of 1817, also an unregistered slave supposedly freed by the Moret Law of 1870
esclavista: a defender of slavery

escribano: a notary
fiscal: as used in this study, a civil magistrate responsible for supervising the application of the laws
golpe de gracia: *coup de grace*
hacendado: as used in Cuba, a sugar planter
hacienda: a large grant of land, an estate, or a plantation used for agricultural or pastoral purposes
ingenio: a sugar plantation that usually included a mill
Junta de Fomento: the economic development board which in 1831 took over the functions of the Real Consulado de Agricultura y Comercio
Junta de Hacendados: an organization of Cuban sugar planters
Junta de Población Blanca: an organization for promoting white immigration
ladino: a Spanish-speaking slave
leyes especiales, las: the special laws in the direction of autonomy promised Cuba by the Spanish constitution of 1837
libertos: freedmen
mariage de convenance: a marriage for advantage (French)
mayordomo (mayoral): an estate manager or superintendent
muerte en garrote vil: death by strangling
negrero: a slave trader
nuevos ricos, los: *nouveaux riches*
Occidente: the administrative unit comprising the western half of Cuba
Oriente: the eastern half of Spanish territorial administration in Cuba
pacto borbónico: the Bourbon family compact arranging for a French prince to assume the Spanish crown
pases de tránsito: travel permits or passports
Patria Criolla, la: the Cuban fatherland
patrocinado: a young Negro, born free, but still under the care of his former master
patrón: a slaveowner converted into a protector of a free-born Negro by the Spanish abolition law of 1870
patronato: the tutelar or patronship system established by law of 1870
peligroso: dangerous
pena de azotes: punishment by the whip
peninsular: a Spanish citizen or immigrant proceeding from the Iberian Peninsula
pico de oro, el: the golden beak, a simile from Spanish cockfights meaning a man of great eloquence in debate
piezas: [African] slaves
plaza sitiada: a besieged fortress
política de atracción: a policy of attraction directed toward disaffected Creoles

Glossary

potestad domínica: the paternal authority over slaves vested in slaveholders by the civil laws
privilegio de ingenios: the sixteenth-century protective legislation for the Cuban sugar industry providing for entailed estates
pronunciamiento: an insurgent declaration in favor of a new plan of government
Real Sociedad Patriótica: the semiofficial society established in 1794 to promote scientific and practical knowledge
reformista: a reformist
reglamento: regulations governing the application of the Moret Law of gradual emancipation
Revolución Gloriosa, la: the Spanish liberal triumph of September 18, 1868
se obedecen pero no se cumplen: the laws are obeyed but not fulfilled
siglistas: supporters of the Creole reformist newspaper *El Siglo*
sitios de labor: small farms often worked on sharecropper basis
trapiche: a small sugar mill usually moved by animal power
vega: a tobacco farm or plantation usually worked by one family
vientre libre: the free birth of slaves
vocal: a councilman or a voting member of an assembly
yanqui: a Yankee imperialist, filibuster, or intruder

INDEX

Aberdeen, Lord (George Hamilton Gordon): and Turnbull, 77; and slave registry, 79
Aberdeen Act: and Brazilian traffic, 90
Abolicionista Español, El: 220
abolition of slavery: and discussion of sources, xiii–xvi; and international movement, 17–20; and Haiti, 18; and American Constitution, 18; and England, 18; and British law of 1807, 19–20; and project of Guridi, 22–23; of Argüelles, 23; of Antollón, 25; and resolution of Vienna, 26; and treatry series, 28–32; of Valera, 37–38; and treaty of 1835, 61–62; and abolition decree of 1836, 63–64; and British proposal of 1840, 69–70; and slave registry crisis, 73–74; in French West Indies, 100; and Cuban annexation, 98–104; and Pezuela's measures, 115–123; and Cuban exiles, 124–125; and Concha's measures, 126–127; and American Civil War, 144–149; and abolition plans of 1865–1866, 149–150, 151; and Spanish Abolitionist Society, 154–161; and Puerto Ricans, 154–161, 202; and United States, 154–163; and law of 1866, 176–181; and Reform Commission, 192–205, 214; and Glorious Revolution, 217–221; and rebel abolition, 224–227, 232; and Moret Law, 243–244, 252–282; and confiscated slaves, 279–281; and military service, 281; and judgment of Latimer, 293; and Peace of Zanjón, 295; and Liberal-Autonomists, 297; and sub-commission of 1879, 300–301; and law of 1880, 301–309; and Alfonso XIII, 302; and abolition of stocks and irons (1883), 311; and abolition of patronato, 311–312; and effect on Spanish dominion, 312–313. SEE ALSO British abolitionism; British government; Cuban slave trade; Cuban slavery; *emancipados;* piracy declaration; Spanish government

Abolitionist: and Vizcarrondo, 158
abolitionist arguments: and slave rebellions, 33, 37, 83–84; and abolitionist examples of Haiti, 58, 300; and white labor, 66, 83–84, 136; and foreign intervention, 83, 178–179, 310; and treaty obligation, 165–166, 178, 201, 256; and cruel treatment, 165–166, 309; and Papal prohibition, 165; of Lincoln, 165, 250; and suicides, 166, 249; and progress, 169, 196–197, 218, 249–250, 256, 269; and foreign abolitionism, 196–197, 256; and enlightenment, 203; and moral obligation, 203; and Christianity, 203, 249, 269; and economic advantage, 210, 221; and humanity, 210, 249; and civilization, 218, 269; and capacity of Negro, 221; of Toussaint L'Ouverture, 250; of Wilberforce, 250; of Phillips Wendell, 250; of United States, 250, 300; of Brazil, 250, 300; of England, 250; of France, 250; and Cuban insurrection, 256; and commercial benefits, 256; and failure of Moret Law, 282; and *emancipados,* 282; and Glorious Revolution, 282; and national honor, 282; of Jamaica, 300

abolitionist deputies: and law of 1880, 309
abolitionist petitions: 299
abolitionist question: and Spanish conservatism, 22; and Cuban insurrection, 231; and Liberal-Autonomists, 297

Abolition Society. SEE Spanish Abolition Society
absolutists: and Glorious Revolution, 217
Academy of Jurisprudence (Madrid): and Spanish abolitionism, 162; and abolition meeting, 219
Acosta, José Julián: and Abolition Society, 154; and Puerto Rican liberalism, 155, 156–157; and abolition, 192–194, 195, 202, 214; and reform reaction, 212–214; and Puerto Rican abolition law, 290
Act of 1837: and colonial exclusion, 187. SEE "Special Laws"
Act of 1845: 91
Additional Article of 1880 law: 303
adelantados: 22
administrative committees; and law of 1880, 307
Admiralty Courts. SEE mixed commissions
Africa: and slave trade, xi; and coast guard, 94, 96; and Moret Law, 275–278; and contract labor, 303
African "apprentices": and Pezuela's measures, 116–117; and traffic, 143
African immigration: in abolition plans, 149–150; and reform commission, 189
African Institution: and English abolitionists, 19
African labor: and missionaries, 4
African *piezas* (slaves): 6
African slave trade: and Old World beginnings, xi, xii; and today, xi; and New World, 3–5; and English abolitionism, 18; and joint resolution of Vienna, 26; and British policy, 31; and Quakers, 168. SEE ALSO Cuban slave trade
African slavery: beginnings in the New World, 3–4, 24; in Spain, 4–5; and Congress of Berlin, 299. SEE ALSO Cuban Slavery
Africanization of Cuba: and Pezuela, 115, 117–118, 120–121; and Davis report, 119; and annexation, 122; and free African immigration, 150; and slave trade, 196; and Cuban abolition plan, 203; and boycott, 203
Agramonte, Eduardo: 279

Agreement of 1810: 31
Agüero, Pedro María de: and annexation, 102; and confiscated slaves, 279
Aguilera, Francisco Vincente: 279
Aimes, Hubert S.: on slave imports, 43, 66; on slave trade, 63; on O'Donnell, 88; on slave landings, 183
Alabama claims: 235
Alarcón, Pedro A.: and law of 1866, 178; and reform question, 179–180
Albacete, Salvador: and confiscated slaves, 280; and abolition, 301
Albaida, el Marqués de: 154
alcabala (excise tax): 25
Alcocer: 288
Alcoy, Conde de (Federico Roncali): and emanicpation, 93; administration (1848–1850), 93–94; on Cuban exiles, 100; and slave trade, 104, 107; on conservation of Cuba, 101, 113
Aldama, Miguel de: and annexation, 100; and *El Siglo,* 133; and Saco, 188; and abolition policy, 225; and his slaves, 225; and Cuban insurrection, 229; and liberal-autonomist movement, 296
Alfonso, José Luis: and annexation, 102, 100; and reforms, 133; and Dulce, 230
Alfonso XII: and Glorious Revolution, 216; and restored monarchy, 293; and abolition promise, 300
Allen, William: 144
Almendares, Marqués de: named reform commissioner, 189; on whip, 200
Alsop, Robert: 144
Alvarado, Pedro de: in Cuba, 9
Amadeo de Savoy, Don: as constitutional monarch of Spain, 264–265; and Moret Law, 266–273; and Sickles' opinion, 271; and Puerto Rican abolitionists, 282; abdication of (1873), 288
Ambrose, Saint: 170–171
American abolitionists: and Cuban independence, 99; and Moret Law, 247; and Spanish government, 269
American abolitionist societies: 300
American citizens: and Cuban rebels, 283

Index

American Civil War: influence on Cuban abolition, 81, 161; and Cuban economy, 138, 183; and Cuban traffic, 139, 144; and Creole abolitionism, 142, 149; and Spanish policy, 145, 149, 175; effect on Cuban slavery, 134–146; and Spanish abolitionism, 152, 161, 210, 250; and Puerto Rico, 155, 289; and belligerency question, 235–236; and Moret Law, 250, 258
American claims: 235
American colonies: as reform examples, 274
American Congress: and Cuban propaganda, 100; and opinion of Calderón; and Cuban insurrection, 233; and protest of Moret Law, 260; and Cuban crisis (1871), 268; and Hayes' message of 1877, 293
American Constitution: and abolition of slavery, 17–18
American deputies: distrust of, 64
American diplomacy. SEE Fish; Grant; United States
American expansionists: 260
American filibusters: 102–104
American flag: SEE flag problem
American foreign policy. SEE United States
American government: and British abolitionists, 270; and Spanish Liberals, 272. SEE ALSO United States
American merchants: and Cuba, 80
American market: and Cuban demands, 303. SEE ALSO Cuban commerce
American North: and Pezuela administration, 115; and filibusters, 123; and Cuban exiles, 124–125; and Concha, 125; and Creole reformism, 140–142, 207; and Cuban sugar, 141; and Spanish policy, 161; and Spanish abolitionism, 209, 245. SEE ALSO American South; United States
American papers: and Spanish diplomacy, 244
American press: and Moret Law, 260
American public opinion: and Fish's demands, 269; and colonial reform, 274; and Cuban rebels, 251, 283
American Quakers: 168

American Republic: and Spanish Republic, 289
American Revolution: 17–18
American ships: in Cuban traffic, 62–63, 94, 144. SEE ALSO flag problem
American shipping: 267
American slavers. SEE American ships
American South: as sugar competitor, 48; and annexation of Cuba, 114; and Pezuela administration, 116; and Cuban exiles, 124–125; and Concha, 125; and Creole reformism, 140–142, 207; and Cuban sugar, 141; as Bastille of slavery, 161; and Spanish policy, 161; and belligerency question, 235, 236; and Cuban abolition question, 300, 305
American tariff: and Cuban demands, 303. SEE ALSO Cuban commerce
American warships: 267
amnesty: and Cuban insurrection, 230, 234; and Peace of Zanjón, 295
Anglo-Brazilian treaty: 31
Anglophile: and Cuban liberalism, 51
Anglo-Portuguese treaty of 1817: and traffic, 31
Anglo-Spanish diplomacy: and the United States, 98
Anglo-Spanish treaty of 1814: 28
Anglo-Spanish treaty of 1817. SEE treaty of September 23, 1817
Angulo de Heredia, José M.: elected to reform commission, 187; and piracy declaration, 196; and gradual abolition, 196–197, 200
Annam: and Cuban reforms, 303
annexation (to United States): and Cuban slavery, 84; and Pezuela's mission, 114; and American reaction, 116–120; and Concha's policy, 123–125; and Reform Commission, 187–188
annexationist movement: emergence of, 65; and propaganda, 98–99, 100; development of, 98–104; and Lopez expeditions, 102–103; and Saco's opposition, 101–102; and failure, 124; and abolition threat, 221; and Grant administration, 236
annexationist party: 210
Annobon (island): and slave trade, 8
anticlerical reforms: 21

anticlericalism: and Spanish abolitionism, 169–171
anti-Spanish Party: 180
Antilles: and Cuban traffic, 144
Antillian commissioners: and election of 1866, 186
Antillón, Isidro: and abolition, 22, 25
Aponte, José Antonio: 46
apostles: and abolition debate, 289
Arango y Parreño, Francisco de: and Cuban progress, 13–14; against abolition, 24, 37; and free white labor, 24, 33; and economic concessions, 32; as commissioner of arbitration, 40; on slave code, 53; and agricultural interests, 56; against traffic, 57; and *Report on Fugitive Slaves* (1796), 165
Archbishop of Cuba: and illegal slave trade, 43
archives: discussion of, xiv–xvi
Argentina: and abolition, 30; and piracy declaration, 121
Argentine Confederation: 32
Argudín, José Suárez: on African labor, 139; and abolition plan, 150; named reform commissioner, 189; against abolition, 201
Argüelles, Agustín: and abolition project, 23; and colonial exclusion, 64; and Moret project, 257
Aristotle: and Inquisition, 20–21; and abolition question, 164, 167, 171
Armas, Manuel de: elected to Reform Commission, 187; and Puerto Rican abolition, 195
Armas y Céspedes, Francisco: 165
armistice: and Grant's Cuban policy, 234
Arrazola, Lorenzo (ministry): 154
Arrow (English steamer): and French revolution of 1848, 100
Article Four (of law of 1880): 309
Article Seven (of 1817 treaty): and *emancipado* problem, 40–43; and Treaty of 1835, 61
Article Nine (of law of 1845): and contraband slaves, 86; and slave registry, 118
Article Twenty-eight: and slave registry, 1886, 181
Article Eighty (of the Constitution of the Monarchy): and Reform Commission of 1866, 190
Artimé y Gassett, Eduardo: and Sickles' advice, 273–274; and Moret Law 276; against Puerto Rican reforms, 283
Asiatics: and Peace of Zanjón, 295
Asiatic cholera: of 1833–1834, 60; and Chinese labor, 210
Asiatic colony: 210
Asiatic immigration: 189, 191
Asiatic labor: number in 1862, 146; and Spanish policy, 179; reform questionaire of 1866, 192; and Reform Commission, 198–199
asiento system: and slave trade, 5–8, in abolition debate, 289
asimilación: 132, 210
Aspinwall, Colonel Lloyd (American ship): detention of, 251
Association against the Slave Trade (1865): rejected, 176; and Reform Commission, 198
Atlantic slave trade: and Portuguese, xi–xii; and the United States, 147
Augustine, Saint: and Spanish abolitionism, 169; and Puerto Rican abolition, 289
Austria: and abolition, 26; and abolition agreement, 32
autonomist doctrines: and legality question, 310
autonomist propaganda: 298
Autonomista, El: 303
autonomy: and law of 1880, 303. See also Liberal-Autonomists
Ayala y Herrera, Abelardo López de: and Colonial reform, 218; and Spanish reaction, 227–228
Ayuntamiento Constitucional (Havana): and Cortes of 1820–1822, 36–38; and threat of rebellion, 71
Ayuntamiento de la Habana: 24, 71
Azcárate, Nicolás: elected to reform commission, 186; and Puerto Rican abolition, 194–196; on slave labor, 199–200; on the whip, 200

Balaguer, Victor: 299
Baker and Dawson: and *asiento*, 8
Baldorioty, Román: and abolition movement, 154; and Puerto Rican

Index

liberalism, 156–157; and Moret Law, 249
Balmes, Jaime: on Spanish Civilization, 20–21; and Spanish conscience, 168; on Christian slavery, 170
Baltimore: and Quaker petition, 269
Baltimore Clipper (newspaper): 104
Banks, Nathaniel: 268
Barbadoes: slave population of, 13, 45; sugar export of, 45
Barcelona: and American trade, 12; and Abolition Society, 158
Barcelona merchants: and flour trade, 174; and tariff, 311
Barras y Prado, Antonio de las: on Creole abolitionism, 129; on Civil War, 142
Barzanallana, Marqués de: 288
Battle of Gettysburg: and Spanish policy, 161
Becerra, Manuel: and Spanish Abolition Society, 154; on Glorious Revolution, 219; and sale of Cuba, 235; his reform policy, 239–243; his resignation, 243
Becker y González, Jerónimo: and Spanish diplomacy, xv; on Spanish slavery, 312
beeswax: exported to Mexico, 10
beet sugar: 48, 134
belligerent rights: and Grant administration, 234–237; and insurrection, 235–236; and Spanish diplomacy, 236; and crisis of 1870, 251–252; and Moret Law, 260; and Cuban rebels, 283
Belvís. See Ruiz Belvis
Benedict XIV, Pope: cited in abolition debate, 165; and slave trade, 174, 197–198
Bentham, Jeremy: and abolitionism, 18
Bergier, Abbot: 170
Berlin: and Creole reformism, 130
Bernal, Calixto: abolition plan of, 149; and Abolition Society, 154; elected to reform commission, 186; and elections of 1879 and 1881, 298
"besieged fortress": 179–180
Betances, Ramón Emeterio: 214
Betancourt, José Ramón: 298
Betancourt Cisneros, Gaspar (*El Lugareño*): and annexation, 98, 102, 124; on traffic, 111

Bible: and abolitionist question, 165
Bishop of Havana: 43
Bishop of Oxford: 123
Bismarck, Prince: 299
"Black hysteria": 77–78
Black Republic: 77–78
black slavery. See African slavery; Cuban slavery
Black Warrior (American ship): and Pezuela, 120; and Soulé, 120
Blanco, Ramón (governor): and distrust of Cuban deputies, 299; on immediate abolition, 301; and British Negroes, 304; and law of 1880, 307
Bolívar, Simón: and abolition, 30; and Cuban planters, 51; and Cuban insurrection, 224
Bona, Félix: 154
Bossuet, Jacques: on slavery, 171
Bourbon Family Pact: and *asiento*, 7
Bourbon Monarchy: and Glorious Revolution, 216; and Amadeo de Savoy, 268
boycott: and Cuban abolition plan, 203; and American pressure, 285
bozales: abuse of, 85; increase of, 105; and "new measures", 113; price of, 1845–1860, 135; and shareholding company, 143
Brazil: and Anglo-Brazilian agreement of 1810, 31; of 1826, 31; and flag problem, 31; as abolition example, 38, 97, 149, 198, 209; and sugar production, 45; and slave population, 45, 89; and Cuban competition, 48, 140; and slave trade, 53; and slave treatment, 53; and Saco, 58; and slave imports, 80; in abolition question, 87; and British abolitionism, 89; and *emancipado* problem, 90; and law of 1831, 90; and coast guard, 94; and Cuban traffic, 112, 144; and piracy declaration, 121; and Russell's proposal, 127; and Puerto Rico, 156; and Moret Law, 261, 267; and Cuban abolition question, 290, 300, 312; and Monarchy, 312
Brazilian parliament: and law of September 4, 1850, 97
Brazilian slave markets: 31

Brazilian vessels: British seizure of, 90
Breda (Netherlands): 5
Brewster de Vizcarrondo, Harriet: and Puerto Rican abolitionism, 157; and Abolition Society, 159
Britain. SEE British government
British abolition bill of 1807: 23
British abolitionism: and international movement, 17–20; and Spanish resistance to, 24, 25–28, 33–34, 143–145; Cuban resistance to, 37–38; and Brazil, 89; and Cuban independence, 99; and pressure on Spain, 122, 143, 294, 299; compared to Spain, 167; and Moret Law, 247, 259–260, 266–267; and *emancipados*, 267; and Granville's policy, 270; compared to Americans, 300. SEE ALSO British abolitionists; British abolitionism; British government; *emancipados*; foreign abolitionism; piracy declaration
British and Foreign Missionary Society: and exposition of 1855, 122
British Antislavery Society: 270
British authorities: and contract labor, 304
British commissioners: and treaty of 1817, 36; and report on traffic, 39. SEE ALSO British government
British consuls. SEE British government
British cruisers: and abolition treaties, 39; and slave imports, 54, 118; and flag problem, 60; and American seizures, 63; and Africa, 96; and Brazil, 97; and captures, 1824–1841, 79
British diplomacy. SEE British government
British government: abolition, and law of 1807, 19–20; and Congress of Vienna, 19, 25–27; and Arguelles proposal, 23; and Treaty of Paris, 25; of 1817, 28–29; and colonial possessions, 30; and treaty chain, 30, 96; and Portugal, 30–31; and Congress of Verona, 31; and diplomatic method, 31–32, 96; and patrol, 61–62; and diplomatic pressure, 31–32, 34, 40–43; and Brazil, 31, 90–91, 97; and right of search, 32, 61, 78, 127–128; and Cortes of 1820–1822, 36–38; and enforcement demands, 35, 59, 60–61, 69; and *emancipado*

problem, 40–43, 276–277; and proposed treaty of 1840, 69–74; and slave registry crisis, 73–74; and Turnbull, 75–77; and American fears, 77–78; and Aberdeen's Policy, 79; and law of 1845, 85–88; and frustrations, 94–95; and American threats, 98–100, 267, 270; and joint intervention (1852), 103, 112; and Pezuela's opinion, 107; and free African labor, 111, 136, 150; and Pezuela's abolition efforts, 113–123; and Concha's, 123–128; and proposed international agreement of 1860, 127–128, 143; and abolition pressure, 143, 175–176, 267–270, 294, 299; and Dulce's policy, 148; and Puerto Rican traffic, 156; and law of 1866, 181; and Spanish liberals, 219; and belligerency question, 235; and cooperation with American policy, 244–245, 269, 281; and Moret Law, 259–260; and census problem, 263–264; and support for Spain, 267, 270, 293; and Granville's policy, 270; and abolition law of 1880, 306. SEE ALSO British Abolitionism; *emancipados*; Spanish government; treaty
British Honduras: 67
British legation: and Brazilian abolition, 89
British market for Cuban sugar: 46, 140
British merchants: and *asiento*, 7; and Cuba, 10
British Negroes: and Turnbull, 77; and contract labor, 304
British Parliament: figures on slave trade, 54, 88–89; and slave sugar, 89; and abolition policy, 95–96, 145. SEE ALSO British government
British planters: and abolitionism, 19–20, 26, 60, 89; and cheap labor, 67, 87; and *emancipados*, 68
British slave trade: and abolitionists, 13, 19; and planter's interests, 19
British squadrons. SEE British cruisers
British West Indies: and Cuban competition, 14; cited in slave debates, 28; and abolition of 1833, 30, 69; and slave conservation, 36
Broglie, Count of: 200

Buchanan, James: and Cuban acquisition, 99, 120, 132; and British threat, 117; as president, 126; and Cuban affairs, 126
Bugallal, Saturnino Alvarez: on American pressures, 288; on German philosophy, 289
Bulwer, Sir Henry Lytton: expelled from Spain, 96; and American policy, 99
Bunch, Robert: on General Dulce, 148
Buxton: 288

Caballero, Fermín: 154
Caballero, José de la Luz: 76
Caballero de Rodas, Antonio: and Glorious Revolution, 217; on significance of rebel abolition, 227; for *vientre libre*, 227; named governor, June, 1869, 231; and Spanish volunteers, 231; 2nd Moret Law, 255-262; his resignation, 262; and Cuban insurrection, 267; and confiscated slaves, 279, 281; against Puerto Rican abolition, 287
Cádiz: monopoly of 12; and revolution, 216-217
Calatrava (Spanish minister): 66
Calderón, Marqués de: 309
Calderón de la Barca, Angel: 103-104
Calhoun, John C.: and Cuban policy, 78; and "Black Republic" scare, 78; and Cuban reform demands, 207
Callahan, James Morton: on Spanish procrastination, 47; on Cuban government, 49
Camaguey (province): and sugar, 224
Comejo, Augustín: 186
Canada: and Cuban reform 65, 206, 303; and belligerency question, 235
Canary Islands: and labor experiment, 108; and Cuban traffic, 144; and literacy question, 221; and immigration, 303
Caneja, Emilio (governor): 310
Cañedo, Valentín: and Pezuela, 115
Canga Argüelles, José: 64
Cánovas del Castillo, Antonio: on Spanish decadence, 31, 167; and colonial policy, 175-181, 185; and American government, 176-177; and law of 1866, 177-181; and colonial reform, 180, 184-186, 190; and eventual abolition, 192; and Unionists, 217; against colonial reform, 243; and Moret Law, 238, 243: and Cuban problem, 265; and Prim, 265; against Puerto Rican reform, 283; and re-established monarchy, 293; and Conservative Party of Cuba, 297; resignation of, 1879, 299; and return to power, 304; against economic concessions, 304; and abolition of stocks and irons, 311
Canning, George: at Congress of Verona, 31; and abolition proposals, 31
capital: and sugar production, 48-51
capitation taxes: and slave procreation, 87-88; and census problem, 277
Caracas Company: 8
Carden, Lionel: on census problem, 277; on *coartación*, 308; on Chinese, 308
Cardenal, Manuel: 257
Cárdenas, Cuba (jurisdiction): and slave insurrection, 87; and Creole conspiracy, 99
Caribbean: and slave trade, 3-9; and British abolition, 89; and status quo, 112
Carlisle, Lord: and British policy, 123
Carlist revolt: and Spanish politics, 21, 64, 66, 84, 215
Carrasco, Antonio: 290
Carrera, Manuel de: and annexation, 100
Casa de Caridad de San Ildefonso: and Vizcarrondo, 157
Casa de Contratación and *asiento* control, 4, 6
Castañón, Gonzalo: 268
Casino Español: in Cuba, 50
Cass, Lewis: and right of search, 78, 147; and Russell's proposal, 128; and Spanish policy, 128
Castañón, Gonzalo: 268
Caste War: and Yucatecs, 109
Castelar, Emilio: and liberalism, 150; and Spanish abolitionism, 54, 169; and anticlericalism, 171; and Glorious Revolution, 217; and Moret Law, 249-250; and Sickles, 272; and Puerto Rican abolition, 286-290; and Spanish Republic, 289
Castellanos, Julian: and abolition, 198
Castleraegh, Viscount (Robert Stew-

art): and British abolition policy, 17, 19, 26–27
Castrillón, Manuel: 276
Castro, Alejandro de: and closing traffic, 182–183; and reform commission of 1866, 189–190, 194, 201, 208, 210–212, 215
Castro, Alvaro de (dean): 4
Cataluña (region in Spain): 108
Catholic amendment: and law of 1880, 305
Catholic church: and Negro slavery, 166–167; and abolitionist conscience, 166–171; and Indian rights, 167; and Protestantism, 168–169
Catholic clergy: and slave trade, 88; as slave holders, 166; and religious instruction, 166–167, 199–200; as abolitionist, 166–167, 169–171; and reform commission of 1867, 199–200; and law of 1880, 305
Catholic countries: 250
Catholic education: 199
Catholic immigration: decree of October 21, 1817, 32
Catholic Kings: 20
Catholic people: 250, 289
Catholic Truths: 165
Catholicism: and immigration, 32; and abolition, 168–171, 197–198, 289–290; and law of 1880, 305; and Spanish slavery, 312
Ceballos, Francisco de: 276
cédulas of identity: and abolition, 312
cédulas personales: and Concha, 126
censorship: and Puerto Rico, 155, 157; and reform commission of 1866, 189; and autonomists, 248–299, 310
census: of 1792, 12; of 1817, 44–45; of 1862, 136; of 1862, 146; of 1870, 263; of 1871, 277; of 1877, 295; of 1878, 294; and Cuban economy, 295
census problem: 263, 275–278
Central America: and American fears, 77–78
Central Committee of Havana: and law of 1880, 306
Central Junta: and Moret Law regulations, 275–276
central sugar refineries (centralization): 138–140
Cepero y Bonilla, Raúl: on Creole reformism, 57, 140–142; on Pozos Dulces, 140–142
certificates of liberty: and Moret Law regulations, 275–278
Céspedes, Carlos Manuel: and Cuban republic, 222–223; and abolition policy, 224–226; and Dulce's conciliation, 230; and Morales Lemus, 231; and Western planters, 240; and Moret Law, 260; and confiscated slaves, 279
Charles III: 12
Charles IV: and slave code of 1789, 52
Chile: and abolition, 30
China: and immigration, 303
Chinese coolies: and British planters, 67; as contract labor, 109, 113; opinion of, 109–110, 137–138; and experiments with, 110, 137–138; treatment of, 110, 137–138, 150; numbers of, 111, 136, 137, 184; and decrees of 1854, 111; and Pezuela's policy, 116; and free African labor, 123; and registry, 126; and planter demands, 135–136; and vagrancy, 136; and vacillating policy, 137–138; and Treaty of Tientsin, 138; and closing of traffic, 184; and reform question, 190–191, 193; and crime rate, 221; and Moret project, 258; and *emancipado* problem, 267
Chinese immigration: proposed, 88; forbidden, 137; reopened, 137
Chinese labor. See Chinese coolies
Christian doctrine: and slave labor, 88
Christian sentiment: and Puerto Rican abolition, 289, 290. See also Catholicism
Christian missionaries: and suppression of traffic, 96
Christianity: and Indian labor, 3, 4; and Spanish decadence, 21; and Spanish abolition, 158, 168–171; and abolitionist question, 199–200, 250; and slave labor, 200; and Quaker petition, 269; and Spanish slavery, 312. See also Catholicism
cholera: 263
Cienfuegos (district): 278
Cienfuegos Jovellanos, José (governor): and Junta de Población Blanca, 33; and census of 1817, 43
Circo Price, El: 219

Index

343

circular of October 27, 1868: on colonial reforms, 218–219
civil codes: SEE codes
Clarendon, Lord (George William Frederick Villiers): and Moret Law, 259–260
Claret, Padre Antonio María (Bishop of Santiago): and Pezuela's abolition policy, 115; and slave welfare, 166
Clarkson, Thomas: and British abolitionism at Vienna, 19; and Treaty of 1817, 29
clergy: SEE Catholic clergy
Club de la Habana, El: and annexation, 99–100; and López, 103
coartación (manumission process): explanation of, 52; and slave code of 1842, 75; in abolition plans, 175; and abolition question, 192, 205, 287; and law of 1880, 308
coartados (freed slaves): and opinion of Turnbull, 52
codes, civil and criminal: and reform, 207, 221. SEE ALSO Cuban reform
coffee: in early Cuba, 10–12; and immigrants, 33, 109; census of 1817, 45; production of (1825–1850), 48; figures for (1817–1846), 80; and census of 1862 and 1877, 295
Coleridge, Samuel Taylor: 19
Coll y Toste, Cayetano: 161
Colomé, Juan A: 264
Columbus, Christopher: and slaving example, 3, 5; and Spanish policy, 47; and Spanish reactionaries, 223; and Puerto Rican abolition debate, 289
colonial abolitionists: 311
colonial bureaucracy: 264–265
colonial deputies. SEE Cuban deputies; Puerto Rican abolitionists
colonial government. SEE Cuban government.
Colonial League (Liga Ultramarina): against Puerto Rican abolition, 286, 287–290; and truce with reformers, 290
colonial legislation (Spanish): 271
colonial ministry. SEE Ministry of Colonies
colonial problem: and the Spanish Cortes, 177; and suppressing traffic, 1865–1866, 176–181. SEE ALSO Moret Law
Colonial Reform Commission (Junta de Información de Ultramar): announcement of, 177; opened November 25, 1865, 185; and colonial reform question, 189–214; and government agenda, 190–193; and Puerto Rican abolition, 193–195; and slave trade, 197; and reports of Dulce and Serrano, 208–210; and failure of independence movement, 213–214; and abolition movement, 214; and Glorious Revolution, 219; and colonial reforms, 239–242; and reactionaries of 1870, 243; and Liberal-Autonomists, 297
colonization. SEE white immigration
commerce. SEE Cuban commerce
commissary judge: 40
commissioner of arbitration: 40
Committee Report (January 29, 1867): on slave trade and Spanish policy, 197–199
Committee on Moret Law: 247–248
Committee of Slaveholders: 258
Comte, Auguste: 169
Comuneros, Los: 288
Concha, Jose de la. SEE Gutierrez de la Concha, José
Condorcet, Marquis de (Jean Antoine Nicolas): 18
confiscated slaves: and rebel abolition, 226, 280; in abolitionist arguments, 282
Congress of Berlin: and abolition, 299
Congress of Verona: 31
Congress of Vienna: and slave trade, 17, 26; and English abolitionists, 19
Conservative Party of Cuba: and Spanish Party, 296–297; and Conservative Party of Spain, 296–297; and autonomists, 297; and election of 1879, 298; and economic concessions, 303
Conspiración de la Escalera, La: 81
conspiración de la mina de la Rosa Cubana, la: and annexation, 99
Conspiracy of José Antonio Aponte: 46; and Spanish liberals of 1868, 216
Constitutional Cortes of 1869. SEE Glorious Revolution
Constitution of 1869: 245

constitutional monarchy: and Glorious Revolution, 216–217; and Amadeo of Savoy, 265
Constitutional Union Party. SEE Conservative Party of Cuba
Consulado (de la Habana): against abolition, 24; in Cortes of 1820–1822, 36–38
Consulado Real, El: 71
contraband: and slave trade, 5, 6, 27; and *asiento*, 7; as safety valve, 8; in treaty of 1817, 29
contraband slaves: and Treaty of 1845, 86; and decree of 1854, 119
contract labor: promotion of, 108–110, 111; failure of, 110; and Pezuela administration, 116; and mixed system, 138; and abolition question, 179; and *emancipados*, 267; and effects of insurrection, 295–296; and abolition law of 1880, 304. SEE ALSO Chinese coolies
contractors *(patron)*: 278–279
coolie labor. SEE Chinese coolies
Cooper, Joseph: 144
Cordero, Rafael: 129
Corn Laws: and Cuban sugar, 84
corporal punishment: and slave code of 1789, 52, 85; and slave code of 1842, 75; and regulation of 1849 (coolie), 110; and reform questionnaire of 1866, 192; and abolition question, 200; and Serrano's report, 210; and Moret Law, 247; and opinion of Moret, 254; and opinion of Crawford, 267. SEE ALSO stocks and irons; whip
Corral, Francisco: 189
Correo, El: 286
Cortes. SEE Spanish Cortes
Cortés, Hernan: in Cuba, 9; and Spanish reaction, 223
Cortina, José Antonio: 309–310
Costa Rica: and Moret Law, 259
cotton: as minor product, 10
Council of Catholic doctors: 305
Council of the Indies: and slave trade, 15, 27; and *emancipados*, 41–42; and alien Negroes, 44; and Moret Law, 264
Council of State (Spanish): and British proposal, 1840, 70; on conservation of slavery, 86–88, 109, 122; and

"free African labor", 110; and British abolitionism, 112, 122; and Ministry of colonies, 174; and Puerto Rican abolition, 241. SEE ALSO Spanish government.
Council of War: 268
Counter Reformation: 20
Court of Madrid: 35
Courts of Vice-Admiralty: 90
Cox, Jacob D.: resolution on Cuba, 300
Crampton, Ambassador J.: 181
Crawford, James F. (consul general): and treaty violations, 69; on slave imports, 126, 143; on *emancipado* abuses, and Cuban slavery, 267
Creole. SEE Cuban Creoles
Creole labor: number of (1862), 136
Creole party: 208
Crescent City (American ship): 116
Crespo, Romaldo (general): 268
criminal code: and treaty violations, 36. SEE ALSO Cuban reformers
criollos. SEE Cuban Creoles
Crittendon, William S. (colonel): 103
Cromwell: 104
Crónica, La (New York): 164
Crowe, A. de C. (Consul General): on law of 1880, 307; on slave interests, 307; and *patronato* abolition, 312
crown. SEE Spanish crown
Cruz, ——— (doctor): 305
Cruz Castellanos, José de la: named reform commissioner, 189; and free Negro labor, 191
Cruz Monclova, Lidio: 207
Cuba (ship): 271
Cuba: and early agriculture, 9–10; compared to Mexico, 14; and reform problems, 21; and abolitionist threat of 1811, 23–24; and white labor, 33; and treaty of 1817, 35–39; and dangers of slave trade, 58; excluded from Cortes of 1834–1836, 64; and British abolitionist societies, 65; and colonial neglect, 67; and reaction to 1840 proposal, 70–73; and Turnbull, 75; and fear of slave rebellion, 81; and slave interests, 83; and law of 1845, 85–88; compared to Brazil, 89; and coast guard, 94; and lack of abolitionist conscience, 122–123; and reform circular of 1868, 218–219; and Spanish Abolitionist Society, 299;

Index

and abolition law of 1880, 302; and abolitionist petitions, 309; and final abolition, 313. SEE ALSO United States

Cuban abolitionists: compared to Puerto Rican abolitionism 155, 195–205; and Montaos plan, 175; and Association against the Slave Trade, 176; and Liberal-Autonomists, 297; explanation of Spanish Party, 298; and law of 1880, 308; and *patrocinados*, 309–310; and abolition of stocks and irons, 311. SEE ALSO Cuban reforms

Cuban annexationist. SEE annexation

Cuban autonomy: rise of, 296–298, 310; and Spanish Party, 298; and legality question, 298, 310. SEE ALSO Liberal-Autonomist

Cuban budget: and the crisis of 1880–1886, 310–311

Cuban commerce: and British stimulus (1762), 10; and sugar trade, 11–12; and the United States, 12, 32, 48, 56, 77, 130, 141, 150, 304, 311; and reform opportunities, 13–14, 32; and direct trade, 32; and tariff, 48, 56, 188, 311; and Cuban reformism, 55–56, 129, 150, 205–206, 213, 303; and figures, 1830–1850, 80; and figures for 1849–1865, 185; and Reform Commission, 190; and Cuban abolitionism, 203, 309; and Liberal-Autonomists, 297

Cuban Commissioners: and election of 1866, 186; and reform questions, 189–214

Cuban corporations: and free white labor, 33; and Cortes of 1820–1822, 36–38; and Creole nationalism, 56; against abolition, 71

Cuban Conservative Party: 305

Cuban Conservatives: 299

Cuban Creoles: and Spanish policy, 22, 44; and political dilemma of, 50–51; and peninsulares, 51, 131; and Tacón, 55–58; division among, 56–59; nationalism of, 56–59, 129–130, 208; exclusion from Cortes, 64–65; and abolition threat of 1840, 70–73; discontent with Spain, 129; and Concha's recommendations, 130; and Serrano's policy, 132–133; and Dulce's policy, 133; and reform demands, 150–151; and insurrection of 1868, 224, 228–229; and promise of Zanjón, 296; and autonomist movement, 296–298, 310; and elections of 1879 and 1881, 298–299; in Cortes, 298, 302–305, 309, 310–311; effect of final abolition, 304

————, reformism: 56–58, 129–134; and influence of Saco, 56–58, 65; and Turnbull, 75–76, 81; and annexation, 98–104; and reform question, 150–151, 180; of the 1860's and autonomist movement, 296

————, abolitionism: emergence of, 57–58, 71, 142; excluded from Cortes, 64–65; and Turnbull, 77; meaning of, 129–130, 142; and American Civil War, 142, 149–150; abolition plans, 149–150; and American South, 207; and Liberal-Autonomist, 297–303; and election of 1879, and 1881, 298. SEE ALSO Cuban liberals; Cuban liberalism; Cuban nationalism; Cuban reforms; Liberal-Autonomists

Cuban delegation: and slave trade extension, 35; and government distrust, 299

Cuban deputies: in Cortes of 1810–1813, 22–24; and 1820–1823, 36–39; and elections of 1879 and 1881, 298; and Article 21, 301; and abolition law of 1880, 302

Cuban economy: in early period, 9–13; and reforms, 12–15, 32–33; effect of Haitian rebellion, 12–13; and status quo policy, 22; immigrant stimulus, 33; census of 1817, 45; prosperity and problems of, 46–50; and cultural development, 56; and Torrente's figures of, 73; and prosperity, 1825–1850, 79–80; and Sagra's ideas, 84; and United States, 89; and Britain, 89; and annexation, 100; and Spanish policy, 105–107; and labor problem, 134–140; and centralization, 138–140; and American Civil War, 183; and status quo, 211, 235, 240; and insurrection of 1868, 224–226; and census of 1862 and 1877 and Cuban abolitionism, 298; and crisis of 1880–1886, 310–311. SEE ALSO Cuban commerce

Cuban exiles: and propaganda, 98–100, 182, 213–214; and annexation, 98–104; and slavery, 105; and Pezuela's abolitionism, 116; and Concha, 123–126; divisions between, 123; and abolitionism, 124–125; and Ferrer de Couto, 164; and protest of Moret Law, 260; and protest of 1880 law, 306; and *Liga Cubana*, 306. SEE ALSO Cuban rebels

Cuban government: and reform question, 24, 57, 117–118, 126–127, 129–134, 189, 206, 210, 212, 301; laxity of, 35; protection of traffic, 35, 53, 54, 55, 57, 59, 69, 111–112, 197; and *emancipado* problem, 40–43, 82–83, 165; and English complaints, 42–43, 65, 69, 75–77; and emergency powers, 44, 65, 132; slave interests, 50, 65; and "Special Laws," 64, 65, 173–174, 189–210; and Saco's protest, 64–65; lack of authority, 112, 126–127, 145, 149, 181, 209; and Concha's administration, 105–106, 124, 130; and Pezuela's mission, 114–123; corruption of, 129; and sale of *emancipados*, 165; and censorship, 188; and tax question, 213–214; and insurrection, 222–232, 252, 265; and Lersundi's policy, 228–230; and Dulce's failure (1869), 230–232; and Spanish Volunteers, 230–232; and Prim's policy, 234; and Moret, 255–258, 274, 281, 294; and census problem, 259–264, 277; and Sickles' advice, 273–274; and Moret Law application, 274, 281, 294; and confiscated slaves, 279–281; and autonomists, 296–299, 309, 310; and contract labor, 303; and law of 1880, 306–308; and abolitionist activities, 309; and economic crisis of 1880–1886, 310–311. SEE ALSO Alcoy; Blanco; Concha; Cuban reforms; Dulce; *emancipados;* O'Donnell; Serrano; Spanish government; Tacón

Cuban historians: and Turnbull, 81

Cuban insurrection 1868: causes of, 222; and abolition, 224–227, 300; and Lersundi's policy, 228–230; and Spanish Volunteers, 228–232; and Dulce's conciliation, 230–232; and canceled elections, 232; and Puerto Rican abolition, 232, 285; and Prim's policy, 234; and Spanish reactionary policy, 240–241; and Moret Law, 246, 262; and Grant, 251–252; and American intervention, 267; and Fish's policy, 269–270, 284; and belligerency question, 283; and Peace of Zanjón, 295; slave population, 295–296; and law of 1880, 301. SEE ALSO belligerent rights

Cuban Junta: and annexation, 124

Cuban liberalism: political dilemma of, 50–53; and emergent nationalism, 56–58; exclusion from Cortes, 64–65; support of slavery, 72; and reform commissioners, 187, 189–214

Cuban liberals: economic and cultural roots of, 56; early leaders of, 56–58; suppressed by Tacón, 56–58; and elections of 1879 and 1881, 298; and attack on 1880 law, 304. SEE ALSO Cuban Creoles; Cuban reforms

Cuban nationalism: and Saco, 58; rise of, 129–130; and slave trade, 139–140; and abolition question, 195; and autonomist movement, 296

Cuban party: 230–232

Cuban plan of gradual abolition (1867): 202–205

Cuban population: in 1602, 9; in 1655, 10; in 1856–1859, 135; in 1862, 136; in 1860, 140; compared to Puerto Rico, 156; in 1868, 221

Cuban press: and law of 1880, 308

Cuban problem: and Amadeo de Savoy, 265. SEE ALSO slave problem

Cuban proprietors: and royal concessions, 11, 13, 26, 49–50; and abolition threat, 17, 70–73, 114–121, 125, 137, 175–176, 179, 220–221, 225; and slave shortage, 26, 134–144; and O'Gaban's defense, 38; and *emancipados*, 41, 278; and investment, 36–37, 48–51; and fear of rebellion, 46; Spanish creditors, 49, 131, 135, 296; political dilemma, 51; and slave code of 1789, 52–53; Saco, 66, 188; reformist sentiment of, 81–82, 131–143; and annexation, 84, 98–104; and law of 1845, 85–88; and slave procreation, 87–88; and census inaccuracies, 89; and traffic, 104; and

Index

Chinese labor, 109, 136; and Pezuela's abolitionism, 114–121, 125; and Concha, 125, 137; and Serrano, 131–133; and Dulce, 133–134; and manumission, 135; and American Civil War, 144; and Puerto Rican slaves, 156; and religious instruction, 166–167; and gradual abolition, 1865, 175–176; divided on abolition, 179; and closing of traffic, 196–198; and reaction to Reform Commission, 212–213; and Cuban insurrection, 224–227, 231; and Moret, 250, 255–259, 275–276; and census problem, 263–265, 277; and *emancipados*, 278; and Puerto Rican abolition, 287; and Colonial League, 287–290; and law of 1880, 301–302, 305, 307–308; and Negro contract labor, 303; and abolition of *patronato*, 309; and slave realtions, 311–312; and immigrant labor, 313. SEE ALSO Cuban proprietors; proslavery arguments

Cuban rebels: and abolition (1855), 124–125; and reform offer, 223; abolition strategy of, 223–227, 280–281; and abolition (1868–1870), 224–226; and Dulce's conciliation, 230–232; and distrust of Spain, 232; and Spanish abolition policy, 240; and influence on Moret Law, 250–256; and belligerency crisis, 251–252; and confiscated slaves, 279–281; and propaganda, 280; and Puerto Rican debate, 288–290; stalemated, 293; and Peace of Zanjón, 295

Cuban reformers. SEE Cuban reforms
Cuban reforms: and Bourbons, 7, 12–13; and Arango, 13–14, 24; and annexation, 98–104; and Concha, 105, 130–131; and Serrano, 132–133, 208–210; and Pozos Dulces, 134–137, 208–210; and economic change, 134–143; and *El Siglo*, 134; and effect of American conflict, 140–144; and Memorandum of 1865, 150–151; opinion of, 173; and Cánovas, 175–181; and Seijas Lozano, 175–176; and O'Donnell, 174; and gradual abolition, 175–176; and Reform Commission of 1865–1867, 185, 189–212, 222; and Saco's importance, 187; and abolitionist views, 194–196; contrast with Puerto Rico, 195–196; and slave problem, 207; and political philosphy, 207–208; and social division, 208; and independence threat, 208; and Glorious Revolution, 215–220, 221; and effect of insurrection, 222–232, 269–271; and Dulce's conciliation, 230–232; and United States diplomacy, 232–237; and Prim's policy, 233–237; and reform committee of 1869, 239; and Sickles, 274; and British policy, 294; and promise of Zanjón, 295; and Liberal-Autonomists, 297–303; and elections of 1879 and 1881, 298–299; in Spanish Cortes, 298, 302–305, 309–311; and law of 1880, 302–306; and tariff, 311

Cuban Republic: proclaimed, 222; and abolition policy, 224–226; and United States, 251–252. SEE ALSO Cuban insurrection

Cuban republicans: and Turnbull, 77; and abolitionist strategy (1855), 124–125

Cuban revenues: 222

Cuban revolution of 1868. SEE Cuban insurrection

Cuban revolutionaries: SEE Cuban rebels

Cuban Senators: 298

Cuban slave market. SEE Cuban slave trade

Cuban slave interests: and Arango's defense, 13–14, 25–26, 27; and Cortes of Cadiz, 22–25; and Spanish policy, 22; and Cuban corporations, 24; and Fernando's defense, 25-26, 27-28; and immigration, 33; and Cortes of 1820–1822, 36–38; investments in slave trade, 36–37; O'Gaban's defense of, 38; Consulado's defense of, 39; and treaty of 1817, 39; prosperity of, 1817–1823, 45–46; and Creole and Peninsular interests, 48–51; and influence of Spanish policy 55, 114, 120, 125, 174, 215, 228–232, 242, 244; and Saco, 58, 83; and abolition threat of 1840, 71–74; distrust of Spain, 73, 84; and law of 1845, 84; and annexation, 99–101; and Alcoy, 104; and Pezuela, 114–

121; and Concha's measures, 123–126; and the Civil War, 140–144, 163–165, 173; and Ferrer de Couto, 164–165; and rebel abolition, 226; and Moret Law suspension, 259; and sale of Cuba, 265; and Puerto Rican abolition, 288–290; and insurrection, 295–296; and law of 1880, 308; propaganda of, 312; and abolition, 313. SEE ALSO Cuban proprietors; proslavery arguments

Cuban slave labor: demand for, 3–8, 13–14, 24, 33, 53, 80, 183–184; and Saco's opinion, 66; and Council of States, 70; and religious instruction, 88; and capitation tax, 108; and conservation attempts, 110–113, 189–205; and mixed system, 135–138; and Reform Commission, 191; and Crime rate, 212; and cost, 240; and effects of insurrection, 295–296; and law of 1880, 302–306, 308. SEE ALSO Cuban slavery

Cuban slave population: and comparisons, 12–13, 14–15, 26–27, 44–45, 156; and abolition plan of 1867, 205

Cuban slave trade: and royal control, 5–9, 10; and "free trade," 13–15; and numbers to 1810, 8; in 1792, 10; in 1789–1791, 13; in 1521–1820, 15–16; and international abolitionism, 17; and Cuban corporations, 24; and license of 1804–1816, 27; and treaty of 1817, 28–29; and treaty chain, 31; and illicit imports, 35, 39, 53, 59; and capital investments, 36–37; in Cortes of 1820–1822, 36–38; and decree of 1826, 36; and patrol problems, 39, 43, 63, 94–95; on alien Negroes, 44; and in 1788–1830, 54; in 1830–1850, 54; Creole reform thought, 57, 134–144, 192–205; in 1835, 59; and treaty of 1835, 61–62; and American agreement of 1842, 63; and bull of Gregory XVI (1839), 64; and papal decrees, 65; and British proposal of 1840, 70–73; and abuse of slaves, 76; and in 1820–1846, 80; and law of 1845, 84–88; in 1845–1848, 88–89; in 1840–1847, 95; and Pezuela's mission, 114–121; and Concha's policy, 123–127; and annexation, 123–125; and Cuban exiles, 123–124; in 1855, 126; and American participation, 127; in 1828–1860, 135; and gradual closing, 135, 138–139, 143–146; and slave prices, 135, 144; and labor shortage, 138–139; in 1858, 143–144; and American Civil War, 143–145, 147; and Puerto Rico, 155–156; in 1811–1825, 165; and Cuban abolitionists, 176; and abolition law of 1866, 176–181; and Reform Commission of 1866–1867, 190, 192–205, 214; and "equilibrium of races," 197; and Dulce's memorandum, 209; and Quaker petition, 269. SEE ALSO Alcoy; British government; Concha; Dulce; O'Donnell; piracy declaration; Serrano; slave interests; slave ships; Spanish government; Tacón; Vives

Cuban slavery: and code of 1789, 52–53, 72; of 1842, 74; and American protection, 77–78; effect of insurrection, 81–82; and Pezuela's mission, 114–121; and Reform Commission, 191–193; and reform dilemma, 207–208; and *emancipados*, 267, 278; judgment of 254, 293; and Liberal-Autonomists, 297; and subcommission of 1789, 300; numbers in 1866, 312

Cuban slaves: and abolition dangers, 59; treatment of, 81–82, 210, 246–247, 275, 308, 312; and Moret Law, 246–247; and census problem, 263–265; number of in 1871, 277; and number emancipated, 1875, 294; in 1878, 294; and effects of Cuban insurrection, 295–296; and abolition law of 1880, 301–302, 307–308; numbers in 1880, 302; number freed, 1880–1883, 307; runaways, 307; and law of 1880, 308; in 1886, 311; and propaganda, 312; and effects of final abolition, 313. SEE ALSO abolition of slavery; Cuban slave labor

Cuban society: and freedmen, 313

Cuban sugar: and American pressure, 285. SEE ALSO Cuban economy

Cunha Reis, Manuel: 150

customs duties: 206

Daily Union (Washington): 104

Index

Danish Antilles: 45
Darwin, Charles: 290
Davis, Charles W.: and census question, 90; and report on Pezuela, 116–120
Debate, El: 286
Declaration of Vienna: 197
decree: of 1527 and licensed slaves, 5; of 1789, 1791, 1804, and opening slave trade, 8, 13, 14, 15; of 1531 and 1598, and sugar mills, 11; of 1764, 1774, 1784, and Spanish-American trade, 12; of 1793, 1804, and abolition in Haiti, 18; of 1817, abolishing tobacco monopoly, 32; of 1818, opening Cuban ports, 32; of 1826, against slave trade, 43; of 1825, on emergency powers, 44; of 1852, and plantation credit, 49; against slavery, 63; of 1836, abolishing slavery in Spain, 63, 181; of 1838, 1865, and connivance with traffic, 64, 148; of 1844, and slave code, 82; of 1854, promoting contract labor, 111, 118; of 1854, and slave registry, 118; of 1861, and exile question, 145; of 1848, prohibiting Puerto Rican slaves, 156; of 1789, and slave refuge in Spain, 168; of 1865, 1867, and colonial reform basis, 190, 210; of 1867, and Cuban tax, 213; of 1868, on *vientre libre*, 218; of 1869, 1870, and *emancipado* liberty, 278; of 1870, and confiscated slaves, 278; liberating rebel slaves, 280-281; and military service, 281; of 1870, and military abolition, 281; of 1843, and British Negroes, 204; of 1886, abolishing *patronato*, 311–312
decadencia española, La: 21
Delicias, Marqués de la: 83
Delmonte, Domingo: on protecting traffic, 55–59; and nascent nationalism, 56; and abolitionism, 57–59; and Turnbull, 76; and American policy, 77; and annexation, 102; and colonial policy, 105; on clerical slaveholders, 167
Democratic Party (United States): and Cuban reforms, 195; in South, 207
Democracia, La (Madrid): 159

Denmark: and abolition, 19
Derby, Lord (Edward Henry Derby): and British policy 294
Diago, Fernando: 110, 138
Diario de la Marina, El: and Pezuela, 115; and *El Siglo* rivalry, 134; and reforms, 303
Diary of the Spanish Cortes: 21
Díaz de Argüelles, Isidro: on Spanish slave policy, 122; named reform commissioner, 189; against piracy declaration, 198
Díaz Quintero, Francisco: 249
diplomacy. See abolition; slave trade
Diputación Provincial (Cuba): and Cortes of 1820–1822, 36–38
Discusión, La (Madrid): and abolition, 153, 159
diseases: and slave labor, 135
Dodge, August Caesar: 125
domestic slaves: and taxation, 108, 113; and Reform Commission, 191–193; and law of 1880, 307–308
Domínguiz Ortiz, Antonio: 63–64
Dominican Republic: and Spanish annexation, 132; and Grant, 236
Dulce y Garay, Domingo: his first administration, 1862–1865, 133–134; and repression of traffic, 147–148, 281; and slave landings, 181; and gradual abolition, 175–176; and slave landings, 181; and Cánovas reforms, 185; and Reform Commission, 185–186, 208–210; and Glorious Revolution, 217; and Cuban insurrection, 230–232; and Spanish Volunteers, 230–232; and Spanish revolutionaries, 241
Dutch: and slave trade, 6–7, and Java labor, 84
Dutch Antilles: 45

East Indian coolies: and traffic, 143
East Indian laborers: and British planters, 67; and traffic, 143
Eastern Cuba. See Oriente
Eaton, John H.: on slave care, 65
Echeverría, José Antonio: and annexation, 100; and *El Siglo*, 133; and Serrano's reforms, 133; on abolitionist trend, 142; elected to reform commission, 187, 189; and Puerto Rican abolition 193–196; and plan of 1867, 202–203

economic crisis of 1880–1886: 310–311
economic reform: and liberal autonomist movement, 296–298; and Cuban conservatives, 299; and law of 1880, 303–304
Economic Society: and Turnbull, 76; and Labra's election, 298–299
Ecuador: and piracy declaration, 121
education: and Liberal-Autonomists, 297
elections: and colonial reform, 185–186, 221; and Cuban pacification, 234; and Liberal-Autonomists, 296–298
Ely, Roland T.: and Cuban archives, xvi; on slave reproduction, 111
emancipation: and rebel abolition, 226; and Confiscation, 226; and war debt, 296
Emancipation Act of 1880. See abolition law of 1880
Emancipation Proclamation: 141
emancipados: rise of problem, 40–43; abuse of, 40–43, 60; and British intervention, 59; and treaty of 1835, 61–62; British shift to Africa, 62, 67; and confiscated slave problem, 62, 279; British colonies, 67; and code of 1842, 74; and Turnbull, 75–77; and Valdés, 79; and numbers, 1862, 79, 146; and slave rebellions, 82; and Palmerston's concern, 82–83; and O'Donnell, 82–83; in Brazil, 90; and Alcoy, 93–94; and Pezuela, 115; in abolitionist debates, 165–166, 282; and Moret plan 245, 266, 276–278; and work contracts, 267, 278; and Crawford's opinion, 267; numbers emancipated since 1867, 294
embargo: and confiscated slave problem, 279–281
emergency powers *(facultades omnimodas):* Tacón's use of, 58–59; and Concha, 105; and reform demands, 207
Emperor Alexander of Russia: 19
Emperor Dom Pedro II: 90, 97
England: and *asiento,* 7, 18; Arango's attack, 38; and Cuban market, 48; and Palmerston, 59; and Cuban annexation, 65; and Russell's proposal, 127; and Fernando VII, 129; and philanthropy, 137; as abolition example, 193; and Spanish indemnity, 211; and Fish's policy, 235; and Moret's policy, 245; and abolition debate, 250; and support of Spain, 270; and reform example, 274; and Puerto Rican abolition, 283–284; and Cuban abolition question, 300
English Parliament. See British Parliament
English: and *asiento,* 7
English abolitionists. See British abolitionists
English Antilles: slave population of, 45; and sugar export, 45
English blockade: and beet sugar, 48
English commissioners: 40–43
English counsuls: and *emancipado* problem, 40–43; and *emancipados* (protests on treatment), 41–43; and abolition efforts, 43; and slave landings, 93
English petitioners: and Moret Law, 266; and American cooperation, 266
English merchants. See British merchants
English Quakers: and abolitionism, 168
English Royal African Company: and *asiento* grant, 7; influence on Cuban trade, 10
English slave trade: abolition of, 19
English South Sea Company: 7
Enlightenment: and abolitionism, 17–20; and Spain, 20
epidemics: of 1853, 114
Época La: 286
equalitarianism: and Puerto Rico, 156; and Colonial reform, 189–190, 206–212, 297
Equator: in abolition treaties, 27–28
"equilibrium of races": and Spanish policy, 197
Escobedo, Nicolás Manuel: 56
escribano (notary): 85
Española: cited in slave debate, 71
Espartero, General Baldomero (Duque de la Victoria): and exposition of 1835, 122; and Puerto Rican abolition, 286–287
Espeleta, Conde de: 80
Estorch, Miguel: 108
Europe: and Creole reformism, 129
European colonists: 108–109

Index

European governments: and Cuban markets, 48
European opinion: and colonial reform, 274
European powers: and joint intervention, 1875, 293; and sympathy 294
Ever-Faithful Isle: 22, 50, 67; economic interests of, 114; and Pezuela, 121; and Cuban insurrection of 1868, 223
Excoriaza, José M. P.: 233
exiles: and Cuban immigration, 33; and Puerto Rico, 212; and Cuban insurrection, 321
exposition. See memorandum

Fabié, Antonio Marie (Spanish deputy): on Civil War, 152; and abolition question, 162–163; on Spanish slavery, 163
farms: and census of 1862 and 1877, 295
Fauli, José Valdés: 133
Feijóo de Sotomayor, Urbano: on Cuban economy, 80; and contract labor, 110
Fernández de Castro, Rafael: 305
Fernández Perdones, Luciano: 150
Fernando (Ferdinand the Catholic King): and slave permits, 4, 266
Fernando III: and slavery in Spain, 5
Fernando VII: apology for slavery, 3, 29; resists abolitionism, 25–28, 54; and liberal Cortes, 36, 39
Fernando Po (island): and slave trade, 8; and contract labor, 88
Ferrer de Couto, José: and defense of slave interests, 164–165; and *La Cronicia*, 164
Figuera, Fermín: and abolition plan, 149; and abolition question, 173
Figureras, Estanislao: 290
Figuerola, Laureano: and Spanish Abolition Society, 154; and Glorious Revolution, 154
filibusters: and López, 102; and "new measures of 1854," 113–114; and Concha, 123; and Vizcarrondo, 157; Spanish reactionaries, 187, 223
Fillmore, Millard: 103
fines: and slave code of 1842, 75
fiscal (public prosecutor): 85

Fish, Hamilton: his Cuban policy, 233–237, 242, 244, 272, 284, 293; and belligerency crisis, 251–252; Moret Law, 252–253, 284; and opinion on Rodriguez, 270; Spanish minister, 284. See also Grant
flag problem: and Portuguese, 30–31, 62; and Brazilians, 31; and search treaties, 32; and French, 35; and Americans, 35, 62–63, 95; and Spanish, 36, 62; and British policy, 60; and nontreaty flags, 60, 62
Fleming: and *asiento*, 5
Florida: and reforms, 33; and Cuban exiles, 98
flour trade: and the United States, 56; and Cuban reform, 150, 173–174, 205
Forbes, Paul S.: 234
forced labor: and Indians, 3–4; and Reform Commission, 189–205
Forcade y Font, José: and traffic, 112
foreign abolitionism: and threat to Cuba, 43; and Spanish government, 122, 176–177, 242, 299; and abolition question, 200; and Spanish abolitionism, 208–209; and Moret Law, 252, 259–261; and census problem, 263; and Puerto Rican abolition, 275, 281
foreign countries: and rebel propaganda, 280
foreign diplomacy: and Puerto Rican abolition, 275, 283–284
foreign immigration: 192
foreign intervention: and influence on abolitionism, 209–210; and Layard's opinion, 266. See also United States
foreign purchasers: and confiscated slave problem, 279–281
foreigners: and Cuban traffic, 15
France: and British agreement, 27; at Congress of Vienna, 25; and Canning, 31; against piracy declaration, 31; and Saco's exile, 69; and joint intervention (1852), 103, 112; and Russell's proposal, 127; as abolition example, 193; and Fish's policy, 235; and belligerency question, 236; and Moret's policy, 245; and abolition question, 250
Francisco (Prince of Portugal): 215
Franklin, Benjamin: 168

Fredericksburg (battle): 286–287
free African labor: and Torrente's plan, 111; British opposition to, 111, 136, 150; in Cuban abolition plans, 150; and contract labor, 303–304; and law of 1880, 304
free birth. SEE *vientre libre*
free black. SEE free African
free-born Negroes (*libertos*): 246, 276
free Chinese: 295
free colored. SEE free Negroes
free labor: and Saco, 66; and abolitionist question, 82–83, 135; and Sagra, 84; attempts to promote, 107–109; and Pezuela's measures, 115–119; and Creole labor, 136; and mixed labor, 138; and Reform Commission of 1866, 194, 198–199; and Puerto Rican abolition, 241–242; and insurrection, 295; and Liberal-Autonomists, 297; and subcommission of 1879, 300; and law of 1880, 306, 308; and plans to abolish *patronato*, 309. SEE ALSO white immigration
free Negro labor: and Pezuela's measures, 116–117; Torrente's defense of, 123; and questionnaire of 1866, 192; and work contracts, 278–279; and Liberal-Autonomists, 297
free Negroes: number in 1792, 12; in 1817, 45; condition of, 52; opinion of, 71; and militia, 115, 287; in 1860, 140; in 1862, 146; and crime, 221; and literacy, 221; and Cuban abolitionism, 297; and abolition question, 201, 297; and assimilation, 313
Free Society of Political Economy (Madrid): and abolition, 162
free thought: and Spanish abolitionism, 169–171
free trade: and British occupation of Havana, 10; and Glorious Revolution, 219; and Cuban demands, 303
free white labor: and immigration, 83; failure of, 136. SEE ALSO free labor
freedom of press and assembly: 221
Freedman's Committee of New York and Iowa: 269
freedmen (*libertos*): and Moret Law, 246, 275–276; numbers emancipated (1875), 294; and abolition question, 301; and law of 1880, 301–302, 207;

and *patronato*, 309, 312; and final abolition, 313
French: and *asiento*, 7
French Antilles: 45
French Assembly: and Haitian abolition, 18; and Cuban rebels, 228
French colonies: 288
French Enlightenment: and Spain, 20
French Revolution: and Cuban reforms, 14; and abolitionism, 17–18; and Spanish politics, 215
French Revolution of 1848: and Spanish monarchy, 96; and abolition, 100
French West Indies: and Cuban competition, 14; and Cuban fears, 100
Friends of New England: 269
Frías y Jacott, Francisco. SEE Pozos Dulces
fugitive slaves: 226

Gaceta de Madrid: and papal bull, 64
Gaceta Oficial: and pacification, 244
Galicia: and free labor, 110
Gallego Diaz (deputy): 253
gallegos: as free laborers, 110
Gálvez, José Mariá: as head of the Liberal-Autonomists, 297; and autonomist struggle, 310
Gandara, José de la: 288
generation of '98: 21
Genoese merchants: and *asiento*, 5
German idealism: 169
Giner de los Ríos, José Luis: 220
Globe The (London): 95
Glorious Revolution of 1868: causes of, 215–216; and Spanish liberals, 216–217, 219; and colonial reform, 217–220; and Cuban insurrection, 220, 223; and Moret Law, 239, 245–246, 249, 253; and reform committee, 239–240; and Puerto Rican reform, 243; and British abolitionists, 270; in abolitionist arguments, 282
Goicouria, Domingo: and annexation, 98–99, 124; and immigration, 108; his execution, 251
Gómez Labrador, Pedro: and Vienna declaration, 17; against abolition, 26
Gómez Reynel, Pedro: and *asiento*, 6
González Álvarez, Ignacio: 189
Gonzáles Brabo, Luis: and status quo, 215; and Glorious Revolution, 215

Index

González de Mendoza, Antonio: and abolition of traffic, 176, 198
González Stéfani, Joaquín: 189
Gospel of Christ: and Quakers, 168
governors: and Moret Law, 278
Gran Antilla. SEE Cuba
Gran Colombia: and abolition, 30; and piracy declaration, 121
Granada (Grenada): 45
Grant, Ulysses S.: and Ambassador Sickles, 233; and Cuban rebels, 236
Grant administration: and Cuban policy, 233–237; and Spanish reform promises, 242; and belligerency crisis, 251–252; and abolition pressure, 285; and joint intervention, 1875, 293. SEE ALSO Fish; Hamilton
Granville, Lord (George Leveson-Gower): and Moret Law, 266–267; and British abolitionists, 270
Great Britian. SEE British government
Greeks: and abolition question, 249; and Cuban reforms, 207
Gregory XVI: and traffic, 64
Grijalva, Juan de: and early Cuba, 9
Grito de Yara: 222
Grotius, Hugo: on slavery, 170
Guatemala: and abolition, 30
Güell y Renté, José: and elections of 1879 and 1881, 298; and abolition law of 1880, 302; on indemnity, 304; and autonomists, 310; and tariff, 311
Guerega, Countess: 83
Guerra y Sánchez, Ramiro: on treaty of 1817, 53; on Creole and peninsular, 56; on Creole abolition, 141
Guerrero, Teodoro: 304
Guizot: and abolition question, 200
Guridi y Alcócer, Miguel: 22–23
Gutiérrez de la Concha, José (Marqués de la Habana): and Lopez expeditions, 103; his first administration (1850–1852), 105, 130; and Creole conspirators, 105; and slave trade, 105, 107; his policies, 122–124; and annexationists, 123–125; on reform need, 129–131; and second command (1854–1859), 123, 137; and law of 1866, 177, 181–182; and Cánovas' reforms, 185; on conservation of Cuba, 196–197; on Spanish party, 230; and Spanish Volunteers, 229–230; and Puerto Rican abolition, 287

hacendados (sugar planters). SEE Cuban proprietors
haciendas: communal ownership, 10–11; insurrection, 295. SEE ALSO *ingenios;* plantations
Haiti: rebellion, influence on Cuba, 13–14, 51; slave population of, 13; and Spanish policy, 15; cited in slave debates, 24, 37, 58, 70, 164, 220, 248; (Creole), 46; and Moret Law, 259; and abolition question, 82, 300
Harris, Vice-Consul: 307
Havana: Royal Company of, 7; and English Royal African Company, 10; English occupation of, 1762, 10–11; and tobacco, 11; commercial system, 12; and slave trade, 13, 15–17, 27, 35, 39; mixed commission, 29, 39, 40–43; railway construction, 49; and merchant capitalism, 50; and Saco's abolitionism, 58; and Treaty of 1835, 62; and *emancipado* problem, 82–83; and Chinese labor, 111; population in 1860, 140; and student executions, 268; and Junta de Hacendados, 296; and Liberal-Autonomists, 297, 310; and economic reforms, 303; and law of 1880, 307; and abolitionists, 309
Hayes, Rutherford B.: and policy change, 293; and law of 1880, 306
Hegel: 167, 289
Hernández Arvizu, Juan: 233
Hernández Iglesias, Fermín: 165
Heron, Sir R.: on treaty indemnity, 29
Hidalgo y Costilla, Miguel: 30
High Court of Admiralty: 90
Hill-coolies. SEE Asiatic labor
His Catholic Majesty: and Treaty of Madrid, 25–26; and slave trade, 43
Hispanic American republics: and Cuban reform, 208; and independence, 214, 223
Holy Office (Inquisition): 21
Holy See: 198–200
Holy Trinity: 289
Hong Kong: 104
Hostos, Eugenio María de: 220
House Foreign Relations Committee: 300

House of Commons: 95
House of Lords: and British policy, 96
House of Representatives: 252
Howden, Lord: 112, 121
Hugo, Victor: and Vizcarrondo, 159
humanitarianism: and abolitionism, 17–20, 167
Humboldt, Alexander von: on coffee plantations, 11–12; on slave imports, 15–16; on sugar exports, 1760–1823, 45; on loans, 49
Humbolt, Wilhelm von: 17
Hutt, Mr.: and traffic, 89

Ibañez Palenciano, Conde de: 305
Iberian Spaniards: and civil rights, 132; and Liberal-Autonomists, 297. SEE ALSO Spain
illicit trade. SEE contraband; Cuban slave trade
immigrant labor: 313
immigration. SEE Chinese immigration; white immigration; Yucatecan Indians
immigration act of 1817: 107
"immortal 400": and López, 103
Imparcial, El: 286
imprisonment: and Moret Law, 247; and economic reforms, 303
indemnity: in abolition plans, 193, 202, 205, 245, 299; and abolition question, 211, 220, 221, 245; and rebel abolition, 225–226; and Grant's policy, 233–234; and Moret Law, 246; and military abolition, 281; and Puerto Rican abolition, 286; and war debt, 296; and Liberal-Autonomists, 297; in law of 1880, 301–304
indemnity (British): in treaty of 1817, 28–29; in Anglo-Portuguese treaties, 30; in slave debate, 73
independence: and Puerto Rico, 155; and Reform Commission, 213–214; and Grant's Cuban policy, 233–234; and rebel abolition, 280
Independencia Española, La: 254
India: and Spanish reply, 77
Indiana: and Quaker petition, 269
Indian coolies: 63, 116, 143
Indians (American): and slavery, 3, 290; and Cuban insurrection, 224
indigo: as minor product, 10
Indo-China: and immigration, 303

Industrial Exposition (London): 144
ingenios (sugar mills): and slave women, 15; reduction of, 1850–1860, 135; problems of, 138; and centralization, 139; and census of 1862 and 1877, 295; and rebel destruction, 295. SEE ALSO plantations
inspectors: and law of 1880, 307
insular government. SEE Cuban government
international abolitionists. SEE foreign abolitionists
international claims convention: 244
interrogatorio. SEE questionnaire on labor regulations
Intransigents. SEE Spanish loyalists; Spanish party
Invincible Armada: and *asiento*, 6
Ireland: and Spanish reply, 77
Irish Quakers: and abolitionism, 168
irons. SEE stocks and irons
Irving, Washington: on traffic, 80
Isabel I (the Catholic Queen of Castille): and slave trade, 5, 266
Isabel II: and treaty of 1835, 61; and Progressive Party, 63; and colonial neglect, 66–67; regency of, 72; and traffic, 112; and liberal revolt, 186, 216; and status quo, 215; exile of, 218, 228; and Lersundi, 218, 228; and student executions, 268
Isidore of Pelusa, Saint: 170–171
Italian Prince. SEE Amadeo
Izaguirre, Eligio: 279
Iznaga, José Aniceto: 98

Jagua (gold mines): and slave trade, 9
Jamaica: and Cuba, 10, 51; and abolition question, 25, 59–60, 70, 73, 82, 149, 288, 300, 313; slave population of, 26, 45; and sugar imports, 45, 89; abolition in, 59, 79; and emancipados, 67, 94
Jameson, R. F.: 40
Jaruco (Cuba): and traffic, 182
Java: cited in slave debate, 84
Jesus Christ: 290
Jesus María (Spanish ship): 76
Jews: and Spanish slavery, 167–168
Johnson, Samuel: and abolitionism, 18
joint commission: 252
joint intervention proposal of 1852: 103, 112

Jorrin, José Silverio: 133
Juaregui, Andres de: 39
judges of the mixed commissions: 39–40
Juluis II: and slavery, 171
Junta Cubana: and slave interests, 220
Junta de Fomento, La (Council for Economic Development): founding of, 12; against abolition, 71; and immigration, 108; and labor problem, 109
Junta de Hacendados (Cuban planters): and Havana, 50; on *vientre libre*, 255–256; Moret project, 255–256, 260; and insurrection, 296
Junta de Información de Ultramar. SEE Colonial Reform Commission
Junta de Población Blanca: founded, 33; abolished, 108
Juntas for the Protection of Freedmen (Juntas Protectoras de los Libertos): and Moret Law, 275–276
Just, Ramón: on reforms, 173

Kansas-Nebraska Bill: 116
Kennedy (British commissioner): on slave repression, 81; and slave landings, 93
Kentucky: and López expedition, 103; and slave reproduction, 111
Key West: and López expedition, 102
Kilbee, J. T.: 40–41
Kindelán y Oregón, Sebastian: 53
King of France: 39
Krause, Karl Christian: 169

labor regulations: and reform questionnaire, 191–193; and Puerto Rican abolition, 202, 241, 242; and Liberal-Autonomists, 297
Labra y Cadrana, Rafael María de: and Vizcarrondo, 157, 160; and abolition movement, 160–161, 169; and Colonial reform, 160; in Cortes, 160–161; and Wilberforce, 160; on traffic, 183; on Spanish slavery, 163, 312; and Glorious Revolution, 217–218, 219; and *La Propaganda*, 220; and Saco, 221; and Reform Commission of 1869, 239–240; and confiscated slaves, 280; and Puerto Rican reforms, 282–283; and elections of 1879 and 1881, 298; and law of 1880, 302; and abolition petitions, 309; and Liberal-Autonomists, 310
Lafayette, Marquis de: 18
laissez-faire philosophy: 205–206
Larroque, Patrice: 170
Las Casas, Bartolomé de: and slave trade, 4, 5, 24; in Cuba, 9; and Arango, 14; and Inquisition, 20–21; and Vizcarrondo, 157; and Indian rights, 167
Las Casas, Luis de: 13
lash. SEE whip
Latin American republics: and contract labor, 88; and Creole reformism, 129–130, 257
Laurent, Francois: 170
Law of Abolition and Repression of Slave Trade (March 4, 1845). SEE law of 1845
law of abolition, 1880: approved Jan. 30, 305; and economic concessions, 305
law of free birth. SEE Moret Law
law of 1526: 5
law of 1831, 1850, 1888: and Brazilian abolition, 90, 97, 311
law of 1835. SEE treaty of June 20, 1835
law of 1845: and free labor, 108; and slave registry, 113; and Pezuela, 118; and slave conservation, 135–136; and law of 1866, 178, 181
law of 1854: and slave registry, 113, 118–119, 182
law of 1866 (for the suppression and punishment of slave trade): 177–181; objections, 181–182; effect, 182–183; and Dulce's memorandum, 209
law of March 22, 1873: and abolition in Puerto Rico, 282, 286–290, 293
law of 1882: and tariff, 311
Laws of the Indies: and slave protection, 65; and abolition question, 163; and Serrano's Memorandum, 210
Layard, Austen H.: and cooperation with American policy, 244; and Moret, 245; and support of Spain, 270; and British abolitionists, 270; on Cuban reforms, 281; on Spanish reactionaries, 287
League Manifesto. SEE Manifesto of Colonial League of January 10, 1873

leased slaves: 295
León, Spain: 158
León, Galindo (Spanish deputy): 162
Lersundi, Francisco: and closing traffic, 182–183; and Glorious Revolution, 218, 228; and reactionary policy, 228–230; against abolition, 287
leyes especiales, las. SEE "Special Laws"
ley Moret. SEE Moret Law
Liberal-Autonomist Party: and reform program, 296–299, 303; and law of 1880, 302–306, 308; and obstacles, 310–311; and tariff, 311
liberal government: SEE provisional government
Liberal Party (Spanish): 272
liberal press (Cuban): 298
Liberal-Reformists: 233
Liberal Union Party (Unión Liberal, Spanish): 132, 174
liberalism: and conduct, 21; and Puerto Rico, 154–157; and Glorious Revolution, 216–220; and Castelar's speech, 250; and law of 1880, 309. SEE ALSO Cuban liberalism; Spanish Cortes; Spanish liberalism
liberated slaves: 278–279
Liberia: and Moret Law, 259
libertos (freedmen): and Moret Law, 246, 275–276; and work contracts, 278–279; and law of 1880, 307
leisure time: and *patronato*, 311
Liga Cubana, La: and law of 1880, 306
Lincoln, Abraham: and Creole reformism, 140; and piracy declaration, 147; and right of search, 147; in abolition debate, 165, 190, 250, 286–287, 288, 305
Lion (British ship): 42
literacy: in Spain and Cuba, 221
Liverpool: and slave trade, 168
livestock: in early Cuba, 10; and census of 1792, 12; of 1817, 45; of 1817–1846, 80; of 1862 and 1877, 295
Locke, John: and abolitionism, 18
Logan's Resolution: 252
London: and indemnity, 29; and abolition, 31; and Creole reformism, 130
López, Narciso: expeditions of, 99–104; and slavery, 102–103; his execution, 103

López de Letona, Antonio: 149
López expeditions: account of, 98–104; and Pezuela, 116; and Concha, 123; and Spanish liberals, 153; and reform question, 180; and Spanish Volunteers, 229
López Domínguez, José: 180
López Roberts, Mauricio: and belligerency question, 236; on *vientre libre*, 242; and American intervention, 243–244, 268; and Zenea's mission, 265; and student execution crisis, 268; replaced, 283; and American opinion, 284
L'opinion nacionale (Paris): 182
Loriga (abolitionist deputy): 302
lottery: in abolition plans, 38, 94, 204–205
Louisiana: and Cuban reforms, 33; and Cuban economy, 89, 140, 141, 185
Louisiana planters: and tariff, 89
L'Ouverture, Toussaint: 18, 250
Löwenhielm, Karl Axel (Comte): 17
loyal slaves: 280
loyalist proprietors: and confiscated slaves, 279; and military abolition, 281
Lutheranism: and Vizcarrondo, 158
Luz Caballero, José Cipriano de la: and Cuban nationalism, 56; and reformism, 129
Luzuriaga, Claudio Antonio: 125

Macao: and immigration, 109
Macaulay, Zachary: on law of 1807, 26; and American denunciation, 78
Macey, George: 169
Machiavelli: 279–281
Madan, Cristóbal: on plantation tax, 54; and annexation, 98, 102
Madden, Robert Richard (Judge): and testimony, 55; on Americanization, 130
Madrid: and revolt of 1820, 36; and reform question, 130, 179–180; and Abolitionist Society, 158; and Liberal-Autonomist, 310
Madrid Atheneum: 249
Madrid government: and Moret Law, 275–276. SEE ALSO Spanish government

Index

Madrid Junta. See Revolutionary Junta of Madrid
Madrid Journal: 273
Mahy, Nicolás: and slave trade, 53
manifesto: of Goicuria, 124; on *vientre libre*, 218; on Puerto Rican abolitionism, 282–283
manumission: frequency of, 52; and labor problem, 137; and church custom, 170; in abolition plans, 194
Manzanedo, Joaquin Manuel (Marqués de): 189
Marchessi, José María: 212
Marcy, William (Secretary of State): and Pezuela, 115–120; on British threat, 117; and Davis' report, 119; and Ostend Manifesto, 120
María de la Gloria: captured slaver, 63
Mario (French ship): detention of, 39
Marqués de las Delicias: 83
Martin, Herrera, J. (Archbishop of Cuba): and elections of 1879 and 1881, 298
Martínez, Campos, Arsenio (General): and peace of Zanjón, 294–295; as prime minister, 299, 304; and abolition project, 300, 301
Martínez de la Rosas, Francisco: and of law of 1845, 84–85
Martos, Cristino: and anticlericalism, 171; and reaction, 241; and Sickles, 271–272, 274; and reforms, 281, 284, 287
Martínez Serrano (Cuban liberal): 76
Mason, John Y.: 120
Masonry: and Spain, 20; and abolition, 100; and Spanish liberals, 169
master. See Cuban proprietors
Matanzas (district): and conspiracy, 81; and abolitionism, 82; population of, 140; and sugar, 224; and law of 1880, 307
matrimony of slaves: 247
Matson, Henry J.: and slave sugar, 95
Maza Arredondo, Fernando de la: 39
medical students (Havana): 268
mechanization: and sugar, 49
memorandum: of Cuban corporations (1811), 24; of Cuban reformers (1865), 150; of Spanish party (1865), 151; of Cuban commissioners (1866), 194–196; of colonial reformers (1868), 219; of Junta Cubana (1868), 220
memorials: against law of 1880, 309
Memoria of Concha: 130
Mendez de Vigo, Felipe: 306
Mendoza, Cristóbal: 279–281
mercantile groups: 265
merchant creditors: and loans, 49–50
Mestre, José Manuel: and *El Siglo*, 133; on Saco, 188
Methodists: and abolitionism, 18
Metternich, Prince Klemen: 17
Mexican government: 109
Mexican War: and annexation, 98–100
Mexico: and Cuba, 14; and abolition, 30; and independence, 33; on piracy declaration, 121; and Spanish intervention, 132; and Spanish reactionaries, 223
Middle Ages: and serfdom, xi; and slavery, 170, 171
militarism (Spanish): 22
military officials: 264–265
militia: and free blacks, 115
Ministry of Colonies (Ministerio de Ultramer): archives of, xiv; created, 1863, 174
Ministry of Martínez Campos: 300
Miraflores ministry: 154
Miranda, Francisco: 224
miscegenation: and Puerto Rico, 114; as abolition factor, 156
mixed commission (court): established, 29, 39; and traffic, 59, 62, 67; in Treaty of 1835, 61–62; and *emancipados*, 67; and Turnbull, 75; and Governor Alcoy, 93; and Crawford, 126. See also *emancipados*
Mobile (Alabama): 103
Moderado government: and Reform Commission, 186–187, 189, 190–193; and suppression of Abolition Society, 187; and ignorance, 191–192; and Glorious Revolution, 216
Modet, José (Spanish deputy): 162
Mon ministry: and status quo, 154
Monarchic Democrats: 217
Monarchists: 265
monarchy of Brazil: and abolition, 312
Montalambert, Count of: 200
Montalvo y Calvo, Ramón: 189

Montaos y Robillard, Don Francisco: abolition plan, 149, 175; and Association against the Slave Trade, 176

Montpensier, Duc de: 216

Moors: and Spanish slavery, 167–168

Morales Bachiller (Cuban liberal): and Turnbull, 76

Morales Lemus, José: as Cuban reform leader, 133, 188, 211; and abolitionism, 194–196, 203; and tax question, 213–214; and insurrection, 229, 231; and Grant, 236; and Moret Law, 266–267; and Liberal-Autonomists, 296

Moreno Nieto, José de: 180

Moret Law of 1870: provisions of, 245–257; debates on, 247, 250–257, 263; and foreign powers, 251–253, 259–261; opinions of, 253–254, 255–258; and application problem, 259–272, 274–276; and census problem, 263–264; and Amadeo de Savoy, 266; and intervention crisis, 268–269, 274–275; and Puerto Rico, 275–276; and *emancipado* problem, 276–277; and confiscated slaves, 279–281; in abolition arguments, 282; and Fish's demands, 284; and numbers emancipated, 294; and Subcommission of 1879, 300–301; and law of 1880, 305, 307

——, Article XVIII: and *emancipados*, 278

——, Article XXI: and abolition question, 247, 253; and amendment problem, 248–249; and Cuban elections, 248–249; and whip, 267

Moret y Prendergast, Segismundo: and Abolitionist Society, 154; named colonial minister, 243; character of, 243; his policy, 243–245; his law, 244–253, 254; on corporal punishment, 254; and proprietors, 255–258; and Moret Law suspension, 259, 261; and Clarendon's defense, 260; and American government, 261; and census problem, 262–264; and Valmaseda, 262; and law of 1880, 305. SEE ALSO Moret Law

Moroccan War (1860–1861): 132

Morón, Cuba: and census problem, 277

Moslem world: cited in debate, 290

Mosquera, Tomás: named colonial minister, 285; and Puerto Rican abolition, 285–286

mulattoes: and Puerto Rican abolitionism, 156, 297; and assimilation, 313

municipal reform: promise of 1868, 221. SEE ALSO Cuban reforms; political reforms

Munne, Juan: 186

Muñoz, Juan I.: 276

Murúa, Antonio: mentioned, 179

Nación La: 288

Napoleon: and Haitian slavery, 18; and Fernando VII, 29

Napoleonic Europe: and beet sugar, 48

Napoleon's invasion: and Spanish factionalism, 21; and reform question, 21, 39

Napoleonic period: 45

Narváez, Ramón María (Duke of Valencia): and expulsion of Bulwer, 96; and sale of Cuba, 105; and status quo, 154, 215; in power, 186; and Reform Commission, 186, 211–214

national integrity: and insurrection, 228; and Colonial League, 287

National Intelligencer (Washington): on Cuban acquisition, 123

nationalism: and Puerto Rico, 135. SEE ALSO Cuban nationalism

Navarro, Bernardo María: 71

Navarro, Rodrigo: 228

Near-Eastern crisis: 114

negreros. SEE slave interests

Negroes: and Las Casas, 24; in Creole reformism, 57; and reform dilemma, 174; and Cuban insurrection, 224; cited in debates, 290, 305; opinion of, 305; and Spanish humanity, 312. SEE ALSO Cuban slavery

Negro labor. SEE Cuban slave labor

Negro marriage: 113

Negro militia: and Pezuela, 121; and abolition question, 287

Negro slavery. SEE African slavery; Cuban slavery

negrophile: and Cuban liberalism, 51

Nesselrode, Karl R.: 17

New Orleans: and Cuban exiles, 98; and López expeditions, 102

New World: and abolition, 313

New York City: and Cuban exiles, 98; and Creole reformism, 130; and annexationists, 99, 213
New York Herald: and slave registry, 182; on Cuban independence (1879), 306
New York Sun: on law of 1880, 307
New York Times: 271–272
New York Tribune: 271–272
North. SEE American North

Occidente Province (Western Cuba): contrast with Oriente, 50; and planter class, 50; and insurrection, 224–225, 226, 240; and census of 1862 and 1877, 295
O'Donnell, Leopoldo (Duque de Tetuan): named governor (1843–1848), 79; and protection of slavery, 79–82, 83, 86–88, 89, 104, 143; slave revolt, 81; and *emancipado* problem 82–83, and treaty of 1845, 86, 88; and Alcoy, 93; and slave trade, 104; as prime minister, 132; returned to power (1865), 154; and liberal revolt, 186
Ofalia, Conde de: 65
O'Farrill, José Ricardo: and Serrano's reforms, 133; and Cuban reforms, 175–176
O'Farrill, Juan: and slave trade, 39
Official Gazette (Havana): 262
O'Gaban, Juan Bernardo (ecclesiastic): defense of slave trade, 38
Ojea, Antonio R.: 186
Olid, Cristóbal de: in Cuba, 9
Oliván, Alejandro: and Reform Commission, 189, 190; and Puerto Rican abolition, 193–194; and piracy declaration, 197; and abolition quesquestion, 200–202
Olivares, Ignacio Gonzales: 191
Olózaga, Salustiano de: and Cuban reforms, 131; and Abolition Society, 154
Order of the Lone Star: 99
Order of Predicators: 4
organic law proposal (1860): 132
Oriental labor. SEE Chinese labor; Indian coolies
Oriente Province (Eastern Cuba): contrast with Occidente, 50; and planter class, 50, 139; population of (1860), 140; and Cuban Republic, 222–223; and insurrection, 224–226, 295; and sale of Cuba, 264–265
Original Sin: and abolition debate, 289
Ortega, Manuel de: elected to Reform Commission, 186; and Puerto Rican abolition, 194–196, 198
Ortiz Fernández, Fernando: on Cuban slavery, 4; on sugar industry, 11, 13; on traffic, 1850–1880, 183
Ostend Manifesto: and Soulé 120; and American opinion, 123; and Buchanan, 126
Otoala, Juan: 276

Padial, Luis Ricardo: as abolitionist deputy, 233; and Reform Commission, 239–240; and reactionaries, 242; and Moret Law, 249
Paine, Tom: and abolition, 18; and Goicouria, 124
Pais, El (Havana): 310
Palmella, Duke of: 17
Palmerston, Viscount (John Henry Temple): on *emancipado* problem, 41, 67, 82, 90; as foreign secretary, 60; and treaty evasion, 60; and new pressures on Spain, 60; and Turnbull, 75–77; and proposal of 1840, 75–77; and O'Donnell, 82–83; and abolitionist natives, 87; and Brazilian abolition, 90–91; and flag problem, 94–95; and Parliamentary testimony (1850), 96; ultimatum on slave trade, 97–98
papal concordats: 21
papal declarations: against slavery, 64, 165, 171, 197–198
Parejo, Antonio: and traffic, 112
Paris: and Creole reformism, 130
Parker, Vice-Admiral: 74
Parliament. SEE British Parliament
Partido Conservador. SEE Conservative Party of Cuba
pases de tránsito: 182
Pastor, Manuel: and traffic, 112; his abolition proposal, 201–202; and tax question, 213–214
Pastor, Luis María: and Puerto Rican abolition, 193; and use of whip, 200; and reform committee of 1869, 239–240
Patria Criolla, La: 37

Patriarch of the Indies: 305
patrocinado (free-born Negro): in Moret Law, 246, 248, 258; and Cuban plan, 258; and law of 1880, 306–307, 308; and abolitionists, 309–310; and coercion, 311
patrón (master): in Moret Law, 246, 248, 275; and work contracts, 278; and abolition abuses, 309
patronato (tutelage): in Moret Law, 245, 246–248, 275; and Liberal-Autonomists, 297; and Cuban Conservatives, 299, 305; and subcommission of 1879, 300; and abolition question, 301; in abolition law of 1880, 301, 302–306; abolition of, 309, 311
Paul, Saint: and abolition question, 164; on slavery, 170–171
Paul III: 197–198
Paula Jiménez, Francisco de: 189
Peace of Utrech: 7
Peace of Zanjón (1878): provisions and effects of, 295; and Cánovas, 299; and American government, 299–300
Pearl of the Antilles: development of, 9; and abolition threat, 71; and sale of, 120. SEE ALSO Cuba
peninsulars. SEE Spanish peninsulars
peonage labor: and Latin America, 30
Perier, Carlos María: 305
Perry, Horatio J.: 120–121
Peru: compared to Cuba, 14; and abolition, 30
Pezuela, Juan de la (Marqués y Conde de Cheste): on policy, 107; as governor, 114–121; his abolitionist measures, 115–120, 182; and retreat, 120; and defiance of United States, 120–121; and Concha, 124; and Cuban reforms, 131; and Puerto Rican liberalism, 155; and Spanish Cortes, 177
Pezuela y Lobo, Jacobo de la: on Cuban development, 9; on treaty of 1817, 26–27, 28; on slaves captured, 54
Philip II: and *asiento*, 6
Philadelphia: 157; 269
Philippine Islands: and reform question, 21, 218; and treaty of 1817, 28; and immigration, 86; and Oriental labor, 88; and reform circular of 1868, 218
Philippines Company: and *asiento*, 8
Phillips, Wendell: cited in debate, 250
philosophy: and Creole nationalism, 56
Pidal y Mon, Luis: 290
Pierce administration: 116, 120, 125
Pierce, President Franklin: 117
Pinar del Río (province): 307
Pintó conspiracy: 123
piracy declaration: and Canning, 31; proposals of, 95, 145; and Brazil, 95, 97; and Spanish refusal of, 97, 145, 175–176; and Pezuela's administration, 121–122; and Serrano, 145, 120; and United States, 147; in abolition plans, 149; and law of 1866, 190; and Reform Commission, 196–198; and Dulce, 209
Pius II: 165, 197–198
Pi y Margall, Francisco: 171
Pizarro, José: 29
plantations: number in 1762, 10; and loans, 49–50; and taxes, 54; and treaty of 1845, 85–88; and labor problem, 134–146, 295; and insurrection, 226, 295, 296; and *emancipado* problem, 276–277; and law of 1880, 307. SEE ALSO *ingenio*
plantation economy: 12, 30
plantation labor: 313
planters. SEE Cuban proprietors
plebiscite: and insurrection, 234; and pacification, 234
poetry: and Turnbull, 76; and abolitionist propaganda, 159
Poey, Juan: and Chinese coolies, 137; and Moret project, 257
policy of assimilation: 151
policy of *atracción:* and O'Donnell, 132–134; and Dulce, 133
policy of nonbelligerency: 236
Política, La: and Saco, 220
political economy: 56
political parties: 208
political reforms. SEE Cuban reforms
Politics of Aristotle: 164
Polk, President James: 99
Polo de Bernarbe, Don José: 283, 284
population of Cuba: in 1602, 9; in 1609, 9; in 1655, 10; in 1792, 12; in 1868, 221. SEE ALSO Cuban slaves
Portel Vilá, Herminio: 278–281

Index

Portugal: union with Spain, 6; and abolition treaties, 30; use of flag, 31
Portuguese: and slave trade, xi–xii, 5, 6, 7, 30, 31; and British abolitionism, 25–26; and Anglo-Portuguese treaties, 30; and piracy declaration, 121; and Cuban traffic, 126; and Russell's proposal, 127
Portuguese Africa: 31
Portuguese Angola: and *asiento*, 6
Portuguese Brazil: 30–31
Portuguese flag. See flag problem
Portuguese Guinea Company: 7
Portuondo, Bernardo: and elections of 1879 and 1881, 304; and abolition, 304, 309; and economic concessions, **304**
potestad dominica: and Spanish slavery, 72; and Moret Law, 258
Power, Ramón: and abolition, 22
Pozo de la Merced, Marqués del: 303
Pozos Dulces, Conde de (Frías y Jacott, Francisco): and annexation, 98–99, 124; and *El Siglo*, 133; on Chinese coolies, 137; and Lincoln, 140–142; elected to reform commission, 186; and Saco, 198; and immigrant labor, 191, 191–199; and Puerto Rican abolition, 193–195; Africanization, 196; and Dulce, 230; and autonomist movement, 296
Prendergast, Luis: and law of 1880, 307; and autonomists, 310
Prensa, La (Havana): 175
Preparatory Law for the Abolition of Slavery in the Spanish Antilles. See Moret Law
priest. See Catholic clergy
Prim, General Juan: and Masonry, 169; and liberal revolt of 1866, 186; and Glorious Revolution, 216–217; and Progresistas, 217; and colonial reform, 221, 265; and insurrection, 223, 230, 234; and Grant administration, 234–237; and abolition question, 237; and constitutional monarchy, 237, 239, 264; and Spanish Volunteers, 241; and Moret, 243; assassination of, 264; and Amadeo de Savoy, 264; and Cánovas, 265
privilegio de ingenio: and feudal concessions, 11; abolished, 49

proclamations: of 1849 and López expedition, 102; of 1868 and Cuban insurrection, 222, 225; of Bayamo and rebel abolition, 225; of Lersundi and insurrection, 229
procreation of slaves: encouraged, 15, 24, 29, 33, 36, 113, 136; and proslavery, 70; and American example, 70; and Reform Commission, 191–192, 193–194
pro-Cuban sentiment in the United States: and Moret Law, 251
Progresistas: 216
Progressive ministry: fall of, 273
Progressive Party: and abolition in Spain, 63; significance of, 64
pronunciamientos: 216
propaganda: and conservation of Cuba, 43; and foreign abolitionism, 43; and republicanism, 43; and Cuban exiles, 98–100; and Spanish Abolitionist Society, 159–160; and Cuban autonomists, 298; of slave interests, 312. See also Cuban exiles; Spanish abolitionists
Propaganda, La (Madrid): 159
property: decree of 1819, 32–33; and *privilegio de ingenio*, 49; and confiscated slaves, 279–281; and rebel destruction, 295; and tax of 1867, 303
proprietor. See Cuban proprietors
proslavery (or status quo) arguments: and Haitian example, 24, 70, 71, 204, 220, 288; and French example, 24, 228, 288; and patriotism, 28, 33–34, 38, 39, 71, 100–101, 178, 198; and British example, 26, 28, 36, 42–43, 73, 86; and Cuban economy, 35–36, 39, 70, 71, 73, 93, 101, 174, 178, 203, 211, 287, 301; and civilization, 38, 72, 164, 194–195, 198, 204; and indolence, 38, 70, 71; and Spanish humanity, 38, 70, 72, 73, 163, 164, 170, 193, 198, 204, 254, 287, 305, 312; and labor problem, 66; and American example, 70, 201, 207, 227, 287, 305; and Santo Domingo, 70, 196; and white labor, 70, 86–87, 136; and vagrancy, 70, 71, 203, 301; and conservation of Cuba, 71, 86, 93, 100, 101, 174, 178, 220, 288–290; and threat to white race, 72, 73, 100, 220–221, 257; and Christiani-

zation, 73, 164, 170, 287, 312; and insufficient indemnity, 73, 211, 220, 256; and foreign abolitionists, 73, 288, 305; and threat of annexation, 93, 101; and Negro's nature, 164, 170, 257, 305; and biblical justification, 170–171; classical, 170–171, 207–208; and Africanization fears, 209, 220–221; and manumission, 287; and American pressure, 288, 305

prostitution of female slaves: 246

Protestantism: and international abolitionism, 17–20, 167; and Puerto Rican abolitionism, 158, 169

Provisional government: and Glorious Revolution, 217–219; and reform, 217–221; and Cuban insurrection, 223, 229, 230; and belligerency question, 235–236; and American government, 242; and Amadeo de Savoy, 264

Prussia: and abolitionism, 26; and Fish's policy, 235

Puig, Padre: 289

Puerto Cabello: and slave trade, 13

Puerto Rican abolitionists: and demands of 1868, 220; explanation of, 154–161; and Sanromá, 169–171; and reaction to Saco, 221; in Cortes, 232–233, 242, 249, 282; and reform promises, 237; and plan of 1869, 241–242; and Moret Law, 249, 267, 282; and Spanish abolitionism, 267; and Don Amadeo, 282–283; and radical party, 282–283; and Puerto Rican abolition, 282–283, 286–293, 301–302; and foreign diplomacy, 283–284; and Liberal-Autonomists, 299; and abolition of stocks and irons, 311

Puerto Rican abolition plan of 1867: 202, 205

Puerto Rican Commissioners: and election of 1866, 186; and reform question, 189–214; and abolition proposal, 192–194; and plans of 1867, 202

Puerto Rican conservatives: 233

Puerto Rican Creoles: 154–161

Puerto Rican deputies: and Cortes of 1810–1812, 22. SEE ALSO Puerto Rican abolitionists

Puerto Rican economy: 156

Puerto Rican government: and reforms, 155, 157; and Zorrilla's promises, 285

Puerto Rican liberals: 233

Puerto Rican people: 275–278

Puerto Rican population: 156

Puerto Rican proprietors: and slave trade, 155–156; and abolition, 154–157, 276, 291

Puerto Rican reforms: and abolition movement, 154–161; and Reform Commission, 185–214, 239; and reform question, 218–219, 221; and Cuban insurrection, 241–243; and Spanish reactionaries, 241–243; and American government, 241–243; and Provisional government, 242; and Glorious Revolution, 243; and Zorrilla promises, 285; and Colonial League, 287–290. SEE ALSO Puerto Rican abolitionists

Puerto Rican republicans: 222

Puerto Rican slave trade: 183

Puerto Rican slavery: and abolition, 157, 287, 291

Puerto Rico: and reform problems, 21; and Spanish policy, 25; and abolition, 27; and contrast with Cuba, 53, 154–161, 221; excluded from Cortes, 64; and colonial neglect, 67; and mixed courts, 76; and Pezuela, 114; and sugar production, 140; and population, 156, 222; and economy, 156; and independence movement, 213; and elections, 221, 232–233, 243; and rebellion at Lares, 222, 243; and British abolitionism, 266; and Fish's policy, 269–270; and Moret Law, 275; and foreign abolition, 281; in abolition argument, 282; and American reform pressure, 284; and Liberal-Autonomists, 299; and abolition law, 1880, 302. SEE ALSO Puerto Rican abolitionists; Puerto Rican reform

punishment. SEE corporal punishment; laws; treaties (of abolition)

Quakers: and English abolitionism, 18, 157, 168; Torrente's attacks on, 73; and Spanish government, 269

Quakers of Pennsylvania: 168

Index

Queen Mother: and traffic, 104
questionaire. SEE Colonial Reform Commission
Quiñones, Mariano: and abolitionist movement, 154; abolition proposal of, 192–194, 202
Quitman, General John A.: and Pezuela's policy, 119; expedition of, 123

Radicals (Spanish): in power, 273; and Sickles' advice, 274; and Puerto Rican abolition, 282–283, 285, 286
Radical government: and Moret Law regulations, 273; and Cuban reform, 281
railroad: in Cuba, 67
Ramírez (deputy): 304
Ramírez, Alejandro: and economic progress, 13; and Junta de Población Blanca, 33; and commissary judge, 40
rationalism: and abolitionism, 17–20, 167; and Glorious Revolution, 219
Rauch, Basil: on slave trade, 105; on Spanish policy, 114
Rawlins, John A.: 236
Real Consulado de Agricultura, Industria y Comercio (Royal Consulate of Agricultural, Industry, and Commerce): founded, 12
Real Sociedad Patriotica, La: 71
reactionaries: and Cuban immigration, 33. SEE ALSO Cuban slave interests; Spanish reactionaries
rebel guerrillas: and insurrection, 267
rebel proprietors: and confiscated slave problem, 279, 280–281
rebel slaves: and Peace of Zanjón, 295
rebellion. SEE slave rebellion
Rebellion of Lares (1868): and Puerto Rico, 222; and Spanish reactionaries, 243
referendum: and pacification, 234–235
Reform Commission. SEE Colonial Reform Commission
reform committee of 1869: 239
reforms. SEE Cuban reforms; Puerto Rican reforms
Reformation: and Spain, 20
registration law of 1880: 307
registry. SEE slave registry
regulations: of mixed tribunals, 61; of 1849, and punishment of coolies, 110; of Moret Law, 264, 274–277; for law of 1880, 305, 306–308
Relampago, El (Spanish ship): 42
religion. SEE Catholicism; Christianity
religious corporations: 41
religious freedom: and reform, 221
Remington rifle: 230
remonstrances: and American Quakers, 269. SEE ALSO memoranda
Renaissance: 290
Report on Fugitive Slaves (of Arango): and abolitionist question, 165
Report of Subcommission on Slavery: and gradual abolition, 300–301
Republic of Texas: and American fears, 77; and British abolitionism, 78
Republican Junta of Cuba: 279–281
Republican Society of Cuba and Puerto Rico: founded in 1865, 213
republicans. SEE Cuban republicans; Spanish republicans
republicanism: threat to Cuba, 43; and Tacón, 67; and Puerto Rico, 155; and Glorious Revolution, 216–220; and Cuban revolutionaries, 223; and Cuban rebels, 283
Republican Party (Spanish): and Glorious Revolution, 216; and Sickles, 272
Revista Economica de las Antilles: mentioned, 310
revolt: and Spanish liberals of 1820, 36. SEE ALSO Cuban insurrection; slave rebellion
Revolt of Yara. SEE Cuban insurrection
Revolution of 1789: 219
Revolution of September. SEE Glorious Revolution
revolutionaries. SEE Cuban rebels; Glorious Revolution
Revolutionary Junta of Madrid: and Glorious Revolution, 217; and abolitionist manifesto, 218
Revolutionary Junta of Havana: 231
Ricafort, Mariano (captain general): and Creole toleration, 55
Richardson, Doctor: 76
right of search: 78; in treaties, 32; in treaty of 1817, 28–30; in Treaty of 1835, 61; and France, 78; and the United States, 147. SEE ALSO British government; United States

rights of man: and abolition, 313
Rio de Janeiro: 89
Riquelme, José Luis: 178
Rivero, Nicolás María: and Spanish liberalism, 150; and masonry, 169; and abolition manifesto, 218; and reaction, 241; and Sickles' opinion, 272
Robertson, William H.: and abolitionism, 18; and Pezuela administration, 116–119; and annexation, 116; and report on Governor Pezuela, 117
Rodríguez, Antonio: 198
Rodríguez, Gabriel: and Spanish Abolitionist Society, 154; on abolition, 242; opinion on Fish's policy, 270
Rodríguez, José Ignacio: and Governor Dulces, 230; and amendment and Moret Law, 249
Rojo Arias (deputy): 289
Roman world: cited in debate, 290
Rome: and slave trade, xi; and slavery, 207; and captain general, 268
Romero Ortiz, Antonio: and anticlericalism, 171; and Puerto Rican abolition, 195; against piracy declaration, 198; on whip, 200; on American pressure, 288
Romero Robledo, Francisco: and reaction, 228; against reform, 242–243, 248
Romney (British ship): and Cuban intervention, 59; and *emancipados*, 76
royal cedula. SEE decree
Royal Company of Havana: 7–10
royal decree. SEE decree
royal license: and slave trade, 4–5. SEE ALSO decree
Royal French Guinea Company: 7
royal orders. SEE decree
royal tobacco monopoly: abolished, 32
Ruíz, Joaquín M.: 189
Ruíz Belvis, Segundo: and Puerto Rican abolition, 192–194, 195, 202
Ruíz Gómez, Servando: 303
Ruíz Zorilla, Manuel: and Masonry, 169; and Glorious Revolution, 217; and Puerto Rican abolition, 282–283
Russell, Lord John: 112, 127, 145
Russia: and abolition, 26, 32; and piracy declaration, 121

"sacks of coal": and slave landings, 182

Saco, José Antonio: definition of slave, xi; on slave numbers in Jamaica and Cuba, 27; on *emancipados* as slaves, 41; on Negrophiles, 51; on British abolitionism, 23, 55; and Creole culture, 56; and nationalism, 56–58, 139; attack on slave trade, 57–58, 183, 196; exile of, 58, 67; on treaty evasion, 64; on colonial despotism, 65, 227; his history of slavery, 67; and Sagra, 83–84; and annexation, 101–102, 221, 222; and free labor, 108; and *El Siglo*, 133; against coolie labor, 138–139; against free African labor, 150; on Church as slaveholder, 165, 171; on Spanish policy, 175; on Seijas Lozano, 175; and Reform Commission, 186, 187, 188, 206–207; against abolition, 205, 220; and Creole fears, 220; refuted by Labra, 221; against revolution, 222; rejected by Cuban revolutionaries, 223
Sagasta, Práxedes Mateo: and Abolition Society; and Glorious Revolution, 217; and Sickles, 272; fall from power, 273; and autonomist movement, 296, 310
Sagra, Ramón de la: on suppression of traffic (1845), 83–84; compared to Saco, 83–84; and free labor, 84; and Cuban studies, 84; on Chinese labor, 110; on Cuban economy, 140; named reform commissioner, 189; and of Asiatic labor, 191; and Puerto Rican abolition, 193
St. Vincent: slave population of, 45
Salamanca (university): 20–21
Saldanha: and Vienna declaration, 17
sale of Cuba. SEE United States
Salisbury, Lord (Robert Arthur Talbot Gascoigne): and abolition policy, 299; and law of 1880, 306
Salmerón, Nicolás: and Abolition Society, 154; and anticlericalism, 171
Sánchez Bustillo, Cayetano: 301–304
Sandoval, Alonso de (Jesuit): 167
Sandoval, Ignacio: 276
San Juan (Puerto Rico): and slave trade, 13; and Vízcarrondo, 157
San Luis, Count of: 113
San Martín, Antonio X. de: and Reform Commission, 187, 197, 199–200
San Martín, José de: and abolition, 30

Index

San Miguel, Marqués de: 264
Sanromá, Joaquín: and Abolitionist Society, 154, 187; on Vizcarrondo, 158; and Spanish abolitionism, 169–171; and abolition studies, 169–171; and anticlericalism, 171; and reform committee of 1869, 239–240; and Puerto Rican abolition, 286, 289
Sánta Clara (district): 307
Santiago de Cuba (district): and English Royal African Company, 10; and Saco, 188; and census problem, 277; and insurrection, 295; and law of 1880, 307
Santo Domingo: and slavery, 4, 13; and reforms, 33; and abolitionist propaganda, 43; and Cuban fears, 58, 81; and Spanish defeat, 150, 213; and proslavery arguments, 164, 248; and Cuban revolutionaries, 223; and Cuban abolition, 300. SEE ALSO Española; Haiti
Santo Spiritus (district): 118
Santos Guzmán, Francisco de los: 302
Saragossa: 158
Saunders, Romulus: 89
Scelle, George: 8
scholasticism: and Spanish conscience, 167, 169
Secretariat of High Civil government: and slavers, 209
Sedano y Cruzat, Carlos de: and British policy, 121
Segovia, Antonio María: 154
Seijas Lozano, Manuel: and reform, 173–174; and colonial policy, 175–177; and abolition, 176, 192
Select Committee of the House of Commons: and right of search, 96
Select Committee of Lords: 96
Sepúlveda, Doctor Juan Ginés de: 167
Serrano y Domínguez, Francisco (Duque de la Torre): his administration, 1859–1862, 131–132; and Cuban reforms, 131–132, 150, 187, 221; and abolition question, 145, 149, 287; and Tassara, 161; and Canovas reforms, 185; his reform memorandum, 208–210; and Glorious Revolution, 216–217; and insurrectionaries, 223, 230
Seville: and slavery, 5; and Abolitionist Society, 158; and reform question, 179–180
Seville merchants: and *asiento*, 6
Seward, William Henry: 147
Sickles, Daniel E.: as ambassador, 233; and Cuban policy, 234, 235, 244, 272, 273–274, 284; and Bacerra's reforms, 240; and Spanish liberals, 241, 242; and Moret Law, 252–253, 260, 273; and protest of Moret Law, 260; on insurrection, 267–268; and British abolitionists, 270; press interviews of, 271; his meddlesome activities, 272
Sierra Leone: and mixed commission, 29, 39; and slave trade, 95
siglistas: and Governor Dulce, 134
Siglo, El (Havana): founded in 1863, 133; and reform question, 133, 212; and *El Diario de la Marina,* 134, 212; and American Civil War, 141; and Reform Commission, 187
slave: definition, xi; and Spanish humanity, 72
slave census: proposed, 1840, and reaction, 70–73; of 1842, 74–75; inaccuracies of, 89–90, 277; Spanish refusal of, 97; and Moret Law, 246, 258, 261, 262–264, 276; and Junta de Hacendados (1870), 255; of 1870, 258. SEE ALSO slave registry
slave code: of 1789, 52–53; of 1842, 53; and proslavists, 72, 164; of 1844, 74; abolitionists, 164; and Arango's report, 165
slave conspiracy: in code of 1842, 74
slave debates: and Concha's policies, 126; and Peace of Zanjón, 295; and law of 1880, 302–307
slave economy. SEE Cuban economy
slave epidemic: 114
slave institution: and Spanish, 311–312
slave insurrection. SEE rebellion
slave interests: of Puerto Rico, 25–26, 27. SEE ALSO Cuban slave interests
slave marriage: 15
slave merchants: and exile, 148
slave mortality: 26, 312; and population, 294
slave problem: and piracy dilemma, 1865–1866, 174; and military abolition, 281; and Spanish statesmen, 312

slave procreation: and O'Donnell, 86–87; and Spanish Council, 87–88; and United States example, 87; and labor shortage, 109–111; failure of, 111; and closing of traffic, 184

slave proprietors. See Cuban proprietors

slave property: 290

slave question: and conservative Spain, 39; and Spanish-American relations, 269–270; recedes military abolition, 281; and American demands, 284; and abolition law of 1880, 301–306, 310–311; and Catholic clergy, 305; and Spanish statesmen, 312

slave rebellion: fear of, 33, 37, 43, 51, 53, 58, 70, 74, 82; and Turnbull, 74–75, 81; and Spanish policy, 84; and annexation, 102–104; and Cuban insurrection, 226; and confiscated slaves, 279–281; and British Negroes, 304

slave registry: and crisis of 1840, 73–74; and Pezuela's mission, 113, 118–119; and proprietors, 119; and law of 1866, 181–182; and Concha's opinion, 182; in Cuban plan of 1867, 204; and Moret Law, 246, 275–278; and law of 1880, 306–307; and abolitionists, 309. See also slave census

slave regulations: and abolition of stocks and irons, 311. See also Moret Law

slave ships: and flag problem, 32, 35, 60–62, 63, 94; and treaty violations, 35, 39; numbers of, 35, 59, 144; capture of, 40, 42, 54, 63, 144, 278; and American participation, 63, 126, 127; and Spanish ports, 69; and declaration of piracy, 95, 97; and Governor Pezuela, 118; and closing of traffic, 182–183; and Dulce's report, 209

slave sugar: and House of Commons, 95; and American pressure, 285

slave trade. See African slave trade; Cuban slave trade; slave ships

slave holders. See Cuban proprietors

slavers. See slave ships

slavery, slaves. See Cuban slavery

slavist. See slave interests

slavocrats: and Spanish policy, 127; and *El Diario de la Marina*, 134

slavophiles: and reform, 1869, 242

Smith, Adam: and abolitionism, 18

social question: and Reform Commission, 1865–1867, 189–205; and Moret Law, 245–251, 255–259; and Junta de Hacendados, 255–258; committee on, 259

Sociedad Abolicionista, La: 288. See also Spanish Abolition Society

Sociedad Económica (Economic Society): founded, 12; against abolition, 24

Sociedad Protectora de Documentos Históricos de Puerto Rico, La: 156–157

Societé des Amis des Noirs: 18

Society for the Abolition of the Slave Trade (English): 18–19

Someruelos, Marqués de (Salvador de Muro): and abolition alarm, 23–24

Soto, Domingo de (friar): 167

Sotolongo, Pedro de: named reform commissioner, 189; and Puerto Rican abolition, 195; and Moret project, 256, 258

Soulé, Pierre: and Ostend Manifesto, 120; and *Black Warrior*, 120; and acquisition of Cuba, 116

South. See American South

South America: and independence, 33. See also Latin American republics

Southern Confederacy. See American South

Southerners: and Cuban exiles, 98–99

Spain: and slave trade, 3–8; of the Golden Age, 20; and reform dilemma, 20–22, 122–123; and conservation of Cuba, 22; and *emancipado* problem, 40; policy of, 59; and Carlist War, 66, 84; and British abolitionism, 23, 84; and Brazil, 91; and annexation threat, 101–102; and emergent abolitionism, 153–154; and religious conscience, 167–168; and Glorious Revolution, 215–217; and literacy question, 221; and support of Britain, 270; and rebel propaganda, 279–281; and autonomist movement, 296; and abolitionist petitions, 309; and colonial tariff, 331; and final abolition judgments, 312–313. See also Spanish government

Index

Spanish abolitionists: and conscience, 20–22, 55, 166–171; in Cortes of Cadiz, 22–25; and Argüelles proposal, 23; influence of Puerto Ricans, 154–161; and United States, 154–161, 288–289; and Puerto Ricans, 154–161; and comparisons, 167–169; and foreign influence, 168–171; and *emancipados*, 166; and ideology, 166, 169–171; and influence of the Glorious Revolution, 217–220, 242–245; and Cuban insurrection, 227, 237, 240–245; and reform promises, 237; and British conciliation, 244–245; and Moret Law, 247, 249–250; and British abolitionists, 270; and confiscated slaves, 279–281; and radical party, 283–284; and Puerto Rican law, 288–290; and propaganda, 290; and British policy, 294; and abolition law of 1880, 302, 304; and abolition of stocks and irons, 311

Spanish Abolitionist Society: founded 20, 154–161; principles of, 158; branches of, 158, 159, 299; propaganda of, 159–160, 220, 282, 288, 289; and law of 1866, 177-178, 181–182; and Saco, 187; suppressed, 187; and Reform Commission, 201; outlawed, 215; and Glorious Revolution, 219; and activities, 1868, 220; and census problem, 263; and Puerto Rican law, 288–290; and the United States, 289; and Peace of Zanjón, 295; and Liberal-Autonomists, 299; and law of 1880, 301; on abolition abuses, 309

Spanish ambassador: 293
Spanish America: 3–8
Spanish-American relations: and Sickles' opinion, 271–272
Spanish army: 287
Spanish Antilles: and Indian labor, 3, 4–8; and abolition problem, 43; and Fish's policy, 270; and tariff, 311
Spanish bankers. See Spanish merchants
Spanish bonds: 96
Spanish colonial system: 304
Spanish colonist: 108–109
Spanish conservatives: and traditional Spain, 21; and restoration of 1823, 39; and law of 1866, 178–181; and Cuban revolution of 1868, 223; and Moret Law, 248–249; and law of 1880, 305

Spanish Constitution: 274
Spanish Cortes: of Cadiz and abolition question, 22–24, 36–38, 63–64, 288; of 1865–1866 and abolition question, 52, 162–163, 173–174, 177–181, 242–253; of 1834–1837 and "Special Laws," 64, 173–174, 187, 309; and status quo, 125; and colonial exclusion, 132, 187, 195; and colonial reform question, 150, 173–174, 177–181, 239; and law of 1866, 177–181; and Glorious Revolution, 216–217; and Junta Cubana, 220; and of Puerto Rico, 232–233, 282; and Moret Law, 247, 250–257, 263, 267; and sale of Cuba, 264–265; and Sickles' opinions, 271–272; and confiscated slaves, 279; and Colonial League, 287; and Puerto Rican abolition, 285, 286–290; and republic, 288; and autonomist movement, 296–298, 310; and Cuban election of 1879, 298–299; and law of 1880, 302–306, 309; of 1879–1880, and abolition of *patronato*, 309

Spanish Council of State. See Council of State
Spanish court: and slave revenue, 105
Spanish Crown: and slave trade, 5–8; and immigration control, 5
Spanish doctors: and abolitionism, 312
Spanish dominion: 312
Spanish Empire: and *asiento*, 8–9; and Puerto Rican abolitionists, 242
Spanish flag. See flag problem
Spanish government:
——————, and abolition question: and conscience, 20–22, 55, 122–123, 166–171; and Argüelles proposal of 1811, 23, 64–65; and Congress of Vienna, 25; and Council of the Indies, 27; and colonial interests, 27; and treaty of 1817, 28–30, 35, 39, 53; and *emancipado* problem, 40–43; and treaty of 1835, 61–63; and British protests, 69, 96–98; and Governor Tacón, 67; and proposed treaty of 1840, 70–71, 73–74; and slave registry crisis of 1840, 73–

74; and Turnbull, 75–77; and O'-Donnell, 79–82; and treaty of 1845, 86–87; and gradual abolition, 82–83, 174–175; and American intervention, 107, 113–114, 260–261, 266–270; and weak policy, 112, 127–128; and Pezuela's abolition mission, 113–123; and Concha's measures, 123–128, 145; and proposed conference of 1860, 127; and Russell, 127–128, 145; and search, 128; and British pressures, 143, 175, 294, 299; and Serrano's proposals, 145; and abolition of traffic, 147–148; and Dulce's policy, 148; and slave interests, 174–175; and law of 1866, 176–181; and abolition proposals of 1866–1867, 192–194, 201–206; and Cuban insurrection, 240–241, 269–270; and Becerra's plan, 241; and Puerto Ricans, 242; and Grant's administration, 242–243; and Moret Law of 1870, 243–254, 255–272; and tutelage system, 258; and British support, 267, 270; and American abolitionists, 269; and confiscated-slave problem, 279–281, 286; and Colonial League, 287; and Peace of Zanjón, 294–295; and petitions, 299; and Alfonso XII, 300; and law of 1880, 302–306, 307–308; and immigrant labor, 303–304; and British Negroes, 304; and final abolition, 312–313. SEE ALSO piracy declaration

———, colonial policy: and Arango's reforms, 14–15; and status quo, 22, 44, 47, 151, 154, 173–174, 215, 235, 240, 248, 286–287; and conservation of slavery, 22, 65, 70, 86, 96, 100–101, 105–106, 113–114, 126, 136, 191, 196–198, 221; and promotion of white labor, 33, 107–109; "besieged fortress" policy, 44; and procrastination, 47; and colonial taxes, 54, 213; and peninsular interests, 56; and distrust of Creoles, 56, 151; and colonial exclusion, 64–65, 173–174; and neglect of Cuba, 65–67, 173; and conservation of Cuba, 66, 96–98, 100–101, 196–198; and slave procreation, 70, 197; and American interests, 78, 84, 98–104, 125, 233–237, 241–245, 252, 311; and annexationist threat, 84, 98–104; and abolition law of 1845, 85–88; and resistance to British, 86, 105, 112–113; and oriental labor, 109–110, 136; and *atracción*, 132–134; and "Special Laws," 173–174, 184–185; and colonial reform question, 173–185; and Reform Comission, 185–187, 189–214; and equilibrium of races, 197; and Cuban insurrection, 221–224, 227–233, 233–238, 240–245, 286; and Spanish Volunteers, 234; and Puerto Rican reform, 241–245, 275, 290; and British support, 270; and Sickles' opinions, 271–272; and war debts, 296; and Liberal-Autonomists, 296, 297–299; and crisis of 1880–1886, 310; and economic reforms, 304, 311; and final abolition, 312. SEE ALSO *asiento;* Cuban government; censorship; Cuban slave trade; decree; emergency powers

———, and influence: of slave interests, 33–34, 48–51, 57, 71–75, 93, 114, 118–120, 151, 174–175, 211–214, 221, 228, 240–241, 287; of Cuban revenues, 54–56, 105, 235, 240; of Cuban officials, 55, 59, 114; of Spanish patriotism, 57, 164; of Spanish pride, 70, 164, 240; of the United States, 70, 113–114, 147–148, 161–163, 176–177, 233–236, 251–253, 260–261, 276; of the Civil War, 145, 148, 161, 235–236; of Spanish liberals, 153–154, 160, 171; of conservatives, 171, 281. SEE ALSO Puerto Rican abolitionists; Spanish abolitionists, Spanish liberals; Spanish party; Spanish reactionaries; Spanish Volunteers

Spanish Indies: 3–8
Spanish immigration: and labor problem, 33; and report of 1867, 199
Spanish Inquisition: 20–21
Spanish intendent (Wenceslao de Villaurrutia): on policy, 72
Spanish insurrection: 281
Spanish jurists: and slavery, 312
Spanish labor: 113, 116
Spanish liberals: and reactionary elements, 21–22, 163, 222–224, 228–

Index

229, 240–241; in Cortes of Cadiz, 22–25; in Cortes of 1820–1822, 35–38, 39; and Liberal Union Party, 153; influence of, 153–154; and Puerto Rico, 155; and Abolitionist Society, 156–161; and Labra, 160–161; and American Civil War, 161; and Glorious Revolution, 216–220; and Cuban insurrection, 241–242; and Sickles, 241, 271–272; and British policy, 293; and Liberal-Autonomists, 296–298, 299; and Cuban autonomist, 310

Spanish liberalism: and abolitionism, 168–171; philosophical origins, and anticlericalism, 169–171; rationalism, 169–171; and Masonry, 169–171; and German idealism, 169–171

Spanish loyalists: and Cuban insurrection, 226; and confiscated slaves 279–281. SEE ALSO Spanish party; Spanish Volunteers

Spanish merchants: and slave trade, 8, 57; and planter loans, 49, 135; and Cuban reforms, 57, 131; and tariff, 104, 311; and loyalty to Spain, 114; and Moret project, 256; and Puerto Rican abolition, 287; and insurrection, 296

Spanish monarchists: 305

Spanish monopolists: and *asiento*, 6

Spanish navy: 63

Spanish officials. SEE Cuban government

Spanish party: founding of, 33–34, 49–51, 134; influence on Spain's colonial policy, 50, 151, 227–232; and patriotism, 57; and Pezuela, 114–120; and *El Diario de la Marina*, 134; and Creole reform, 134, 208; and Dulce, 148, 230–232; and exposition of 1865, 151; and reform question, 180, 185–186; and arbitrary tax, 213; and Cuban insurrection, 223, 231, 234–235, 296; and Governor Lersundi, 228–238; and Spanish reactionaries, 228–232; and Moret Law, 248; and Puerto Rican law, 290; and autonomists, 297, 310; and abolition policy, 299; and law of 1880, 308. SEE ALSO Spanish Volunteers

Spanish patriotism: and traffic, 105. SEE ALSO Cuban slave interests; proslavery

Spanish peninsulars: and economic interests, 48–51; and relation to Creoles, 49–51, 56–59; and Casino Español, 50; and Spain's Cuban policy, 50, 56; and Creole reform question, 133, 180; and American Civil War, 142; and abolitionism, 176; and elections, 185–186. SEE ALSO Cuban government; Cuban reforms; Spanish government

Spanish people: in abolition debate, 288

Spanish political parties: 265

Spanish press: and sale of Cuba, 235; and Moret Law, 254; and Cuban reforms, 303

Spanish reactionaries: and Moderados, 187; and Cuban insurrection, 222–232, 240–246; and Lopez de Ayala, 227–228; and Saco's opinions of, 227; leaders of, 228; and Governor Lersundi, 228–232; and Spanish Volunteers, 229–233; and expulsion of Governor Dulce, 230–232; and Spanish liberals, 241; and Puerto Rican reform, 242; and Moret Law, 245, 248–249, 250–251; and Puerto Rican abolition, 285–290; and Colonial League, 287; and Liberal-Autonomists, 297. SEE ALSO Spanish Volunteers

Spanish regulars: and insurrection, 266; and Sickles' opinion, 271–272

Spanish Republic: and abolition in Puerto Rico, 282, 288–290; and the United States, 289; collapse of, 1874, 293; and Catholic sentiment, 305

Spanish Republicans: and Puerto Rican abolition, 286; and the United States, 289

Spanish Senate: and law of 1880, 305

Spanish ships: and slave traffic, 27, 69, 117, 118, 144

Spanish slavery: and Indians, 3–4; opinions of, 120, 305, 311–312; and abolition conscience, 167–168; and tutelage system, 258

Spanish-speaking slaves *(ladinos)*: export of, forbidden, 5

Spanish statesmen: 312

Spanish theologians: 312
Spanish Volunteers: origins, purpose of, 229; and López expedition, 229; and Cuban insurrection (1868-1878), 229–232, 267; and government policy, 229–232, 241, 268; and expulsion of Governor Dulce, 230–232; and Spanish casinos, 231; and Amadeo of Savoy, 265; and Zenea's execution, 265; and execution of students, 268; and Sickles' opinion, 271; and Cuban reform, 281. SEE ALSO Spanish party
Spanish West Indies: 128
"Special Laws": and colonial reform question, 64, 65, 67; and exclusion of colonies, 173–174; and slave question, 174; and Cánovas' reforms, 184–186; and Reform Commission, 185, 190
Spencer: and Spanish abolitionism, 169
steam engines: and sugar mills, 49
status quo. SEE proslavery; slave interests; Spanish government; Spanish reactionaries
Sterling, Domingo: named reform commissioner, 189; and Puerto Rican abolition, 193–195
Stewart, Lord: 17
stocks and irons: in slave code of 1789, 52; and Moret Law, 247; and abolitionists, 309; abolition of (1883), 311; and propaganda, 312
stock raising. SEE livestock
Suárez Inclán, Estanislao: against Puerto Rican abolition, 286; and American pressure, 288; on coercive measures, 311
subcommission on cuban reform: and report on slavery, 300–301
sugar (cuban): and slave trade, 3–9; beginnings of, 10; and royal subsidies, 11; and exports in 1763, 11; and census of 1792, 12; and industrial requirements, 13, 135, 138–140; and reform opportunities, 13–14; and census of 1817, 45–46; and problems, 47–50, 135–140; and slave interests, 49–51; and Torrente's figures, 73; and prosperity, 1771–1846, 80; and cost of slave labor, 135; and reduction of *ingenios*, 1850–1860, 135; and Sagra's figures, 140; and Civil War, 183; and insurrection, 224; and census of 1862 and 1877, 295; and law of 1880, 301; and crisis of 1880–1886, 310–311. SEE ALSO contract labor; Cuban slave labor; Cuban slavery; free labor; immigration
Sugar Duties Act of August 18, 1846: and Cuban sugar, 89
sugar industry. SEE sugar
sugar planters. SEE Cuban proprietors
Sumner Charles: and Moret Law, 260
Superintendent of Liberated Africans: and Turnbull, 75–77; abolished, 77
supertintendent of emancipated Negroes: suggested, 41
Superior Tribunal of Justice: 126
suicide: of slaves, 110; and abolitionism, 159, 249; and religious instruction, 166
Sweden: and abolition, 19–26
Swedish Antilles: 45

Tacón Miguel: and Creole suppression, 55–58, 65; administration of, 55–59, 67; and *emancipado* problem, 58–59, 60; and Alcoy, 93
Talleyrand, Prince Charles: and Vienna declaration, 17; and British abolutionism, 19
tariff: and protection, 56, 311; and United States, 89; and Cuban reforms, 150, 209, 303
Tassara, Gabriel: on Russell's proposal, 128; on abolitionist policy, 161–162
taxation: and slave trade, 8, 14; and conservation of slavery, 33, 87–88, 108, 191; and Cuban oppression, 65; and Reform Commission, 189, 205–206, 212–213; and Moret Law, 246–247; and insurrection, 222, 225, 303; and law of 1880, 303; and Crisis of 1880–1886, 310
tax revenues (Cuban): and Spain, 54; slavery, 71; and Spanish volunteers, 229, 230
Te Deum: 291
Ten Years' War (1868–1878): 229. SEE ALSO Cuban insurrection
Terry, Tomás: elected to reform commission, 186; and abolition, 194–196, 198, 309
Texas: and Cuban annexation, 96

Index

Thomas, Saint: and slave trade, 63, 170–171; and abolitionism, 169
Thrasher J. S.: on slave numbers, 80
Times (London): 95–96
Title XIII of the Penal Code: 247
tobacco: and slave trade, 3–9; development of, 10–11; and census of 1792, 12; and Arango's reforms, 14–15; and royal monopoly, 32; and immigrants, 33, 109; figures for 45, 47–48, 80, 295
Tolmé, Carlos: 109
Topete, Juan Bautista: and colonial policy, 87; and Glorious Revolution, 217; and *patronato*, 248
Toreno, Count of: and treaty, 37
Torrente, Mariano: on slave conservation, 110–111; and defense of Spain, 123
trade. See Cuban commerce
trading companies (European): 6–7
traffic. See slave trade
trapiches: and centralization, 139
treaty of June 20, 1835 (law of 1835): and suppression of Cuban traffic, 61–62, 63, 67, 68–69, 107; and Negro contract labor, 304
treaty of Madrid (1814): 25
Treaty of Paris (1814): 25
treaty of September 23, 1817 abolishing Spanish slave trade: provisions of, 28–30; and free white labor, 33; and Cortes of 1820–1822, 35–38; and application problem, 35, 39, 53; and *emancipado* problem, 40–43; and supplementary treaty of 1835, 61–62; and free African labor, 304
treaty of 1795: 252
Treaty of Tiensin of 1864: 138
Treaty of Vienna (1815): 94
treaties (other): Anglo-Portuguese of 1815 and 1817, 30; Anglo-Brazilian of 1810, 31; of 1826, 31; Argentine of 1825 and 1839, 32; Gran Columbia of 1826, 32; Mexico of 1826 and 1842, 32; France, 1833, 32; Bolivia, Tuscany, and Asiatic cities, 1837, 32; Kingdom of Naples, 1838, 32; Haiti, Venezuela, and Chile, 1839, 32; Uruguay, 1839, 32; Texas, 1840, 32; Ecuador, 1841, 32; Dominican Republic, 1850, 32; Webster-Ashburton Treaty of 1842, 32, 78; proposed Anglo-Spanish of 1840, 70; rumor of secret treaties, 119; and proposed treaty for legalizing slavery 164
Tribunal of Commerce of Havana (Tribunal de Comercio de la Habana): against abolition, 71; and status quo, 72
Trinidad: slave population of, 43, 45; and sugar exports, 45; and Asiatic labor, 179
Trinidad (Cuban district): 118
Trist, Nicholas P.: 63
Trollope, Anthony: on Valdés, 79; on Negro freedom, 313
Tucker, Commander: 69
tutelage. See *patronato*
Turnbull, David: on slave treatment, 50, 52, 53; on treaty of 1835, 62; and radical measures, 69; expulsion from Cuba, 71, 76, 77; and Torrente's attacks, 73; abolitionist activities of, 75–77, 81; expulsion from economic society, 1838, 76; Varona's opinion of, 76
Tyler, President John: 102

Ulloa, Agustín (minister): 162
"unconditionally Spanish party": 134
Unión Liberal. See Spanish liberals
University of Havana: and nationalism, 56; and elections, 298
unregistered slaves: and numbers emancipated, 294. See ALSO slave census; slave registry
Upshur, Abel P.: 78
Urban VIII: 165, 197–198
Uruguay: and abolition, 30
Usera, Jerónimo de: named reform commissioner, 189; and piracy declaration, 198
United States: and American slave trade, 19; and Webster-Ashburton Treaty, 32, 63, 78; and influence on abolition question, 43, 84, 176, 203, 209, 241–243, 245, 256, 276–277, 284; and Cuban traffic, 63, 143–144, 147; and Cuban acquisition, 66, 77, 98–104, 116–120, 121, 123–127, 234, 265; and "Black Republic hysteria," 77–78; and right of search, 78, 127–128; and Palmerston, 78; and abolitionist debate, 87, 288–290,

250; and intervention, 104, 114, 161, 243–245, 260–261, 266–270, 283–285; and slave breeding, 111; and Pezuela's mission, 116–120; influence on Spanish policy, 113, 116–120, 161, 176–177; and piracy declaration, 121; and Concha's policy, 125–126 and Russell's proposal, 127; and Creole reformism, 129–130; as abolitionist example, 149, 193, 198, 209, 250; and Puerto Rican abolitionism, 157, 283–291; influence on Cuban reform, 207–208, 304; and rebel abolitionism, 226; and Cuban insurrection 230–234, 242, 252, 226, 283–285; and Spanish liberals, 241; and Moret Law, 245, 253, 259–261; and English petitioners, 266; and Cuban policy, 266; and Layard's interpretation, 266; and student executions, 268; and rebel propaganda, 280; and Spanish reactionaries, 281, 288–289; and Spanish abolitionists, 288–289; and autonomists, 297; and British abolitionists, 299. SEE ALSO American North; American South; Cuban commerce; Fish; Grant; Peace of Zanjón

vagrancy: and Saco's abolitionism, 58; and slave labor, 135; and Oriental labor, 136; and reform questionaire, 192; and abolition question, 198, 203; and work contracts, 278–279; and insurrection, 296; and law of 1880, 307–308; and abolition, 312
Vail, Aaron: on Turnbull, 76
Valdés, Gerónimo (captain general): and opposition to British, 69, 70–71; and conflicting orders, 73–74; and *emancipados,* 79; and slave trade, 80; and colonial policy, 87
Valdés Fauli, José: 133
Valdivieso, Nicolás Martínez: 189
Valdosera, Count of: 301–302
Valencia, Spain: and Spanish Abolitionist Society, 158; and reform question, 179–180
Valencia merchants: 243
Valera, Juan: 154
Valiente y de las Cuevas, Porfirio: quote by, 35; on treaty of 1817, 35;

on protecting traffic, 55; and annexation, 124
Valmaseda, Count of (Blás Villate y de la Hera): and Moret Law, 262; and Zenea's execution, 265; and insurrection, 267; on military abolition, 281
Varela y Morales, Father Félix: and abolition proposals, 37–38, 166; and University of Havana, 56; and nationalism, 56; and Creole liberalism, 57
Varona, Enrique José: on Turnbull, 76
Vázquez Queipo, Vicente: on free labor, 108; named reform commissioner, 189; and law of 1880, 306
Venetians: and slavery, 171
Venezuela: and piracy declaration, 121
Verdad, La (New York): and annexation, 98; and Cuban exiles, 100
Victoria de Cuba: and census, 277
Victorian England: 76
Vienna. SEE Congress of Vienna
vientre libre (free birth): in abolitionist projects, 22–23; and Cuban plan of 1867, 204; and Serrano's memorandum, 210; and Glorious Revolution, 218; and Governor Caballero de Rodas, 227; and Becerra's plan, 240; and Spanish diplomacy, 242; and Moret Law, 242, 246, 253; and proprietors, 255–256, 257; and subcommission of 1879, 301
Viera Antonio: 168
Villa Clara, Cuba: work contracts, 278
Villalva, Marqués de (planter): 309
Virginia: and slave reproduction, 111
Vitoria, Francisco de (friar): and Inquisition, 20–21; and Indian rights, 167; and Puerto Rican debate, 290
Vives, Francisco Dionisio: and emergency powers, 44; and slave trade, 55; and Creole toleration, 55; and *emancipados,* 60
Vizcarrondo y Coronado, Julio L. de: and Abolitionist Society, 154–161; and Puerto Rican abolitionism, 156–161; his education, 157; and Protestantism, 158, 169; and Victor Hugo, 159; and Labra, 160; and anticlericalism, 171; and abolitionist manifesto, 217–218
Voice of America: 214

Index

Volunteers. See Spanish Volunteers
Voz de Cuba, La: 309

wages: and *patronato*, 311
war: threat of, 98
war debts: and abolition, 296; and Cuban reforms, 304; and crisis of 1880–1886, 310–311
War of Jenkin's Ear: 7
wars of independence (Hispanic America): and Cuban immigration, 33
war taxes: and Cuban reforms, 303
war with Mexico: and Spanish relations, 98–99; and Cuban exiles, 98–99
Webster-Ashburton treaty of 1842: 32, 78
Wellington, Duke of: and Vienna declaration, 17; and British abolitionism, 19
Wesley, John: and abolitionism, 18
Western Cuba. See Occidente
Western Committee: 269
Western planters: 240
Weyler y Nicolau, Valeriano (general): and Cánovas, 185
whip: 52–53, 267, 200, 210, 247, 253, 267. See also corporal punishment
white immigration: royal restrictions on, 5; and Arango's proposals, 24, 28; and decree of 1817, 32; and Spanish policy, 32–33, 86–88, 137–138; and Junta de Población Blanca of 1815, 33; and refugees, 33; and restrictions, 44; and Saco's proposals, 58, 66, 137; Council of State on, 70; figures on, 86; failure of, 86, 136; and contract labor, 88, 108–109, 135–140; promotion attempts, 107–109, 113, 183–189; experiments with, 110; and labor shortage, 135–140; and Pozos Dulces, 137–138, 199–200; and Serrano's policy, 137–138; and African immigration, 150; and abolition question, 179; and Reform Commission, 189, 191, 192, 198–199; and Dulce's Memorandum, 209; and Serrano's Memorandum, 210; and Liberal-Autonomists, 297
white labor. See free labor; white immigration
Wilberforce, William: abolition proposals, 13, 19; and British planters, 19–20; and Labra, 160; and abolition debate, 250, 288
work contracts: and freedmen, 278
work regulations: 301

Yankees: and Spanish reaction, 187
yanquis: fear of, 43, 161; and Cuban acquisition, 43, 99
Yucatecan Indians: and contract labor, 109; number of, 109; and decree of 1854, 111; immigration of, 113, 117; and Concha's registry, 126; and Creole reformers, 134; and planters' needs, 136; numbers in 1862, 146

Zanjón agreement: and law of 1880, 301. See also Peace of Zanjón
Zaragoza, Justo: xv
Zenea, Juan Clemente: 265
Zeno y Correa, Manuel: 193, 195
Zorilla, Ruís: and anticlericalism, 171; and Sickles' opinion, 272; in power, 273; and Cuban reform, 281; and Puerto Rican reforms, 283–284, 285
Zulueta, Julián: and Chinese coolies, 137; and slaving expeditions, 137; exiled, 148; and Moret project, 257

www.ingramcontent.com/pod-product-compliance
Lightning Source LLC
Chambersburg PA
CBHW020120240426
43673CB00038B/540